THE
GREAT
SOCIETY
READER

AS YOUR PRESENT PRESIDENT — IT IS INCUMBENT UPON ME TO PLAY A VARIETY OF ROLES IN THE COURSE OF A SINGLE DAY.

POLICEMAN TO THE WORLD. —

SOCIAL WORKER TO THE — POOR.

LOVER OF PEACE. —

SEEKER OF CON-SENSUS. —

EDUCATOR —

CIVIL RIGHTS LEADER. —

AT THE CLOSE OF DAY — WHAT A RELIEF IT IS TO BE ABLE TO GIT IN MY PAJAMAS —

AND JUST BE — MYSELF.

JULES FEIFFER

© 1966 JULES FEIFFER, DECEMBER 18, 1966.
THE HALL SYNDICATE, INC.

THE
GREAT
SOCIETY
READER

The Failure of
American Liberalism

Edited by
MARVIN E. GETTLEMAN
and **DAVID MERMELSTEIN**

RANDOM HOUSE
New York

FOR OUR PARENTS

Pauline Antopol Gettleman
Arthur Abraham Gettleman

A N D

Ida Helen Mermelstein
Samuel Mermelstein

PREFACE

This book is only incidentally about Lyndon Baines Johnson, the thirty-fifth man to hold the office of President of the United States of America. It has the more ambitious and more important aim of illuminating the nature of American liberalism, the rhetoric as well as the reality. It so happens that in the mid-1960s American liberalism is represented by the man who promoted the notion of a "Great Society." Thus, in the pages below, it is often President Johnson whose words set forth the main features of the government's programs. This is entirely fitting. We have also included official or semi-official statements of those close to the Administration.

We do not intend merely to present the views of the government spokesmen. It is obvious that government policies are advanced in response to (or anticipation of) certain pressures in society. Our aim is to reveal the context of Administration policy, and the whole range of unresolved problems smoldering behind the political slogan "Great Society."

By the term "Great Society" we understand not only what seem to be the humanitarian aspects of President Johnson's domestic program—so many of which have already been sacrificed to the war in Vietnam—but also the overall slogan of a coordinated policy. The extravagantly publicized welfare programs of the Great Society—the campaign for civil rights legislation and the war on poverty—are only part of the story. Any comprehensive account must also deal with the Johnson Administration's fiscal strategy, its approach to business and labor and its ideology. All these can be most fruitfully seen as the mature expression of an evolving American liberalism.

What is more, we perceive this program for the creation of a Great Society in America as having consequences extending well beyond the three-mile limit. United States policy abroad, especially in Asia and Latin America, is intimately entwined with what goes on at home. For this reason a substantial section of this book is given over to consideration of international affairs.

Limitations of space have forced another set of choices on us. We could not deal with all aspects of President Johnson's program for a Great Society. Sacrificed were analyses of the Administration's housing, education, and conservation programs, its policy on public utilities, and many other issues. Instead of attempting to treat them all, we have chosen a limited number of problems, the ones we considered most important, and have dealt with them in greater depth.

The editorial format we have chosen is quite different from usual readers in which "liberal" and "conservative" views are presented with the clear implication that the possible range of relevant opinions is thereby exhausted. We emphatically reject the notion that the liberal/conservative dichotomy reveals much that is important about contemporary America.

In the readings themselves (some of which have been specifically written for inclusion in this book) varying viewpoints are expressed—libertarian, liberal and socialist. We have also aimed at presenting selections that offer the reader a contrast between the Administration's views and radical perspectives. The way we have exercised our editorial prerogatives has much to do with the political beliefs of the editors. In the introductions to each part of this volume, we have attempted to set forth these beliefs—and our reasons for holding them— as fully as possible within a restricted amount of space. If lack of balance is charged we may fairly say that our book is offered as an antidote to competitive readers and textbooks in which radical ideas are rarely even mentioned, let alone discussed at length.

We hope that this volume will prove useful to students in courses on contemporary America, current economic problems and political science. In fact, the book is an outgrowth of our own teaching experiences. But we hope as well that this varied collection of documents and analyses will also be meaningful to other readers. Sometime soon after this book appears, Lyndon Johnson's programs will face a test at the hands of the American electorate. We have aimed at providing easily available material in order that a judgment of the Great Society may be made with heightened awareness and understanding.

In the course of putting this book together, we have had the assistance of many persons. Our colleagues at the Polytechnic Institute of Brooklyn have been of great help. We wish to mention Professors Helmut Gruber, John Langrod, Eleanor Leacock, Leonard Leeb, Shane Mage, Louis Menashe and Murray Rothbard in this connection. Our secretaries, Mrs. Jean Lester, Mrs. Nita Woods, and Miss Myra Shapiro, have also rendered invaluable aid. Welcome advice and other forms of help also came from Michael Barth (City College of New York), Susan Brown, William Cannon (U. S. Bureau of the Budget), Ronnie Dugger (of the *Texas Observer*), Joan Faber, Ray Franklin (Queens College), Paul Goodman, Joanne Grant, Tom Hayden, James A. Jarman (Library of the Polytechnic Institute of Brooklyn), Helen Kramer (State University of New York at Stony Brook), Leslie Mermelstein, John Owen (The Johns Hopkins University), James Petras (University of California, Berkeley), Ronald Radosh (Queensborough Community College), Robert Scheer and Sol Stern (*Ramparts*), I. F. Stone, and Adam Walinsky (office of Senator Robert F. Kennedy).

Editorial assistance of our publisher, Random House, was superb. John J. Simon saw this book through its early stages; Berenice Hoffman has worked closely with us and we are deeply indebted to her.

In the course of our work we found it necessary to visit Washington, D. C., and thanks to the graciousness of co-directors Marcus Raskin and Richard Barnett, we enjoyed too briefly the hospitality and rare intellectual comradeship of the Institute for Policy Studies. Other members of the Institute— Milton Kotler, Christopher Jencks and Arthur Waskow—freely gave of their time and experience.

The length of this list reminds us of the extent of our obligations. But despite the generous help we have received, the editors alone are responsible for whatever shortcomings this book may display. The products of the collaboration between an historian and an economist, all selections and editorial comment are the results of joint effort. Neither blame nor credit is divisible.

MARVIN E. GETTLEMAN
DAVID MERMELSTEIN

July, 1967
New York City

CONTENTS

PART I

LBJ
AND
THE
GREAT
SOCIETY

INTRODUCTION

In a major address intended to generate support for an ambitious domestic program that would cost many billions of dollars, President Lyndon Johnson on May 22, 1964, publicly committed his Administration to strive to create a "Great Society" in the United States. He also invited citizens in general to join him in shaping "the civilization that we want." [1] To the extent that he defined his notions of the "shape" of the Great Society, it was a vision of abundance and justice, freedom and efficiency, harmony yet diversity. Fully within the tradition of American liberal rhetoric, the Great Society is the self-conscious successor to John Kennedy's New Frontier, Harry Truman's Fair Deal, Franklin Roosevelt's New Deal, Woodrow Wilson's New Freedom, and Theodore Roosevelt's New Nationalism. As a political rallying cry, the Great Society, like its predecessors, is loaded with ambiguities. It is the aim of this book to try to dispel some of the ambiguity and to clarify the likely consequences, the long-term significance of the Great Society program.

In his public pronouncements on this program, President Johnson hardly mentions the rest of the world, except to note that people out there stand in rapt admiration of what the USA has achieved.[2] The implication is that the Great Society is a purely domestic policy, not affecting, and largely unaffected by, foreign affairs. We reject this implication. Johnson himself has affirmed, in another context, the contrary principle: "that

[1] The text of the May 22 speech, along with some amplifying statements, appears below. See reading 1.

[2] He said on June 26, 1964, that "[The] almost 3 billion people in the rest of the world who have never known the pleasure and prosperity that is ours, who have never shared the freedom that belongs to us—they watch our every move to see which direction our life will take in the hope that they, too, some day, may enjoy the blessings that are ours." See below, reading 1, for the context in which this statement was made.

our foreign policy must always be an extension of this nation's domestic policy." [3] This seems the more fruitful approach, and we shall attempt to illuminate the connection between the program of domestic reform and foreign policy.

The man who became President of the United States, and who now considers himself leader of the Free World, launched his political career in Texas. For two generations his family had been deeply involved in the political life of that state. Far from being radical "populists," [4] the Johnsons were in fact part of "a local [Democratic] establishment that made the political decisions and ruled the scene in Blanco and Gillespie counties." [5] Coming from a family of local notables helped open many doors in the early political career of Lyndon Johnson. Through friends and relatives he obtained a teaching position in Houston and then became involved in local politics. A group of influential Texans, including Roy Miller, lobbyist for the powerful Texas Gulf Sulphur Company, made it possible for the twenty-four-year-old Lyndon to come to Washington in 1932 as secretary to a Congressman.[6]

Working for Congressman Richard Kleberg, a wealthy Corpus Christi rancher, Johnson displayed the brash audacity that attracted much attention in the early days of the New Deal. According to an unfriendly critic, he "took to the techniques of influence and pressure like a kitten to a warm brick." [7] Among those on whom these techniques apparently worked were Sam Rayburn, who had known Lyndon Johnson's father, and Franklin Roosevelt, who selected Johnson as Texas State Director of the New Deal National Youth Administration. After two years in this strategic post, he was able to win election to Congress,

[3] Remarks at the University of Denver (August 26, 1966); in *Weekly Compilation of Presidential Documents*, II (September 5, 1966), p. 1,167.

[4] The notion that Johnson enjoyed a "populist" political ancestry has been repeated again and again in journalistic accounts. See, for examples, William S. White, *The Professional: Lyndon B. Johnson* (New York, 1964), p. 71; Michael Davie, *LBJ: A Foreign Observer's Viewpoint* (New York, 1966); Rowland Evans and Robert Novak, *Lyndon B. Johnson: The Exercise of Power* (New York, 1966), pp. 6, 7, 15, 18, 37, 55, 73, 211, 212. There is no substance to this view.

[5] William C. Pool, Emmie Craddock, and David E. Conrad, *Lyndon Baines Johnson: The Formative Years* (San Marcos, Texas, 1965), p. 33.

[6] The best account of Johnson's early years is contained in Pool, Craddock, and Conrad, *Lyndon Baines Johnson: The Formative Years*.

[7] J. Evetts Haley, *A Texan Looks at Lyndon: A Study in Illegitimate Power* (Canyon, Texas, 1964), p. 11.

and in 1937 Johnson began his twenty-three-year career on Capitol Hill.

The record he compiled during those years was one of a country liberal, favoring such programs as rural electrification, Social Security, soil conservation, farm price supports, and power projects built with federal aid. On the other hand, Johnson was a willing supporter of business interests seeking to restrain the power of labor unions. His support for such measures as the Taft–Hartley Act enabled him to boast to his employer–constituents in August, 1959, that he had always favored "strong, effective regulatory legislation to protect Americans from improper labor practices." [8] It also seems that Johnson played a major role in the passage of the restrictive Landrum–Griffin Act in 1959.[9]

For at least the first seventeen years Johnson spent in Congress, his record on civil rights was that of a typical Texas politician. He repeatedly voted with the Southern bloc against bills to outlaw lynching and the poll tax. Running for the Senate in 1948, he denounced in the strongest terms the civil rights portions of Harry Truman's Fair Deal policy:

This civil rights program, about which you have heard so much [Johnson explained to an Austin audience], is a farce and a sham—an effort to set up a police state in the guise of liberty. I am opposed to that program. I have fought it in Congress. It is the province of the state to run its own elections. I am opposed to the anti-lynching bill because the federal government has no more business enacting a law against one form of murder than another. I am against the FEPC because if a man can tell you whom you must hire, he can tell you whom you cannot employ. I have met this head-on.[10]

[8] From a letter from Johnson to his constituents, reprinted in the *New York Times* (January 6, 1960).

[9] See Alan K. McAdams, *Power and Politics in Labor Legislation* (New York, 1964), and the brilliant biographical essay on Johnson by I. F. Stone in the *New York Review of Books* (July 30, 1964).

[10] Quoted in Ronnie Dugger, "The Johnson Record—II," *Texas Observer* (June 10, 1960). We are heavily indebted to this article as well as to Mr. Dugger's "The Johnson Record—I" *Observer* (June 3, 1960) and "Johnson of Texas: A Summing Up," *Observer* (June 24, 1960). These articles, along with Dugger's "Before We Cheer" in *The Progressive* (May, 1964), add up to the most substantial analysis of pre-presidential Johnson we have seen. Mr. Dugger is currently preparing a book of his own on Johnson, which promises to be of considerable value.

A political scientist, studying the roll-call votes during the 85th Congress, concludes that during 1957-58 even Barry Goldwater displayed less hostility to civil rights legislation than did Lyndon Johnson.[11] Later of course, when the Texan began to seek ways to escape from his identification with the South, his position began to soften, and as President he was capable of great eloquence in behalf of the Negroes' cause.[12]

In areas other than civil rights, Johnson adopted more and more of what are considered "liberal" positions as he approached the White House. On medical insurance, for example, he moved from a denunciation of President Harry Truman's health insurance program of 1948 (Johnson called it "socialized medicine")[13] to rhapsodic celebration in 1964 of a medical care program that, in Johnson's words, will help ensure older Americans "that the ravages of illness will not destroy the rewards of a lifetime of labor." [14] The transformation of Lyndon Johnson from a Texas-style moderate liberal to a national political figure demanded the shaping of a political ideology to suit his wider constituency.

One reason why he could accomplish the required transformation was a singular lack of commitment to any fixed ideology whatever. His recent biographers point out that Johnson is a man "of infinite practicality, unencumbered with theory." A cool, calculating pragmatist, he could take on the particular coloration that suited his growing ambitions.[15] But insight into the process by which Johnson escaped the local and regional interests that carried him through the early part of his career should not be vitiated by assuming that afterward he emerged as President into some limpid realm of pure freedom.[16] It is our hypothesis that Johnson's political ascent can

[11] Charles H. Gray, "A Scale Analysis of the Voting Records of Senators Kennedy, Johnson, and Goldwater, 1957-1960," *American Political Science Review,* LIX (September, 1965), pp. 617-18.

[12] See below, reading 20.

[13] See Ronnie Dugger, "The Johnson Record—II," *Texas Observer* (June 10, 1960).

[14] Remarks at a convention of the Communications Workers of America, Cleveland (June 17, 1964), in *Public Papers of the Presidents, Lyndon B. Johnson, 1963-64,* p. 779.

[15] Evans and Novak, *Lyndon B. Johnson,* pp. 10 and *passim.*

[16] This interpretation is implicit in Evans and Novak's *Lyndon B. Johnson: The Exercise of Power.* See the critical review of this book by Marvin E. Gettleman in *The Nation* (January 30, 1967).

best be understood in terms of a shifting and widening of the interests he served. Instead of the parochialism and limited perspective of *nouveaux riches* Texas oil barons or ranchers, the global outlook of national corporation leaders became Johnson's political idiom as he pursued his national political ambitions.

The details of the Texan's progress toward the White House provide a series of fascinating case studies in the American political process. On this level the political biography of Johnson by Rowland Evans and Robert Novak[17] gives us an excellent survey of wheeling and dealing. It is clear that throughout his Congressional career—in the House of Representatives from 1937 to 1948 and in the Senate from '48 until he was chosen to be Vice President in 1960—Johnson learned to practice with near perfection the art of political manipulation. Focusing on the busy surface of his Capitol Hill life, many students of American politics have pictured him as some sort of legislative wizard, almost single-handedly toppling Joseph McCarthy, and bringing about in 1957 the passage of the first federal civil rights act since the Reconstruction Congresses of the nineteenth century.[18] And it is true that Johnson was a capable politician. But he was not above using McCarthyite tactics himself in order to discredit Leland Olds, an able public servant who had devoted himself to the consumer interest, and hence came afoul of business groups.[19] Nor was his legislative wizardry always salutary in its effect on the functioning of the legislative process. Johnson's recent biographers conclude that the "system" he set up as majority leader to make the Senate a productive legislative body virtually destroyed the tradition of informed, meaningful debate in the upper house,[20] a tradition that has just now begun to be invigorated by Senatorial opposition to Johnson's foreign policies.

As Vice President, Johnson was able to exercise only a small

[17] *Lyndon B. Johnson,* esp. Chaps. II-XIII.

[18] These inflated claims, along with more modest ones, are made in Robert L. Branyan and R. Alton Lee, "Lyndon B. Johnson and the Art of the Possible," *Southwestern Social Science Quarterly* (XLV, December, 1964), pp. 213-45; White, *The Professional,* Chaps. 10-12; Evans and Novak, *Johnson, passim.*

[19] Joseph P. Harris, "The Senatorial Rejection of Leland Olds: A Case Study," *American Political Science Review* (XLV, September, 1951), pp. 674-92; Evans and Novak, *Lyndon B. Johnson,* pp. 35-39.

[20] Evans and Novak, *Lyndon B. Johnson,* pp. 115-16.

fraction of the political power he had enjoyed in the Senate. His acceptance of the role of underling to John F. Kennedy, a man he did not admire, is difficult to explain. Other factors may have played a role, but the most plausible explanation is that Johnson wanted to use the Vice Presidency as a steppingstone to the White House. He even hoped at the outset of his Vice Presidency to continue to exercise power in the Senate. But he was rebuffed by his former colleagues in the upper house. Thus chastened, he was also eclipsed nationally by the grace, charm, and intellectuality of the Kennedy clan.[21]

After a thousand days in office John F. Kennedy was assassinated, and Lyndon Johnson ascended to the presidency of the United States.[22] There were obvious differences in style between the two men. The younger man, born to wealth and educated at Harvard, demonstrated a kind of poise and ironic detachment along with driving political ambition. Johnson, no less ambitious, certainly, but to many people far less attractive personally, quickly began to draw critical comment in the press, which stressed his vanity and obsessive ego involvement. John Osborne's article (reading 3, below) graphically reveals some of these traits.

Johnson had striking early success in getting Congress to pass legislation he wanted. His predecessor, on the other hand, experienced defeat after defeat. The list of Kennedy's thwarted legislative plans—a civil rights bill, Medicare, aid to education, the tax cut—read like the roster of Great Society bills passed later under Johnson's Administration.

In the area of foreign affairs, contrasts are far more subtle. Kennedy, for at least the first two years of his presidency, was

[21] On Johnson's career between 1960 and 1963, see Leonard Baker, *The Johnson Eclipse: A President's Vice Presidency* (New York, 1966).

[22] One of his first acts was to appoint a special commission, headed by Chief Justice Earl Warren, to investigate the assassination. The "Warren Commission" produced in ten months a report, authoritative in tone and impressive in sheer bulk of evidence, that fastened the guilt upon Lee Harvey Oswald, a lone assassin. It was easy at first to dismiss criticism of these findings as the demented doubts of compulsive conspiracy hunters. But with the appearance of Edward Jay Epstein's *Inquest: The Warren Commission and the Establishment of Truth* (New York, 1966), a new phase was opened. Epstein suggested that whatever "truth" the Warren Commission uncovered was but the byproduct of the highly political aim of restoring public calm in the wake of national disaster. In the short run, it worked. But a reckoning with the deeper truth that the Warren Commission seemed to overlook cannot long be postponed.

an energetic "Cold Warrior." He bore a vast responsibility for endorsing the US-aided invasion of Cuba in 1961, as well as the sharp escalation of the war in Vietnam late that same year.[23] Yet in the last months of his Administration he seemed to be striving not to intensify the Cold War but instead to find a way to remove some of its more damaging aspects.[24] The accession of Lyndon Johnson did not end these efforts immediately. A major step was the quiet burial of proposals to establish a multilateral nuclear submarine fleet among the North Atlantic Treaty nations, proposals that the Soviet Union and even some of America's allies found highly objectionable.[25] The presidential campaign of 1964 gave Johnson the occasion to speak eloquently for peace against an opponent who seemed to want to risk war. He told an audience in Albuquerque, New Mexico, that men like Senator Barry Goldwater who voted against the Nuclear Test Ban Agreement could not be trusted to lead the nation:

We cannot and we will not play the war game of bluff and bluster. We want to speak softly and act prudently. We want to be prepared, the mightiest nation in the world, with all the bombers we need and all the rockets that are necessary.

But we don't think that we ought to rear back and throw out our chest and shoot from the hip and say, "We are going to rattle our rockets and we are going to bluff you with our bombs, and we are going to issue ultimatums to all the other 120 nations that 'You do it like we do or else,'" because we don't think that will keep peace in the world.

So what we are going to do is to keep the strength that makes our adversaries sure that America can defend herself and will. . . . We will keep the course that makes our adversaries and our allies alike sure that the number one thing that we are dedicated to in America is peace on earth, good will toward men. We will keep the peace.

[23] Arthur M. Schlesinger, Jr., a former Kennedy aide, glosses over this latter point in his critique of Johnson's Vietnam policy, reading 31, below.

[24] This interpretation is offered in William G. Carleton, "Kennedy in History: An Early Appraisal," *Antioch Review*, XXIV (Fall, 1964), pp. 277-99.

[25] See Philip Geyelin, *Lyndon B. Johnson and the World* (New York and Washington, D. C., 1966), chap. 7.

Now that, most of all, is what this election is all about, keeping the peace.

Which man do you think can keep the peace?

Which man do you want to have his thumb close to that atomic button?

Which man do you want to reach over when that line rings, when that phone jingles, and it is the "hot line" and it is Moscow calling? Who do you want to have pick up and answer it and speak for you? [26]

To these questions the nation overwhelmingly responded: "Lyndon Johnson."

Elected to the presidency in his own right, with something of his debt to John Kennedy erased by the verdict at the polls, Johnson began to reveal his own brand of foreign policy. Most clearly in the case of Vietnam, but also evident in the overall international posture of the United States under Lyndon Johnson, was the determination to crush Communist insurgency by military force. Where Kennedy had favored a subtle blend of military and political tactics to win the allegiance of people, and thus turn them from Communism, Johnson has all but abandoned "counterinsurgency" for traditional and purely military means.[27] Successive stages in the military escalation in Vietnam have been introduced with perhaps as much concern for political and economic developments in America as for the imperatives of the situation in Asia. The schedule of escalation seems to accord with the needs of the domestic economy,[28] as well as the perennial "necessity" to avoid the "danger" of peace breaking out.[29]

It is not clear that John Kennedy (or any other Kennedy) would have been able to avoid committing America to a global policy of counterrevolution. Far more powerful forces than mere personal idiosyncrasies are at work. In the chapters that

[26] Remarks at the University of New Mexico (October 28, 1964), in *Public Papers of the Presidents, Lyndon B. Johnson, 1963-64*, II, p. 1,491.

[27] On the shift in military strategy between the Kennedy and Johnson administrations, see Robert Scheer, "The Winner's War," *Ramparts* (Winter, 1965). Reprinted in *Ramparts Vietnam Primer* (San Francisco, 1966), pp. 70-75.

[28] See below, Part II, introduction.

[29] On this aspect of American diplomacy in Vietnam, see Franz Schurmann, Peter Dale Scott, and Reginald Zelnik, *The Politics of Escalation in Vietnam* (Boston and New York, 1966).

follow we try to clarify these forces. At home and abroad the Kennedy and Johnson Administrations reveal more similarity than difference. In both cases there is the same commitment to a program of domestic reform in the tradition of Franklin Roosevelt's New Deal. The all-American, bipartisan Cold War policy of "combating Communism" remains the unchallenged frame of reference for US foreign policy. Johnson's plea for a "Great Society" in the mid-1960s is the most recent manifestation of a continuous tradition of American liberalism, which when linked to the vast dynamo of American power has momentous effects on the world. To study these effects, and the society that produces them, is our aim in the pages that follow.

© 1965 JULES FEIFFER, SEPTEMBER 9, 1965.
THE HALL SYNDICATE, INC.

1 / *LYNDON B. JOHNSON*

HERALDING THE
GREAT SOCIETY

President Johnson's first announcement of the phrase "Great Society," which became the hallmark of his program, was made at the University of Michigan commencement exercises in 1964. A crowd of over 90,000 people gathered in the football stadium at Ann Arbor to hear the President speak and see him receive an honorary Doctor of Civil Law degree. When Johnson arrived by helicopter at the university, demonstraters protesting the war in Vietnam and inadequacies in his domestic program greeted him on campus.

It is reported that the Ann Arbor speech, as well as some of the other Great Society pronouncements, was written by presidential speechwriter Richard Goodwin, who later broke with the Johnson Administration over Vietnam policy. It is likely that Goodwin wove into these speeches some of the notions of Barbara Ward, the British journalist, "a frequent White House caller" (Charles Roberts, *LBJ's Inner Circle* [New York, 1965], pp. 96-100). When Miss Ward aired her conception of the Great Society, it was a nebulous inspirational idea of Man striving to realize the divine impulse within him (see her *Nationalism and Ideology* [New York, 1966], chapter 11), not too different from Johnson's own concept.

The phrase itself has a rich and fascinating historical genealogy. It seems first to have been used during a revolutionary epoch in medieval England. During the agitated "July Days" of 1381 a united front of aggrieved peasants, London artisans and various others arose. Its energies were directed against the feudal establishment of the day. With the colorful Wat Tyler as its leader, this group took the name "Great Society." Though evidently in advance of its time, and eventually suppressed by the state, for months the revolutionary Great Society of 1381 was able to enforce a strict discipline over its members, while carrying out a full-scale assault on the foundations. of English feudalism. For a good description see G. M. Trevelyan, *England in the Age of Wycliffe* (1899; reprinted, New York, 1966).

This original use of the term "great society" bears little resemblance to Lyndon Johnson's usage. But a more proximate usage by Adam Smith in 1776 defined "great society" as the global economic community, knit together by bonds of international trade (*Wealth of Nations*, book IV, chap. 2). In a similar vein, a twentieth century Englishman, the Fabian Graham Wallas, published a book entitled *The Great Society* (New York, 1914), which discussed the interconnected world urban community. Wallas had a vivid perception of the fragility of his Great Society: a high degree of division of labor intensifies class struggle and makes the costs of social disunity great. Although it is doubtful that he has studied Wallas's book deeply, President Johnson too has frequently commented on the need for unity in America.

Selections from Lyndon Johnson's Great Society speeches, printed below, provide no more than a tantalizing introduction to his policies and their significance. Note for example the explicit acceptance of a benevolent, energetic government as a desirable achievement in a democracy:

A compassionate government keeps faith with the trust of the people and cherishes the future of their children. Through compassion for the plight of one individual, government fulfills its purpose as the servant of all the people. [Lyndon B. Johnson, My Hope for America (*New York, 1964*), p. 59.]

Assured that state power is in capable hands in America,

Johnson does not fear its vigorous exercise. But for our deeper understanding of the Great Society programs of the 1960s, we have to examine the question of how this power is to be exercised, and in whose interest. The President's speeches do not enlighten us on these matters.

◇ ◇ ◇

THE GOALS: ANN ARBOR

(MAY 22, 1964)*

I have come today from the turmoil of your capital to the tranquility of your campus[1] to speak about the future of your country.

The purpose of protecting the life of our nation and preserving the liberty of our citizens is to pursue the happiness of our people. Our success in that pursuit is the test of our success as a nation.

For a century we labored to settle and to subdue a continent. For half a century we called upon unbounded invention and untiring industry to create an order of plenty for all of our people.

The challenge of the next half century is whether we have the wisdom to use that wealth to enrich and elevate our national life, and to advance the quality of our American civilization.

Your imagination, your initiative, and your indignation will determine whether we build a society where progress is the servant of our needs, or a society where old values and new visions are buried under unbridled growth. For in your time we have the opportunity to move not only toward the rich society and the powerful society, but upward to the Great Society.

* From *Public Papers of the Presidents of the United States, Lyndon B. Johnson, 1963-64*, I, pp. 704-07.

[1] In fact, the Ann Arbor campus was soon to become a center of turmoil, with the birth there of the teach-in movement, in less than a year. For a comprehensive account, see Louis Menashe and Ronald Radosh, *Teach-ins USA* (New York, 1967).—Eds.

The Great Society rests on abundance and liberty for all. It demands an end to poverty and racial injustice, to which we are totally committed in our time. But that is just the beginning.

The Great Society is a place where every child can find knowledge to enrich his mind and to enlarge his talents. It is a place where leisure is a welcome chance to build and reflect, not a feared cause of boredom and restlessness. It is a place where the city of man serves not only the needs of the body and the demands of commerce but the desire for beauty and the hunger for community.

It is a place where man can renew contact with nature. It is a place which honors creation for its own sake and for what it adds to the understanding of the race. It is a place where men are more concerned with the quality of their goals than the quantity of their goods.

But most of all, the Great Society is not a safe harbor, a resting place, a final objective, a finished work. It is a challenge constantly renewed, beckoning us toward a destiny where the meaning of our lives matches the marvelous products of our labor.

So I want to talk to you today about three places where we begin to build the Great Society—in our cities, in our countryside, and in our classrooms.

Many of you will live to see the day, perhaps fifty years from now, when there will be 400 million Americans—four-fifths of them in urban areas. In the remainder of this century urban population will double, city land will double, and we will have to build homes, highways, and facilities equal to all those built since this country was first settled. So in the next forty years we must rebuild the entire urban United States.

Aristotle said: "Men come together in cities in order to live, but they remain together in order to live the good life." It is harder and harder to live the good life in American cities today.

The catalogue of ills is long: there is the decay of the centers and the despoiling of the suburbs. There is not enough housing for our people or transportation for our traffic. Open land is vanishing and old landmarks are violated.

Worst of all expansion is eroding the precious and time-honored values of community with neighbors and communion with nature. The loss of these values breeds loneliness and boredom and indifference.

Our society will never be great until our cities are great. Today the frontier of imagination and innovation is inside those cities and not beyond their borders. . . .

A second place where we begin to build the Great Society is in our countryside. We have always prided ourselves on being not only America the strong and America the free, but America the beautiful. Today that beauty is in danger. The water we drink, the food we eat, the very air that we breathe, are threatened with pollution. Our parks are overcrowded, our seashores overburdened. Green fields and dense forests are disappearing.

A few years ago we were greatly concerned about the "Ugly American." [2] Today we must act to prevent an ugly America.

For once the battle is lost, once our natural splendor is destroyed, it can never be recaptured. And once man can no longer walk with beauty or wonder at nature his spirit will wither and his sustenance be wasted.

A third place to build the Great Society is in the classrooms of America. There your children's lives will be shaped. Our society will not be great until every young mind is set free to scan the farthest reaches of thought and imagination. We are still far from that goal. . . .

Each year more than 100,000 high school graduates, with proved ability, do not enter college because they cannot afford it. And if we cannot educate today's youth, what will we do in 1970 when elementary school enrollment will be 5 million greater than 1960? And high school enrollment will rise by 5 million. College enrollment will increase by more than 3 million.

In many places, classrooms are overcrowded and curricula are outdated. Most of our qualified teachers are underpaid, and many of our paid teachers are unqualified. So we must give every child a place to sit and a teacher to learn from. Poverty must not be a bar to learning, and learning must offer an escape from poverty.

But more classrooms and more teachers are not enough. We must seek an educational system which grows in excellence as it grows in size. This means better training for our teachers. It

---

[2] William J. Lederer and Eugene Burdick's novel, *The Ugly American* (New York, 1958), dramatized the failures of official US policy in Vietnam.—Eds.

means preparing youth to enjoy their hours of leisure as well as their hours of labor. It means exploring new techniques of teaching, to find new ways to stimulate the love of learning and the capacity for creation.

These are three of the central issues of the Great Society. While our government has many programs directed at those issues, I do not pretend that we have the full answer to those problems. . . .

But I do promise this: We are going to assemble the best thought and the broadest knowledge from all over the world to find those answers for America. I intend to establish working groups to prepare a series of White House conferences and meetings—on the cities, on natural beauty, on the quality of education, and on other emerging challenges. And from these meetings and from this inspiration and from these studies we will begin to set our course toward the Great Society.

The solution to these problems does not rest on a massive program in Washington, nor can it rely solely on the strained resources of local authority. They require us to create new concepts of cooperation, a creative federalism, between the national capital and the leaders of local communities.

Within your lifetime powerful forces, already loosed, will take us toward a way of life beyond the realm of our experience, almost beyond the bounds of our imagination.

For better or for worse, your generation has been appointed by history to deal with those problems and to lead America toward a new age. You have the chance never before afforded to any people in any age. You can help build a society where the demands of morality, and the needs of the spirit, can be realized in the life of the nation.

So, will you join in the battle to give every citizen the full equality which God enjoins and the law requires, whatever his belief, or race, or the color of his skin?

Will you join in the battle to give every citizen an escape from the crushing weight of poverty?

Will you join in the battle to make it possible for all nations to live in enduring peace—as neighbors and not as mortal enemies?

Will you join in the battle to build the Great Society, to prove that our material progress is only the foundation on which we will build a richer life of mind and spirit?

There are those timid souls who say this battle cannot be won; that we are condemned to a soulless wealth. I do not agree. We have the power to shape the civilization that we want. But we need your will, your labor, your hearts, if we are to build that kind of society.

Those who came to this land sought to build more than just a new country. They sought a new world. So I have come here today to your campus to say that you can make their vision our reality. So let us from this moment begin our work so that in the future men will look back and say: It was then, after a long and weary way, that man turned the exploits of his genius to the full enrichment of his life.

AMERICA MOVING: DETROIT

(JUNE 26, 1964) *

In 1960, in this city, John Fitzgerald Kennedy began his campaign for President. He asked you then to make a choice for progress. You made that choice. The result has been four years of unmatched progress in this nation.

This year you and all the American people are going to choose four more years of progress. And who knows, if things work out, I might be with my old friend Walter Reuther back in Cadillac Square on Labor Day! And may I express the hope that you will be there, too. I know that your great and popular and wonderful Senator Phil Hart will be there with me. And I know that Neil Staebler, who will make one of the best governors Michigan ever had, will be there with me, too. And Pat McNamara, one of the finest men that I have ever served with in all my public career—he will be there with me, too.[3]

I am proud and inspired and stimulated that there is a Ford

* Remarks at a Democratic Party fund-raising dinner, in *Public Papers of the Presidents, Lyndon B. Johnson, 1963-64*, I, pp. 819-23.

[3] Walter Reuther, President of the United Auto Workers of America, AFL-CIO; Philip A. Hart was (and is) US Senator from Michigan, as was Pat McNamara until his death in 1966; Staebler was beaten soundly by Republican George Romney in the Michigan gubernatorial race in 1964.—Eds.

in my future. And with Jack Gordon here tonight, I hope there is a Chevrolet, too.[4] For Lady Bird and I have waited so, so long, to be a two-car family. With the help of all of you, all good Americans, doing what we conceive to be best for our country, we will continue to work together for the people of Michigan and the people of America.

It is perhaps typical of the others [the Republicans] that their major issue in this year of change and crisis, this year of great hazard and emerging hope, their great issue is who is going to stop what.

I have no opinion about the outcome of that battle. But I can tell you that, if we stand together, if we are united, if we join hands, there are some things that no party, no group, or no person is going to stop. No one will stop America from moving toward a world where every child will grow up free from the threat of nuclear war.

Do we stand together on that?

No one will stop America from wiping out racial injustice and liberating every citizen, of every race and color, to share in all the blessings of our freedom. No one will stop America from feeding the hungry, and caring for the helpless, and giving dignity and self-respect to the old.

Do we stand together on that?

No one is going to stop the great forward march that we began four years ago. Because you are not going to let them. The American people are not going to let them. And as long as I am President of the United States, so help me God, I am not going to let them. . . .

I am proud to say tonight that we are, tonight, entering our fortieth straight month without any indication of a recession. And we shall never again permit this country to retreat toward the ravages of economic decline.

We can all, each of us, take great pride in our own tax paying, profit-sharing, private-enterprise system of government where incentive has its reward, and all the nations of the world look to us with envy.

[4] References here are to two leading automotive magnates. Henry Ford, II, chairman of the board of the Ford Motor Company, a nominal Republican, had just announced that he would support Johnson in 1964. John Gordon, president of General Motors Corporation, soon followed suit. On the significance of big business support for Johnson, see below, reading 11.—Eds.

In every area of activity that we chose to be part of, we have moved farther and faster than at any time in our history. These have been exciting and these have been rewarding years. But the job is not yet done. We have barely begun our drive toward prosperity. Men of little vision and men of small vitality have always underestimated the American potential for progress. If we work together in a policy of prosperity, we can build an America where every man can meet his desires for a decent life, where no man lacks the dignity of labor.

This is the kind of America that we are going to build. This is the policy we have. This is our policy for prosperity.

First, we will continue to direct the enormous impact of the federal budget toward stimulating growth and toward controlling inflation.

Second, we will work with industry and labor to discourage destructive inflation. The responsibility for prices and wage decision belongs to private enterprise. But we have a common interest in controlling inflation. For inflation undermines alike the profits of business, the wages of workers, and the savings and the profits of all of our people.

Third, we will encourage and expand investment in material and human resources. We will stimulate them. We will take great pride in aiding them and supporting them. This is the core of the poverty program. Our war against poverty seeks to give the desperate and the downtrodden the skills and the experience that they need to lift themselves from poverty. We are going to pass this program, and in our lifetime we, God willing and with your help, we are going to wipe out poverty in America.

Fourth, with the help of people of all faiths, doing it in the American way, we will bring resources together with needs, matching skills to jobs, incentives to lags, and focusing our help where help is most needed.

Fifth, we will encourage technology and modernization, through research and tax incentives. At the same time we will not forget our responsibility to find jobs for those thrown out of work by machines.

These policies offer us the prospect of an abundance beyond the furthest aims of an earlier generation. . . .

But abundance is not an end in itself. Our concern is with the quality of the life of our people, not with just massive statistics, not with just mounting bank balances. The purpose and the values of our party and our nation can never be listed in the ledgers of accountants. They are inscribed in the hearts of our people, in the history of our nation, and the heritage of our civilization.

So the ultimate test of our beloved America is the larger purpose to which we turn our prosperity.

We must first turn it toward relief of the oppressed, the underprivileged, and the helpless. We must, in the words of the Bible, "Learn to do well, seek judgment, relieve the oppressed, judge the fatherless, plead for the widow."

In this pursuit we will turn special attention to the problems of older Americans. Retirement should be a time of serenity and fulfillment, not deprivation and fear.

We are going to provide hospital care through Social Security to older Americans under a Democratic Administration, and that Administration will never permit a lifetime of savings to be wiped out by the ravages of illness.

And we will go on from this to increase benefits and build better housing, and expand employment opportunities, and do all in the power of a nation grateful for a lifetime of service and labor.

But this is only part of our service.

We stand at the edge of the greatest era in the life of any nation. For the first time in world history we have the abundance and the ability to free every man from hopeless want, and to free every person to find fulfillment in the works of his mind or the labor of his hands.

Even the greatest of all past civilizations existed on the exploitation of the misery of the many.

This nation, this people, this generation, has man's first chance to create a Great Society: a society of success without squalor, beauty without barrenness, works of genius without the wretchedness of poverty. We can open the doors of learning. We can open the doors of fruitful labor and rewarding leisure, of open opportunity and close community—not just to the privileged few, but, thank God, we can open those doors to everyone.

For we will not allow the ancient values of the human spirit and the visions of the human heart to be submerged in unbridled change.

This is a vision and a task that is worthy of the highest labors of any generation. This is the vision and this is the task that the American people are asking of us tonight. And I pledge to you in your name and in mine, and in the name of our party and our country, we will be ready. . . .

In this land in which we live we have much to be proud of, much to protect and a great deal more to preserve. It is the kind of people like you who have made the sacrifice to come out here and spend this evening listening to speeches and to reach down in your pocket and pay the fare that supports one of the two great parties in America that are responsible for this great system that we have. . . .

And the almost 3 billion people in the rest of the world who have never known the pleasure and prosperity that is ours, who have never shared the freedom that belongs to us—they watch our every move to see which direction our life will take in the hope that they, too, some day, may enjoy the blessings that are ours. . . .

THE PRESIDENT
AND THE PRESS*

One of the key elements that makes modern authoritarianism a more menacing phenomenon than ancient dictatorship, is the current possibility of going far beyond tyranny (against which it is at least possible to rebel) to attack the very notion of independent truth. The technology of modern mass communications is changing man's very perceptions. And the question of who controls this technology becomes increasingly urgent.

Ben Bagdikian recognizes the dangers inherent in the situation where a President controls the very sources of information by which his policy must be judged. Staff writer for the *Saturday Evening Post*, Bagdikian has been the recipient of numerous journalism awards. He has written *In the Midst of Plenty: The Poor in America* (Boston, 1964), and has edited *Man's Constricting World in an Expanding Universe* (Providence, R. I., 1959).

◊ ◊ ◊

For a time during World War II this writer was an instructor in aerial navigation, an exercise that required one student navigator to direct the plane to a practice target while a second navigator, in the same plane but out of touch with the first, tracked where the plane had been and where it was headed. One night the first navigator said the plane would hit the target

* From "L.B.J.: Press Agent—But Still President," *Columbia Journalism Review* (Summer, 1965), pp. 10-13. Copyright © 1965 by Ben H. Bagdikian. Reprinted by permission of the Sterling Lord Agency.

at 11 PM and the target would be El Paso. Asked where we would be at 11, the second navigator wrote, "Albuquerque." At 11 o'clock a large city loomed out of the night. Both men looked jubilant. On the ground I had to tell the second man we were not in Albuquerque but in El Paso. He was stunned. He pulled out his log, full of statistics like compass headings and celestial fixes, waved it in front of my face and cried, "But that's impossible! I've got the figures to *prove* we're in Albuquerque!" He did have the figures to prove it. But the sign on the tower said El Paso and all the natives claimed to be Texans.

This episode came to mind when the President in his June 1 [1965] press conference described the care with which he decided to send the marines to Santo Domingo: "I had 237 individual conversations during that period and about 35 meetings with various people. . . ."

The President is a lover of statistics and of appearances and in the fierce gamesmanship that has developed in the White House he has proved himself an indefatigable practitioner of the art of public relations. This has presented special problems for the press corps, but not simply because a President tries to put himself in the best light, because all do that. It has dawned only recently on Washington correspondents just how deeply committed the President is to his public relations practice.

Joseph Kraft, writing in *Harper's*, believes the President's troubles with the press "stem largely from the inability of the press to see the President as just another flack."

What happens if the press has to view the President of the United States as "just another flack"?

The problem is not the existence of public relations in the White House, which has to consider its "image" if for no other reason than to know whether it is being understood. But there is flackery and flackery and the White House has pushed the techniques of PR to the point of negative returns.

Some White House deceptions are forgiven as part of the job. President Eisenhower would have been wiser to refuse comment on the U-2 shot down over Russia. As a national leader the President has to keep himself open to negotiations for the national good and if he publicly associates himself with all the dirty tricks that go on behind the scenes he damages his power—not because he tells the other side anything it doesn't privately know, but because he becomes a public symbol of the dirty tricks with whom other national leaders cannot negotiate. Precisely because the President is more than a promoter of his own program and reputation, more than proprietor of government agencies, but also a symbol of national aims and values, it is important that he be listened to—and speak—as something more than a shrewd public relations man.

Some of the deceptions have been important. For weeks President Johnson told the public it was being misled by reporters who said the government was considering widening the war in Vietnam. The reporters were correct and the President wrong. The White House has implied that it consulted the Organization of American States before committing troops to the Dominican Republic, but it never told the OAS beforehand that it was considering troops.

Other illusions are of interest chiefly within the trade, such as the time the President gave a backgrounder in Texas but asked correspondents to put on a Washington dateline (which most did).

The problem is partly the astonishing portion of presidential attention given to public relations. No President has monitored his public image with more zeal. He often pulls popularity poll results out of his pocket. He adds up hours of time given to the press and it is enormous, though much of it is ritualistic or nonuseful. In one extended session a French correspondent whispered to an American that he had a Paris deadline coming up and had to leave. The President was holding forth on the White House south balcony. The American whispered back that the Frenchman couldn't possibly leave. "But we've been here for an hour and a half and he is saying nothing and I have a deadline." The American hissed, "Would you leave if Charles de Gaulle were doing this?" The Frenchman stiffened and whispered, "Charles de Gaulle would not spend fifteen minutes talking about the rust on his balcony."

The President and his staff seem to ring like burglar alarms whenever and wherever the name "Johnson" appears in print or is uttered on the air. A small item in a West Texas paper mentioned Billie Sol Estes in connection with the President in a three-paragraph story on the inside; the editor claims he got a telephone call from the White House in time to kill the item in later editions. One television correspondent was awakened in the middle of the night by the White House, which had heard that he planned to make some critical remarks the next day. A newspaper correspondent wrote a critical morning story and got three telephone calls from White House aides before breakfast. The *New York Review of Books*, a medium-highbrow publication, ran a scathing review of Johnson's Vietnam policy[1] and its editors got a phone call from a White House aide suggesting that in the future they have Vietnam books reviewed by Joseph Alsop (who approves of the Johnson policy).

The President has three television sets for simultaneous viewing of the three networks, plus an AP and UPI ticker. Apparently he watches them more closely than some of the editors. One night a startled wire service editor in Washington got a White House call later preserved in the house organ, *U.P.I. Reporter*, as follows:

"Hello?"

"Hello, Pat, this is Lyndon Johnson."

"Yes, Mr. President."

"Say, I have here . . . (pause) . . . A101N from Johnson City, Texas, about the homestead, by Kyle Thompson. Let's see . . . (pause) . . . you say in there that there's going to be a fee for the tour. Well, that's not right at all. The idea is to give it to the people."

"Just a minute, Mr. President, and I'll get the story."

"You see what it says. It says 'the home was opened to the public for fee tours.' That isn't right. You see, it's for free. That's the idea. Do you see that?"

"Yes, Mr. President. It looks like they dropped the 'r' in the word 'free.' I guess they omitted it in transmission."

"Well, Pat, it sure does mean just the opposite of what we mean."

"It sure does, Mr. President. I'll fix it."

"Well, we want it to be free."

"Certainly, Mr. President. I'll straighten it out right away."

"I'd appreciate it if you would clean this up for me."

"I certainly will, Mr. President."

---

[1] The reference is to I. F. Stone's "Vietnam: An Exercise in Self-Delusion," *New York Review of Books* (April 22, 1965)—Eds.

"We hope you will take the necessary steps to straighten this out."

"Yes, sir, Mr. President."

"Thank you, Pat."

"Thank you for letting us know, Mr. President."

But the problem is not just quantity of presidential time and intervention. Some of it is less meticulous than his editing of UPI typos and some of it has such an implausible ending that it can only harm his credibility. He likes to be the miracle worker, so takes pains to knock down stories predicting what he will do. In December he complained that the Washington *Evening Star* reported falsely that he would propose a 3 per cent pay raise for Federal workers. The *Star* dutifully reported the presidential complaint. Then the President proposed a 3 per cent pay raise for federal workers.

At about the same time, the President complained that the Washington *Post* falsely reported that he planned to ask for a $4 billion cut in excise taxes. "The President is described as feeling that the $4 billion figure couldn't be further wrong," the news story said. The then press secretary, George Reedy, said, "That figure bears no relationship to any decision that has been made." The President proposed an excise tax cut of $3,964,000,-000, which bears a relationship to $4,000,000,000 as 99.1 to 100.0.

Nor is it unknown that a responsible White House aide will confirm a reporter's story before it is printed, and after the published story causes unexpected embarrassment another equally responsible White House aide will tell reporters that the story is wrong and was never checked with the White House.

While doing all this, the President maintains sympathetic relations with editors and publishers beyond anything known before. Lyndon Johnson is the only Democratic President in this century who seems to be on better terms with newspaper publishers than with the working press. This isn't bad; it is merely astonishing. I. F. Stone, an incorrigible heretic in a town with increasing pressures for journalistic orthodoxy, has written, "Johnson sometimes seems to think the Constitution made him not only Commander-in-Chief of the nation's armed forces but editor-in-chief of its newspapers."

Among the institutional casualties of this crushing program of public relations are the press briefings by the press secretary, which have decreasing content, and the presidential press conference, which becomes increasingly rhetorical. Even the semi-confidential backgrounder has often been reduced to an absurdity. On April 7, for example, such a session was held to give prior interpretation of the President's Johns Hopkins University speech offering unconditional discussions on Vietnam. The briefing was given in the White House by Secretary of Defense Robert McNamara, then-Acting Secretary of State George Ball, and special assistant McGeorge Bundy. Ordinarily it is not cricket to print names of briefing officers but in this case the White House disclosed them by staging a make-believe start of the briefing for television and radio for the 6 PM newscasts to help build public interest in the speech.

When it came to the non-attributable Q-and-A, the cameras were shut off but the same spirit of charade continued to pervade the session. Max Frankel of the *New York Times* asked why the government had waited so long to make public its aims and its basis for settlement in Vietnam. Secretary Ball said that there was no delay, that the government had always had the position presented in the President's speech.

"Are you saying," Frankel asked, "that this speech is not news, that we should treat it as old stuff?" Ball replied that the government had always held the same position, though the "formulations" might be new and, he added as a parting shot, "it may be a little clearer to you." To which John Scali, ABC diplomatic correspondent, rose to say, "Since this has all been said before, would the Secretary please refresh the reporters' memories on the last time anyone in the government offered unconditional discussions on Vietnam?" There was general laughter and no answer.

The White House seems so obsessed with keeping the news record favorable that it is defensive about first-hand journalism that it could find useful. The press helped dispel some of the wild confusion within government on the Dominican *coup d'état* with reporting from the scene that was better than official diplomatic and military reporting.

The same was true in Vietnam. John Mecklin, chief information officer in Saigon during the time when David Halberstam of the *Times* and Malcolm Browne of the AP were official dirty words, writes in his book, *Mission in Torment,* that Halberstam and Browne were essentially correct in their reporting[2] and the government essentially wrong.

The White House obsession with PR would be easier to handle if it came from another source. Most correspondents learned to cope with flackdom a long time ago: they react when special pleaders originate news; they recognize the implausibly rosy release; they instinctively check with the opposition; they treat with contempt a man who deliberately flim-flams them.

What is special here is Kraft's observation: most reporters have trouble looking at the President as just another flack. He is not just another flack. He is a PR man in his obsession with image, his unrestrained attempts to create illusion for tactical reasons, and his concern with appearances no matter how implausible. But he is also President of the United States, carrying the burdens of his office seriously.

The problem is that Lyndon Johnson appeals to reporters with all the dignity and power of his position as President and when this does not produce the results he wants, begins manipulating them and the news in ways that are not highly regarded even at the Press Club bar. He is trying to have it both ways. The weakness of many correspondents is that the President is too valuable a source in the competition for news to be ignored as a lesser PR man would be. But deeper than that is the conflict the President creates in many serious correspondents who respect the office of President and the man in it, but whose professional standards tell them that what is going on is common, ordinary press agentry.

The President and his aides often seem to ignore the demands of professionalism upon correspondents, which require exercise of independent judgment based not on personality or pressure but on honest discrimination. Too often correspondents are asked to choose between disrespect for the reader and disrespect for the President.

One simple answer may be to report the unabashed interven-

[2] See Malcolm Browne, *The New Face of War* (Indianapolis, 1965), and David Halberstam, *The Making of a Quagmire* (New York, 1965). —Eds.

tion of the White House into the news process. The dialogue in *U.P.I. Reporter* was seen widely in the trade, but it was not on the UPI wire. Ordinarily this would be healthy avoidance of narcissism. But perhaps the time has come to report the President not only as originator of news but also as editor of it.

CONCERN ABOUT LBJ*

Uneasy observers of the American scene, concerned about the quality of political leadership produced in the United States, have been able to draw some reassurance from the history of the presidency. As interpreted by such writers as Harold Laski (*The American Presidency*, New York, 1940, pp. 40-53), this history reveals that while great men may not always occupy the White House, in times of need appropriate leaders seem to appear. The presidency of Lyndon Johnson severely strains this interpretation.

While certainly a master of political maneuvering, Johnson appears to few as a man of presidential stature. Of course, there are exceptions to this generalization. One of the former members of Johnson's "inner circle" professed reverence for his chief.

He is a sensitive man, a cultivated man, a warm-hearted and extraordinary man . . . [Jack Valenti asserted] the full spirit of the man never seems to be captured. . . . All around him [after the assassination] everyone was in various states of shock, nearing collapse. But the new President sat there, like a large gray stone mountain, untouched by fear or frenzy, from whom everyone began to draw strength. . . .

He began to give orders in clear, audible tones, yet the voice was soft, the words unhurried. And suddenly, as though the darkness of the cave confided its fears to the

* *New Republic* (July 24, 1965), pp. 12-14. By permission.

trail of light growing larger as it banished the night, the nation's breath, held tightly in its breast, began to ease and across the land the people began to move again. . . .

The President, thank the good Lord, has extra glands, I am persuaded, that give him energy that ordinary men simply don't have. He goes to bed late, rises early, and the words I have never heard him say are, "I'm tired." . . .

I sleep each night a little better, a little more confidently, because Lyndon Johnson is my President. For I know he lives and thinks and works to make sure that for all America and, indeed, the growing body of the free world, the morning shall always come.[1]

Valenti's position is exceptional; much of unofficial Washington is buzzing with gossip about Lyndon Johnson's less-than-praiseworthy characteristics. Even within the government, fear of the President's obsessions is widespread. Consider the *Wall Street Journal* dispatch of July 14, 1966:

Sooner or later at a capital cocktail party some John Jones takes a verbal poke at the President of the United States. Whereupon the party clown cups his hands and calls out, "That was John Jones talking just now, Mr. President."

The implication—that the room is bugged and that Lyndon Johnson is listening in the White House—always gets a laugh. Yet, like most topical humor, it has a serious foundation. Among government officials and employes, Congressmen, reporters, businessmen, there is a fear of Lyndon Johnson. . . .

When employes are afraid of the man at the top, they are overzealous in carrying out his wishes. Almost Orwellian in its humorless urgency was the fervor with which government officials, from Cabinet members on down, twisted the arms of their underlings to buy US savings bonds.

No one seems to know why the matter was so important to the President in the first place—whether he hoped the government would set an inflation-fighting example

[1] Quoted in *New York Times Magazine* (February 20, 1966), p. 72.

for private firms, or wanted a demonstration of old-fashioned patriotism and loyalty to the boys over there, or simply saw it as a test of loyalty to himself. But there's no doubt Mr. Johnson hit the subject hard and often—talking about it at Cabinet meetings, posting huge charts in the White House showing agency-by-agency progress, getting almost daily intelligence briefings from Postmaster General Lawrence O'Brien, in charge of the 1966 bond drive within the federal establishment.

And the fervor fanned down the line. Mr. O'Brien, in a memo to all Cabinet officers and agency heads, stressed that the President was personally following the campaign's progress. "He will accept nothing less than the minimum immediate goal of 75 per cent," Mr. O'Brien wrote, ". . . will consider adequate nothing less than realization of our long-range goal of 90 per cent, and will be satisfied with nothing less than achievement of the 100 per cent record established by the White House."

Cabinet members talked up bond sales at their top staff meetings; even Secretary of State Rusk and Defense Secretary McNamara took time off from departmental discussions of Vietnam and NATO to discuss the progress of the bond drive. At the Federal Aviation Agency, according to men there, a bulletin-board notice about payroll deductions warned employes: "If you don't sign up, you will have an interview with your section chief, who will try to convince you. If he doesn't convince you, you will have an interview with Administrator McKee, and he will convince you."

At Andrews Air Force Base, a briefly circulated form (recalled as soon as a newsman started asking questions) contained alternative boxes for the employe to check and return: "I am now supporting the President by buying U.S. savings bonds on an allotment from my pay" or "I do not accept my responsibility to support the President in this savings bond campaign."

All over the country were reports of postmasters and other federal supervisors threatening that non-buyers would be passed over for future promotions. A notice from the postmaster in Boise declared, "It is my firm belief that any employe who cannot be loyal to his employer

should not be working for him." In York, Pa., postal work-
ers who did not give consent for bond deductions were
told they would be called in for a conference with the
postmaster "every day until you give it."

Ultimately, outcries from federal employe unions forced
Mr. O'Brien to concede "isolated but nevertheless disturb-
ing reports of overzealousness" on the part of some offi-
cials, and to caution all government men against going
too far. He reminded them that each individual "has a
perfect right to refuse to buy and to offer no reason for
that refusal." But again, the damage had been done, a
new wave of uneasiness set in motion.

Fear can be a potent instrument of presidential power,
insuring obedience and cooperation as dramatically as
would ideological agreement or personal affection. But
even apart from the obvious damage it can do to the
American democratic tradition, it poses a threat to the
President himself. If the opportunity arises—a broad Re-
publican resurgence in this year's Congressional elections,
a strong challenge from the GOP or from his own party
in 1968, a stirring of revolt within the bureaucracy as his
White House tenure nears an end—the intimidated might
strike back.

The characteristics of Lyndon Johnson, the man, have
political significance. It is a reflection on the American
political system that a man with such character defects
as are sharply etched in the selection by John Osborne,
printed below, can occupy the nation's highest office. (Osborne has been reporting the Washington scene for various national magazines for two decades. He is at work on
a biography of the late James Forrestal.) But not all of
Lyndon Johnson's difficulties can be traced to personal
shortcomings; few of them will be eliminated simply by
a change in White House personnel. Subsequent sections
of this book will deal with these larger problems.

◇ ◇ ◇

In the spring of 1964, when President Johnson was still shed-
ding the role of subdued successor and, by comparison with his
later self, was restrained in many respects, Joseph Kraft dealt
in one of his newspaper commentaries with a phenomenon

which has grown in interest and importance since then. "The real source of uneasiness about the President," Kraft wrote, was Mr. Johnson's "capacity for immoderation." Much that has happened since bears out the statements in the same column that "the President is a man who gets wound up. Power excites him, and success even more. He is subject to self-intoxication . . . the President's hectic activity expresses a condition that gives ground for concern . . . [a] concern that springs from living in a delicate world under the direction of a leader capable of excess."

There is no disputing that there *is* uneasiness about Mr. Johnson. In recent weeks it has been expressed in print by journalists like James Reston, Joseph Alsop and Eric Sevareid. It is constantly reflected in accounts of the Johnson White House, larded as they usually are with stories of his temperamental outbursts, his brutal treatment of offending assistants, and his passion for secrecy, a characteristic which in many of the accounts is made to seem downright pathological. It is also reflected in the defensive explanations of his associates, usually anonymous, such as this one quoted by the *Washington Post:* "He's thoughtless and thoughtful, cruel and compassionate, simple and immensely complicated. I don't know anyone who doesn't feel ambivalently about him."

The concern that Mr. Johnson continues to arouse is important quite apart from the question of whether it is justified. It breeds and magnifies doubts, in the United States and abroad, as to the President's prudence, his wisdom, his fitness to be a chief custodian of the world's security. It colors the response to and judgment of his policies and actions, however sound they may actually be. It is, in brief, a phenomenon in itself, a very definite factor in the world of 1965.

The burden of what may be termed the White House case in defense of Mr. Johnson is that it is a synthetic uneasiness, attributable to faulty reporting and interpretation and to malicious gossip, rather than to any defect or quality of his. Our subject here is not Mr. Johnson's famous "war with the press," a normal conflict which he and self-conscious journalists have absurdly inflated. But some attention to the reporting of the Johnson presidency is necessary if the sources of the concern and uneasiness about him are to be usefully studied.

It is probably true, as one of his favored assistants complained the other day, that the press has failed to capture and convey "the full spirit of the man." It could hardly be otherwise, considering that even Mr. Johnson cannot have reporters and television cameramen at hand through the whole of his long days and broken nights. But the President is not a victim of a press vendetta. If there is a legitimate complaint, it is rather that the coverage and commentary accorded him have on the whole been excessively tender. In part because so much they hear and observe around the Johnson White House is disturbing, unpleasant and potentially damaging to the country— and also because the boldest of reporters are constrained at times to protect their positions and sources—the journalists covering the Presidency nowadays probably write and speak with more care, and pull their punches more often, than they have in any regime in memory. To this must be added the skill of Mr. Johnson, the rancher from the Pedernales, at roping in susceptible journalists. Eric Sevareid and the *New York Times* have recently referred to "house-trained reporters" and "sycophantic journalists" who specialize in the Johnson story as Johnson wants it told, and some of his colleagues have dubbed a notably subservient columnist "Lord Toady of Toady Hall."

What, in fact, is the source of the most serious concern about Mr. Johnson? It is not what is reported of him second-hand, but what he is seen to do and heard to say, occasionally by millions on television and more often by reporters and others in actual contact with him. Some of these things have to do more with manner and taste than with substantive performance, but they nonetheless contribute to concern. Before cameras and in view and hearing of many people, Mr. Johnson did yank a puppy's ears and make it cry and he did say, "I like to hear them yelp," while his pleasure was recorded in an unforgettable photograph. At the Texas ranch, reporters see with their own eyes that Mr. Johnson can hardly drive past placid cattle, dozing in the heat, without turning his car from the road and dashing amongst them, his horn blaring, just to watch them mill and run. Standard ranch-hand fun, of course, but more than one reporter watching his President have it has been moved to sympathy for the cattle. Mr. Johnson led a troop of strangers through his house in Texas and summoned his wife from a bathroom to the bedroom door and pointed to a Senator's photograph and brayed, "That's Lady Bird's boy friend."

A crowd of reporters observed the event and one of them described it with scarifying precision.

On a more substantial but not necessarily more revealing level, there is a disturbingly constant note of plain brutality in the accounts, including very friendly accounts, of the way Mr. Johnson handles his staff and conducts his business. When they try to describe the Johnson staff operation, conscientious reporters are impelled to note that most of it proceeds beyond their view and that they can never appraise it with sure knowledge. Only one Johnson assistant was placed where they could watch him, day in and day out. He was George Reedy, the press secretary, and reporters who dealt with him knew that he was outrageously abused and misused—and, perhaps more to the point, that his operation was extremely inefficient. A *New York Times* story intended to reassure the public contained this revealing sentence: "Mr. Johnson has given increased freedom to his staff except for George E. Reedy, whom he has not given the chance to do his job either freely or well." A *Washington Post* story at around the same time, retailing one of many examples of Mr. Johnson's bullying of Reedy, quoted the President in a solemn statement of management principle: "You never want to give a man a present when he's up—you want to do it when he's down." Now that Bill Moyers has taken over Reedy's job things may improve, of course, but the treatment of Reedy contributed to the concern about Mr. Johnson.

Mr. Johnson on occasion has used his Secretaries of State and Defense as if they were staff lackeys, rousing them from bed after midnight and summoning them either to help redraft a speech, or to the White House to listen to him talk. He once made most of his Cabinet sit in a group for White House reporters, without preparation, in a transparent pretense that they were showing the public how Cabinet meetings go. The President enhanced the humiliation by marching out, with the Secretaries of State and Defense in tow, and leaving a staff assistant to "preside," indicating with a pointed pencil the turn of each hapless head of a great department to recite for the embarrassed reporters. The accurate reports of this performance in the next morning's papers threw the President into one of his rages and, in ways both visible and audible to the White House correspondents, affected Mr. Johnson' temper and work throughout the day. This is the sort of thing that keeps Washington gossiping, and laughing, but also worrying.

The decision to land troops in Santo Domingo was reached in an atmosphere of frenzy. Mr. Johnson, in one of his numerous monologues on the subject, said that the decision was preceded by 235 individual conversations and some 35 meetings in four days. Weighed with the known fact that he spent a portion of those days at Camp David, away from Washington, his statistics hardly supported the impression of coordinated staffing and calm consideration which he sought to convey.

At a suddenly called press conference on June 17 [1965], which proved to be a truly disturbing display of the presidential consciousness in public stream, a question about the current effects of Vietnam and Santo Domingo sent Mr. Johnson off on a long and occasionally incoherent repetition of much that he had said before about the beginnings of the Dominican involvement. It was evidence enough that Mr. Johnson in private has reverted again and again and again to that decision, as if to convince himself and all within hearing that he was right and his critics wrong. Recounting on the same occasion his efforts to find the right man to push development of a supersonic airliner, the President gave a recital which must have been totally unintelligible to anyone who did not already know what he was talking about. And anyone who expects ordered thought and reasoning from the President when he is talking to the world could not have been reassured by his reference, filling more than a column of newspaper print, to the congressional resolution of 1964 supporting the American presence in Vietnam. Quite apart from his citation of it in support of action that was not dreamed of when it was passed, such passages as the following are cause for wonder: "First, the authority of the President is very clear and unquestioned without a resolution. The Commander in Chief has all the authority that I am exercising. . . . Any time they want to take the authority the resolution gives me, they can take it away. It is just an expression and they just approved our position that we were taking."

Mr. Johnson sometimes favors interviewers with three or four hours of his time. Judging by what is written and said in the wake of these marathon sessions, they often show the President at his defensive worst, endlessly explaining what does not need to be explained and betraying an extreme sensitivity.

The White House staff assistant who is said to be the "most intimate" and the "most active" of all of Mr. Johnson's helpers is Jack Valenti, who was recently quoted as saying of himself that "every time I see a story about myself I'm described as a fast-talking Houston ad man who wears metallic suits." Mr. Johnson has said that Mr. Valenti is "a valuable hunk of humanity," that he "can write a speech as well as anybody," and that he would be accepted as a qualified intellectual if he had not been born on the wrong, or southern, side of the Mason and Dixon line.

Mr. Valenti recently began a speech in Boston with this sentence: "The presidency is a mystical body, constructed by the Constitution, but whose architecture was conceived in the inner crannies of a people's soul." Thus launched, he referred to President Johnson as "a father to lead us" and said that the President, fortified by "Godly osmosis" and "extra glands," not only deserves but has the total confidence of the masses. In one of his less turgid passages, the most widely quoted one of the speech, he also said with manifest conviction that he knows Mr. Johnson to be "a sensitive man, a cultivated man, a warmhearted and extraordinary man." The pathetic thing is that Mr. Valenti may have been right. But how is one to believe it of a President who tolerates, much less invites, this kind of crass, extravagant and quasi-literate adulation? Can it be that this President, so competent and masterful and overwhelming, is plagued and eaten and driven to immoderation by some inward insecurity? The Valenti speech and a good deal else, including the subsequent cry from the White House that Mr. Johnson "is never forgiven anything while his young predecessor was forgiven everything," suggests that this may be the case.

PART II

THE MACRO-ECONOMICS OF THE GREAT SOCIETY

INTRODUCTION

Why has a nation, long committed by its traditional ethic to public frugality and the balanced budget, seized upon the startling idea that spending without taxation may be a virtue instead of a vice? To some the answer is simple. "The New Economics of the 1960s is the triumph of an idea," writes Robert Lekachman in his recent study of modern economic thought and policy. "And the idea itself is above all the product of the creative genius of a single man—John Maynard Keynes as he was christened; Lord Keynes, Baron of Tilton, as he came to be." [1] Keynes himself had underscored the importance of theoretical formulations for public policy in a vivid image. "Madmen in authority," he wrote, "who hear voices in the air, are distilling their frenzy from some academic scribbler of a few years back." [2] But the significant thing to note is the adoption of Keynesian ideas, not by "madmen" but by the sober political leaders of the United States of America in the wake of the Great Depression of the 1930s.

Neo-classical economic theory—that which followed Mill but preceded Keynes—had been increasingly structured during the twentieth century toward answering technical questions on economic efficiency. The theory was virtually useless when it came to policy issues in what is now called macro-economics. [3] Full employment, orthodox theory maintained, was the norm toward which the economy gravitated. After a half-dozen years of depression nightmare when more than ten million Ameri-

---

[1] Robert Lekachman, *The Age of Keynes* (New York, 1966), p. 6.

[2] John Maynard Keynes, *The General Theory of Employment, Interest, and Money* (New York, 1936), p. 383.

[3] Macro-economics is the study of aggregates of prices, production, employment, etc., as opposed to micro-economics which puts the economic behavior of individual business firms and households under the scholar's "microscope."

cans were out of work, this theoretical formulation was nothing more than a cruel joke.[4]

Keynes's new theory was striking in its contrast. The economy, he asserted, would equilibrate—exceptional circumstances aside—at a low level in which vast numbers would remain unemployed. Aggregate demand—or in less technical words, the total volume of consumer, business, and government spending—determined total output and employment. It was the last of the three components, government spending, that provided the key to prosperity. Budgets need *not* be balanced and *deficits* were laudable fiscal policy in times of depression.

To the American businessman, the "new economics" had something subversive about it. Capitalism, in Keynes, was stripped of its supposed benevolence; left to itself it brought only chaos and depression. To challenge the private-enterprise system in this fashion was to deny to its chief beneficiaries both a sense of worth and purpose.[5] Moreover, as seen through the prism of those who captained industry, Keynesian economics seemed to endanger the very survival of their system. Only later did the businessman come to realize that Keynesian economics could create a new, acceptable foundation for capitalism.

Until the post-World War II period, the greatest peacetime adventure in American government intervention had been Franklin Roosevelt's New Deal. But the New Deal cannot be looked on as simply the application to America of Keynes's doctrines. Roosevelt never comprehended them, and some of his

[4] Qualifications are in order. Keynes held that neo-classical economists accepted Say's Law. This generalization is usually interpreted to mean that unemployment cannot occur under conditions of competition. It may well be true, as many economists now insist, that Say's Law had been abandoned long before Keynes. We may even accept, for the sake of argument, recent resuscitations of classical economics to the effect that the latter may have been valid theory, granted (1) its (incorrect) premise of perfectly competitive markets or (2)—for economists only!—time enough for the expansion due to the Pigou and Keynes Effects. But whatever the various technical controversies, of much interest to economic theorists and historians, they have no bearing on the argument stated above. Neo-classical economic theories, whatever can be read into them today, *at the time* were static and micro-economic. Because of this, those neo-classical economists, concerned with policies to restore prosperity *at the time*, were completely at sea.

[5] Joseph Schumpeter makes a similar point in his classic study, *Capitalism, Socialism, and Democracy* (New York, 1942).

major advisers became Keynesians only in 1938. The timid fiscal policies of the peacetime New Deal fell far short of filling the full Keynesian prescription,[6] and it has by now become a commonplace to observe that World War II, and not the Roosevelt Administration's economic reforms, pulled the country out of the Great Depression.[7]

There was no difficulty in justifying huge expenditures on armaments during these war years, and since then military items have been almost sacred items in the budget. All this suggests the acceptance in America of a greatly expanded role for government. Certain kinds of government spending, of course, are still denounced as the menacing harbingers of collectivist tyranny,[8] but others are considered legitimate. The differences were clarified by the authoritative corporate journal *Business Week* in an analysis of President Harry Truman's Fair Deal welfare program.

. . . *[There is] a tremendous social and economic difference between welfare pump priming and military pump priming. It makes the government's role in the economy—its importance to business—greater than ever.*

Military spending doesn't really alter the structure of the economy. It goes through the regular channels. As far as a businessman is concerned, a munitions order from the government is much like an order from a private customer.

But the kind of welfare and public works spending that Truman plans does alter the economy. It makes new channels of its own. It creates new institutions. It redistributes income. It shifts demand from one industry to another. It changes the whole economic pattern. That's its object.[9]

Does this mean that Keynesian techniques can only work under conditions of war and cold war, and that America is in

[6] Lekachman, *Keynes*, Chapt. 5.

[7] The real achievement of FDR's New Deal should not be slighted. By energetic activity in Washington, the New Dealers *gave the impression* that at last a humane and flexible government was going to restore prosperity. The initiative was thereby taken from those who were attempting to offer a more radical alternative. Thus the New Deal was essentially a political (not economic) response to the Great Depression, and a brilliantly successful strategy to save capitalism.

[8] Barry Goldwater, *Where I Stand* (New York/Toronto/London, 1964), *passim*.

[9] *Business Week* (February 12, 1949), p. 20.

the state of a perpetual war economy? That group of influential fiscal experts, the President's Council of Economic Advisers, would say no. The council seems oblivious of the extent of the military impact on the economy. Its Report of January, 1965, states: "These four years of expansion have demonstrated that the American economy is capable of sustained balanced growth in peacetime." [10] This, at a time when over $50 billion was being spent annually on armaments! Council Chairman Gardner Ackley smugly concluded that "The employment gains of 1964 and 1965 clearly demonstrate that our economy is capable of reabsorbing large numbers of unemployed into productive jobs without serious strain or inflationary pressures" (see reading 5, below). Ackley's statement must be qualified. No one has seriously suggested that America cannot put its labor force back to work. The issue is back to work on what. The council seems unable to recognize that their interim goal of 4 per cent unemployment was achieved only because of the war in Vietnam.[11] The reader should compare the statements of policy makers Ackley and Schultze (see readings 5 and 6) to those of Leo Huberman and Paul Sweezy (see reading 8). Huberman and Sweezy continue the analysis along lines similar to ours here, and in addition subject the full economic upswing to a penetrating probe.

We do not suggest that the entire Johnson prosperity can simply be credited to the war in Vietnam. The Internal Revenue Act of 1964, Johnson's famous tax cut, played its role.

This significant piece of legislation has had lavish praise heaped upon it. Harvard Professor Seymour Harris has called it "one of the great achievements of modern public policy." [12] And Robert Lekachman has viewed the measure as a great *tour de force* of Keynesianism.[13] There was, however, nothing es-

[10] *Economic Report of the President* (1965), p. 38.

[11] The Labor Department, in what must be emphasized as a most minimal estimate, stated "that about half a million jobs in 1966 might be attributable to defense expenditures for Vietnam. This would amount to only seven-tenths of 1 per cent of total employment in the private sector of the economy." (*Hearings on the January 1966 Economic Report of the President,* Joint Economic Committee [February, 1966], p. 357.) But it is this very decline from 5 per cent unemployment to 4 that has brought forth the hosannas of the council.

[12] Testimony in *Hearings on the January 1965 Economic Report of the President,* Joint Economic Committee (February, 1965), part 2, p. 4.

[13] Lekachman, *Keynes,* p. 284.

pecially earth-shattering about the size of the tax cut, though it was large—$11.5 billion—and exceeded the Eisenhower tax cut of 1954 by a few billions. Neither was any new principle of equity established by the legislation of 1964. The overall tax structure has not become more progressive. In fact, as Leon Keyserling shows (reading 7, below), it has become less so in recent years. No attempt was made to plug the fabled loopholes so graphically described in Philip Stern's *The Great Treasury Raid* (New York, 1962). Oil barons, for example, still enjoy the gracious government gift of a 27½ per cent depletion allowance. Tax reform was just not intended. In the words of a knowledgeable *Newsweek* correspondent, the act finally signed by President Johnson "almost exactly fitted the demands of the Ford-Saunders businessmen's committee: a whale of a big tax cut, and a minimum of reforms." [14]

The ultimate significance of the Kennedy–Johnson tax cut lay in other directions. In an earlier age, a reduction of taxes would never have been considered, let alone enacted, in the face of an impending budget deficit of $10 billion.[15] For most Keynesians, the long-awaited triumph in the Congress of the "new economics"—the adoption of modern fiscal planning—was a dream finally come true. But if this was Keynesianism, it had departed sharply from its early years when Keynes advocated welfare spending, not tax cuts.[16] In recent years, cutting taxes was the characteristic demand of Republican conservatives, not liberal Democrats. Other, more "liberal" Keynesians, such as John Kenneth Galbraith and Leon Keyserling, urged more traditional Democratic priorities.

Galbraith's *Affluent Society* (Boston, 1958) stresses the greater need for public expenditures. He identifies an imbal-

[14] Hobart Rowen, *The Free Enterprisers: Kennedy, Johnson, and the Business Establishment* (New York, 1964), pp. 243, 246. Initially, President Kennedy's proposed tax revision included tax reform as well as tax reduction. Under tremendous pressures put on him by a special committee set up, in Rowen's words, by "the top brass of American business"— the Ford (Henry Ford II)–Saunders (Stuart T. Saunders, president of the Norfolk & Western Railway Co.) Committee—Kennedy abandoned most of the proposed reforms. The Act, with the "reform" features removed, was signed into law by President Johnson in February, 1964.

[15] An exception would be the case in which budget expenditures were simultaneously being drastically reduced.

[16] True, when Keynes wrote *The General Theory*, there wasn't much in the way of taxes to cut.

ance between a relative surfeit of private goods on the one hand, and a scarcity of schools, transportation facilities, and public services on the other. Similarly, Keyserling has frequently and vigorously objected to a fiscal policy that overlooks key societal needs. Both call for the recasting of America's priorities and the reallocation of resources in a way that goes beyond the Johnson Administration's Great Society program.[17] Thus, the left wing of the Keynesian school objects to the exclusive adoption of such policies as the tax cut of 1964 on the grounds that they ensure the perpetuation of a social imbalance.[18] Those who persist in seeing a steady leftward drift in American economic policy should recognize the ultimate significance of the Kennedy–Johnson tax cut. It marks the abandonment of the traditional liberal-labor program and the acceptance of the substantive proposals of old-fashioned conservatives.

Examination of macro-economic strategy in other areas reveals essentially the same picture. The Johnson Administration's specific labor policy is properly dealt with elsewhere in this volume.[19] But the general way in which employment prob-

---

[17] It should not be thought that Galbraith and Keyserling are alone in their reformist endeavors. Many others are contributing to the explorations of the alternatives to current domestic and foreign policies. For the recent deliberations of a high-level academic group, see *The National Priorities Problem: Choices and Consequences, Papers Presented to a Meeting at Columbia University, September 30–October 1, 1966* (available from room 320, Mudd Building, Columbia University, New York City, 10027; the newly reactivated periodical, *New University Thought* [P.O. Box 7431, Detroit, Michigan, 48202] promises to publish these papers shortly). The major difficulty in this approach is the implicit assumption that demonstrations of the desirability of change will convince rational policy makers in Washington. (See the discussion of the problem of rationality below, pp. 344ff.). No attempt is made to link their analysis to the interests of any group or class who could bring about the desired changes.

[18] See Keyserling's critique, reading 7 below; Galbraith's in "An Agenda for American Liberals," *Commentary*, XLI (June, 1966). In the interest of accuracy, it should be pointed out that Keynes's reasons for favoring welfare spending differed from those offered by Galbraith. Keynes simply wanted to put the unemployed back to work. Unlike Galbraith, he apparently saw no problem of social imbalance. He wrote: ". . . I see no reason to suppose that the existing system seriously misemploys the factors of production which are in use." (*The General Theory*, p. 379.)

[19] See Part III, readings 10 and 12.

lems are handled demands separate consideration as a major component of macro-economic policy.

Economists—especially of the Keynesian variety—agree that no single policy or combination of them can simultaneously reduce both unemployment and inflation. They are competing and contrary ends, and governmental initiative determines to a large extent the balance or compromise between putting people to work and keeping prices down. The choices made reflect, not the will of some neutral force we call "the government," but the values and interests of those who hold power. On the matter of unemployment and inflation, decision-makers are not of one mind. Under the Eisenhower Administration, higher unemployment rates and lower prices were favored. Kennedy and Johnson and their advisers seem to have a slight tendency in the other direction—lower unemployment and an increased measure of inflation.[20] A relevant consideration influencing these choices is the sensitivity of various politicians to groups who may be adversely affected by inflation—recipients of fixed incomes and lenders. Mild inflation is no great threat to other strata; and high interest rates aimed at curbing inflation may in reality be intended to keep unemployment high enough to reduce the demand for labor and thereby enhance employer discipline over the worker. Whatever the differences among the policy makers in Washington, it is clear that they are narrow enough to exclude serious consideration of policies that would reduce unemployment to the rates achieved in other capitalist countries, such as Japan and West Germany.[21] Instead, during the period of escalation of war in Southeast Asia but prior to the weakening in aggregate demand that began late in 1966, Johnson's macro-economic policy contained a strong dose of extremely tight money, mixed with an unprecedented personal campaign by the President himself to restrain capital spending.[22] Substantial unemployment, particu-

[20] When all is said and done, this may be the major policy difference between the Republican and Democratic parties.

[21] Albert Rees, after adjusting West German and Japanese statistics to make them comparable to US figures, indicates that in 1960 the unemployment rate in each country was 1 per cent. "Dimensions of the Employment Problem," in Arthur M. Okun, ed., The Battle Against Unemployment (New York, 1965), p. 24.

[22] See John D. Pomfret, "Johnson Striving to Cool off Boom," New York Times (April 6, 1966), p. 27.

larly of blacks,[23] in the midst of general prosperity, is therefore the reality of Lyndon Johnson's Great Society.[24]

Related to the problem of unemployment is the thorny issue of the balance of payments. Despite a substantial excess of merchandise exports over imports, a large overall deficit has plagued the United States since 1958. Many factors contribute to and complicate this situation, but most economists agree that essentially foreign aid, overseas investment, and the worldwide US military establishment are responsible for the problem.[25] The war in Vietnam intensifies an already alarming situation.

Various strategies have been proposed to deal with the balance of payments problem. Such techniques as interest equalization[26] and voluntary foreign-investment ceilings will alleviate the problem somewhat, and have already done so.[27] But the deficit cannot conceivably be erased without a massive reduction in American overseas military involvement, and this in turn hinges on a change in foreign-policy objectives that do not appear likely in the near future. The US policy of combating socialist or left-wing revolution in the third world maintains the excessive dollar outflow.[28] Consequently a crisis looms

---

[23] See below, Part V.

[24] The sharp debate among economists on the extent to which recent unemployment is structural—due to the changing nature of technology—or caused by a deficiency of aggregate demand, should not hide the fact that an aggressive enough fiscal policy will reduce unemployment. Employers will, as they did during World War II, train the unskilled "unemployables." Needless to say, such a fiscal policy would have to be accompanied by a large degree of economic planning, including price controls, in order to stop inflation. For this reason such a policy is not considered.

[25] John Kenneth Galbraith, "The Balance of Payments: A Political and Administrative View," in Douglas F. Dowd, ed., *America's Role in the World Economy: The Challenge to Orthodoxy* (Boston, 1966), pp. 44-56; see also *The Economist* [London], CCXXI (November 19, 1966), pp. 808, 811.

[26] US government taxes on foreign securities purchased by American investors.

[27] During the early 1960s, higher interest rates were imposed to induce volatile funds to remain in this country, and though every effort was made to minimize their effect on employment-creating investment, by keeping short term rates high and not long term rates, the effect was to exacerbate an already shameful unemployment picture.

[28] See the discussion of the Johnson Administration's foreign policy, below, Part VI; and Hans Morgenthau, "Globalism: Johnson's Moral Crusade," *New Republic*, CLIII (July 3, 1965), pp. 19-22.

ahead for the American economy and threatens the stability of the Western bloc economies.

Finally, there is the central issue of America's economic growth. A highly complex question, susceptible to subtle economic theorizing, economic growth was made an issue by John F. Kennedy during the election campaign of 1960.[29] The record since Kennedy's election has been one of marked improvement. The annual rate of growth of Gross National Product during the Eisenhower years was only 2.1; during the Kennedy–Johnson period it is substantially higher, about 4.5 per cent.[30] The gain is mainly ascribable to the sopping up of unemployed workers. But we have already noticed the Johnson Administration's unwillingness to reduce unemployment much further because of the "danger" of inflation.[31] From here on in increases in the rate of growth of the US economy must be accomplished primarily through greater investment, a task of herculean dimensions.[32]

[29] See Seymour E. Harris, *The Economics of the Political Parties: With Special Attention to Presidents Eisenhower and Kennedy* (New York, 1962), p. 223.

[30] These rates of growth, compounded annually, were calculated on data adjusted for changes in price, i.e., GNP in 1958 prices. The eight years of Eisenhower, 1953 to 1960, were compared to the first five years of Kennedy and Johnson, 1961 to 1965.

[31] See above, p. 49. Inflation itself tends to be countered by higher interest rates, which in turn reduce the capital expenditures on which economic growth in good part is based.

[32] One estimate shows the staggering amount of net investment necessary to raise the growth rate. To add 1 per cent to the overall 3 per cent growth rate for the period 1929-57, the ratio of net investment to national income would have to increase from 6 per cent to 20 per cent! See on this, E. F. Denison, *The Sources of Economic Growth in the United States* (Committee for Economic Development, Supplementary Paper no. 13 [New York, 1962]), pp. 116 and *passim*. That any such increase in investment requires a complementary increase in overall demand is soberly noted by the Council of Economic Advisers, who fear that the current level of investment, to say nothing of a huge increase, is unsupportable:

The current strength of investment demand provides new evidence and, at the same time, raises new issues concerning the longer-term prospects for capital outlays. Nagging doubts about a possible secular weakening of capital spending have been resolved. Yet, it is obvious that business fixed investment cannot continuously grow twice as fast as GNP, as it did in 1964 and 1965, and that it cannot always be a propelling sector of demand. Nor is it certain that the economy can regularly maintain the current 10½ per cent investment share at full employment, a share which

In the spring of 1967, against a background of serious long-term problems, the daily operation of the American economy is closely geared to the war in Vietnam. To a large extent, the war had escalated without economic pain. This was possible because of the existence of underutilized industrial capacity and unemployed labor. Further escalation forces a sharper choice between guns and butter. A likely result may be less butter, brought on by higher personal taxes. To some extent recent inflation itself has already served as a barely hidden tax. Yet, if the tempo of escalation is carefully measured, increased arms spending may offset nicely whatever tendencies exist to recessions.[33] Thus the war in Vietnam, activating a kind of militaristic Keynesianism, has become an integral part of the macro-economics of the Great Society.

Something has been lost in the process. Keynes originally urged vigorous government intervention into a faltering economy to restore prosperity. Modern Keynesians among Lyndon Johnson's advisers have pushed macro-economic manipulation to great heights of sophistication. But these techniques have become the adjunct of a permanent war economy, and whatever humanitarian focus they once had has all but dissipated.

---

matches the postwar peak." (Economic Report of the President [1966], p. 57.)

[33] As long as increased productivity and the increased reservoir of youth make possible a potential increase in GNP of $50 billion per year, a $5-10 billion increase in war spending need not require the loss of output elsewhere. It may even provide the stimulus that makes possible the $50 billion increase itself. For a similar argument, see *Fortune* (July, 1966), p. 15.

4 / COUNCIL OF ECONOMIC ADVISERS

THE ECONOMIC GOALS OF THE GREAT SOCIETY *

Included below are three official statements by the Johnson Administration on what it conceives to be its economic policies and goals. The first is a listing of the broad, overall goals, while the second is limited to the contributions of federal fiscal and monetary policies. The last selection includes a rather more technical discussion of recent refinements to the "new economics." The Council of Economic Advisers, an agency established by the Employment Act of 1946, consists of three leading economists who are aided by a small professional staff. The 1965 and 1966 council consisted of Gardner Ackley (chairman), Arthur Okun, and Otto Eckstein. Ackley and Okun have remained on the Council and are on leave from the University of Michigan and Yale University, respectively, while Eckstein has since returned to Harvard University. His replacement, James S. Duesenberry, is a Harvard colleague.

---

* The first selection is from the *Economic Report of the President* (1966), pp. 5-6; the second, from the *Economic Report of the President* (1965), pp. 61-62; the third, from the *Economic Report of the President* (1966), p. 180.

THE PRINCIPLES OF
ECONOMIC POLICY

In a time of high prosperity, economic policy faces new problems. But it is still guided by the basic principles that have served us so well.

Twenty years ago next month, the Employment Act of 1946 —which prescribes this report—became law. The principles of our policy emerge from that act and from our two decades of experience under it.

The essential and revolutionary declaration[1] of the Employment Act was that the federal government must accept a share of responsibility for the performance of the American economy. The nature of that share has been more and more clearly defined over the years, by the recommendations of four Presidents and the enactments of ten Congresses.

I [2] see these as the main tasks of federal economic policy today:

1. to attain full employment without inflation; to use fiscal and monetary policies to help to match total demand to our growing productive potential, while helping to speed the growth of that potential through education, research and development,

---

[1] The complete declaration, with all its qualifying clauses, is rarely considered to be revolutionary:

The Congress declares that it is the continuing policy and responsibility of the federal government to use all practicable means consistent with its needs and obligations and other essential considerations of national policy, with the assistance and cooperation of industry, agriculture, labor, and state and local governments, to coordinate and utilize all its plans, functions, and resources for the purpose of creating and maintaining, in a manner calculated to foster and promote free competitive enterprise and the general welfare, conditions under which there will be afforded useful employment opportunities, including self-employment, for those able, willing, and seeking to work, and to promote maximum employment, production, and purchasing power.

For a complete discussion of the origins and wording of this act, see Stephen K. Bailey, *Congress Makes a Law* (New York, 1950).—Eds.

[2] This is a polite fiction; the Council of Economic Advisers puts its words into the President's mouth, so to speak.—Eds.

manpower policies, and enlarged private and public investment;

2. to help to open the doors of opportunity to all, through developing human resources and removing barriers of discrimination, ignorance, and ill-health;

3. to help to solve social and economic problems that neither private action nor state and local governments can solve alone —an efficient transportation system, the protection of our environment, the health of our agriculture, the reconstruction of our cities;

4. To achieve and maintain equilibrium in the Nation's external payments, and to press for improvements in the international economic order;

5. to maintain and enhance healthy competition;

6. to achieve national purposes as far as possible by enlisting the voluntary cooperation of business, labor, and other groups.

Recognition of these responsibilities of the federal government neither lessens the responsibilities nor impairs the freedoms of individuals and private groups; nor does it challenge the authority of state and local governments.

The tasks involve new and growing problems of an increasingly complex and interdependent economy and society. Only the federal government can assume these tasks. But the federal government by itself cannot create prosperity, reduce unemployment, avoid inflation, balance our external accounts, restore our cities, strengthen agriculture, eliminate poverty, or make people healthy.

Only through a creative and cooperative partnership of all private interests and all levels of government—a creative federalism—can our economic and social objectives be attained. This partnership has written the story of American success. And a new vitalization of this partnership and a new confidence in its effectiveness have produced the extraordinary economic and social gains of recent years.

CONTRIBUTION OF FEDERAL FISCAL AND MONETARY POLICIES

Federal policies have made a major and continuing contribution to the great achievements of the American economy during the past four years. These policies were not laid down in one master plan early in 1961 and then carried out on a predetermined schedule. There have been delays, surprises, and a need to adapt policies to changing events; but policies have had a unified direction and strategy. They have consistently reflected a number of basic ideas shared by those responsible for federal economic policies. These basic ideas include the following:

1. a firm belief that the United States must make optimum use of the tremendous productive capacity of its economy; conversely, an abhorrence—for both human and economic reasons —of the waste of resources and opportunities involved in a prolonged underutilization of that capacity;

2. a recognition that federal purchases, taxes, and transfer payments are a major force, along with monetary policy, in determining the strength of the total market demand for productive resources;

3. a full understanding of the key role of private investment in total market demand and in the long-term growth of incomes, and of the need for adequate profit incentives to stimulate this investment;

4. a recognition that expanding consumption is necessary if increasing investment and overall growth are to be maintained;

5. a belief that vigorous efforts are necessary to restore equilibrium in the balance of payments;

6. a determination to achieve reasonable price stability in order to preserve equity at home and to improve our international competitive position both at home and abroad;

7. a conviction that, if they are to be effective, policies cannot respond passively to what has already transpired, but must try to foresee and shape future developments, remaining flexible and ready to change speed or direction yet holding to fixed goals;

8. a belief that the American people share these ideas and are ready to support imaginative but carefully considered innovations in public policy.

ECONOMIC POLICY TODAY

Two decades of economic analysis and policy experience have shaped the development of a revised economic policy. By some, current policy has been labeled the "new economics." It draws heavily on the experience and lessons of the past, and it combines both new and old elements. Current policy represents a coordinated and consistent effort to promote balance of overall supply and aggregate demand—to sustain steady balanced growth at high employment levels with essential price stability.

This approach to policy has several key aspects, not entirely novel by any means. First, it emphasizes a continuous, rather than a cyclical, framework for analyzing economic developments and formulating policies. Stimulus to demand is not confined to avoiding or correcting recession, but rather is applied whenever needed for the promotion of full utilization and prosperity. Second, in this way, it emphasizes a preventive strategy against the onset of recession. Third, in focusing on balance of the economy, this policy strategy cannot give top priority to balance in the budget. When private investment threatens to outrun saving at full employment, a government surplus is needed to increase total saving in the economy while restrictive monetary policy may also be called for to restrain investment outlays. When, as in recent years, private saving at full employment tends to outrun actual private investment, the balance should be corrected by budget deficits and expansionary monetary policy.[3] Fourth, it considers the budget and monetary conditions in the framework of a growing economy, recognizing

[3] The preceding two sentences seem to imply that a balance in the budget should not be given any priority at all. Only by sheer chance would a balanced budget occur simultaneously with a "balanced economy." This sweeping disregard of balancing the budget is what distinguishes the economic policy statements of Johnson and Kennedy from those of Eisenhower.—Eds.

that revenues expand and thereby exert a fiscal drag on demand unless expansionary actions are taken; similarly, it recognizes that money and credit must expand just to keep interest rates from rising. Fifth, this strategy emphasizes the use of a variety of tools to support expansion while simultaneously pursuing other objectives. Manpower policies, selective approaches to control capital outflows, as well as general fiscal and monetary measures, are all part of the arsenal. Sixth, it calls for responsible price–wage actions by labor and management to prevent cost inflation from impeding the pursuit of full employment. Finally, it makes greater demands on economic forecasting and analysis. The job of the economist is not merely to predict the upturn or the downturn but to judge continuously the prospects for demand in relation to a growing productive capacity.

EXPANSIONARY FISCAL POLICY DOES WORK*

Each year, the Joint Economic Committee of the Congress currently chaired by Representative Wright Patman, Democrat of Texas, holds hearings on the *Economic Report of the President,* written by the President's Council of Economic Advisers. On Tuesday, February 1, 1966, the first witness to appear was Gardner Ackley, chairman of the council. Before joining the Johnson Administration, Ackley, a specialist in *Macroeconomic Theory,* the title of his 1961 book, was Professor of Economics at the University of Michigan. Included below is Ackley's initial statement as well as a revealing colloquy over unemployment with Senator William Proxmire, Democrat of Wisconsin.

◇ ◇ ◇

Employability of the unemployed

The employment gains of 1964 and 1965 clearly demonstrate that our economy is capable of reabsorbing large numbers of unemployed into productive jobs without serious strain or inflationary pressures.

In 1962, after five years of high unemployment, it was impossible to be certain that the majority of the unemployed were readily employable. The possibility could not be ruled out that, in the interim, the character of job requirements at high em-

---

* Reprinted from *Hearings on the January 1966 Economic Report of the President,* Joint Economic Committee (February, 1966), Part I, pp. 4-14, 50-51.

ployment might have changed more rapidly, or in different directions, than the skill composition or the industrial or geographic distribution of the labor force.

Since 1961, the council has steadily maintained that a 4 per cent unemployment rate could be achieved readily, and without excessive strain, through an adequate expansion of total demand; and that even lower rates are attainable in combination with policies of manpower development, training, education, and area redevelopment. The record of the past several years provides unmistakable support for this position.

Relevant evidence is found in the experience both of the highly skilled groups—who might have been a bottleneck for expansion—and of the low-skilled and depressed-area groups— whose employability might have been subject to particular question.

For example, in 1961 there were only 160,000 technical and professional workers unemployed, giving an unemployment rate for these workers of only 2 per cent. In the four succeeding years, employment of professional and technical workers expanded by 1,178,000. Since the number of such workers unemployed fell only by about 25,000, it is clear that at least 1,150,000 of the newly employed professional and technical workers were new entrants into the labor force, or were trained or upgraded from among other employed or unemployed workers. In 1965, the unemployment rate of professional and technical workers was 1.5 per cent. Although there continue to be specific shortages—such as teachers and medical personnel—our further expansion is not being restrained by any shortage of technical and professional workers.

The experience of the unskilled and geographically displaced is equally revealing. From 1961 to 1965, there was a net employment gain for "blue collar workers" of 2.6 million or 10.9 per cent, and for "laborers, except farm and mine," of 380,000, also 10.9 per cent, well in excess of the average employment gain of 8.1 per cent. Employment of nonwhites increased 11.5 per cent, and of teenagers almost 20 per cent. The unemployment rate of laborers fell from 14.5 per cent to 8.5 per cent; of nonwhites from 12.5 per cent to 8.3 per cent. The rate for teenagers declined from 15.2 per cent to 13.6 per cent, despite a net increase of one million teenagers in the labor force over this period. These rates are all too high. But we are confident that strong labor markets in 1966—along with active manpower policies—will again reduce these rates substantially.

In September 1961, 25 major labor market areas had unemployment rates of 7 per cent or more (table 1).[1] Many seemed to be areas of permanent distress, which no amount of general prosperity could erase. By September 1965, only 2 areas (both in Puerto Rico) had rates in excess of 7 per cent. Not only did the average unemployment rate decline over these 4 years, but the wide dispersion of unemployment rates was greatly reduced, with 121 of the 150 labor market areas showing rates between 2 per cent and 4.9 per cent in September 1965.

The lesson seems clear. The millions of "excess" unemployed were indeed employable, and the great flexibility and mobility of our labor force, and the ingenuity of our employers permitted their re-employment without severe strains or bottlenecks. . . .

Expansionary fiscal policy does work

Deliberately expansionary fiscal policy has been a major propelling force for the economy in the last five years.

At the end of 1960, the federal budget was essentially in balance (on the national income basis), while the economy was far out of balance and plagued by recession. Fiscal policy was clearly too restrictive. Over the past five years, federal outlays have risen $32 billion, not quite matching in percentage terms the growth of GNP. Meanwhile, tax cuts have directly added more than $16 billion to the private income stream. The combination of expenditure increases and tax cuts substantially exceeded the normal high employment growth of revenues, thus providing a sizable net stimulus to private purchasing power.

The response of the economy has been dramatic. By increasing after-tax incomes of individuals, consumer expenditures and business sales have been directly lifted. In this way, and through the depreciation reform, the investment tax credit, and the reduction in corporate taxes,[2] the profitability of private

---

[1] Omitted.—Eds.

[2] The new rates for tax-deductible depreciation, which increased the annual cash flow to corporations by $2.5 billion in 1963, were announced by the Treasury in July 1962. The investment tax credit, which allows corporations a deduction from their taxes for making investments

investment has been distinctly raised, contributing importantly to the strong expansion of business fixed investment we are now seeing. Statistical analysis shows that the direct and indirect effects of the 1964 tax cut alone were contributing about $30 billion to the level of GNP at the end of 1965 through higher consumer outlays and business investment. The strong rise of GNP has in turn generated sharply rising federal revenues in spite of tax rate reductions, In spite of—indeed in part because of—the massive tax cuts, federal revenues by the end of 1965 were, in fact, more than $30 billion higher than at the beginning of 1961.

Noninflationary expansion can benefit all groups

The course of the economy during the past five years demonstrates that economic expansion, accompanied by generally stable prices, can greatly benefit all groups in the society.

The advance of the economy—greater employment, higher productivity, larger volume of sales—has permitted large gains in real incomes for both labor and businesses. Both groups have benefited greatly, not at each other's expense, but by sharing the dividends of progress. We have had ample evidence in the past that attempts to gain excessively large wage increases do not in fact add to real wages, but rather raise prices. Similarly, price increases designed to widen profit margins have simply added to the costs of business, and swelled labor's demands and justification for bigger wage increases. This time, we have avoided either the wage-push or the profit-push engines of inflation. We have taken our gains in sound dollars and found that there was an abundance to go round.

Thus, in the five years between 1960 and 1965, all economic groups have made significant gains, even after adjustment for changes in prices. The average weekly spendable earnings of a manufacturing worker with three dependents rose by 13 per cent, after adjustment for the increase in consumer prices. Because of inflation, his gain in the previous five years has been less than 4 per cent. After adjustment for changes in prices, the

in machinery and equipment, was given to corporations by the Revenue Act of 1962, while the reduction in rate of taxes on corporate profits was a product of the Revenue Act of 1964.—Eds.

average income of self-employed and professionals rose by 14 per cent, and average net income per farm by nearly 34 per cent. As always during a period of recovery from recession or slack, corporate profits showed the largest gains. From 1960 to 1965, profits before taxes increased by over 50 per cent, after-tax profits by almost 67 per cent, and corporate dividends by 41 per cent. Adjusted for the rise in consumer prices, dividends have increased almost 35 per cent.

Labor gained in this expansion without pushing up unit labor costs. Wage settlements generally remained close to the good rate of advance in productivity. Overall unit labor costs rose on the average by less than 1 per cent a year and in manufacturing they showed essentially no trend. Business gained without relying on general price increases to widen profit margins. Between 1960 and 1964 the wholesale price index remained stable; it rose only during the last year, adding 2.0 per cent, largely as a result of special circumstances. Consumer prices rose at an average of only 1.2 per cent a year between 1960 and 1964 and by 1.7 per cent in 1965. To some extent, this rise was offset by unmeasured improvements in product quality. The acceleration in prices last year was mainly caused not by a cost push in the industrial sector but by farm and food price rises reflecting production cycles in agriculture. The absence of inflationary pressures during the past five years made possible the pursuit of expansionary policies that have brought great benefits to all the groups participating in the production processes of the economy. . . .

The challenge of defense

This year, we face not only the normal problems of prosperity but some special ones as well. The economic impact of Vietnam presents an important new challenge to our improved but imperfect abilities to maintain stable and sustained prosperity. In the past, defense build-ups have often disrupted the American economy and have rarely been taken in stride.

To be sure, we have the recent favorable example of the $7 billion increase in defense outlays of 1961-62, associated with the Berlin crisis. However, it impinged on an economy that was barely emerging from recession and that had a wide margin of idle men and machines. But it would be just as misleading to compare present problems with the Korean crisis. The mobilization requirements then were of a totally different order of magnitude from anything now reasonably foreseen for Vietnam. In ten months, from June 1950 to April 1951, the Armed Forces expanded by almost 1.5 million men. This time, slightly more than 300,000 men are being added during fiscal 1966 and another 100,000 in fiscal 1967. Similarly, the increase of $23.5 billion (annual rate) in defense outlays from the third quarter of 1950 to a year later simply dwarfs the $6 billion annual increase in today's much larger economy. In that one-year interval, defense outlays rose from 4.8 per cent to 11.3 per cent of GNP. This year, defense outlays will reach 7.7 per cent of GNP compared with the 7.4 per cent ratio in the first half of 1965, the low point of recent years.

The current buildup should not produce the economic dislocations and disruptions—real or psychological—that marked the start of the Korean conflict. The present situation obviously does not call for the same type of emergency restraint that was necessary then. The tools for dealing with our foreseeable defense needs are fiscal and monetary policies, fortified by the competitive workings of the price system, by limited use of existing authority for priorities and allocations, and by responsible wage and price decisions in areas of market power.

In short, by standards of mobilization the current defense needs are modest. By standards of fiscal stimulus, however, they are substantial and significant. The $6 billion of added outlays this year will have an important broad influence on all industries and all areas of the nation. But this stimulus has been appropriately offset within the fiscal program for 1966. Along with the incalculable human costs of armed conflict, defense needs are imposing the real economic costs reflected in the fiscal program: postponed tax reductions, more rapid tax payments, less rapid progress toward the Great Society. We are paying these costs to avoid the high toll of inflation. By making the proper adjustments we have good prospects for preserving a balanced noninflationary economy.

The new assignment of fiscal policy

Fiscal policy has demonstrated its ability to stimulate the economy when total spending lagged behind productive capacity. Now that demand and supply are in better balance, fiscal policy is called upon to contribute to smooth sustained expansion without adding further stimulus. This is a new assignment and a demanding one. But the principles to promote overall balance of supply and demand which have been successfully applied in the past are still there to guide us.

The enlarged defense requirements of Vietnam certainly complicate the task by enforcing a large increase in government purchases of goods and services. The normal growth in federal revenues generated by an advancing high-employment economy allows considerable room for increases in expenditures without making overall fiscal policy more expansionary. Our fiscal drag[3] is welcome this year. But the margin it provides does not match the required addition to defense outlays along with the highest priority expenditures for federal civilian programs.

The only way to prevent fresh new fiscal stimulus under these circumstances is to introduce restraint from the tax side. The appropriate restraining influence comes from the President's proposals to reschedule excise tax cuts and to put tax collections on a more current basis. With these measures, the fiscal program will not further stimulate the economy over the budget planning period of the coming year and a half. It approximately balances the stimulus of added expenditures and the restraint of increased taxes through both normal revenue growth and new legislation. The high-employment surplus[4] in the national income accounts budget was virtually removed in the second half of 1965. Over the next year and a half, the fiscal

[3] Fiscal drag refers to the fact that increases in potential GNP automatically generate increases in potential federal taxes. Since increased tax revenue, taken by itself, slows down spending, the economy "drags" or tends to grind to a halt. When too much spending is taking place, and inflation threatens, fiscal drag is "welcome," in the eyes of Keynesian economists, for the very fact that it does slow down the economy. For further discussion of this concept, see the following footnote and the authoritative comments of former Council chairman, Walter W. Heller, *New Dimensions of Political Economy* (Cambridge, Mass., 1966), pp. 64-73.—Eds.

[4] The "high-employment surplus," which the CEA often calls the "full-employment surplus," is the surplus in the federal budget that would exist if unemployment were reduced to 4 per cent. The council argued that the budget had been restricted because a positive full-employment surplus existed—even though the actual budget was in deficit, and a deficit budget is ostensibly a fiscal stimulant.—Eds.

program remains essentially at that position, tending to become somewhat more restrictive toward the end of that period. The President's program is a consistent and appropriate application of unwavering principles to a changed economic environment. We do not claim that this is a sure-fire formula for stable growth—but we know of no better strategy, and we believe this one should succeed.

CHAIRMAN PATMAN. Senator Proxmire?

SENATOR PROXMIRE. Mr. Ackley, I agree with you that we have had a wonderfully balanced and full prosperity. There is a tendency in these question periods to emphasize the negative rather than the positive.

Also, I think that your statement to us this morning in laying to rest some of the myths was very helpful. I don't agree, and I am sure that no member would agree fully, on all points, but I think that we have made great progress, and the speech of President Kennedy, made at Yale in 1962,[5] was directed at this same kind of thing. I think that by following up in 1966 and showing the progress that has been made by economic developments, you have served a real purpose this morning.

I would like to ask you about your *Annual Report of the Council of Economic Advisers*, pages 41-42, where the GNP potential seems to be based on a 4 per cent unemployment level. Since we have reached that, I wonder if the high-employment surplus is still based on that figure; 4.1 per cent was the last figure I recall, and as I understand it, it is expected to be less than 4 per cent in the coming year.

MR. ACKLEY. We could, of course, recalculate the high-employment surplus on some other percentage of unemployment. We have not done so. We have continued to calculate it on that basis of 4 per cent.

SENATOR PROXMIRE. Why not? Everything in your report, and also the statement that you made this morning, and that we have heard from Secretary Wirtz and others, seems to sug-

---

[5] Kennedy's June, 1962, Commencement address at Yale University challenged a number of long-standing conservative "myths": "that government is big and bad—and steadily getting bigger and worse . . . that federal deficits create inflation and budget surpluses prevent it." *Public Papers of the Presidents, John F. Kennedy, 1962*, pp. 470-75.—Eds.

gest that we can get the 3½ per cent without inflation. Why not give serious consideration to a somewhat lower level?

MR. ACKLEY. We have deliberately refrained from setting a new target for unemployment now that we have approximately achieved the old interim target, Senator, primarily because we are not sure enough what kinds of problems we will meet as we move down to 3½ per cent. If, as we hope and expect, a 3¾ per cent average unemployment rate for 1966 is possible, with relative stability of prices, then I think it might then become appropriate to aim for 3½ per cent or even possibly 3 per cent.

SENATOR PROXMIRE. This is a "supercautious" policy. In other words, you don't consider a target until after you have hit it, gone through it, and devastated it, and then you consider it may be a target.

It would seem to me in view of the fact that there was a great question—and I remember, Chairman Martin and others questioned—whether we would get down to anything like 4 per cent, or even 5 per cent, without inflation. We had inflation, but, of course, it has been very moderate. We have gotten down to 4 per cent now and as I say, you have very well documented arguments that we can reduce unemployment further, if we follow wise policies, without inflation.

I would simply recommend that you give real consideration to 3½ per cent.

MR. ACKLEY. We certainly will.

FISCAL STRATEGY OF
THE 1967 BUDGET*

On February 2, 1966, the Joint Economic Committee
heard its second witness, Charles L. Schultze, director of
the Bureau of the Budget. Like Ackley, Schultze had been
an economics professor (at the University of Maryland)
and had published a recent book on *National Income
Analysis* (Englewood Cliffs, N. J., 1964). Excerpts from
his prepared statement are reprinted, followed by a discussion on the space race with former Senator Paul Douglas of Illinois and an exchange with Senator William Proxmire of Wisconsin over the school milk program.

◇ ◇ ◇

Fiscal strategy of the 1967 budget

The central story of the 1967 budget, in its fiscal aspect, is
the change in emphasis from economic stimulation to economic
restraint. Fiscal policy is a two-edged weapon. This Administration—as you are, of course, aware—has not hesitated to
employ fiscal policy, primarily through tax reduction, as a
means of preventing the waste of unemployed resources.

The fiscal 1967 budget shows that we are also prepared to
shift the emphasis of fiscal policy away from economic stimulation toward restraint as conditions in the economy change.
Reasonable men may differ on whether the shift in emphasis

* Reprinted from *Hearings on the January 1966 Economic Report of
the President,* Joint Economic Committee (February, 1966), Part I, pp.
106-17, 156-59, 163-65.

is too great or too little. But the fact of the shift is undeniable.

Five years ago, the American economy was operating significantly below its potential. The unemployed rate in February 1961 was 6.9 per cent; industrial plant and equipment was operating at only 78 per cent of capacity, compared to the optimum rate of 92 per cent which, on the average, most firms desire to maintain; the gap between actual output and the economy's potential was $50 billion.

One of the principal reasons for that waste of economic resources through enforced idleness was the fiscal drag created by a tax structure under which the revenues generated under high employment conditions were too large relative to governmental expenditures.

Sound fiscal policy called for elimination of this fiscal drag. Two routes were open: a reduction in tax rates or an increase in expenditures relative to GNP. The Administration chose the former route. Tax reductions of some $20 billion were proposed and adopted by the Congress. Expenditure increases in the administrative budget were held below the rate of increase in GNP. In fact—leaving aside the added costs of the recent buildup in Vietnam—all other federal expenditures in the administrative budget will have risen only about half as rapidly as GNP in the six years between fiscal 1961 and 1967.

It is, naturally, difficult to prove causality in economic affairs. Nevertheless, I think the results of this policy speak for themselves.

Real gross national product has risen without interruption and at an average annual rate of over 5 per cent since 1961. Even while new industrial capacity rose rapidly, idle capacity was sharply reduced. The unemployment rate has fallen virtually to 4 per cent. Productivity has increased at a very substantial clip, and living standards have risen with it.

We face the year ahead with a substantially different set of conditions than those under which previous budgets in recent years have been formulated. The major factor, of course, is the economic impact of the conflict in Vietnam.

The costs of these operations will add some $10½ billion to federal expenditures between 1965 and 1967. These increases come at a time when economic activity—while still not completely up to economic potential—is closely approaching it.

Taken together with the projected course of private spending, they call for a fiscal policy shift away from economic stimulation in the direction of economic restraint.

At the same time, the 1967 budget had to be formulated under conditions of great uncertainty. No one can honestly claim to predict with accuracy the course of future events in Vietnam. We have presented budget estimates which reflect all the costs of Vietnam operations as we can best foresee them.

Expenditures, however, may ultimately turn out to be either higher or lower than those estimated in the budget. The actual course of events turns heavily on the actions of our adversaries. Under these circumstances, a fiscal policy had to be developed which permits an unusual amount of flexibility.

The 1967 budget, therefore, is designed to effect a shift in emphasis toward restraint under conditions of unusual uncertainty about future events:

First, outside of Vietnam, budget expenditures will rise by only $0.6 billion—about one-half of 1 per cent. This increase reflects not an arbitrary holding the line on every program, but a selective mixture of expenditure increases and decreases which approximately offset each other. I will discuss this at greater length at a later point.

Second, several measures have been proposed to increase revenues:

1. A graduated withholding plan for personal income tax collections;

2. A step-up in the already scheduled acceleration of corporate income tax payments;

3. A rescission of the excise tax cuts on passenger automobiles and telephone services which took effect January 1, plus a temporary postponement of further scheduled reductions.

In total, these measures are estimated to yield $1.2 billion in the current fiscal year and $4.8 billion in 1967.

Third, the combined impact of expenditure restraint and tax revenue increases will reduce the administrative budget deficit to $1.8 billion in 1967 and produce a cash surplus of half a billion dollars in the same year.

Since this budget was announced a number of criticisms have been leveled at it on the ground that the major tax measures it proposed yielded only temporary increases in revenues.

The fact is correct. The inference is wrong. These particular tax increases were chosen by the President precisely because their effects are temporary. I mentioned earlier the uncertainties facing us as the budget was formulated. The nature of the tax measures is a response to those uncertainties.

If a settlement is reached in Vietnam we will not have have made any unneeded changes in our tax structure. Conversely, if events in southeast Asia so develop that additional funds are needed, the President has stated, in his budget and economic messages, that he will not hesitate to ask for them, and at the same time to propose such fiscal actions as are required to maintain economic stability.

This budget, then, does provide for a significant shift in the thrust of fiscal policy—away from stimulation and toward restraint—in a way which takes into account the uncertainties of the situation. It is, I submit, a highly responsible budget.

Budget totals: Using the three major federal financial measures, the totals in the 1967 budget are given in Table 1.

TABLE 1.—BUDGET TOTALS
[In Billions]

	1965 actual	1966 estimate	1967 estimate
Administrative budget:			
Receipts	$93.1	$100.0	$111.0
Expenditures	96.5	106.4	112.8
Deficit	−3.4	−6.4	−1.8
Consolidated budget:			
Receipts	119.7	128.2	145.5
Expenditures	122.4	135.0	145.0
Deficit	−2.7	−6.9	+.5
National income basis:			
Receipts	119.6	128.8	142.2
Expenditures	118.2	131.0	142.7
Deficit	+1.2	−2.2	−.5

Administrative budget receipts are estimated at $111 billion in fiscal 1967, an increase of $11 billion over 1966. Of this increase, 3.6 billion reflects the effect of President Johnson's proposed revenue measures, while the remainder results mainly from the vigorous economic growth during the past year.

Total administrative budget expenditures are estimated to rise from $106.4 billion in 1966 to $112.8 billion in 1967. The administrative budget deficit, therefore, is expected to be $1.8 billion in 1967, substantially less than the estimated deficit for the current year and only about one-half the actual 1965 deficit.

In fiscal year 1966, $4.7 billion of administrative budget expenditure is for special Vietnam costs while $101.7 billion is for all the other functions of the government. In 1967, $10.5 billion is estimated for special Vietnam costs and $102.3 billion is for regular budget expenditures.

Thus, of the $6.4 billion increase in total administrative budget expenditures from 1966 to 1967, $5.8 billion represents the added costs of Vietnam. Expenditures for all other functions of the government are expected to increase by only $0.6 billion.

Some five years ago, the Bureau of the Budget—under one of my predecessors, Mr. Maurice Stans[1]—issued a report on the longer run outlook for federal expenditures. The report pointed out that the likely growth in federal nondefense expeditures, arising chiefly from the rising population and income of the nation, should be expected to run $2 to $2½ billion per year. Had the President in his 1967 budget allowed this growth of expenditures to be added to the additional costs of Vietnam and refrained from requesting the tax measures he has proposed, the 1967 budget would have showed not a $1.8 billion deficit, but something in the neighborhood of $9 billion.

Containing federal expenditures, outside of Vietnam, to an increase of only $0.6 billion was not, as I indicated earlier, accomplished by an arbitrary holddown of every program. The change of $0.6 billion actually reflects many increases and decreases.

For example, the 1967 budget provides for $5.3 billion of expenditure increases. These increases include:

1. $3.2 billion for Great Society programs, primarily in education, health, and the war on poverty;

2. $0.8 billion for higher interest costs and $0.3 billion for the

[1] Maurice H. Stans, director of the budget under President Eisenhower, was firmly committed to the principle of the balanced budget.—Eds.

added costs over 1966 of the military and civilian employee pay raises enacted last October; and

3. $1 billion for other unavoidable workload and contractual commitments, such as expenditures for construction projects started in earlier years.

Against these increases there are reductions of $4.7 billion included in the 1967 budget. These consist partly of:

1. $1.6 billion in defense activities excluding the added Vietnam costs and

2. $1.5 billion in savings through pruning lower priority programs, through management improvements, and the nonrecurrence of certain costs. The remaining $1.6 billion reduction stems from increased sales of mortgages and other financial assets or conversion of direct federal loans to guaranteed private loans—the substitution of private for public credit.

On the more comprehensive consolidated cash budget basis —including such trust funds as social security, medical care for the aged, aid for highway construction, and so on, which are financed by special trust fund receipts—payments to the public in 1967 are estimated to be $145 billion. Cash receipts are projected at $145.5 billion in 1967.

Thus, in spite of the heavy added costs we are incurring in Vietnam, it is estimated that we will realize a $0.5 billion cash surplus in 1967, the first such surplus in seven years.

On a national income accounts basis, federal outlays are estimated to rise to $142.7 billion in 1967. This concept most clearly indicates the direct economic impact of federal finances on the economy. It excludes financial and other transactions which do not directly enter into the national income accounts. The major part of federal national income account expenditures is for direct purchases of goods and services, which will amount to an estimated $74.4 billion in 1967.

Federal receipts on a national income account basis will rise from $128.8 billion in 1966 to $142.2 billion in 1967. While 1966 expenditures will exceed revenues by $2.2 billion on the national income accounts basis, the deficit will be reduced to only $0.5 billion in 1967.

Program strategy of the 1967 budget

As President Johnson said in his budget message, a budget is not simply a financial schedule. It is also a plan of action for the future. It reflects more than dollars and cents, it reflects the hopes and aspirations of hundreds of millions of people.

The President's program in the 1967 budget is based on two major premises:

1. The United States will do everything within its power to seek peace. But, we are also prepared to bear the cost of meeting our commitments abroad.

2. We will continue to press forward with high priority programs which will move us toward the Great Society. We will do so, however, in a manner which clearly recognizes the claim of our commitments abroad upon our great, but limited, resources.

The estimates presented in the 1967 budget provide for both of these purposes. But, as I indicated earlier, there are many uncertainties which could greatly alter the course of events, particularly with respect to our commitments in Vietnam. We have done our best to make the most realistic and reliable estimates possible.

While the composition of the total spending proposed for a given year is an important aspect of a budget, another significant element is the change from year to year. In spite of added costs for meeting our heavy military needs, the budget provides for continued progress toward the Great Society through the war on poverty and through stepped-up efforts in education, health, manpower and training, and housing and community development.

It is a difficult task to allocate scarce resources among many competing needs and provide a desirable balance between the various programs. One way—perhaps the easiest—is to simply stand pat and avoid any significant changes in the composition of the budget program.

A more difficult approach—the one which was followed in the 1967 budget—is to change the composition of federal spending by doing more of some things of immediate urgency and less of other lower priority things. This, essentially, is what we accomplished with the increase of $5.3 billion in 1967 expenditures and the decrease of $4.7 billion, resulting, as I stated earlier, in only a net increase of $0.6 billion in budget expenditures, excluding special Vietnam costs.

There are two additional factors which have helped to finance program expenditures within a relatively stable total level. First, upon the continued insistence of the President, every agency and department of the government has intensified its efforts to obtain a dollar's value for a dollar spent in each of their functions. As a result, savings are being made through management improvements, reorganizations, and better utilization of manpower resulting in increased productivity. On the basis of specific cost reduction reports from each government agency, we estimate that the 1966 and 1967 budget programs would each cost $3 billion more, if agencies were operating at their 1964 level of efficiency.

Second, expenditure reductions are being made from increased sales of mortgages and other financial assets or conversion of direct federal loans to guaranteed private loans. This substitution of private for public credit, wherever consistent with program objectives, is a continuation of a policy supported by the last three Presidents.

Table 2 illustrates the results of the change in composition of our federal budget over the past three years. Between 1964 and 1967, administrative budget expenditures, excluding the special costs of Vietnam, will rise by $4.6 billion, an increase of only 1½ per cent per year.

Within the total, however, there are sharply varying trends. Between 1964 and 1967, expenditures for the major Great Society programs will increase by $6.2 billion. Interest costs will increase by $2.1 billion. All other federal administrative budget expenditures, however, will decline by $3.7 billion over this three-year period.

SENATOR DOUGLAS. Now, may I ask you whether you see any soft spots in the budget? Do you think we should spend approximately $5 billion a year to put a man on the moon by 1970?

What is the use in getting to the moon before another country for prestige reasons when there is no advantage to either country getting to the moon?

MR. SCHULTZE. Well, if all we were doing with this program

TABLE 2.—THE CHANGING FEDERAL BUDGET

[Fiscal years. In billions]

	Administrative budget expenditures, excluding special Vietnam costs				
	1964 actual	1965 actual	1966 estimate	1967 estimate	Change, 1964 to 1967
Interest	$10.8	$11.4	$12.1	$12.9	+$2.1
Health, labor, education, housing and community development, economic opportunity program, and aid to the needy	6.7	7.3	10.8	12.9	+6.2
All other	80.2	77.6	78.8	76.5	−3.7
Total	97.7	96.4	101.7	102.3	+4.6

was getting to the moon and it had no side benefits, your question would disturb me.

SENATOR DOUGLAS. I have talked to scientists and the scientists tell me there are no scientific advantages in getting to the moon. I think there are no military advantages in getting to the moon.

You can hit any spot on earth from the earth just as well as you can from the heavens, and, besides, you can do your photographic work at 186 miles up; you don't have to go 240,000 miles up.

MR. SCHULTZE. I think that the additional factor to be put in here, however, is that this effort has generated tremendous advances in technology—in industrial management and the like—which admittedly can't easily be quantified or identified. But in evaluating—however one comes out—the merits of this program, this has to be taken into account.

SENATOR DOUGLAS. Taking a chance on failure.

MR. SCHULTZE. No, sir, I don't really think so. I recently, for the first time, had a chance to visit all these installations, and I must say I was tremendously impressed.

SENATOR DOUGLAS. Oh, yes, one is overawed by them, but what is the need or use? I have seen a marvelous blind chess player—marvelous fellow—playing twelve games at once, but what is the advantage of that?

MR. SCHULTZE. I am not sure, Senator, I don't want to be facetious, but I suspect that the first fellow who put the wheel together probably had a neighbor who said: "What are you going to use that darn thing for?"

I admit that you can't really put your finger on this. I admit that reasonable men can differ about how many dollars should go into the effort.

SENATOR DOUGLAS. Is it not really romance and prestige that is behind the drive for putting a man on the moon—simply romance and prestige?

Wouldn't it be better to improve the conditions of people on earth than to put a man on the moon or go to the older planet or planets? Shouldn't we consider the human conditions of mankind and not merely general prestige? That is one question.

MR. SCHULTZE. I just want to point out in this context, Senator, that we do have some $21 billion going toward the direct improvement of the poor, one way or the other.

SENATOR DOUGLAS. I know, but as you will very carefully say, part of that is from the trust fund, as I understand it.[2] While there is an increase in the fiscal year, since most of the poverty program started late in fiscal year 1965, there is a slowing down of the momentum which has been accumulated in the last six months.

MR. SCHULTZE. Two points to that, Senator. First, there is clearly a slowing down in the rate of acceleration.

SENATOR DOUGLAS. A slowing down in the total, isn't it?

MR. SCHULTZE. No, sir.

SENATOR DOUGLAS. So far as the last six months are concerned?

MR. SCHULTZE. Of this year?

SENATOR DOUGLAS. Of the last three or four months.

MR. SCHULTZE. No, sir; I don't think so. In fact, I looked only

[2] Senator Douglas is probably alluding to the fact that the Social Security program is a trust fund expenditure, paid for in advance, more or less, by the recipients.—Eds.

recently at their rate of obligations in the first six months compared to what their rate will be in the last six months, and—this is obligations—it will be higher in the last six months.

SENATOR DOUGLAS. Very little higher, if any, and in some programs a slowing down.

MR. SCHULTZE. There are a few, that is correct; but in the bigger ones, there is not a slowing down.

SENATOR DOUGLAS. May I ask about a point that I heard my friend and colleague, Senator Proxmire, inquiring about when I came in, the supersonic air transport. How much is that going to cost?

MR. SCHULTZE. The expenditures that we have in the budget for the supersonic air transport are $115 million, I believe.

SENATOR DOUGLAS. Yes, but what is beyond that, in future years? What is the ultimate total cost of developing supersonic air transportation?

MR. SCHULTZE. The experts and the people in charge of the program are still working out the details on this and I don't have a final figure, sir.

SENATOR DOUGLAS. I have heard figures; $1 billion, $2 billion.

MR. SCHULTZE. It is in that general range, I think, but I am not that close as to a specific estimate.

SENATOR DOUGLAS. What were the results of the Oklahoma City experiment?

MR. SCHULTZE. I can't answer that, Senator.

SENATOR DOUGLAS. The chairman comes from the borderline of Oklahoma, Arkansas, and Texas, but my information is it knocked out all kinds of windows and created all kinds of disturbances. What speed will the supersonic have?

MR. SCHULTZE. Mach 2.5 or 2.6, which is 2½ times 700 miles an hour. It gets up in the neighborhood of 1,800 to 2,000 miles an hour.

SENATOR DOUGLAS. I want to ask what is the use of going 2,000 miles an hour when you can go 750 miles an hour; considering all the incidental disadvantages, vibration, and shock?

MR. SCHULTZE. Senator, you are asking me for a reasoned analysis and exposition of the SST program for which, at the moment, I am not prepared.

It seems to me that a reduction in the time from here to London, let's say by roughly half—which I think is what would be involved—is over a period of years a significant saving in time.

SENATOR DOUGLAS. That is flying time.

MR. SCHULTZE. This is block time.

SENATOR DOUGLAS. But it is not a commensurate reduction in total time because of the time getting to the airport and getting on.

MR. SCHULTZE. It is about three hours.

SENATOR DOUGLAS. That would be a reduction of only about 20 per cent so far as that is concerned. It will take more time to get to an airport than to fly across the Atlantic. I want to say that one can get mesmerized by these new developments.

MR. SCHULTZE. As I say, and as I answered in the case of the space program, there are very substantial intangible benefits; and I don't mean just the benefits that come out of this in terms of science, technology, and the whole industry. I can't give you the dollar cost-benefit relationship—one tangible, one intangible—obviously, but I think it is an important advance.

SENATOR DOUGLAS. I remember when this man-to-the-moon business first came up I asked Mr. Bell, who was your predecessor, how much it would cost. He said a minimum of $20 billion. And I questioned whether it was worthwhile. One of my colleagues said: "Well, people questioned the expenditure to finance the experiments by Alexander Graham Bell and the telegraph." I replied: "That cost $40,000, and there is quite a difference between $40,000 and $20 billion."

My time is up. Now I simply want to say that a little critical judgment is needed on these measures. The public, the business community, the political world, is just carried away with the fascination of these subjects, and yet we ignore the human beings who live here in the United States of America, 20 million of whom live in abject poverty and 35 to 40 million living in poverty.

You can easily shift your sense of values from the human value to the spectacular mechanical value.

What profits a civilization if it has 20 million people in abject poverty and sends one man to the moon?

Thank you.

SENATOR PROXMIRE. One of the most puzzling decisions to me that the Administration has made in recent years is their decision not only to refuse to permit the school milk program to go ahead on the basis that Congress decided it should when they appropriated $103 million, but their decision to virtually kill the program in coming years.[3]

This is a conservative program, a well-established program, an accepted program, not criticized by the NAM, the chamber of commerce, or other groups.

It is a program that makes all the sense in the world because you have a surplus product here that is otherwise going to be stored away under price support programs. The government is going to save very little by cutting back on this program because they are just going to have to turn around under the 75 per cent price-support situation and buy the milk and store it and waste it.

I just can't understand the reasoning behind this.

MR. SCHULTZE. I hesitate to get myself in a position of arguing with someone who knows so much about it, but let me try at least some of the reasons that went into it. Let me assure you that it was not done until a good bit of careful consideration went into it—much of which you may disagree with, but it was carefully considered.

First, as you, of course, are aware, the whole emphasis in this reduction is to leave school milk in two situations: No. 1, where there is no school lunch program in a school. As you undoubtedly know, the school lunch program provides for a mandatory half pint of milk for the school lunch program to qualify. So that in case where there is a school lunch program, pulling out the special milk program will still leave milk.

Second, it will also continue to go to needy school districts on a formula that either hasn't been fully worked out or, if it has, I am not yet quite aware of it.

What this essentially does is to reduce the government's contribution in paying for milk for those who can well afford it.

That is point No. 1.

Point No. 2, on the basis of estimates of the Department of Agriculture only about one-fifth—I think I am right on that—there would be a reduction of about one-fifth in the amount of milk consumed in participating schools, and in most cases the reduction will not affect needy districts.

[3] The reduction was $82 million, from $103 to $21 million. The school lunch program was also reduced.—Eds.

It is not being taken out of areas where there is no school lunch program. Purchases and consumption of milk will continue.

In turn, since the government will have to pick up that one-fifth——

SENATOR PROXMIRE. Is there any documentation at all to that conclusion?

MR. SCHULTZE. I am sure the Department of Agriculture is prepared to provide that documentation in their presentation to the Appropriations Committee.

This is essentially the analysis they give us.

SENATOR PROXMIRE. The department told me last night what they intend to do is just leave it to the school administrator to decide which children are poor and which children are not poor.

How would you like to be a school administrator under those circumstances, to say this child's parents are poor? They can't afford to buy milk. In the first place, that requires a means test. We have never had a means test for children before.

We opposed a means test for adults for the medicare program and as one of our principal points of opposition. Now we are going to apply it to children and we are going to make the school administrator separate his flock in this way.

It seems to me he will be unpopular with both sets of parents —those who are not going to qualify because they are able to pay for it, and those who qualify because they are labeled poverty stricken—can't even pay a nickel a day for Johnny's milk.

What is going to happen under this program—on the basis of everything I have seen, and I have all kinds of letters from administrators all over the country—is that the administrators are going to say, "We don't want the school milk program." They will argue, "The school milk program is divisive and very bad for morale, and even though milk is important, it is just not that important."

MR. SCHULTZE. Senator Proxmire, as I said earlier, I must confess I don't know the specific administrative details which will be followed. I know that the objective of the cut was to continue to make milk available to children who need it, but not to have the federal government making contributions where they are not needed.

I know from earlier childhood experience that this kind of

thing can be done without embarrassment to children because I was in a school where a similar thing was done.

It wasn't for milk. It was for other contributions. I know it can be done that way. We never knew who paid or who didn't pay. It was a parochial school where you paid, and it was so worked out that those who weren't going to pay got tokens and nobody ever knew the difference. So I know it can be worked out.

I must confess, I can't guarantee that this will work perfectly. I don't know all the specific administrative arrangements, but this was the objective of the reduction.

SENATOR PROXMIRE. Who do you eliminate? People in the Department of Agriculture tell me, "You don't want Rockefeller's children to have free milk, do you?" Well, of course, this is the kind of argument that is ridiculous. The fact is that the great majority of people with children in grade school are at the toughest parts of their lives. They started their family formation a few years before, of course.

They are usually in debt. The wife has had to stop working because she has the child at home. They are people whose budgets are strained; and in view of the fact there is no opposition to the program, in view of the fact that you use up the surplus commodity, in view of the fact that it provides a very desirable and necessary element in the child's diet, it is very, very hard for me to understand it.

You say that the schools that have a school lunch program are the only ones who are going to be directly affected by it. Of course, there are many, many schools that don't have a school lunch program now and that don't qualify as needy schools.

It is my understanding that this would only be used in areas where either you have, as you said, a situation where most of the children come from needy families.

MR. SCHULTZE. Right.

SENATOR PROXMIRE. Or a situation in which you have the administrator apply some kind of a test or some kind of a judgment on his part.

MR. SCHULTZE. But, my understanding was that the primary way this would be done would be by school districts rather than by individual children, although, as I say, I am not sure of the exact specifics.

SENATOR PROXMIRE. It is perfectly obvious there is going to have to be a lot on discrimination. In almost every school district, including Montgomery County, the richest county in the country, there are many thousands of families whose incomes are extraordinarily low, and in each school district—you bring it down on the school districts—with few exceptions you find that in almost every school district, even though many of the families are well-to-do, there are other families that are not.

MR. SCHULTZE. But I would ask you to look at it in two lights. First, we have turned down many programs and we have cut many programs, and there isn't one of them that doesn't have some benefit.

This is a question of putting this into the context of a very difficult budgetary year, looking across the board at relative priorities and looking at benefits compared to costs. This is not to say that milk to needy children doesn't have a high priority.

SENATOR PROXMIRE. Milk to children; period.

MR. SCHULTZE. The other kids will get the milk.

SENATOR PROXMIRE. Well, I am not so sure.

MR. SCHULTZE. They will get the milk.

SENATOR PROXMIRE. You admitted yourself that the Department of Agriculture's own estimate is that a fifth to a sixth of this milk isn't going to be consumed.

MR. SCHULTZE. But that is a relatively small proportion, Senator.

SENATOR PROXMIRE. Maybe a small proportion, but if you have 4 million children involved that is 800,000 who aren't going to get it.

MR. SCHULTZE. That won't get the same amount. This is an estimate of total consumption at home and in the school. In many cases, it can continue in the school, but with full contribution.

In other cases, it will be gotten at home. I would be the first to admit that there is no administrative arrangement we have for helping the needy which doesn't give problems.

There is no question about that. I would be frank to admit it. But, again, we can't—it seems to me—make budgetary decisions on the basis that only when we can get 100 per cent perfect administration can we take a step.

It would be impossible. So, I realize your great interest in this program. I know you disagree vigorously with what we did, but I did want to indicate that we didn't do it arbitrarily.

We didn't do it simply on the basis of finding something to slash. We did give this a lot of consideration.[4]

[4] Congress refused to go along with the President's proposal for sharp budgetary cuts for school milk and the long-standing program was restored.—Eds.

ECONOMIC PROGRESS
AND THE GREAT SOCIETY*

Formerly chairman of the influential Council of Economic Advisers (under President Harry Truman), Leon Keyserling is currently president of the Conference on Economic Progress, a nonprofit, nonpolitical organization engaged in economic research. Considered by many to be a liberal gadfly, Keyserling has continued to maintain the original Keynesian position that government spending is the key to prosperity. Included in this volume are excerpts from two of his recent statements: a critique of the Kennedy–Johnson tax proposal of 1963, which passed into law early in 1964 without its reform features; and an analysis of the recent Reports of the Council of Economic Advisers and the economic policy of the Johnson Administration.

*The tax proposal overstresses investment
and understresses consumption*

In evaluating the tax proposal, it is necessary to examine it both without and with the reform elements which it contains. The proposal without the reforms is examined first.[1]

* Reprinted from *Taxes and the Public Interest*, published by the Conference on Economic Progress, June 1963, pp. 58-69; and *Hearings on the January 1965 Economic Report of the President*, Joint Economic Committee, Part 3, pp. 94-133.
  [1] The alternate analysis that Keyserling made, with the tax reforms included, has been omitted because these reforms did not become part of the law.—Eds.

Looking at the first chart following this chapter,[2] the tax concessions to investors in 1962, by congressional and Treasury action, have an annual value of about 2 billion dollars, and it is essential to consider this in connection with the new tax proposal. The proposed cut in corporate taxes is estimated at an annual value of more than 2.5 billion. The proposed personal tax cut, estimated at an annual value of 11 billion dollars, brings the total to 15.5 billion without the reforms.

It is very difficult to estimate what portion of the 11 billion dollar personal tax cut would be spent immediately by consumers, and what portion would be saved for investment purposes. But about 5 billion dollars of this cut would go to taxpayers with incomes of $10,000 and over, who constitute approximately one-fifth of all taxpayers. Certainly, no argument can be made for assigning more than 45 per cent of the total personal tax cut to the top-income fifth, except on the ground that they would utilize a large part of this cut for saving and investment. For if it were assumed that they would utilize a major portion of this cut to improve their immediate living standards, no considerations of equity or social justice would countenance failure to give a much larger part of the cut to the four-fifths lower down in the income structure, particularly the two-fifths of our total population who still live in poverty or deprivation. Assuming therefore that the taxpayers in the top fifth would use about 3.5 billion of their 5 billion cut for saving and investment purposes, this, added to the 4.5 billion in corporate tax cuts, lifts to 8 billion the portion of the total tax cut assigned to the investment function.

This would leave 1.5 billion dollars of the 5 billion personal tax cut granted to the upper-income fifth available for enlargement of their personal consumption. Adding the 6 billion dollars of the 11 billion proposed personal tax cut which would go to taxpayers with incomes below $10,000, and who might be expected to spend all or most of it for immediate consumption, brings up to 7.5 billion the portion of the total tax cut assigned to the consumption function. . . .

In view of the actual nature of our economic difficulties, such a pattern of tax change might well provide some temporary quickening of the rate of economic activity, both on economic

[2] This chart, as well as others referred to in the text, has been omitted.—Eds.

and psychological grounds. But in the longer run, the imbalances which this pattern of tax change would maintain or even augment would offer but slight realistic prospect of improving our long-term economic growth rate. Without the reforms, of course, the imbalance would be greatly worse than with the reforms.

The faulty distribution of the proposed personal tax cuts

Excluding the proposed tax reforms, the second chart following this chapter shows that only 3.7 per cent of the total personal tax cut would go to the 32.8 per cent of all those filing tax returns whose incomes are below $3,000. The 12.3 per cent who have incomes of $10,000 and over would receive 45.5 per cent of the tax cut; the 1.9 per cent with incomes of $20,000 and over would receive 21.1 per cent; and the 0.3 per cent with incomes of $50,000 and over would receive 8.3 per cent. . . .

Effect of the proposed tax cuts upon disposable incomes

Superficially, it may be argued that the foregoing distribution results inevitably from the fact that, under the current tax system, the higher income people pay progressively higher tax bills, and therefore should receive progressively larger shares of the tax cut. But it is essential to look more carefully at what the tax cuts really mean. Without the reforms, as shown on the fourth chart, taxpayers in the various income brackets would receive tax rate reductions of about the same size, measuring the proposed tax rate against the existing tax rate. Thus, the effective tax rate for the $3,000 taxpayer would be reduced 20 per cent and the tax rate for the $200,000 taxpayer 22.8 per cent. But the so-called tax reduction indicated by this customary measurement is merely a mathematical formula for determining *how much actual tax reduction each taxpayer gets.* What really counts, both economically and socially, is *the effect of the tax cuts upon disposable (after-tax) incomes.*

Measured in this proper way, as shown also on the fourth chart, without the reforms the $3,000 income taxpayer would receive an increase in disposable income of only 0.4 per cent;

the $5,000 income taxpayer, 1.8 percent; the $10,000 income taxpayer, 3.5 per cent; the $50,000 income taxpayer, 9.7 per cent; the $100,000 income taxpayer, 16.3 per cent; and the $200,000 income taxpayer, 31.1 per cent.[3]

HIGH UNEMPLOYMENT, THE HUGE PRO-DUCTION GAP, AND THEIR CONSEQUENCES*

The Report of the Council of Economic Advisers persists in stating the volume of unemployment as being in the neighborhood of 5 per cent of the civilian labor force. But I have not found economists prepared to defend this figure. Taking into account not only full-time unemployment as officially recorded, but also the full-time equivalent [4] of the part-time unemployment which is also revealed in government statistics, and the concealed unemployed which results from those who are not in the civilian labor force only because of the high level of unemployment and the scarcity of job opportunity, my estimate is that the true level of unemployment averaged 6.3 million or 8.3 per cent of the civilian labor force in 1964, and 6.2 million or 8.1 per cent of the civilian labor force, seasonally adjusted, in fourth quarter 1964. These estimates are set forth on my chart 1.[5]

A number of years ago, before this committee, I began to make the point that the count of unemployment should include the full-time equivalent of part-time unemployment. It is only more recently that other economists have come to assert the validity of this proposition. Three years or so ago, I began to point out, before this committee, that the concealed or hidden

[3] Using the same assumptions as to family size and deductions as in earlier chapters. [He assumes that the taxpayer is married, with two children. A flat 10 per cent deduction is allowed for taxes.—Eds.]

* From Keyserling's testimony before the Joint Economic Committee.

[4] The following example may help make this concept understandable. Suppose the work week were 40 hours. If 4 individuals worked only 10 hours each but all wanted to work full time, the full-time equivalent is 3, obtained by adding up the undesirable leisure, 120 hours, and dividing by 40.—Eds.

[5] Again, the chart mentioned, as well as the other charts Mr. Keyserling referred to in these hearings, has been omitted here.—Eds.

unemployment should also be counted. At long last, in its current report, the council admits categorically (p. 83) that "many who are not currently counted in the labor force would be at work if unemployment were reduced to 4 per cent." The President, on page 7 of his report, puts it even more strongly. He says that there are about 1 million "hidden unemployed" who would enter the labor force if the unemployment rate could be brought down just 1 percentage point. For these reasons, and thinking in terms of a full employment environment, rather than just bringing unemployment down by 1 percentage point, I do not feel that there can be serious challenge to my estimate that concealed or hidden unemployment is now in the neighborhood of 1.5 million.

Yet, for all practical purposes of analysis and policy, the council continues to talk about 5 per cent unemployment. I cannot understand why they persist in this.

The lower half of the same chart 1 contains my estimate that the production gap in 1964 was about $82 billion, or about 11.9 per cent of maximum production, and was about $87 billion, or 12.4 per cent of maximum production, in fourth quarter 1964 (annual rates). In contrast, the Council of Economic Advisers (p. 39) estimates the production gap now at between $25 and $30 billion. But the council arrives at this estimate by projecting a 3.5 per cent annual growth rate from early 1955, as being consistent with our growth potential. I submit that this is grossly in error, for two reasons. First, we were nowhere near optimum resource use in early 1955. And second, for reasons which I shall disclose shortly, the use of a 3.5 per cent figure as representing our potential growth rate from year to year is indefensibly low, and does not square with various findings of the council itself.

The inadequate growth rate since 1953, and its current persistence

My chart 3, with which the committee is familiar in its earlier versions, contains in its first sector data which lead me to insist that, in recent years, we have needed an average annual growth rate in the neighborhood of 5 per cent to keep our resources reasonably fully employed. But from 1953 through 1964, the annual average was only 3 per cent. As shown by the bottom sector of the same chart, which shows the growth rate trends in twelve-month periods, the last twelve-month period shown, ending with fourth quarter 1964, reveals a growth rate of only 3.9 per cent, representing a sharp shrinkage in the growth rate in each of the twelve-month periods following the period from second quarter 1963 to second quarter 1964. And this 3.9 per cent growth rate should properly be contrasted, not with the 5 per cent or so which we would need subsequent to full economic restoration, but rather with the 8 to 9 per cent that we need for at least two years to achieve full economic restoration.

Actually, despite all the talk about the longest recovery on record, what has really been stretched out is a period of high level stagnation, and what has really been deferred into the indefinite future is the achievement of anything approximating full economic recovery.

It is striking that even the Council of Economic Advisers, despite the glowing optimism of its report, admits this. For on page 39, the Council says: "The remarkable characteristic of the current expansion is not the degree to which it has carried us toward our objective of full employment. Previous expansions have done as well or better in this respect. Rather, its most remarkable feature is its durability." I do not find much comfort in such long durability of 8 per cent unemployment, or even 5 per cent unemployment. This is not the purpose of the Employment Act.

The council has virtually abandoned the central purpose of the Employment Act, which is to budget maximum employment, and propose policies accordingly

The central purpose of the Employment Act [6] is not to bring forth mere business forecasts, nor to take pride in the fact that previous forecasts have been nearly correct. The central purpose of the Employment Act is to state the requirements for maximum employment, production, and purchasing power,

[6] The key section of the Employment Act is reprinted above, p. 54. —Eds.

and to devise policies accordingly. This the council does not even pretend to do.

A simple mathematical demonstration, profoundly important but overlooked in most of the commentaries, should drive this point home. On page 91, the council says this: "Apart from increases in participation rates that would be induced by improved employment opportunities, the expected annual growth [in the civilian labor force] to 1970 is 1.7 per cent, or about 1.4 million persons, a major acceleration from the yearly average of 1.2 per cent, or 0.9 million persons, in the past 9 years." (On p. 61, the council estimates the average annual increase in the civilian labor force through 1970 at 1.5 million.)

Then (p. 54), the council says that productivity in the private economy advanced during the four years 1961-64 at an average annual rate of 3.5 per cent. To this the council adds (p. 83) that "productivity would be higher in a full-employment economy than it is today . . . in periods of underutilization, output per worker is depressed." Thus, the council now admits a main point which I have been stressing all along.

Adding the 1.7 per cent to the 3.5 per cent, even without allowing for compounding, and even without allowing for the more rapid growth in productivity and in the civilian labor force which the council itself says would result under conditions of full utilization, the resultant figure is 5.2 per cent. This squares precisely with my own estimates, frequently reiterated, that the growth rate in our output potential is now in excess of 5 per cent, and that consequently we must actually grow more than 5 per cent a year merely to hold our own with respect to unemployment. This seems well supported by recent developments, especially when full account is taken of the extent to which the true trends in productivity and in the labor force have been concealed by underutilization.

Yet the council, which until this year was arguing that our growth potential was about 3½ per cent a year, now says (p. 81) that it is about 3¾ per cent a year. How the council gets 3¾ per cent by adding 1.7 per cent and 3.5 per cent is beyond me, unless the council takes as our productivity growth potential the average of the last forty years instead of the average of the last four years—a manifestly unsound approach, especially in view of the new technology and automation.

This entirely insupportable figure of 3¾ per cent apparently explains the council's optimism in the face of its forecast (p. 85) that recommended policies are likely to yield a 1965 GNP about 4½ per cent higher than in 1964 in dollar terms, and it appears somewhat less than 4 per cent higher in real terms.

Nor is this all. The council says that the labor force is going to grow by 1.7 per cent or 1.4 million a year. But absorption of this growth would take no account of the excess unemployment, which is currently at least 3 million on a true unemployment basis. To get back to maximum employment within two years, the growth in job opportunity would need to be about 3 million a year (counting both the growth in the labor force and the current excess unemployment). This means that employment would need to expand by more than 4 per cent a year. Adding this 4 per cent to the 3½ per cent annual growth in productivity, we need, even according to the council's analysis, an annual growth rate in the neighborhood of 7½ per cent a year for at least two years, if we have any serious intent to make real inroads upon unemployment and to restore maximum employment even by 1967. (My estimate is 8 to 9 per cent, because I factor in the effect of faster growth and fuller utilization upon productivity trends.)

This figure of 7½ per cent makes even more unacceptable the council's mere forecast that the economy is likely to grow somewhat less than 4 per cent in 1965. In short, the council admits categorically that, while it expects full-time unemployment in 1965 to be somewhat lower than in 1964 as a whole, it is not willing to forecast that it will be lower than it is now. Thus, the council says (p. 85): "In constant prices, the increase in output is likely to exceed the growth of potential, reducing the gap moderately." Adding to this the fact that the council is grossly underestimating the current potential growth rate, it is incontestable that the council has virtually abandoned any effort to do very much about reducing unemployment, or for that matter, about the production gap. I submit respectfully that this committee should consider placing major emphasis, in its forthcoming report, upon this virtual abandonment of the high purposes of the Employment Act. . . .

Why massive tax cuts cannot reduce unemployment very much

The general theory in back of the tax cuts is that tax reductions increase aggregate demand, and that more aggregate demand means more employment. This completely neglects the fact that the economic disequilibrium results not from total unavailability of adequate purchasing power, but rather from its maldistribution. If this were not the case, we could get full employment by giving another $20 billion of tax reduction to corporations and persons of high income. But they could not invest it, and they would save rather than spend much of it (even if they did spend it for consumption, the social results would be unconscionable, when we have so much poverty and such great national public needs).

The report of the Council of Economic Advisers accepts without question this whole fallacious doctrine of the efficacy of expansion of aggregate purchasing power, regardless of its distribution. Thus, the council says (p. 98) that further federal fiscal stimuli will be needed, but that the criteria in choosing between more tax reduction and more public outlays are "not primarily economic."

This bland assumption by the council that there is not much economic difference between a given volume of tax cuts and the same volume of increased public outlays is utterly insupportable on purely economic grounds, quite aside from the social question. This bland assumption ignores the very nature of the new technology and automation. As shown by my chart 12, the trends in technology and automation, in most basic sectors of the private economy, are such that no feasible increases in demand for their products can result in much additional employment. For example, in the automobile industry, less than 59 workers in 1963 turned out as much or more than 108 turned out in 1947. This means, very simply, that the creation of the 25 to 27 million new jobs which the government itself says are needed over the next decade will depend upon a pronounced shift in the structure of demand, toward those types of products where the nation's unmet needs are so great that the increased demand for products can run far ahead of the increases in technology and productivity in these particular sectors. This means relatively more emphasis upon rehousing slum dwellers, rebuilding our cities, improving our mass transportation, developing and replenishing our natural resources, expanding both facilities and personnel with respect to education and health services, etc. To illustrate these needs, my chart 13 indicates my estimates as to the relative opportunities for employment expansion from now through 1975. Manifestly, this calls for relatively more emphasis upon increased public outlays than upon tax reduction. Moreover, the shift in the product mix thereby obtained would be entirely compatible with the war against poverty and the real needs of the Great Society.

Professor Galbraith, in his recent testimony, argues for more public spending instead of more tax cuts. I agree with his conclusion, but dissent in large part from some of his implications. His argument is that most of the unemployment today is due to the unfitness of the unemployed for available jobs, and that more public spending would help to train and educate them so that they would be fit for these jobs and obtain them. While I agree as to the need for more education and training, all experience indicates that the main problem is to create the jobs. The jobs draw in the people, and they get trained mostly on the job, and in any event we do not know what to train them for until we know what jobs are opening up. Therefore, as against the school which places major emphasis upon the structure of the labor force, I agree that the problem is to create enough aggregate demand to restore full employment. But we cannot get enough aggregate demand without drastic changes in the structure of demand. Viewing technological factors as well as the nation's needs, we must get the changes in structure of demand to which I have referred above, in order to move toward full employment. And these changes in the structure of demand cannot possibly be accomplished by more and more tax reduction; they require, for the reasons already stated, vastly increased public outlays. The fact that this shift in public policy would also administer so much better to the needs of the poor and deprived, and to the growing gaps in our public services, illustrates my favorite thesis that the economic problem and the social problem, the employment problem and the poverty problem, are really all one problem in the United States. Fragmentizing them into isolated compartments points us in the wrong direction on all fronts.

The neglect of the problem of the needed shifts in the structure of demand is well illustrated by the council's treatment of the housing problem. My own estimates indicate that an adequate program of rehousing the one-fifth of the nation who still live in slums, and corresponding rebuilding of our decaying municipal areas, could during the next decade meet a full half of the whole requirement for net additions to employment. It could simultaneously make the largest single attack upon the problem of poverty, which is so deeply rooted in the slums. It could simultaneously, through the uniquely high "multiplier" effect of housing outlays, contribute most to the maintenance of adequate economic growth.

But due to failure to quantify on a long-range basis the various components in our resources and needs, the council nowhere identifies the vital importance of the housing problem. Merely qualitative reference to this problem is not enough, without identification of the amounts and types of housing required, and the changes in both public and private economic policies, including fiscal and monetary policies, essential to achieve these goals. As a striking evidence of this oversight, the council (pp. 48-49) seems entirely complacent about the tapering off of housing starts, and equally complacent about its own forecast (p. 86) that no substantial expansion of housing outlays is expected in 1965. . . .

The fundamental problem of income distribution

My core concern about the report of the Council of Economic Advisers is that it really overlooks or skirts what seem to me to be the big and difficult problems of our economy. As I have indicated, these problems raise the question of the attainment and maintenance of economic equilibrium at maximum resource use. This issue, in turn, is fundamentally one of income distribution. It is income distribution that allocates resources. And in a country as highly developed as ours in a material and technological sense, it is the allocation of resources which determines how close we come to full resource use.

It is by now apparent that my analysis leads to the conclusion that we are chronically plagued by the problem of excessively slack resources, mainly because of faulty income distribution, compounded by national economic policies which have in part contributed to this faulty distribution and in any event failed to make appropriate efforts, within the ambit of our institutions and ideals, to help correct this maldistribution.

I, therefore, find it desirable to bring before this committee a few outstanding illustrations of this distributional problem, especially as they are areas of concern to me, but to which the council's report pays little or no attention. I deplore the recent tendency of so many outstanding economists to shun the whole problem of income distribution, possibly on the ground that it is a thorny and controversial subject, when it is a problem at the very heart of our economic and social performance.

1. My chart 19 indicates that, as of 1962, the top quintile of all U.S. multiple-person families had more than eight times as much more income as the lowest quintile, and very considerably more than the lowest three income quintiles. With respect to unattached individuals, the top quintile had more than 26 times as much income as the lowest quintile, and considerably more income than the four other quintiles put together. I do not regard this pattern of income distribution as conducive to optimum economic performance, and it is certainly not compatible with our social conscience when more than 34 million Americans live in poverty, and when about twice this number live either in poverty or deprivation. . . .

The council is not adequately budgeting our resources and needs

The whole import of what I am saying is that, contrary to the express intention of the Employment Act, the council is not making long-range quantifications of our needs and resources, as guidelines to economic policy. If it would do so, the whole context of policy would undergo drastic change, as it would at once become apparent from these long-range quantifications that recent and current trends in policies are not suitably adjusted to our economic purposes and goals.

THE KENNEDY–JOHNSON BOOM *

Business Week, an influential magazine read by many American business executives, ran an unusual feature in its issue of April 13, 1963. Under the title, "Viewing U.S. Economy With a Marxist Glass," *Business Week* offered an analysis of the *Monthly Review,* an independent socialist magazine, and its editors Paul M. Sweezy and Leo Huberman:

"Sweezy, whose article on how giant corporations compete, 'Demand Under Conditions of Oligopoly' [*Journal of Political Economy,* XLVII (1939), pp. 568-73—Eds.], is required reading for most Ph.D. candidates in economics, spent twelve years on the Harvard faculty. He quit Harvard after a World War II OSS stint because 'I got bored.' Now, like Huberman, he gives most of his time to *Monthly Review.* At the moment, though, he's enjoying a small academic boom. He taught at Cornell in 1961 and at Stanford in 1962; this year he has been invited to lead seminars at other top schools, such as MIT.

"Huberman formerly taught economic history at Columbia. An old-line American-style radical, he was once labor editor of the now defunct New York newspaper *PM.* His skill is as a writer and popularizer rather than theorist; his economic history of the West, *Man's Worldly Goods,* first published in 1936, has sold over 500,000 copies."

Business Week goes on to say of them that they ". . . peddle a brand of socialism that is thorough-going and tough-minded, drastic enough to provide the sharp break

* From *Monthly Review,* XVI (February, 1965) and XVII (February, 1966). Slightly abridged, by permission.

with the past that many leftwingers in the underdeveloped countries see as essential. At the same time they maintain a sturdy independence of both Moscow and Peking that appeals to neutralists. And their skill in manipulating the abstruse concepts of modern economics impresses would-be intellectuals. . . . Their analysis of the troubles of capitalism is just plausible enough to be disturbing."

In the reading that follows, Sweezy and Huberman give an analysis "just plausible enough to be disturbing" of how the American economy is becoming ever more dependent on war to bring about prosperity.

◇ ◇ ◇

The business-political Establishment which runs this country has digested Keynesian economic theory and has begun to put it into practice. It likes the results. Listen to Douglas Dillon, Wall Street financier turned Secretary of the Treasury, speaking at the Harvard Business School last June 6 [1964]:

In the relatively short span . . . of less than three and one half years, both American economic policy and practice have taken new and dramatic turns for the better. Our economy is no longer on the wane—but surely and strongly on the rise. And we can now look forward, in all sober confidence, to the continuation of a peacetime economic recovery of greater durability and strength than in any comparable period in this century.

Equally important, the past three and one half years constitute a significant watershed in the development of American economic policy. For they have borne witness to the emergence, first of all, of a new national determination to use fiscal policy as a dynamic and affirmative agent in fostering economic growth. Those years have also demonstrated, not in theory, but in actual practice, how our different instruments of economic policy—expenditure, tax, debt management, and monetary policies—can be tuned in concert toward achieving different, even disparate, economic goals. In short those years have encompassed perhaps our most significant advance in decades in the task of forging flexible economic policy techniques capable of meeting the needs of our rapidly changing economic scene. (Treasury Department News Release.)

The achievement of which Mr. Dillon and his colleagues in business and government are proudest is a continuous and, relative to the immediately preceding years, high rate of growth of Gross National Product (GNP = total output of goods and services). In 1960, the last Eisenhower year, GNP was $502.6 billion. Estimates for 1964 put the figure at $624 billion. The increase in the four years of the Kennedy–Johnson Administration was thus 24 per cent—or, expressed as an average of the annual increases, 5.6 per cent per annum. This is unquestionably high by relevant historical standards, and it is scarcely surprising that it evokes hosannas from the Establishment's scribes and pundits. "Americans have received a $40 billion lift this year," writes Edwin L. Dale, Jr., in the *New York Times* of December 26 [1964]. And he continues:

The $40 billion represents the growth in the economy in 1964 over 1963, as measured by the gross national product. . . .

The growth in 1964 is nearly as large as the entire gross national product of Canada, which will be about $45 billion this year.

It is about half the gross national product of France.

It is also . . . probably more than the Soviet Union's economy grew this year and last year combined, and possibly more than the last three years combined.

What government policies have contributed to this speeding up of the overall rate of economic growth? At first blush the answer might seem to be very simple, and entirely in accordance with Keynesian prescriptions: deficit financing. The record of federal government cash surpluses (+) and deficits (−) during the last five years is as follows (in billions of dollars):

1960	+3.6
1961	−6.8
1962	−5.7
1963	−4.6
1964	−5.2 [1]

[1] Estimate based on first three quarters. Unless otherwise indicated, all figures in this piece are from the December, 1964, issue of *Economic Indicators*, monthly publication of the Council of Economic Advisers. [The final figure for 1964 was as estimated, 5.2.—Eds.]

That a shift from budgetary surplus to deficit and the continuation of sizable deficits should, other things being equal, produce an acceleration of economic growth has by now attained the status of an axiom; it might seem therefore that the question is answered and there is little more to say except that Keynes and his followers have been proved right.

In reality matters are not quite so simple. The "other things being equal" proviso is an indispensable part of the axiom, and in practice other things rarely are equal. In fact, opponents of Keynesian policies, at least the more sophisticated among them, have always argued that deficit financing, if continued for any length of time, must have an adverse effect on other variables of the system and thus defeat its own ends. In particular, they reason that businessmen are a conservative lot who believe in balanced budgets, perhaps not every year but certainly over a period of years, and that therefore a continuation of deficits is bound to undermine their confidence and precipitate a decline in private investment. This did not happen during the last four years; on the contrary, business expenditures for plant and equipment are estimated to have been a good 25 per cent higher in 1964 than in 1960, the last year of a (more than) balanced budget. What explains this apparent enthusiasm of businessmen for the policy of continuing deficits? This is evidently as important a part of the whole picture as the facts of the deficits themselves.

The approved answer to this question is that American businessmen have finally become enlightened. They have, so to speak, studied Samuelson's *Economics*,[2] and they know that the supposed need to balance the budget is an old wives' tale. And so, when Kennedy brought the Keynesians to Washington with him, the stage was all set for the grand experiment: businessmen were not only ready to acquiesce but actively to co-operate.

There is undoubtedly something to this theory: the men who run the giant corporations which dominate the American economy have certainly shed the blinkers of old-fashioned fiscal orthodoxy. But this is not to say that they are enthusiastic about a policy of deficits as such. It is safe to assume that if at any time

[2] Paul Samuelson's *Economics: An Introductory Analysis* (New York/London/Toronto, many editions from 1948 on) is a leading college textbook written from a Keynesian perspective.—Eds.

either Kennedy or Johnson had proposed to open up a deficit by sharply increasing expenditures of a "welfare state" variety while leaving taxes unchanged, the men of the corporations would have been strongly opposed; and if the program had nevertheless been adopted by the Congress (a most unlikely assumption of course), business confidence and private investment would undoubtedly have suffered in accordance with the anticipations of the traditional anti-Keynesian theory. In other words, it all depends on *what kind* of deficits are at issue. Once we look at the matter from this angle, we shall have little difficulty in understanding the wholehearted enthusiasm of the Big Business community for the Kennedy–Johnson policy of deficits.

In the Harvard Business School speech quoted above, Treasury Secretary Dillon gives an account of the genesis and development of this policy. The problem when the Kennedy administration took office, he says, was "sluggish growth and inadequate incentives for investment. Postwar expansionary forces had been dissipated. Tax rates were siphoning off too much income to allow the private economy to reach full employment. The result was inadequate demand—with increased unemployment and ever more frequent recessions." [3]

Under these conditions, a basic decision was taken to rely on fiscal policy. But this posed the "big question" which was "whether to increase government expenditures or to reduce taxes—or, to come to the heart of the matter: whether to rely upon the latent energies of the private sector or to expand government activity."

The reasoning at this point is crucial to an understanding of all that followed:

Larger government expenditures, if well timed, could, of course, have boosted demand and thereby cut unemployment.

[3] Secretary Dillon is referring to the following unemployment rates:

1951	3.3	1956	4.2	1961	6.7
1952	3.1	1957	4.3	1962	5.6
1953	2.9	1958	6.8	1963	5.7
1954	5.6	1959	5.5	1964	5.2
1955	4.4	1960	5.6		

"Ever more frequent recessions" is indicated by the fact that the expansion of 1949-53 lasted 45 months; that of 1954-57, 35 months; and that of 1958-60 only 25 months.—Eds.

But unless such expenditures could be clearly justified on their own merits, their long-run contribution to productivity and investment would be uncertain at best. Thus they seemed to offer less benefit . . . than the path we chose: tax reduction.

The phrase "unless such expenditures could be clearly justified on their own merits" is obviously question begging, but in context its meaning is plain enough: unless those responsible for investment decisions approved, additional government expenditures could not be counted on to produce the desired expansionary effect. From the outset a veto power was conceded to the men of the corporations: the expansion of demand (deficit) would have to be achieved by methods tailored to their interests. Hence tax reduction, and hence also the kind of tax reduction decided upon. We return to this presently.

The decision to rely on tax reduction did not mean the renunciation of all increases in spending. In our system, it takes a long time to pass new tax legislation and still longer for it to begin working as intended. In the meantime, an increase in spending was urgently called for, with the proviso of course that it should be justified in the eyes of Big Business. Fortunately, from Mr. Dillon's point of view, there were in 1961 "overriding national priorities, all of which cost money: the need to bring our military defenses to a higher plateau of readiness, the special requirements of the Berlin crisis, the rapidly expanding space program. And, of course, the interest on the national debt." Yes, of course. These are the expenditures which are "justified on their own merits," and Dillon proudly boasts that the rate of increase of spending for arms, space, and interest on the national debt has been double that of the second Eisenhower Administration. For all other purposes, he is equally proud to report, the increase in spending during the Kennedy–Johnson Administration comes to "one third less than the comparable increase during the earlier 4-year period." In retrospect, Ike is beginning to look like a rabid pacifist and New Dealer!

While the full tax-cut program was in preparation, certain preliminary steps were taken. Let Dillon tell the story:

It was necessary to get the major increases in defense and space spending behind us before we could safely implement our full program of tax reduction. But rather than wait, we promptly undertook two major moves to improve the climate for business investment—moves that could be instituted without any excessive loss of revenue. They were the Revenue Act of 1962, with its central provision of a 7 per cent investment tax credit, and the administrative liberalization of depreciation—both landmarks of progress in our drive to spur the modernization of our capital equipment. Together they increased the profitability of investment in new equipment by more than 20 per cent. This was equivalent in terms of incentives to invest to a reduction in the corporate profits tax from 52 per cent to 40 per cent.

But, says Dillon, the "biggest impediment to a more robust private sector still remained—the high individual and corporate income tax rates." The crowning act of policy was therefore the tax law of 1964, designed to "break the grip of these high tax rates on our economy"—and in the process distributing some $11½ billion of largesse, mostly to the rich but with a sop to the little fellow thrown in as a political lubricant.

As a final assessment, Dillon approvingly cites a study by George Terborgh, an ultraconservative economist at the Machinery and Allied Products Institute, which shows that the tax measures adopted in 1962 and 1964 by the Kennedy–Johnson Administration will together have an effect on after-tax returns to capital comparable either to a cut in corporate income tax rates from 52 per cent to 34 or 29 per cent (depending on the ratio of equity to total capital), or to a reduction in the cost of new capital equipment of 16 per cent. "It is hardly surprising," Dillon adds, "that investment activity is responding to incentives of this magnitude—even though it will be some time before the cumulative impact is fully realized—and that investment spending is now spearheading the recovery." Quite so, it is hardly surprising.

It is also hardly surprising that businessmen are so enthusiastic about *this kind* of deficit spending: boiled down to essentials it amounts simply to using the borrowing power of the federal government to subsidize corporate profits. But let no one be so naive as to conclude that some other kind of deficit spending—for example, the use of the government's borrowing power to provide decent jobs or incomes for the poverty-stricken, free medical services, good education—would command similar enthusiasm from the lords of the economy. Deficits incurred for *such* purposes would obviously be wasteful and confidence-destroying. And, as every right-thinking person knows, there could be no greater folly than to harm, or even threaten, that delicate plant which is the confidence of the billionaire corporations and the millionaires who run them.

Against this background, let us examine a little more closely the main characteristics of the great Kennedy–Johnson boom.

In the first place, the real beneficiaries have been, as intended, the corporations. Aggregate corporate profits after taxes have increased as follows (in billions of dollars):

1960	22.0
1961	21.9
1962	25.0
1963	26.7
1964	32.0 [4]

This, however, underestimates the real increase, since the liberalization of depreciation rules in 1962 enabled the corporations to shift approximately $2.5 billion from (taxable) profits to (nontaxable) depreciation. If we make a rough adjustment by adding this figure to the totals for 1962 and later years, we find that the increase in profits from 1960 to 1964 was $12.5 billion, or 57 per cent. This is more than double the increase of GNP which, as noted earlier, was 24 per cent in the same period.

Not all industries shared equally in this bonanza, of course. It is therefore worthwhile to cull out industry profit data from a twelve-page news release issued by the White House on October 22 (less than two weeks before the election) setting forth "a compilation showing some of the economic gains achieved by twelve major industries in the United States during the Kennedy–Johnson Administration." The figures are percentage increases in after-tax profits during the four-year period 1961-64, arranged in descending order of magnitude:

[4] Annual rate in the third quarter.

Motor vehicles and parts	120.3
Transportation equipment	89.9
Textiles	80.0
Non-electrical machinery	79.0
Nonferrous metals	46.0
Iron and steel	41.9
Chemicals	35.2
Petroleum	34.8
Paper and paper products	28.5
Electrical utilities	21.3
Food and beverages	17.6

Note: No profit figures are given for mining, which is the twelfth industry.

Wage-earners, even those fortunate enough to hold steady jobs, have done less well than even the least favored of these industries. Average weekly earnings in manufacturing went up only 15.8 per cent between 1960 and the first three quarters of 1964. And if this is adjusted to take account of the 5 per cent increase in consumer prices which has taken place since 1960, it will be seen that real weekly earnings have gone up only about 11 per cent. During the same period labor productivity in the private economy is supposed to have risen by 3.6 per cent a year, which aggregates to just over 15 per cent for the four years.[5] Overall productivity figures of this sort, throwing together as they do all kinds of productive and unproductive labor, are not very meaningful and certainly vastly understate the increase in productivity of rationally organized production workers. Still they show that from labor's point of view, and judged even by the Establishment's own distorted standards, the Kennedy–Johnson Administration could appropriately be labeled the Raw Deal.

But perhaps at any rate some progress has been made toward reducing the distressingly high rate of unemployment which developed in the late 1950s? Unfortunately, no. To be sure, the official unemployment rate shows a modest decline from 5.6 per cent in 1960 to 5 per cent (seasonally adjusted) in November 1964. But at the same time the number of people looking for work also declined so that what is called the labor

[5] See Charles E. Silberman, "The Real News About Automation," *Fortune* (January 1965), p. 125.

force participation rate fell by 1.3 percentage points in the same period. If we assume that most of these dropouts from the labor force are as much unemployed as ever but have given up looking for jobs because they know from experience that none exist, we have to conclude that the true unemployment rate has risen to something over 6 per cent after four years of uninterrupted expansion.

Nor are matters much better when it comes to the rate of utilization of the economy's material productive capacity. The McGraw–Hill index of capacity utilization stood at 81 in 1960 and rose slowly to 86 at the latest survey in September, 1964.[6]

Overall, therefore, it appears that the slack in the economy today is as great as it was four years ago. And if we keep in mind the experience of the Second World War—when GNP nearly doubled at the same time that 10 million persons in the most productive age groups were being drafted into the armed forces—we can be sure that the commonly accepted measures of unemployment and unused capacity give no more than a faint inkling of what could be produced at the present time with a full, but not overstrained, utilization of available resources. It is surely well on the conservative side to assume that GNP could be rapidly expanded by $100 billion,[7] an increase of 16 per cent over the present level. If this amount were distributed, directly and indirectly, to the two-fifths of the nation living in poverty or deprivation, their real income would be doubled.[8] Such is the potential of the American economy. Such could be the *immediately* attainable goal of a real war on poverty.

The reality of course is entirely different. Far from disappearing, the problems of poverty and deprivation have grown along with the magnitude of corporate profits in the years of the Kennedy–Johnson boom. In New York City, for example, where so many of the giant corporations have their headquarters and so much of the nation's wealth is concentrated, the

---

[6] Periodic McGraw–Hill mimeographed releases, the latest dated November 6, 1964.

[7] See Keyserling's estimate, reading 7.—Eds.

[8] In round figures, the lowest 40 per cent of income receivers get about 20 per cent of total personal income. At the end of 1964, total personal income was running at a rate of just over $500 billion. The present personal income of those living in poverty and deprivation is therefore in the neighborhood of $100 billion.

Department of Welfare is asking the city government to approve a budget for the next fiscal year of half a billion dollars, 20 per cent more than its current budget and 15 per cent of the total proposed expenditure by the city in the coming period. In justifying his department's request, Welfare Commissioner James R. Dumpson explained to the city's Budget Bureau that the larger amount was needed to care for the steadily rising number of people receiving public assistance.

The commissioner said that the rise, which he put at about 5,850 a month, could be attributed to "chronic unemployment among the unskilled, low wages for many employed persons, the unavailability of sufficient low-cost housing, our failure to achieve open occupancy for all people in available housing, increased cost of care for the medically indigent aged, and the continuing breakdown among families." [9]

But maybe this situation will be changed by President Johnson's war on poverty which, in his State of the Union Message, he promised to double in 1965? Well, maybe—a little. But Commissioner Dumpson has already made full allowance for that possibility. If the federal program is implemented, the rate of increase of welfare caseloads might be reduced by half. "If it were not for that possible reduction, he said, the department would have to ask for $20 million more a year." [10]

The conclusion is inescapable: only the rich gain from the kind of boom which can be induced by methods acceptable to the business-political Establishment which rules this country today. The wages of the employed worker have not kept pace with gains in his own productivity. There are more, not fewer, unemployed. Poverty and deprivation are spreading like an unchecked cancer. There is, in truth, only one group President Johnson could have been referring to when he declared in his State of the Union Message: "We are in the midst of the greatest upward surge of economic well-being in the history of any nation." It is the group to which the multimillionaire President himself belongs.

What about the future?

It is not our purpose to add one more "forecast" to the collection which crowds the news and financial columns at the turn of the year. It is enough to point out that not even the peren-

[9] *New York Times* (December 29, 1964).
[10] *Ibid.*

nial optimists expect GNP to go on expanding at the rate of the last four years much longer. *Fortune* magazine, capitalism's most ardent apologist, says that "a new period, of subnormal growth, is now in prospect for the US economy after this quarter. Following four years of rapid gains in output . . . this means a real change in trend. . . . The odds are still against recession in the next eighteen months, but the chances of it will be rising in 1966." [11] Others figure the odds differently, but let us suppose that *Fortune* is right and that what we face now is once again a period of sluggish growth such as characterized the late 1950s.

What cannot be overemphasized is that such a prospect, in the conditions of the 1960s, is little short of catastrophic. The labor force is today growing 50 per cent more rapidly than it was a decade ago, and the speedup will continue for years to come. At the same time, automation is penetrating more and more areas of the economy—in no small measure, ironically enough, because of the tax-stimulated investment boom of the last few years—and will certainly be throwing more and more workers into the industrial reserve army in the period ahead. If a 5½ per cent rate of growth of GNP has been unable to hold the unemployment line, one can imagine what the consequences will be of a decline to, say, half that figure. Even without a recession, unemployment could easily reach the 10 per cent level in the next couple of years. With a recession—and it would not have to be a severe one in terms of total output—we could be back where we were in the 1930s.

The somber truth is that this country is headed into a time of troubles from which there is absolutely no escape within the framework and confines of the capitalist system.

———

[One year later, in February, 1966, Huberman and Sweezy updated their previous analysis of the nation's economy.]

THE BOOM CONTINUES

Our last analysis of the state of the United States economy appeared just a year ago. There we diagnosed the long up-

[11] *Fortune* (January, 1965), p. 27.

swing of the Kennedy–Johnson years as the result of a new fiscal policy of deliberate deficits engineered by a combination of higher government spending and lower taxes, chiefly on corporations. We quoted Douglas Dillon, then Secretary of the Treasury, to the effect that the cumulative effect of tax changes in 1962 and 1964 would be equivalent to a reduction of the corporate income tax from 52 per cent to 34 or 29 per cent (depending on the ratio of equity to total capital) or to a reduction in the cost of new capital equipment of 16 per cent. "It is hardly surprising," said Dillon in June of 1964, "that investment activity is responding to incentives of this magnitude . . . and that investment spending is now spearheading the recovery."

As all this implies, the biggest beneficiaries of the boom up to that time had been the corporations. Total corporate profits increased by an estimated 57 per cent in the period 1960-64, while Gross National Product was rising less than half as fast, by 24 per cent. Simultaneously, real wages were going up by less than the productivity of labor, and poverty was becoming an increasingly obtrusive and serious problem. We concluded by pointing out—quoting *Fortune* as an example—that most observers of the economic scene anticipated an imminent slowdown in the rate of expansion, and that such a change in the economic climate would bring with it a rapid increase in unemployment.

Looking back from the vantage point of a year later, we can see that these anticipations were wide of the mark. The boom has continued, and even accelerated. Between the third quarter of 1964 and the third quarter of 1965 (the latest for which figures are available at the time of writing) GNP rose by 6.9 per cent, well above the average of the preceding four years. At the same time, the basic character of the boom not only has not changed but has become markedly accentuated. In the same period corporate profits went up by no less than 19.5 per cent, nearly three times the rate of increase of GNP; and expenditures on plant and equipment, still "spearheading the recovery," were up 12 per cent. And once again real wages (weekly earnings of workers in manufacturing adjusted to take account of the rise of consumer prices) lagged behind, rising by only about 3 per cent, which once again is probably lower than the rise in labor productivity. If ever confirmation were needed that this economy and this Administration belong to the big corporations, the last year has certainly provided it and with plenty to spare.

There remains, however, the question as to why the predictions of a slowdown, and possibly a recession, in 1965 were wrong. By the end of 1964 the upswing had been under way 46 months, only four months fewer than the longest peacetime expansion on record (1933-1938), and for this reason alone it was surely reasonable to expect a leveling off in the near future. How are we to explain that in fact the upswing has continued through 1965, and at the beginning of 1966 shows few of the usual symptoms of an approaching turning point?

Given the complexity and elementality of capitalist economic processes, no one can answer a question of this kind with any certainty. Nevertheless, two important factors are pretty clearly involved, and it seems plausible that, taken together, they provide the explanation.

In the first place, it now seems obvious that the power of the investment boom initiated by the large tax cuts of 1962 and 1964 was considerably greater than was generally realized a year ago. Huge outlays on Research and Development in recent years—now running, according to a *Fortune* article (September 1964, p. 158), at some $20 billion per annum—have brought all sorts of new technologies to the stage of practicality. Apparently all that was needed to touch off an investment boom of unprecedented magnitude and duration was a substantial reduction in the costs of the equipment embodying these technologies—a reduction which the tax cuts effectively accomplished.

Second, and perhaps even more important, has been the sharp escalation of the war in Vietnam which began with United States bombing of the North in February. In last November's issue of MR we printed a dispatch by *New York Times* financial correspondent M. J. Rossant (taken from the Toronto *Globe and Mail,* since the *Times* was then on strike) which began:

It was a close call. Little by little it has become clear that the longest peacetime expansion in U.S. history was in danger of petering out until the escalation of the war in Vietnam gave it a new lease on life.

This may be something of an exaggeration, but there is undoubtedly much truth in it. Not that military spending (euphemistically labeled "National Defense" in the official statistics) has gone up all that much during the past year: the annual rate in the third quarter was only about a billion dollars (or less than 2 per cent) more than in the first quarter—certainly not enough in itself to have any decisive effect on the state of the economy. But almost from the beginning of the escalation, it has been clear that the planned scale of the United States intervention in Vietnam would involve the spending of many billions more in the near future. A story in the *Wall Street Journal* of December 21, for example, has the following to say on the outlook for military spending:

In late November, the President announced from Texas that current-fiscal-year [July, 1965, through June, 1966] defense spending, budgeted last January at $49 billion . . . , would actually wind up at $52 billion to $53 billion. Aides now say it will be closer to $53 billion and, depending on how fast the Pentagon can spend extra billions it will seek in January, could go higher.

For the new fiscal year [ending in mid-1967], most expect the defense figure to be somewhat below the $60 billion now rumored, but admit it's approaching that figure unbelievably fast. Any decision to increase the troop build-up in Vietnam beyond present plans would probably force an increase in total U.S. ground forces, swelling military spending still further.

The apparent certainty of massive increases in government spending of course cannot but play a major part in shaping the expectations of businessmen about future demand, the profitability of new investment, the need for inventories, and so on; and these expectations in turn determine current decisions. It is thus entirely reasonable to assume that the escalation of the war in Vietnam has been an important, and perhaps decisive, factor in keeping the investment boom going and hence in prolonging the upswing.

As to how much longer it may last, we quite frankly would not even hazard a guess. The latest McGraw–Hill survey of investment plans for 1966 (press release of November 5, 1965) indicated that the overall level of spending on plant and equipment would be 8 per cent above 1965, and at this writing there is unfortunately no sign of an end to the escalation of the war in Vietnam. Since, despite the long boom, the economy has plenty of unemployed men and idle plant, it is probably safe enough to say that an early end to the upswing is not likely. But beyond that nothing is safe. . . .

PART III

BUSINESS AND LABOR

INTRODUCTION

This has been the age of American celebration. Certain intellectuals have vied with one another in proclaiming the demise of serious class conflict and the consequent irrelevance of radical theories to the happy reality of life in these United States. President Johnson has repeatedly referred to "the confirmation of the vitality, the strength and the promise of the free enterprise system" implied "by the ability of labor and management to work out their destinies in a free and peaceful manner."[1] Economists lovingly dwell on the "income revolution" of the late thirties and forties, which in their view created a substantially egalitarian society.[2]

But significant evidence exists to dispute this rosy picture. The corporate rich continue to enjoy a wildly disproportionate share of wealth and power. The top 1 per cent of adults in America own nearly 26 per cent of all personal wealth. The ownership of corporate stock—a key form of "wealth" in America—is even more highly concentrated. Currently about 1 per cent of the adults in the United States hold two-thirds of all stock, and there are no signs that this pattern of distribution of wealth is becoming equalized.[3] A recent headline in the finan-

[1] Statement on labor-management relations (January 2, 1964) in *Public Papers of the Presidents, Lyndon Baines Johnson, 1963-64*, I, pp. 107-108.

[2] See discussion in Herman P. Miller, *Rich Man, Poor Man* (New York, 1964), Chap. IV, and the literature there cited.

[3] Robert Lampman, *The Share of Top Wealth-Holders in National Wealth, 1922-1956* (publication of the National Bureau of Economic Research, Princeton, 1962), pp. 24-25. There was some decline in overall personal wealth concentration since 1922—the figure then was 31.6 per cent—although Lampman believes that half of this decline would disappear if the figures were presented on a family basis. In other words, for various reasons such as tax considerations, husbands have distributed their wealth to their wives. Another estimate of stock distribution similar to Lampman's is J. Keith Butters, et al., *Effects of Taxation—Investment by Individuals* (publication of the Harvard Business School, Cambridge, 1953), p. 382.

cial section of the *New York Times,* above an article describing a Ford Foundation study of concentration of stock ownership, accurately describes the current situation: "Multimillionaire Stockholders Still Rule Big Business." [4] Thus, despite significant quantitative change in income distribution, the old pattern of domination and control that characterized nineteenth-century capitalism remains with us.

The changes that have taken place are accounted for by the ideologists of business as stemming from some combination of government benevolence and business "enlightenment." [5] The political theory implicit in such arguments is that the state acts, not essentially in the interests of any particular class, but as the mediator effecting compromise among conflicting interests and groups that might otherwise tear society apart. The state steps in—as with a progressive, or not so progressive, income tax[6]— to curb extremes of inequality, with the desire to benefit society at large.

The notion of a state neutral among various groups in society has serious flaws. It fails to see that the apparent benevolence of the occasional use of state power can be accounted for as concessions wrested from the ruling group, or attempts on the part of this group to mollify potential sources of discontent. But such an alternate view, which derives in part from the Marxist tradition, is suspect in the United States, where because of Cold War exigencies such ideas are considered simply the intellectual tools of "the enemy." [7]

In reply it can be said that such political considerations are alien to the search for valid social theory; that just because

[4] *New York Times* (September 13, 1963). The study, prepared by Jean Crockett and Irwin Friend of the University of Pennsylvania, shows not only highly concentrated stock ownership, but that the millionaire capitalist continues to be the principal power behind the scenes in key top corporations.

[5] See, for example, A. A. Berle, Jr., *The 20th Century Capitalist Revolution* (New York, 1954); John Kenneth Galbraith, *American Capitalism: The Concept of Countervailing Power* (Boston, 1956); and David Lilienthal, *Big Business: A New Era* (New York, 1953).

[6] The negligible degree of progressiveness in the overall tax structure of the US is widely recognized by economists. See, for an example, *Allocation of the Tax Burden by Income Class* (New York: Tax Foundation, 1960).

[7] William A. Williams, *The Great Evasion: An Essay on the Contemporary Relevance of Karl Marx and on the Wisdom of Admitting the Heretic into the Dialogue About America's Future* (Chicago, 1964).

Marx rather than Smith authored an idea, the truth of that idea is in no way affected. And although "evil" men use, or are thought to use, certain concepts, the concepts nevertheless should be judged independently.[8] Furthermore, a point of view from which government is seen as the organ of class domination need not be traced to any Marxian influence. Our colleague, Professor Murray Rothbard (in reading 35 below), argues substantially this position from an intellectual commitment to laissez-faire, free-market economics.

But the most important reason for rejecting the concept of a neutral state presiding over a society in which power among the various classes is balanced and harmonized, is that it does not square with the facts. As David Bazelon shows (reading 11), big business has entrenched itself in Washington so firmly that viewing the federal government as "the executive committee of the capitalist class"[9] begins to look more and more like a good working hypothesis.

In the Cold War era, big government's aggrandizement of power has proceeded hand in hand with the growth of big business. No one has expressed this point better, or with more authority, than President Dwight D. Eisenhower, in his famous Farewell Address of January, 1961:

> *Until the latest of our world conflicts, the United States had no armaments industry. American makers of plowshares could, with time and as required, make swords as well.*
>
> *But we can no longer risk emergency improvisation of national defense. We have been compelled to create a permanent armaments industry of vast proportions. Added to this, three and a half million men and women are directly engaged in the defense establishment. We annually spend on military security alone more than the net income of all United States corporations.*
>
> *Now this conjunction of an immense military establishment and a large arms industry is new in the American experience.*

[8] To hold otherwise would be to commit a logical fallacy, that of confusing the *genesis* or *application* of ideas with the *truth* or *validity* of these ideas.

[9] Or, as Marx and Engels put it a hundred years ago: "The executive of the modern state is but a committee for managing the common affairs of the whole bourgeoisie." *The Communist Manifesto,* in Max Eastman, ed., *Capital and Other Writings by Karl Marx* (New York, 1959), p. 323.

The total influence—economic, political, even spiritual—is felt in every city, every state house, every office of the Federal Government. We recognize the imperative need for this development. Yet we must not fail to comprehend its grave implications. Our toil, resources and livelihood are all involved; so is the very structure of our society.

In the councils of Government, we must guard against the acquisition of unwarranted influence, whether sought or unsought, by the military-industrial complex. The potential for the disastrous rise of misplaced power exists and will persist.

We must never let the weight of this combination endanger our liberties or democratic processes. We should take nothing for granted. Only an alert and knowledgeable citizenry can compel the proper meshing of the huge industrial and military machinery of defense with our peaceful methods and goals, so that security and liberty may prosper together.[10]

This was a solemn, authoritative warning to the American people of the dangers inherent in the close ties between military production, foreign policy, and the power of the big corporations that get the choicest government contracts. These companies have a direct interest in the Cold War; profits after taxes of the Boeing Aircraft Company's government business, for example, exceeded 35 per cent of stockholders' equity during the 1950s.[11] Other figures, too, speak eloquently of the progress and success of big business in America. Between 1929 and 1962 manufacturing concentration so increased that the one hundred largest corporations hold approximately one-half of all manufacturing assets.[12] Richard Barber, a staff member of the Sen-

[10] *Public Papers of the Presidents, Dwight D. Eisenhower, 1960-61,* VIII, p. 1,038.

[11] Report of Senator McClellan's Committee on Missile Profits (March 31, 1964), quoted in *I. F. Stone's Weekly* (April 13, 1964).

[12] This statement is based on Dr. Gardner Means' careful study, presented to a congressional committee during 1964 (*Economic Concentration,* Hearings before the Subcommittee on Antitrust and Monopoly of the Committee on the Judiciary, U.S. Senate, Part I, 1964, p. 18). The increase in total assets was from 40 per cent to 49 per cent. Dr. Means' access to the records of the Bureau of Internal Revenue for 1929 undercuts Dr. Adelman's study for the period 1931-60 (presented in the same volume, pp. 223-41), which showed virtually no change in concentration. Adelman picked 1931 as his base because of the absence of published data prior to this date.

ate Subcommittee on Antitrust and Monopoly, gives one reason why this is so:

Last year a thousand companies disappeared through merger in the U.S. and in 1966 they will be joined in the graveyard by an estimated 1,300. Not only is the absolute number of mergers high by any standard of comparison (fewer than 200 firms a year vanished a decade ago), but a great many large firms are involved. In 1965 Pure Oil (with assets of $750 million), Richfield Oil (assets: $500 million), Consolidation Coal (assets: $465 million), and ABC–Paramount, were acquired by, respectively, Union Oil, Atlantic Refinery, Continental Oil, and ITT. Between 1948 and 1965 more than 800 companies with assets of at least $10 million each were assimilated into larger empires, mostly those ruled by the 200 biggest manufacturing corporations. At this rate Art Buchwald may well be right in thinking that "the whole country will soon be merged into one large company!"

Barber also points out that the opposition of the Justice Department to mergers between competitors having as little as 8 per cent of the market means that the dominant firms "are tacitly immunized from antitrust persecution that would seriously curb or reduce their power." [13]

Despite this overwhelming evidence of growth in size and power of big business in America, many writers (such as Arthur Krock in the *New York Times*) continue to argue that the labor unions wield an inordinately large amount of power in present-day America. The generally accepted scholarly view, however, stresses the weaknesses and increasing impotence of what can hardly any longer be called a union "movement." Professor Lloyd Reynolds of Yale University, in his standard study of labor economics, expresses this view. "The most striking feature of the past decade," writes Reynolds, "is the stagnation of union membership. After twenty years of rapid expansion, membership has stopped growing and the percentage of the labor force in unions has dropped." [14]

[13] Richard J. Barber, "The New Partnership: Big Government and Big Business," *New Republic* (August 13, 1966), pp. 17-19.
[14] Lloyd G. Reynolds, *Labor Economics and Labor Relations* (4th ed., Englewood Cliffs, N.J., 1964), p. 48. Among the reasons adduced by Reynolds to explain this decline are: a decline in the numbers of workers in manufacturing, mining, and transportation (areas of traditional union

Of course labor leaders enjoy high symbolic status, and President Johnson periodically genuflects to the "great strength and freedom and respect" enjoyed by America's labor movement.[15] But this movement proved too weak to block enactment of the Taft–Hartley Act in 1947 (when even a New Deal Congressman from Texas, Lyndon Johnson, voted for it), or the Landrum–Griffin Act of 1959. Labor leaders have been unable to convince the President to give high priority to the repeal of section 14b of the Taft–Hartley Act, which permits state "right-to-work," or anti-union, shop laws.[16] The article by James Wason printed below (reading 10) puts this problem into historical perspective by showing labor's inability to bring the major political parties to contemplate seriously a solution to the unemployment problem, which everyday further vitiates union strength.

An interesting test case of the relative strength of business and labor was provided by the now defunct wage–price guidelines of the Kennedy–Johnson Administration, discussed below (reading 12) by our colleague, Professor Shane Mage. It is clear that when productivity is increasing by 3.2 per cent a year and prices are rising at a rate of 3.3 per cent, then wages ought to rise by 6.5 per cent—if the theory of the guidelines is to be followed. Otherwise, not only will capital's share rise relative to that of labor, but insistence upon a 3.2 per cent increase for labor is tantamount to saying to the worker, "no increase this year"; all this at a time when corporate profits are setting new record highs.[17]

Is it any wonder, then, that even George Meany, the

---

strength), and the expansion of industry to the South, where the union movement remains weak. He also mentions the complacent attitudes of union leaders, who, having won their victories in the thirties and forties, seem unable to mount new, significant organizational drives.

[15] Remarks at a reception for labor leaders (July 24, 1964), in *Public Papers LBJ, 1963-64,* II, p. 897.

[16] See Lloyd Reynolds' *Labor Economics and Labor Relations* for a summary of these complicated laws and a description of the way in which they have tended to protect the power of employers at the expense of unions.

[17] In fact, even though the work week was slightly longer, the average factory worker took home *less* "real" income in 1966 than in 1965. This was primarily due to sharply rising consumer prices, though increased Social Security withholdings also played a role. See *Economic Report of the President,* 1967, p. 248.

staunchly conservative president of the AFL-CIO, has chafed at Johnson's bit and felt compelled to mutter vague threats of opposition to the President.[18] But traditional ties and allegiances to the Democratic Party are so strong that these mutterings are expressions of political impotence. Labor has been unable to generate the marvelous political flexibility of big business, which, courted by President Johnson and virtually betrothed to the Democratic Party, nevertheless retains enough of an instinct of infidelity to enable it to play one party against the other, and consequently exert considerable political leverage. (See David Bazelon's analysis, reading 11.) What we seem to have, then, is a coalition between liberal big government and the giant corporations, with organized labor as a junior partner.

The obvious question is: can the Johnson coalition last? Labor's discontent with its junior status is likely to continue. The nature of work, in response to automation, is sure to change. The number of jobs in the public sector will increase,[19] and schoolteachers, workers in welfare, transportation, sanitation, and hospitals will have to fight the labor battles of the future. In addition, unmet social needs are already developing new political movements: of the poor, the Negro, and the city dweller in his frightful slum, with his overcrowded school, breathing foul air, and burdened by polluted water. It is unlikely that such forces can be contained within a Johnson–style coalition.

What might the future hold? One thing seems clear: any attempt to hold the coalition of big business and "liberal" planners together in the face of mounting opposition will necessitate a more tightly controlled society. A possible drift in this direction has already been noted by Arthur F. Burns, the distinguished conservative economist and former Chairman of the Council of Economic Advisers under President Eisenhower, when he remarks that "recent history suggests, the guidepost policy may, under the pressure of events, move our nation's economy in an authoritarian direction." [20] It is evident to radicals as well, especially those who attack U.S. foreign policy.

Thus, the Great Society seems to be laying the foundation

[18] See the New York Times (August 7, 1966).
[19] See the Manpower Report of the President, 1963, pp. 4-5, as well as that of 1966, p. 41, both of which clearly show this trend.
[20] Harvard Business Review (March-April, 1965), p. 62.

for an increased exercise of government power. But, despite the confusion generated in this country by the tendency to label centralized government as socialistic, the increasing use of government power does not define socialism. The quality of this power, and the ways in which it will be exercised by a state more and more tied to the needs of the giant corporations, suggest perhaps another parallel—corporate Italy under Mussolini. In his famous Charter of 1927, Il Duce spelled out the alliance between government and business in which labor will be disciplined, government will coordinate and aid production, and private enterprise will be safeguarded.[21] Contemporary historians have clarified the significance of this closeness between big business and fascist government. H. Stuart Hughes has written: "This convergence between the fascist parties and the interest of the business class—more particularly the larger industrialists—was the central feature of the fascist regimes in practice." [22] It is possible that there will be further evolution in this direction in the United States. This conclusion is not based upon any mechanical analogy with Fascist Italy, but rather from sober analysis of the actual political and economic conflicts at the present time in America. What seems to be in the making now is a growing polarization of society. The big business establishment, along with its political allies in Washington, are beginning to be ranged against the outcasts of the Great Society—students, the poor, the Negro masses, disaffected workers, and others unable to endorse the consensus of establishment liberalism.[23] Increasing doses of government authoritarianism will probably then be administered to quell the incipient conflict. This in turn cannot help but lead to magnified conflict. Ironically, maintenance of the Johnsonian consensus by the leaders of corporate America may best be served by the removal of Johnson himself. Businessmen may choose to support a liberal Republican in 1968 to brighten up that tarnished foreign and domestic image of the United States. On the other hand, they may once again acquiesce in the

[21] The Fascist Charter is reprinted in Alexander Baltzy and A. William Salomone, eds., *Readings in Twentieth-Century European History* (New York, 1950), pp. 245-47.

[22] H. Stuart Hughes, *Contemporary Europe: A History* (2nd ed., Englewood Cliffs, N.J., 1966), p. 247.

[23] See the analysis by Tom Hayden (reading 34, below) of the sources of discontent within the Great Society.

nomination of a Goldwater-type Republican whose mere existence will aid Johnson in assuming the role he had in 1964 of restraint and moderation. But it is not likely in the long run that this will succeed; the incipient conflicts in America, we believe, can no longer be contained within the traditional liberal consensus.

OUR FREE ENTERPRISE SYSTEM*

During an election campaign many speeches are made which at the time receive little prominence. In 1964, one of these was by Lyndon B. Johnson to a group of business, industrial, and civic leaders in Hartford, Connecticut. In it, he gives his conception of the free enterprise system and its four important segments: the capitalist, the manager, the worker, and the government. This speech, slightly abridged, is reprinted below.

◇ ◇ ◇

As we meet here, there are two great philosophies that are rivals in the world—and one or the other will ultimately prevail.

One philosophy is the democratic philosophy that has been practiced in this country from the time of our first President, George Washington, up until this moment. Although I have only been your President for ten months—I was called upon to shoulder awesome responsibilities without a moment's notice—I have had the support and the prayers of the members of this great business fraternity from coast to coast without regard to their business affiliation, their religious affiliation, or their party affiliation.

Because I have had that support as your President, as President of all the people, this whole nation—Democrats and Republicans and whatnots—enjoys a period of prosperity that has never been equaled before in the annals of the history of this country.

Now while we are enjoying all of that prosperity, we see

* From *Public Papers of the Presidents, Lyndon B. Johnson, 1963-64,* II, pp. 1,147-51.

communism challenging us and challenging freedom on many fronts. I am proud to say to you that we are standing up, we are resisting, and we are trying to halt the envelopment of freedom anywhere in the world. Although there are more than 120 nations in the world, and although there are dozens of nations that have been born in the last decade, we have not lost a single nation to communism since 1959.

Now these two philosophies are in a struggle. They are after each other's jugular, and if we survive it will not be because we have more people than they have, because they outpopulate us. There are many more millions in the Soviet Union than we have in the United States. They have more than 600 million acres of tillable land and we have less than 200 million, so they have a lot more tillable soil. They outnumber us in many of our greatest resources and their potential in other ways far exceeds ours.

So in resources, in human beings, in tillable acres, we are all at a disadvantage. What do we rely on? We rely on the one great advantage that the American people have: that is our system of govenment.

Now, that system is not built on any one party, or any one people, or any one section, or any one religion, or any one group. That system that we know as the free enterprise system is made up of really four important segments.

The first is the capitalist. Some of you have been known as capitalists in your time and some of you not many years ago were even called royalists—"economic royalists," I believe it was. You have been so referred to from time to time in various campaigns in America because sometimes you asked for it, and sometimes you couldn't avoid it.

But the capitalist is the man that, through prudence, accumulates wealth and takes that money and is willing to invest it. It may be to rebuild a whole new area. It may be to put skyscrapers in the sky. It may be to provide production lines for jobs. It may be to build railroads and dams. It can follow many lines.

But he invests that dollar in America with a reasonable assurance that it will not be confiscated and will not be taken away from him by some government that stages a coup in the midnight hours, and that he will be secure in his possessions without fear that some night at midnight someone will rap on his door and serve him a warrant and lead him off to jail. He hopes that he may get a reasonable return on it. Sometimes he does and sometimes he doesn't. Sometimes he gets it all back plus 5 or 6 per cent, sometimes he loses it all.

But anyway, he has hope and he has a chance, he has an opportunity, and he is willing to take care of the rest himself, if you give him that—and he has that in America.

That capitalist is joined by what you call a manager.

That manager is the fellow that gets up at daylight and works to midnight and develops stomach ulcers trying to get a bonus or trying to have a profit-sharing plan, or trying to build a better mousetrap at less cost, trying to compete not only with his fellowman here but with the rest of the world.

He takes his chances where he finds them and if he loses, he fusses with his wife about it, but he takes it in stride. Sometimes he has a good profit. For forty-three months now he has had a rather good record, but the next forty-three might not be so good, so he has to take it.

But he joins with the capitalist and he manages that dollar, he sees where it is invested and he tries to exercise prudence and yet exercise vision.

Then the third segment there is the worker who gets to work at 8 and works to 5, and he has twenty-seven seconds to put the number of rivets in that car or that plane that he needs to. If he doesn't get them in in the twenty-seven seconds he goes to twenty-eight. That car or that plane moves on down the line— and it doesn't have the rivets in it! And you've wound up with a car that is missing a rivet a time or two yourselves. We all do that. But that poor fellow gets a coffee break twice a day. The rest of the time he has twenty-seven seconds to do that job and handle that machine.

He is the worker, and he hopes someday he can have a little hospital care, he can have a little pension, he can have a little social security, he can have a place to take Molly and the babies when he retires. That is his great love. His boys go to war; they fight to preserve this system. He likes his boss and he respects him. He believes in free enterprise, and he does not hate the man who makes a reasonable return.

Now those three—the capitalist, the manager, and the worker—make up free enterprise.

Now, whatever they have after they have produced it, Uncle

Sam steps in and takes 52 per cent of it. He is the first partner. And every dime you make, I've got a 52 per cent interest as President. So I want you to do well. And I think you are doing well, and I am glad that you are.

My 1965 budget—when I came in they anticipated it would be $5 billion more than 1964, because '64 was $5 billion more than '63, '63 was $5 billion more than '62, and '62 was $5 billion more than '61. We have a growing population, we are moving on—we have more schools, more roads, more needs to fill.

But I spent the first 37 days and nights I was in office trying to find some way, somehow, some means to keep that budget under $100 billion, because I thought psychologically it would be a good thing.

I thought if we could not pull down our expenses in a great era of prosperity I did not know when we could pull them down. So instead of a budget of $5 billion more—$103.8 billion —we reduced it. And I had the help of Republicans. President Eisenhower came down and worked with me two days. Bob Anderson, the Secretary of the Treasury under President Eisenhower, came down and worked with me almost a month.

I had the budget directors from other Administrations come in. I got all of the advice I could get, because nobody needed it any more than I did. We finally developed a budget that was $1 billion less in '65 than it was in '64.

While we were doing that, we passed a tax bill. We put some of the money back for the people to spend instead of letting the government spend it for them. We put some of the money back for business to invest in new enterprise instead of the government investing it for them.

So as a result, we have more men working today than we have ever had before. Our profits are higher, our wages are higher, our economics are better, our system is producing.

Don't you tell me for a moment that we can't outproduce and outwork and outfight any communistic system in the world. Because if you try to tell me otherwise, you tell me that slaves can do better than free men, and I don't believe they can. I would rather have an executive vice president, even if he comes from Hartford, Conn., than to have a commissar!

So I say to you men who are the leaders of this community, and through your industries the leaders of the United States, that we are doing reasonably well today but we have got to do better. We have got other fields to conquer. We have other roads to travel. This part of the United States has always led the rest of the nation and the rest of the world in two fields: prudence and progress.

You have something about you that permits you to keep your eyes on the stars, and still keep your feet on the ground. And if you don't have both of them on the ground all the time you at least have one of them on the ground. So don't ever get both of them off the ground at one time.

LABOR-MANAGEMENT UNDER
THE JOHNSON ADMINISTRATION *

The issues that should dominate any relevant discussion of contemporary America are: in whose interest is the society being run? what role will existing and emerging groups play in the decision-making process? what uses will be made of our vast resources? To grapple with these issues in the spirit of the reform administrations of the thirties, or to "pick up where the New Deal left off," means to continue and possibly expand unemployment compensation or higher minimum wages, or some such program. But these would be the application of depression-born policies to an era of potential affluence. Automation too has introduced a new element: the promise to free man from the necessity of toil. In such a situation, a set of "labor reforms" which will do little more than perpetuate the privileged position of a minority of workers is inadequate; what is needed are a new set of social institutions appropriate to a new age.

The essay below falls far short of these conclusions. Instead it amounts to a competent overview of the Johnson Administration's labor policies, which provides a good introduction to the more interpretative essays that follow. James R. Wason served as an economist with the US Department of Labor from 1950 to 1962 before joining the Legislative Reference Service of the Library of Congress. He is the editor of *National Labor Policy*, the handbook

* From *Current History* (August, 1965), pp. 65-70, 115-16.

prepared by the service. Mr. Wason has also been a lecturer at George Washington University since 1956.

◇◇◇

Following the overwhelming victory of President Lyndon B. Johnson in the November, 1964, election, interest in its implications for national labor policy has remained at a high level. The election was a victory for the liberal forces in the United States, with the labor unions prominent among them. Swept into office with President Johnson were a large number of Senators and Congressmen who were elected with labor's support and known to support labor's legislative aims.

This interest has been heightened by the realization that the Democratic Party platform, on which the President had campaigned, pledged the repeal of section 14b of the Taft–Hartley Act, the section of the federal law which makes possible the state "right-to-work" laws. These laws make it illegal to establish contracts between labor and management requiring mandatory union membership by all employees within the contract terms. State "right-to-work" laws are presently in effect in nineteen states. The overwhelmingly liberal complexion of the new 89th Congress makes it a virtual certainty that section 14b will be repealed, provided President Johnson gives his full support to this primary objective of his labor supporters.

In his State of the Union Message, delivered to the newly-convened Congress on January 4, 1965, the President outlined his program for the Congress and for the Administration—the program of the Great Society. In the area traditionally falling within the scope of labor legislation he mentioned three programs:

1. Extending the protection of the Fair Labor Standards Act —the federal wage and hour law—to additional workers;

2. Improving and modernizing the federal-state unemployment compensation system; and

3. Repealing section 14b of the Taft–Hartley Act.

After this beginning, so reassuring to his labor supporters, so disturbing to his conservative opponents and to some others, nothing further happened for several months. The Economic Message did not mention section 14b. It repeated the proposals to extend the coverage of the Fair Labor Standards Act and to make improvements in the unemployment compensation system. It listed them under items for "Maintaining Incomes for the Disadvantaged," along with Medicare, the annual items strengthening the assistance and pension aspects of the Social Security Act, and the antipoverty program. Thus he underlined the importance of the proposals as major parts of his program. But despite, or possibly because of, news stories of its imminent appearance, the Labor Message, with its accompanying draft legislation, did not appear. February, March, and April passed. Congress was now halfway toward a possible August adjournment. On May 18 [1965], the Labor Message went to the Hill.

The labor message

In one sense, the message contained nothing new. It merely repeated the three proposals of the State of the Union Message. Yet, despite the fact that it remained within the pre-existing framework, it contained a number of surprises. In amplifying the three programs the message gave them a significance not generally anticipated.

Up to now the Johnson program had been to carry forward to completion the proposals of the Kennedy Administration. Now, the Johnson program was his own, but its roots were in the Roosevelt Administration; in the Roosevelt second term. Clearly, the President was picking up where the New Deal left off in 1938.

The tone of the message was set in its opening paragraphs:

The last thirty years have seen unprecedented economic development . . . and unparalleled improvement in the general standard of living of the working men and women of America.

Most of this has been accomplished privately. These are the fruits of free enterprise.

This process of . . . growth has been helped by wise legislative enactment. . . .

But progress is never complete. Experience under various existing laws suggests changes which will make them serve even better their purpose, the nation's workers, and the economy.

The tone was not contradicted by the substance of the message.

The Fair Labor Standards Act was last amended in 1961. At that time, provision was made for a minimum wage of $1.25 an hour, to be reached after two years. Coverage was extended for the first time in a major way, mostly to employees of large retail stores and the construction industry. However, to secure these gains the Kennedy Administration had been forced to abandon efforts to cover workers in large laundries, restaurants, and hotels and had accepted some minor, but annoying, reductions in existing coverage.

The first surprise in the Johnson message was in the number of workers for whom coverage was proposed. Instead of the 2.5 million workers to whom coverage had been promised in the State of the Union Message, coverage was proposed for 4.6 million. Not only would employees in large laundries, restaurants, and hotels be covered, but an additional 1.5 million employees in retail stores, nearly 900,000 employees in hospitals, and workers in many smaller industries, employees of logging contractors, taxicab drivers, employees of motion picture theatres, and so on. . . .

On the question of a higher minimum wage the President was caught in a dilemma. In 1964, in connection with the antipoverty program, the figure of $3,000 annually was widely circulated as marking the line between poverty and a minimum acceptable income. A minimum wage of $1.25 an hour, which yields for a year's full-time employment only $2,500, was obviously inadequate. An hourly increase of 25 cents would seem a necessity to reconcile the two figures and the two programs.

Yet, as a longtime member of the Congress, President Johnson was surely aware of the unhappy experience of President Dwight D. Eisenhower when he unwisely committed himself in 1955 to a specific increase in the minimum wage, 90 cents an hour, which was substantially lower than the $1.00 rate then being discussed and considered reasonable by members of the Congress. At that time, when Congress passed a bill increasing the rate to $1.00, the President was left in the unenviable position of either having to veto the increase, or to approve it and admit that his support of 90 cents was, at best, niggardly and, at worst, a dishonest attempt at figure-juggling.

President Johnson wisely chose to avoid this trap. He was well aware that the A.F.L.–C.I.O. was supporting an increase to $2.00 an hour and would hardly settle for less than an immediate increase to $1.50. At the same time, he could have refused to support any increase in the present rate, as his initial failure to mention an increase had led the public to expect. Instead, the President raised the question and then continued:

. . . As average wages rise, the minimum wage level should be increased periodically.

The question is not whether the minimum wage should be increased but when and by how much. The Congress should consider carefully the effects of higher minimum wage costs on the incomes of those employed, and also on costs and prices, and on job opportunities—particularly for the flood of teenagers now entering our labor force.

That President Johnson did not intend to commit himself to any specific increase in the minimum wage by this statement was obvious. But what he did intend became the subject of some controversy. The only thing that was clear was that, by raising the question of an increase in the minimum wage in his message, the President had taken a step closer to the support of such an increase than was indicated by his State of the Union Message.[1]

Actually, a careful reading of what the President actually said may indicate what he had in mind. He advocated increasing the minimum wage to keep it in step with the movement of wages generally. In the past, the general measure of wage movements for such purposes has been the change in average hourly earnings in manufacturing. From the effective date of the $1.25 minimum wage, September, 1963, to March, 1965, manufacturing wages have increased from $2.47 an hour to $2.60, or 13 cents. Rounding this amount to the nearest five-cent interval, as Congress has customarily done, one.gets a rate of $1.40 an hour. Clearly, the reason the President did not mention any amount was that he would thereby run the risk of finding himself in the same position as had President Eisenhower.

What is far less clear, but probably much more significant than this rather obvious tactical maneuver, is the meaning of the President's concluding reference to the need for the Congress to consider carefully the effect of a minimum wage in-

[1] In 1966, Congress, goaded by increased inflation, with the support of the Administration, raised the minimum wage. The compromise enactment placed it at $1.40 in 1967, with a further rise to $1.60 scheduled for 1968.—Eds.

crease on job opportunities for teenagers. Past Administrations, including that of President Eisenhower, had always considered that the minimum wage was the lowest wage to be paid to any worker fully competent to hold a job. Thus exceptions had been made for the handicapped, apprentices and, in a very limited way, for "learners," those workers who required a short break-in period to acquire sufficient skill to earn the minimum wage on certain piece-work jobs. All told, in any year the total number of such exceptions had seldom exceeded 50,000.

For all others, the minimum wage specified in the act was to be the lowest amount paid. If experience or training were not required in order to perform the job properly, there was no reason for paying any lesser rate.

However, the Johnson message could be read as suggesting the need for an entrance rate for inexperienced workers. This, in turn, might open the way for a bi-level minimum wage; an entrance rate for the inexperienced, and a higher rate for the worker with a substantial job history.

If this were what was being suggested to the Congress, it opened the way to an entirely new concept of a minimum wage. If the inexperienced worker, who is usually also the young worker without family responsibilities, is to be paid a lower rate than the experienced worker, then might not it be possible to set the rate for the latter at a level approximating a living wage? This would base the minimum on a concept which had hitherto been considered socially desirable, but economically impossible. . . .

Unemployment compensation

Despite the fact that unemployment has been a major problem for every President in the past generation, the major program designed to alleviate the conditions of the unemployed—the federal-state unemployment compensation system—has not been changed in any substantial way since its inception in 1935, thirty years ago. As a result, its current benefits are, in many ways, less adequate than its original benefits.

President Johnson's proposal that all states be required to pay unemployed workers benefits equal to at least 50 per cent of their average weekly wage is, for example, only the restoration of the original minimum jobless payment standard, met by most states in 1935. Today, only eleven states meet this standard. The President's proposal would require states to increase benefits to this proportion or have their employers forfeit part or all of the tax credit allowances they now receive from the federal government. . . .

Section 14b of the Taft–Hartley Act

President Johnson's statement on the repeal of section 14b contained no surprises, except to a minority of observers who had expected additional proposals:

. . . with the hope of reducing conflicts in our national labor policy that for several years have divided Americans in various states, I recommend the repeal of section 14b of the Taft–Hartley Act with such other technical changes as are made necessary by this action.

It is true that there were no surprises in this part of Johnson's policy on labor. Yet nowhere else in the President's statement is the Johnson approach to our national problems more apparent. Consensus is to be sought and found, not by policies to compromise differences, but by acts to eliminate the bases for these differences.

The President's statement thus starts from the fundamental basis of our national labor policy in the area of union security, that laid down in the Taft–Hartley Act, an act which, as a member of the Congress, the President supported in 1947.

The conflict in our labor policy to which the President referred in his message lies in section 14b of the act, which in effect preserved the right of the individual states to enact "right-to-work" laws forbidding the union shop and other forms of union security. . . .

The labor policy of the Johnson Administration may be compared to a set of nested "boxes." The outer box is our national labor policy of maintaining full employment and economic security under conditions of balanced and sustained growth.

Within this outer box are two boxes, one labeled "manpower policy," the other, "incomes policy." The one marked "manpower policy" concerns the supply side of our labor policy. The primary concern of manpower policy is the maintenance of full employment and, under present conditions, the reduction of unemployment. The one marked "incomes policy" concerns the demand aspects of our economy. Its primary present concern is the maintenance of a reasonably stable price level.

Within these two boxes many programs may be found. Some programs belong in both boxes, as they affect and concern both the supply and the demand sides of our economy. From this multitude of programs, the President singled out a few in his Labor Message for the special attention of Congress in 1965.

It is not difficult to see that the proposals to amend the Fair Labor Standards Act and to strengthen and modernize our unemployment compensation system contribute to maintaining full employment and to the reduction of the problems of unemployment. They may also, however, have adverse effects: for example, on price stability, as the President himself noted with respect to the Fair Labor Standards Act.

These programs thus belong in both the manpower policy and incomes policy boxes. But where does the repeal of section 14b fit into the President's labor policy program?

Wage-price guidelines and union responsibility

The wage-price relationship is one of the dilemmas of our time. Our economy can provide a high level of employment or a high level of price stability, but not both at the same time. We have a choice of holding prices down and having somewhat more unemployment, or of reducing unemployment to a more acceptable level and experiencing at least some increase in prices.

After unemployment drops below a certain level, pressures for higher wages arise from a demand for labor. At this point, unless restraint is consciously exercised, wages rise more rapidly than does the ability of the economy to produce additional goods and services for the consumer to purchase. Prices must rise, because too much money now chases too few goods. Yet if restraint is exercised through fiscal or monetary measures, and the money available to purchase these additional goods is then not forthcoming, the opposite process takes place. Prices fall, because demand is lacking, and men are laid off.

The obvious, possible, but difficult-to-attain solution to this dilemma is to keep the increase in wages in line with the increase in productivity, which is the measure of the ability of the economy to produce extra goods and services. With such balanced growth, some unemployment and some increases in prices occur, but both remain within the limits of tolerance of a stable, growing economy.

The formula for maintaining this balanced growth with relative stability is that contained in the wage–price guideposts. These were originally advanced in 1962, during the Kennedy Administration. They were accepted and firmly restated by President Johnson. As they appear in the 1965 *Economic Report of the President* they are simple and straightforward:

1. The general guide for wages is that the percentage increase in total employee compensation per man-hour be equal to the national trend rate of increase in output per man-hour.

If industry follows this guidepost, unit labor costs in the overall economy will maintain a constant average.

2. The general guide for prices calls for stable prices in industries enjoying the same productivity growth as the average for the economy; rising prices in industries with smaller than average productivity gains; and declining prices in industries with greater than average productvity gains.

If each industry follows this guidepost, prices in the economy will maintain a constant average.

As the report observes, these guideposts "contain an inescapable economic logic." [2] They also present some inescapable problems of implementation. The cooperation of both management and labor is essential to make them effective. Leaving aside the management aspect, how is the cooperation of labor to be secured?

In part, it may be secured by an appeal to the social conscience and civic responsibility of labor's leaders. In part, it may be secured by recognition of their economic self-interest. Wage gains that are wiped out by price increases benefit only management, not labor.

But to exercise responsibility and economic foresight, labor must have the support of its rank and file. This, in recent months, has been something the leaders of labor can no longer take for granted. In major unions such as [those of] the steel workers, the electrical workers, the rubber workers, the paper-

[2] For an alternate view of its logic, see reading 12.—Eds.

makers, rank and file revolts have thrown out incumbent officials and split unions. Today's labor leaders require all the support they can obtain if they are to continue to exercise economic responsibility in the face of internal unrest.

It is in this context that the support of the Johnson Administration of the repeal of section 14b should be seen. Nothing has stirred the labor union officers and the active union members more than the issue of union security. Nothing has done more to contribute to labor unrest than the inability to stop the inroads of runaway shop competition in the "right-to-work" states. If the exercise of economic restraint is to be practical for union officials, labor requires additional union security on a national basis. If additional union security is forthcoming, union officials can then better exercise economic restraint because they will not need the support they might otherwise have to obtain from the rank and file by aggressive efforts to increase wages. They will have the protection of union security clauses in their contracts to prevent losses in membership from labor turnover.

Viewed from this aspect, repeal of section 14b becomes a vital part of the labor policy program of the Johnson Administration. Early action toward repeal may contribute materially, for example, to a final and noninflationary settlement of the pending steel contract negotiations. Support of the repeal of 14b by the President is much more than the paying off of an election debt.

As the President noted in his Labor Message, repeal will reduce conflicts that have divided Americans. It may do more. It may usher in an era of full acceptance by labor of its responsibilities. Once union security becomes a reality in all states, labor will have neither the need nor the excuse for economic aggression that might unsettle the economy. As an equal partner with industry in observing the wage–price guideposts, it will be equally the recipient of governmental pressure to maintain a balanced economy.

On the other hand, a failure to secure repeal would be more than an embarrassing loss of congressional support by the President. Aside from the purely political implications, which could be seriously adverse to both the Administration and organized labor, the economic results which might result from such failure, in the form of increased rank and file unrest, wildcat strikes, repudiation of settlements by the membership of unions, and protracted strikes, could be disastrous. Repeal of section 14b is thus not merely important to the Johnson Administration. It is essential.[3]

[3] But not that essential. With labor safe in his hip pocket, unable to play one party off against the other, Johnson felt free to give only lip service to repeal of section 14b. Without the full support that Wason earlier stated made repeal "a virtual certainty," section 14b has not been repealed and few signs exist in the spring of 1967 that Johnson will try to change its status.—Eds.

BIG BUSINESS AND
THE DEMOCRATS*

Popular political mythology in the United States includes the traditional belief that the Democratic Party represents the interests of the common folk and the Republican Party is the instrument of big business. Academic scholars, such as Professor Seymour E. Harris of Harvard University, have often lent credence to this view. In his *Economics of the Political Parties* (New York, 1962, p. *xxiii*) Harris has stated that "The Democrats represent the little man; the Republicans the more affluent members of society." He notes that Republican politicians often have "excessive recourse" to wealthy contributors to the party coffers (p. 33). He also states that "Excessive mergers, a reluctant antimonopoly policy, the excess of talk over action in maintaining the position of Small Business, and an overidentification of big business interests with the best interests of the nation as a whole—these all reflect the operations of an administration too wedded to the interests of Big Business" (p. 42).

The selection that follows is by David Bazelon, former Fellow of the Institute for Policy Studies in Washington, and author of *The Paper Economy* (New York, 1965) and *Power in America: The Politics of the New Class* (New York, 1967). He argues a substantially different view, namely that the Democrats are rapidly becoming the

* From *Power in America: The Politics of the New Class,* by David Bazelon. Reprinted by arrangement with the New American Library, Inc., New York.

party of big business. Lyndon Johnson's career illustrates this development. Even in Texas, as one perceptive journalist observed, commenting on Johnson's support in that state, there is a strong possibility that business interests are becoming dominant in the Democratic party." (Ronnie Dugger in *The Texas Observer* [June 24, 1960]). If this is the new reality of American domestic politics, then traditional beliefs about the party system will have to be drastically revised. It may very well be true that big business has a decisive voice in *both* major parties, and that what differences do exist reflect splits *within* business—geographical, industrial, ideological.

I

Hardly ever before has so much political history been crowded into so short a period as was jammed into the "fiscal" political year extending from November 22, 1963, to November 3, 1964. The urgent need, in coming to terms with an overflowing period of this kind, is for perspective. Let me then suggest the following hypothesis: the political events of 1964 make possible, and all but insure, the belated completion of the New Deal. To fill out this hypothesis, we must be clear about what the New Deal was, and wherein its lack of completion lay.

In most respects, the New Deal, given the facts of our history, was a profound triumph—equal in stature to the Colonial Revolution and the Northern victory in the Civil War. But it did not solve the problem of the Great Depression: its only broad attempt to do so was the NRA, mere fragments of which survived; and the problem was actually "solved," of course, only by war production. What the New Deal, all on its own, did was to interrupt a cataclysmic deflation. And at the behest of an overwhelming majority of the electorate, it bequeathed to the federal government the responsibility to forestall any uncontrolled deflation in the future.

The completion of the New Deal revolution, which had been delayed for a quarter of a century, required political moves and policy moves which none of the Democratic leaders who expressed the willingness to make showed the capacity to carry through successfully. The major policy move that had to be made was to institutionalize budget deficits in pursuit of full production and employment. The essential political moves that had to be made were the subordination of the Southern minority—in order to "contain" the potentially explosive racial issue —and the inclusion of a significant element of corporate power in the New Deal coalition—in order to engineer the acquiescence of business and finance in efforts toward full production, and to insure the distribution of a sufficient share of the benefits thereof to all the constituent elements of the coalition. The New Deal grouping, great creation that it was, did not have the power—lacking the imminence of economic collapse and without a disciplined congressional majority—to issue orders to the "second government" of big business. Caught between the corporations and the South, the New Deal was stopped short of fulfillment. And with the rise of the military economy, "fulfillment" often enough seemed like a wayward impulse to gild the lily: both taxes and deficits for military purposes were nicely accepted; nor was there any lack of "cooperation" on the part of big business in achieving full production by the military route. So the New Deal was not only caught in the crossfire between business and the South; it was outflanked by the military–industrial complex.

All this has been changed (or at any rate a firm basis for the change provided) by the events of the year just ended. The liberal congressional sweep, the Civil Rights Act, the actual and potential increase in Negro voting, and the defection of the racists to Goldwater, now invite a renegotiation of the role of the Southern bloc within the Democratic coalition. And the tax cut, followed by the five-billion-dollar welfare deficit in the new budget—with assurances of further revenue cuts and deficits later in the year, if the pace of the economy slows—have pretty clearly established, even if only minimally, the long-awaited full-production deficit policy.

But the greatest political event of 1964—if one understands what the New Deal was and what it intended—has been the inclusion of a glittering section of the national corporate community within the Democratic Party. Some people think that this will turn out to be a transitory development occasioned solely by the monumental error of the Republicans in nominating Goldwater. I suggest, on the contrary, that this development was lucky but is not in the least transitory, and that we must now begin to believe in the reality of 1964. But if we are to appreciate the meaning of that reality in all its fullness, we must look as far back as 1912, when the previously governing coalition broke up and the pieces began to arrange themselves in the pattern which eventually became the New Deal.

II

When the Republican Party was founded, Major Alvan E. Bovay chose the word "Republican" because, as he said, "It is the only one that will serve all purposes present and future. . . ." With this end in view, the party had a magnificent beginning: the coalition which elected Lincoln with 40 per cent of the vote was probably the wildest mixture in our history, ranging all the way from elements of the Know-Nothing party to radical intellectual New Englanders. And whether or not it served all purposes, the party served sufficient interests to hold power until 1912, with the slight interruptions of two Cleveland administrations. (Cleveland probably succeeded because he was a Me-too Democrat who cut the price on the same services the Republicans had been rendering to business since Grant.)

By 1912, however, it was all over: the party of Mark Hanna, which had tied itself too tightly to irresponsible big money, dissipated the powerful national coalition it had inherited and created, and the Democrats once again had the opportunity forced on them to take up the burden of American history, as they had done before in the other worlds of Jefferson and Jackson.

Following the defeat of Bryan in 1896 (as James MacGregor Burns has noted), there was a steady decline in the exercise of the franchise which reached its lowest point in 1924. Perhaps this decline should be seen as the dissolution of Republican power, providing the opportunity for the growth of national Democratic power, which culminated, of course, in Roosevelt's triumph in 1932. But the process was in motion before that. Samuel Lubell has pointed out that the Republican hold on the cities was dissolved by Al Smith, not by FDR. The Republican plurality in the twelve largest cities shrank from 1,638,000 in 1920 to 1,252,000 in 1924, and in 1928 the Democrats achieved a plurality of 38,000. Thus, from having been the party of the South and the West, the Democrats were now becoming the party of the North. Hoover's insane devotion to the myth of individualism and the principles of federal non-rule speeded his party's final debacle: the Republicans lost the Negroes and the workers forever, and, along with them, the sincere and well-to-do Progressives. (FDR set out with the determination to catch his cousin's former supporters—the enlightened minority of the middle and upper classes, the idealistic Bull Moosers: Harold Ickes is an obvious example, but not the only one.)

The consequence of the Republican default and the locking of the Progressive middle class into the Democratic Party (there to squirm in the embrace of the South) has been a half-century of floundering. For in the absence of a genuinely revolutionary re-ordering of social power, there could be no adequate national government in the United States *without* a large portion of national corporate power or *with* too much of the South.

Those Progressives who remained with the Republican Party, with its embarrassing ties to the troglodytes and with its pallid Me-tooism, achieved even less than the ones who went over to the Democrats. In explaining the source of Me-tooism, Walter Lippmann has written:

For when the [Republican] party split in 1912, it surrendered to the Democrats the initiative in the selection and formulation of issues in domestic and international affairs. By surrendering the initiative, the party organization surrendered the vital center of American politics to the Democrats.

Eisenhower was the Republicans' last chance to make up for the 1912 mistake and subsequent defaults—their last chance, that is, to retake the "vital center," where the only ready possibility lies of putting together a national majority coalition. That he failed scarcely needs to be demonstrated. How anyone can imagine that anyone else is apt to have anything like as good an opportunity in the foreseeable future, is quite beyond me. The Republicans needed a winner, which they got in Eisenhower; but they needed a master politician rather more, and this they did not get. And even if Goldwaterism within the party is decisively squelched (a very unlikely outcome), that it could ever have taken over at all remains an enduring curse for a party aspiring to the center.

The Kennedy interregnum ended with the accession of a true centrist to power. Whether Johnson can build a genuine and comprehensive center party depends entirely on whether he can hold the corporate power he has brought into the New Deal coalition. For without it, to repeat, there can be no effective national government. To this difficult and crucial matter, therefore, we must now turn.

III

On July 23, 1964 (after the Civil Rights Act had been passed, and Goldwater had been nominated), President Johnson hosted a luncheon attended by 242 business leaders, the ostensible purpose of which had to do with civil rights—the corporate barons were to be asked to use their influence "to persuade others that the law of the land must be obeyed." It was the first such well-attended Presidential luncheon, and the physical planning was unavoidably off-form. The National Airport across the river in Virginia was not able to handle the crush of "more than 90 company planes"; two JetStars and "a dozen humbler" aircraft were diverted to Dulles Airport. The Washington *Post* also reported: "An operations worker . . . remarked that 'every big corporation you can think of' was represented."

Thus, the barons met—with a President who was Democratic. So be it, for the eccentric and *de facto* character of the new Magna Charta.

Whatever fresh and compelling attractions a revived Republican Party may be able to offer big business in 1968 or later, the underlying point is that a startlingly significant vanguard of the corporate barons has begun to move toward Washington— and toward the Democrats, at least for the time being—not to obstruct the social development of the country but to participate in it. A part of the basic thinking behind this new move was indicated by Lammot du Pont Copeland, president of the big chemical company, in a speech to the New York Chamber of Commerce on February 10, 1964:

Whether we like it or not, the federal government is a partner in every business in the country. . . . We are confronted . . .

with a condition and not a theory. . . . As businessmen we need the understanding and cooperation of government in our effort to throw the economic machine into high gear.

A few months later, on July 2, 1964, the president and second leading officer of the Bank of America returned from a trip to Europe and told reporters how impressed they were with the extent of cooperation there between business and government. "They are doing what we are talking about," the president said. The very important news here is that "we" are now talking about it.

There are so many excellent reasons for this shift that it is much easier to explain its happening than it would have been to account for its not having happened. What keeps us from readily recognizing this is the ordinary image of "business" as a monolith, and moreover one with an eternal and unreasoning allegiance to the Republican Party. But business is not a monolith, and the degree of national irresponsibility involved in its traditional attitudes is no longer appropriate to the large national corporations. What I am suggesting, in other words, is that the "natural" division in the business community between small and large, and between old money and new, has now matured—with profound political consequences.

After the Goldwater nomination, the *Wall Street Journal* reported: "A big majority of executives clearly favor the Arizona conservative." But the *Journal* also cited a Research Institute of America survey of 8,000 businessmen to the effect that one out of three would vote for Johnson, whereas four years earlier Kennedy had been supported by only one out of five. Which one out of which three, the *Journal* did not say. Eileen Shanahan, assigned for several months by the *New York Times* to cover the story of business defection during the campaign, wrote directly to this point in her report on the Northeast and Midwest:

The business executives who expect to cast the first Democratic presidential vote of their lives are nearly all affiliated with large companies.

She noted "the general rule that small businessmen are remaining Republican." Additional differences, generally borne out by later reports from other regions, were that Johnson was getting more support in the East, in big cities, among middle-aged rather than younger or older men, and from "businessmen who have previously been involved . . . in public affairs." In her report from the South, she quoted a large-firm executive from Winston-Salem: "Businessmen in the South felt a sense of relief when Johnson came in. We knew him . . . we knew from the start that he was not antibusiness." There was, however, a "less pronounced" shift in the Far West, while the defection was greater in port cities like San Francisco, New Orleans, and Boston, and among businessmen involved in international trade.

Defense contractors, of course, favor government spending and tend to go along with the party in power. The effort of the Goldwater forces to identify *all* of Johnson's business support as being of this character was, however, patent nonsense. In fact, even many engineers (members of a profession that has always been distinguished by its overwhelming Republicanism) were organized in 1964 by the scientific elite into an action group called Scientists and Engineers for Johnson and Humphrey. The Organizing Group of forty-seven scientists was exceptionally distinguished—it included George Kistiakowsky, Jerome Wiesner, Detlev W. Bronk, James M. Gavin, Benjamin M. Spock, Gerard Piel, Harold C. Urey, Paul Dudley White, Warren Weaver, and other leading professors and administrators, as well as scientific corporate officers of IBM, CBS, Hallicrafters, Gillette, Northrop, Hughes Aircraft, Lockheed, Aerojet-General, Litton Industries, North American Aviation, The Martin Company, and RCA.

The most important of the really important business leaders to come out for Johnson, however, was Henry Ford II. He announced for the President early and he later became one of the forty-five sponsors of the National Independent Committee for President Johnson and Senator Humphrey—the elite, and willing-to-be-counted big business group behind the President. Mr. Ford is important not alone for being Mr. Ford, but also for having headed the Business and Finance Committee for the Reduction in 1963, which lobbied among the corporate barons for support of the tax cut. This group was organized in April, 1963—seven months before the assassination, fifteen months before the Goldwater nomination; by May it had announced a membership in excess of four hundred. In this early organizing effort, Mr. Ford was joined by the president of Westinghouse, and by Stuart T. Saunders, then president of the Norfolk and Western Railway and now chairman of the board of the Pennsylvania Railroad. Addressing the Business Council (probably the single most august organization of barons in the nation) on October 17, 1964, Mr. Saunders proclaimed the tax cut to have been an unqualified success—he noted an increase of after-tax corporate profits of 18 per cent over the previous year. The *Times* reported that Mr. Saunders "emphasized, in a news conference following his speech, that he did not want his remarks taken politically" (this—two weeks before the election!)[1]

Henry H. Fowler, a Washington lawyer appointed by Kennedy as Under Secretary of the Treasury, was the Administration liaison in setting up the Committee for the Reduction; he was also one of the organizers of the campaign committee in 1964 (after leaving the government). Mr. Fowler, a Democrat, is reputed to have been the central "executive" figure in the corporate-Democratic rapprochement. (He was recently appointed Secretary of the Treasury by Johnson.) The leading Republican figure seems to have been Robert B. Anderson, Eisenhower's Secretary of the Treasury and Johnson's fellow Texan. Among other things, Mr. Anderson is a partner in the Wall Street firm of Carl M. Loeb, Rhoades—as is John L. Loeb, another organizer of the National Independent Committee. The other three organizers were Sidney J. Weinberg of Goldman, Sachs; Carter L. Burgess, chairman of the board of American Machinery & Foundry; and John T. Connor of Merck & Co. (since appointed Secretary of Commerce).

A list of the forty-five "sponsors" of the political committee was published in the *New York Times* on September 4, 1964, following an organizational meeting at the White House. Perhaps the most impressive grouping in the list was the investment bankers (concentrated in New York and Boston) including, besides those already mentioned, Thomas S. Lamont, Lehman Bros., Lazard Frères & Co., Eugene R. Black, Lewis W. Douglas and Marriner S. Eccles (from New Deal days), and some Boston Cabots. Other well-known names (of individuals or companies represented by a leading executive)

---

[1] Further on the Business Council: M. J. Rossant, writing in the *Times* for August 17, 1964, cited a member as saying that 60 per cent of the group would support President Johnson—a fact which, if true, indicates an avalanche rather than a drift.

were: Kaiser, Curtiss-Wright, Inland Steel, American Electric Power, Burroughs, Ralph Lazarus of Federated Department Stores (current owner of Goldwater's department store), Hunt Foods, American Can, Tennessee Gas Transmission, Western Pacific Railroad, and Texaco.

Not exactly the *Fortune* list of the five hundred leading corporations, to be sure. But it was a list of *public* sponsors—and traditionally, businessmen contribute privately. (Eileen Shanahan reported that "almost none" of the new Democratic supporters "will permit use of his name.") Moreover, there is the fact—noted proudly in the White House release—that three-quarters of these Johnson supporters had always been Republicans.

Within a month, Citizens for Goldwater-Miller responded in kind with a full-page ad in the *Wall Street Journal* (October 1, 1964), listing 519 businessmen who were backing Goldwater. This was also not the *Fortune* list, although it included some national corporations—Armstrong Cork, J. I. Case, Cluett Peabody, Eli Lilly, Quaker Oats, and others. Upon closer analysis, the hidden surprise in this list is that the Goldwater supporters were heavily concentrated in Illinois, California, and Ohio. (There was also an intriguing concentration among steel and steel-related businesses.)[2] Along with Texas, with its well-known concentration of right-wing wealth, *these were the four big states the Goldwater strategists said they had to win in order to put their man over.* The persuasive implication here is that the Goldwater maneuver from the beginning involved a schism in the business community—more specifically, a power-play by regional interests to shift the *business* balance of power, using the Republican Party as the vehicle. Or was it a response to a power shift begun in the East?

Probably both. In the East—and for the more national corporate interests—the basic policy toward the government was undergoing a change; elsewhere, the considerable growth of regional business wealth was producing a natural assertion of new independence and power. For representative individuals, think of Douglas Dillon and George Humphrey—each a leading spokesman on the basic divisive issue of a purposeful fed-

---

[2] I am indebted for these notions to a former student of mine, Elinor Graham. [Cf. reading 18.—Eds.]

eral deficit. (Miss Shanahan said: "It is on the issue of government deficits that the division of opinion between small and large businessmen emerges most dramatically.") On this issue, under George Humphrey's tutelage (along with the pull of his own primitivism) Eisenhower failed—*failed as a centrist*. And the tragi-comedy of Richard Nixon, of course, is that he made himself into a centrist of the Republican party, not the American nation: a serious oversight for a shrewd politician. It remained for Kennedy to plow the ground, and Johnson to harvest the seed grain, of the new American center. Each in his own way (which turned out to be marvelously complementary) understood the New Deal heritage and its imperatives, and the consequent vulnerability of the Republican posture.

Business, then, is not a monolith. The classic view, which produced the image of the business monolith, is simply the distinction between property owners and the propertyless; the distinction to replace this classic one concerns personal proprietorship and sparsely populated areas as against highly organized property tenure and use in densely populated centers. With the natural caveat that young people are not very realistic, and old men hate to change their views, this formulation can be useful in evaluating diverse business opinion.

IV

In years to come, it will be recognized that 1958 is a pregnant date like 1929 and 1896 and 1912 and 1964. What happened in 1958 was that the postwar inflationary boom came to an end—by something like "administrative decision." In 1958, the powers that could have done so in 1928, made the decision they should have made then, and they made it in the light of the political decision the American people had meanwhile made in 1933: that is, the *repeal* of natural deflation. Since there was so much more to be destroyed in 1958, and since big money and big business had been through it once before, they agreed to slow down the inflationary boom that had been presided over by the congressional Republicans and then the Eisenhower Administration. Indicating the administered quality of this decision is the fact that the corporate powers initiated an expensive advertising campaign around the slogan—"*Infla-*

tion is the cruellest tax of all." What led them to this departure was the built-in (by the New Deal) and unintended (by Eisenhower) deficit of $18 billion in the first six months of fiscal 1959 which, after much effort, was cut down to a $12 billion deficit for the full year. This was a unique financial event in American history. It meant that big business and big money were finally accepting the facts of life, including the fact of the New Deal (which in this particular context means cooperation between government and industry to prevent the busts that must, if things are left alone, follow the booms). For American society, it was like being born again.

When U. S. Steel, reportedly squeezed by its own inefficiency, attempted to get a spiral going again after a few years, President Kennedy reacted as if the non-boom policy were not an act of unilateral discretion on the part of the barons, but was a kind of *joint* program of business and government. The emotional reaction to this presumption was, of course, extreme, but the policy was not abandoned (for all that U. S. Steel got itself a piece of a price rise a year later). And the policy still is in effect, as are the administration's wage–price "guidelines." These are a highly amateur effort at price control, or reasonableness, which can be "enforced" only by voluntary cooperation on the part of business. The point is that this cooperation has been given.

Why? To answer that question, we must first grasp that there are two kinds of inflation. The ordinary one concerns prices; the overlooked one concerns paper (stocks, bonds, private and public debt). In the postwar period, paper inflation has far outdistanced price inflation, although the latter has been by far the more notorious.

Prices have, roughly, trebled since the bottom of the Depression and doubled since the war. Total public and private debt, however, went from $200 billion in 1935 to something under $1200 billion in 1962—at least twice as great an advance as the increase in prices. Meanwhile, the market value of stocks listed on the New York Stock Exchange went from about $46 billion in 1940 to $76 billion in 1950, $170 billion in 1955, $219 in 1957, $196 in 1958 (notice the decline), up again to $277 in 1959, and to $346 in 1963. In other words, while prices were doubling since the war, values on the New York Stock Exchange went up seven times over; total private debt went up five times over; state and local debt better than quadrupled; and federal public debt went up only about 20 per cent—including deficits attributable to all cold war expenditures.

All this means that the increase in corporate profits and in the value of corporate stocks has been tied only loosely to increased prices in the postwar period; and since 1958 in particular, corporate values have continued to go up even though prices have remained fairly steady. There was no reason, then, for the corporations to object to holding the line on prices, especially since: (1) prices rise by standing still if (as was indeed the case in the period under consideration) costs go down and sales increase; (2) financial decisions concerning inventory and expansion and so on can become more sophisticated and less expensive if there are no recessions to discount; and (3) the government's anti-recession policy was heavily slanted in favor of direct and immediate advantages for business.

Last year in the middle of May, Dr. Donner of General Motors pointed out that the company had not raised its basic auto prices since 1958. Then he pledged that "we're going to do our part" to hold the line on prices. A few months later, in January of this year General Motors announced the greatest annual profits of any single corporation in the history of the human race. Now what could possibly induce GM to yearn for Goldwater purism under such circumstances? It is only the liberal intellectual's traditional and excessive downgrading of business intelligence that even raises the issue.

Following the decision to forego a runaway boom, the big corporations were willing to settle for high-level stagnation— about 80 per cent of capacity—and preserve the achieved level of paper values and the growth that could reasonably be expected therefrom. Then, when the recession began in 1960, some enlightened elements began to see that the choice lay between an uncertain course of continued high-level stagnation, and embarking on a series of planned deficits. The Democrats, under Kennedy and Dillon, demonstrated that there was no good reason whatever to settle for stagnation and frequent recessions. With covert and then overt deficits, they gave business and most of the rest of the country almost five years of good growth and no recession. This "New Economic Policy," which was sold as a tardy imitation of proven centrist procedure in Europe, has worked extremely well, bringing about the longest postwar period without recessions.

That it is genuinely entitled to be called a New Economic Policy seems clear. Under the thinnest veneer of a reform bill, a $10-billion-plus tax cut was advertised and finally enacted (more recent indications put it at $14 billion). Thus was taken the first step toward a purposeful non-military deficit. This was then buttressed by another advertising program which encompassed the embarrassingly small ($1 billion) "war on poverty." Meanwhile, a great deal of conversation and newspaper speculation about defense cut-backs occurred. And there were rumors about further tax cuts. All this was designed to induce spending wherever possible in the private sector, and to prepare the necessary groundwork for *non-military public spending*, should the political occasion arise. (Thus the post-Cuban *détente* with the Russians might be deepened without economic disaster.)

But the substance of all this indirection should not be lost sight of: consistent administrative deficits were incurred—$3.9 billion in 1961, $6.4 in 1962, $6.3 in 1963, $8.2 in 1964, and $6.3 estimated for 1965. If by one means or another—indeed, if by any means—a ten- to twenty-billion-dollar annual non-military deficit is institutionalized, we will have finally passed a major post-New Deal point of departure, and later historians will treasure the indirection as consummate shrewdness.

This policy has corralled enlightened, national business for the Democrats. It was Kennedy's creation—and Johnson executed it. Business opposed Kennedy no matter how hard he tried to please them, and he tried very hard (the story is well detailed in the recent book by Hobart Rowen, *The Free Enterprisers: Kennedy, Johnson and the Business Establishment*). But business accepted Johnson—*and* the policy, when offered by him—almost immediately. This is where Kennedy's "style," especially including that of the intellectuals around him, was quite important: businessmen detest intellectuals.

In long-term perspective, Harry Truman understood (and tried to fulfill) the New Deal as the near-triumph of Populism. John Kennedy saw it as the near-victory of enlightened managerialism. But President Johnson sees it more shrewdly as the great national political coalition that, in its essence, it truly is. A more elegant style must wait on the future.

V

If the NEP continues to work, the corporate barons will have to remain in politics in a new way and more seriously than before. The consequence is that they will be unable to ignore the governing and majority party—i.e., the Democrats, who have the more modern, more usable coalition. But not only is it more modern and usable; it is already there—and when a big corporation enters a new field, it always begins by buying into a good going concern.

Thus Lyndon Johnson, Me-tooing Eisenhower politically and accepting the direction of Kennedy's shrewdly constructed economic policy, has now put together the elements of a competent Establishment. A significant sector (still a minority) of national corporate power has now joined in responsible national government, accepting the Democratic Party as the vehicle. For liberals who have never faced the overriding facts of corporate power, and whose politics is derived from a glowingly fuzzy remembrance of New Deal things past, the event—when they own up to it—will be spiritually disquieting in the extreme. For their more realistic companions, who recognize the New Deal to have been a major innovative effort to save the corporations from themselves, the event will be taken with a deep sigh of relief—and as an occasion for some fresh political thinking. The simplest and most important facts of our political life are and have been for some time: (1) that there can be no adequate government of the United States without the participation and cooperation of the major corporations—they are in fact all by themselves the major part of *"the* government of the United States"; and (2) that there has not yet been created in this country a power equal to the task of issuing *orders* to the corporations. Therefore, it has been and remains necessary to negotiate their compliance with federal policy.

What died in 1964 was 1940 Me-tooism. The Republican Party cannot avoid survival of some kind; the important question is whether the Me-too group (otherwise known as the moderates) can devise and execute a *new* Me-tooism. The old one is properly dead. Since it was a calculatedly pale reflection of Democratic initiative, the new form of the latter must emerge clearly before it can be newly recalculated. Barring the intervention of genius, this is at least four to eight years off.

Meanwhile, the Republican Party is, from the most generous point of view, riven. The Goldwater group, broadly conceived, severely limits the flexibility required to create the new and necessary Me-tooism. This group does not appear to be impressed with its defeat, apart from a disappointment with Goldwater himself. They can hardly be thrown out, and it is difficult to believe that they will quietly return to their previous captive status in the party. Moreover, the "success" of John Grenier's Southern strategy is a new, intractable factor that will plague the moderates. It took in economic earthquake and a lot of history to bring the majority of the Negroes into the Democratic party while it included the Southern racists. Now the racists are oozing away from the Democrats to the Republicans at just the moment when the national racist policy of the Goldwater campaign has produced a massive defection of Negroes from the Republican party. How can the moderates get them back, especially now that the Administration has put real force behind Negro registration in the South? And how can the moderates win in the cities without the Negroes? Paradoxically, urban Republicans may have to become, like Javits and Lindsay, *more* liberal than the ordinary run of Democrat in order to win in the North.

The utter collapse of the moderate or Me-too wing of the Republican party became widely known after the California primary in the spring of 1964, and the subsequent cancellation of Rockefeller's self-financed campaign. At that point, even amateurs and outsiders could see that the money for stopping Goldwater had not arrived. Eastern and national corporate money abandoned the Republican Party because the Goldwater group raised the ante: there is today too much primitive money, West and local, for the corporations to try to match. To buy into the Democratic coalition costs less; also, you win.

VI

The President now has at least two secure years in which to consolidate and further prove-out his creation. My guess is that he will succeed. By backing Negro voting rights in the South, he has already forced the racists deeper into the Republican Party. What remains is for him to clear the decks of hangover

New Deal legislation and to use federal money to back up the working congressional majority he is so eminently able—by training, talent, and unprecedented opportunity—to weld together. He may even reach out imaginatively to a Northern and urban Democratic-Republican coalition in Congress to replace the deeply damaged Southern Democratic-Republican coalition. This would certainly be a proper accompaniment to the new Establishment government. And it would follow naturally enough as a reasonable deal on behalf of the President's new business allies and as generally realistic politics, if the Northeastern Republican party (with urban allies elsewhere, as in Michigan) remains in business but does not re-achieve its dominance of the national party. This seems to me a likely event: the barons of the National Independent Committee agreed as an organizing principle to support *only* Johnson and Humphrey, leaving themselves free to continue with their usual localistic interests. In some instances, this might not even be so bad from the President's point of view, since it would give him a fairly good handle in local party affairs (and even more of a handle in Congress).

Another important point: if enough big businessmen (a majority is not necessary) enter into the politics of the Democratic Party at the Presidential level—and abandon their backing of the fanatical free enterprisers in and out of Congress—they could easily build a congressional majority behind "their" President. One million dollars a year—chewing-gum money—puts $20,000 into each of 50 congressional campaigns; five million dollars a year—pipe-tobacco money—puts $25,000 into enough campaigns to elect a majority of the House; etc. Thus, the Establishment could create an *ad hoc* parliamentary system as backing for whatever it happened to be establishing that year.

The political possibilities are numerous and interesting; the eventualities will depend, however, on the success of the new centrist *policy* behind which the New Deal–Establishment coalition—with whatever additions, subtractions, and rearrangements—is forming. And it is so forming only because the policy works so well; therefore, no longer than that. Runaway technological unemployment, renewed price inflation, or inadequate deficits could undermine the NEP.[3] But in this wealthy country

[3] As throughout, I am foregoing discussion of the possible effects of foreign/military matters.

only superhuman and super-shortsighted greed could engender the kind of anti-historical stupidity that might make such matters unmanageable. Clearly the next step, after institutionalizing the deficit through the 1966 election, is indicative planning —that is, voluntary planning executed by the government with the cooperation of the big corporations. Then very likely, later, wayward *individual* producers will have to be forced to stay within the wage-price guidelines (general price control is out of the question).

Meanwhile, everyone becomes more and more committed to the continuance of the incredibly continuing prosperity. These commitments are substantial, and need have nothing to do with ideology; it will be the *present*, not the *future*, that is being "proven." Business, even in the South, cannot countenance actions which interfere with good business (including sales to Negroes). Therefore, one may expect non-militant and unexciting compliance with the Civil Rights Act and what we may call "calculated utilization" of the antipoverty program. In addition, since an educated work force becomes increasingly important to industry, one must be a psychoanalyst to imagine determinative reasons for business's refusing to allow the government to bear more and more of the cost of educating our substantially undereducated population. Moreover, now that big business, in dealing with the unions, has had enough experience with fringe benefits, it may even allow the government to assist it in covering the health and retirement costs of the working population. And finally, why should business not wish the government to underwrite purchasing power to protect the achieved level of capital values, especially including that involved with consumer debt?

If the President can divide Eastern and bigger business from smaller and Western, older from newer money, managerial from fee-simple types, and include those he gathers in the Democratic Party while holding most—but not all—of the current Democratic coalition, he will have at last re-created a national Establishment party which could and probably would govern this mass technological society.

And the "captured liberals" in the Democratic Party—where will all this leave them? The enactment of the hangover New Deal program will leave them bereft—specifically, of a program. There are, however, four considerations, or issues, or sources of issues, to replace it: (1) Johnson's policy may prove to be too little and too late, or not flexible enough to arrest urban decay and contain technology; (2) the institutionalized deficit may not be allowed to grow large enough; (3) the Establishment pie, granted a successful baking in its own oven, may not be divided properly; and (4) there may arise what we might begin calling crypto-political matters of culture—e.g., not whether there is a program in education and housing, or its dollar value, but what *kind* of education and housing it is apt to, or did, produce.

There is enough here to keep any middle-aged liberal busy who may be unhappy with the bland corporatism of the emerging Establishment party. One may add, finally, that the *new* generation has not yet had *its* politics: it is only the Depression-and-War generation that will now close out the remaining New Deal business.

THE "NEUTRALITY" OF THE WAGE-PRICE GUIDELINES

In his *American Capitalism: The Concept of Countervailing Power* (revised ed., Boston, 1956) Harvard Professor John Kenneth Galbraith restates the classical tenet of all liberal economic theory at least since Adam Smith: that the state is a kind of neutral broker among the contending economic interests in a society. His view is that the state does (or should—the distinction is not always clear) step in to place its weight on the side of groups like farmers and workers when other interests, such as business, become too strong.

One of the many difficulties in Galbraith's view is that while the motivations of the members of various interest groups are clear—they seek the advance of their interests—the motivation of members in this neutral agency, the state, remains unclear. Are they collectively the selfless seekers of the good of the overall system, the modern counterparts of Plato's philosopher kings?

A more realistic view is suggested in the following essay. It shows how despite a public declaration of neutrality toward the two parties—business and labor—the actual course of policy, as well as its theoretical assumptions, favors one group over the other.

The author, who holds degrees from the University of Chicago and Columbia University, is assistant professor of economics at the Polytechnic Institute of Brooklyn. His essay was written specifically for inclusion in this book.

◇ ◇ ◇

In no other sphere of economic policy have the Kennedy and Johnson Administrations followed such a confusing and obscure course as in their so-called "wage–price guideposts." This fact, however, does not make the problem of the "guideposts" an uninteresting or unimportant one. On the contrary, analysis of this area should cast considerable light on what might be called contradictions of our overdeveloped economy.

The basic objective, as seen by the Council of Economic Advisers, is to combine high employment with stable prices. We have no need to examine, at the outset of this discussion, whether this is a "real" economic problem: the experience of the postwar era testifies uniformly that prices have tended to rise at all times and to rise quite rapidly at times of high employment (such as 1966). It is, however, essential to start with an analysis of the council's rationale for its assertion that prices *should* remain stable.

Is inflation a bad thing?

". . . [T]here are compelling reasons," the council states, "why we can ill afford to neglect prices." [1] What are the compelling reasons?

1. "First, inflation redistributes real incomes and wealth arbitrarily. When prices rise, those groups that are able to expand profits and wages most rapidly improve their situation at the expense of those whose incomes respond slowly" (p. 116).

Coming from a group of economists, this is indeed a peculiar argument. What is "arbitrary" about a group's being able to expand its income "most rapidly"? Such ability can stem from only one economic factor: a particularly intense demand for the product or service it provides (monopoly power is irrelevant here indeed, competitive industries such as agriculture tend to experience wider income fluctuations than monopolistic ones like metallurgy). But since economic theory tells us that the function of income differentials is to direct resources to the uses that correspond best to social desires *as measured by the market,* the fact that rising price levels have such a differential effect is if anything beneficial to the economy.

2. "Inflation erodes the real value of public assistance and

---

[1] *Economic Report of the President* (1964), p. 116.

makes it difficult for local governments to maintain adequate standards of education and other essential services" (p. 116).

It is impossible to be charitable toward this arrant sophism. Government services are paid for out of taxes, and the US tax structure is such that "inflation" causes a *greater* share of the real national income to be available for public purposes. Political authorities, it is true, may not choose to use the available funds on "education and other essential services," but then the problem is hardly one of inflation.

3. "It also reduces the purchasing power of retirement pensions and other fixed incomes—in effect, subjecting them to a discriminatory tax" (p. 116).

This at least *seems* true—but is in fact quite evasive. The vast bulk of retirement pensions comes from the federal government through the Social Security system, and there is no reason whatsoever why these payments should not be tied automatically to the consumer price index, as indeed should have been done in the first place. As for "other fixed incomes"—the interest received by that small class of "coupon-clippers"—need we recall to our "Keynesian" advisers a certain phrase about the "euthanasia of the rentier"? [2]

4. "Fixed-income assets lose value while the prices of equity securities and other properties rise" (p. 116).

This is true, but quite trivial. The interest of the bankers is not that of the productive economy, and the problem with capital gains is not their existence but their grossly discriminatory favored position in our tax structure.

5. "A . . . cost of inflation that we cannot afford is its adverse impact on our balance of trade and on our balance of payments" (p. 116).

This final argument, seemingly plausible, is in reality per-

[2] In his classic and seminal work, *The General Theory of Employment, Interest, and Money* (New York, 1936), John Maynard Keynes, in exploring the implications of the lower rate of interest his theory called for, felt it would mean "the euthanasia of the rentier, and, consequently, the euthanasia of the cumulative oppressive power of the capitalist to exploit the scarcity-value of capital." Continuing, Keynes remarks, "Interest today rewards no genuine sacrifice, any more than does the rent of land. . . . But whilst there may be intrinsic reasons for the scarcity of land, there are no intrinsic reasons for the scarcity of capital" (pp. 375-76). Though Keynes saw the euthanasia as "nothing sudden," it is dubious that the rentier would view his gradual disappearance as a painless act of mercy.—Eds.

fectly absurd. Any "balance of payments" difficulties the US may have do not involve that part of the balance affected by price changes, called "current account," the major part of which is the balance of trade, where the US always has a substantial surplus. More important, the whole question has meaning only so long as the US remains tied to the archaic and dangerously restrictive gold-exchange standard. A country with a "floating" exchange rate need have no worries about its balance of payments.

Why then all this concern about moderate "inflation"? A politician might answer: "People are prejudiced against inflation and we have to pretend to share their prejudices." I cannot advance any definitive answer, but would raise this one question: is it perhaps in order to justify policies like the "guideposts"?

It should in any event be made quite clear that the guideposts are relevant only to conditions of *gradually* increasing prices. No economist considers tolerable a "runaway" inflation of the sort that Germany underwent in 1922-23, or even the annual doubling of the price level that Brazil has experienced in recent years. But these pathological conditions require a vast and growing disproportion between the creation of new monetary tokens and the productive capacity of the economy. Such a specter is totally irrelevant to the US, where monetary and fiscal authorities are able to restrain or even contract the money supply, and where productive capacity is growing very rapidly indeed. Our "inflation" has involved mainly a broadly diffused process whereby the banking system "institutionalizes" price increases by uncovering more and more efficient ways of using the existing stock of money (in technical terms: by accelerating the income velocity of the money supply).

This situation is usually called a "cost-push" inflation, meaning that price increases are caused, not by cost increases following from increased sales and output at a given price, but by autonomous decisions by workers or capitalists to increase their incomes even if sales of their product do not increase or are actually reduced by the price change. There is little doubt that most of the price increase we have experienced during the past decade stems from a process of this sort, since unemployment has been above the high level of 4 per cent throughout the period, eliminating excessive *aggregate* demand as a cause of rising prices. In such a state of affairs an attempt to stabilize the price level by blocking such autonomous cost and price increases makes at least *formal* sense, and this is indeed the professed objective of the "guideposts."

What are the "guideposts"?

The 1965 *Report* states the guideposts in these terms:

"1. *The general guide for wages is that the percentage increase in total employee compensation per man-hour be equal to the national trend rate of increase in output per man-hour.*

"If each industry follows this guidepost, prices in the economy will maintain a constant average.

"2. *The general guide for prices calls for stable prices in industries enjoying the same productivity growth as the average for the economy; rising prices in industries with smaller than average productivity gains; and declining prices in industries with greater than average productivity gains.*

"If each industry follows this guidepost, prices in the economy will maintain a constant average." [3]

If these guideposts were scrupulously adhered to, the *Report* claims, the division of income between labor and capital would remain unchanged. This is of course a tautology, but a pointed one. Labor is told that a single figure, the "trend rate of increase in output per man-hour," should govern all contract negotiations (with rare and minor exceptions), while capital is assigned no such single standard: price behavior is to be related also to industry productivity changes.

This in fact represents a built-in bias against labor, and a very powerful one. Wages have to be negotiated, and the guidepost is a weapon in the hands of employers who want to resist any increase in wages over this limit, particularly where arbitration or "fact-finding" is invoked. But, except for spectacular gestures by a President, price decisions are entirely unilateral. Steel, aluminum, and tobacco corporations have, it is true, *partially* rescinded price increases after Johnsonian lectures. (There is however no proof that such an outcome was not orig-

[3] *Economic Report of the President* (1965), p. 108. (Italics in the original.)

inally envisaged.) But who can imagine Johnson intervening to force an industry "with greater than average productivity gains" to *reduce* prices?

What happens, of course, is that the Great Society prices continue to creep up (at a rapidly accelerating rate in 1966). The "guideposts" for wage increases may allow an increase in *real wages*, but one that lags considerably behind productivity gains: the difference goes to swell capital's relative share of the national income.

The foregoing analysis brings into question the assertion in the 1966 *Report* that "public policy is and should remain neutral with respect to wage and price decisions that attempt to change the distribution of   industry's income between labor and capital. But when such decisions lead to inflationary pressure they properly become a subject of public concern." [4] Labor, because it has no conceivable means of compelling price reductions, can "change the distribution of income" in its favor *only* by winning wage increases far enough above the rate of productivity increase to overcompensate for price increases. These are precisely the sort of wage increases that Johnson and his advisers consider "a subject of public concern."

How has productivity actually changed?

The above demonstration of the bias in the guideposts has implicitly accepted the conceptual and statistical accuracy of the CEA's estimates of the rate of productivity increase. These estimates, however, are far from the least dubious of the advisers' procedures.

The advisers' productivity estimates seem to be obtained by dividing the total output of the private economy (estimated in constant dollars) by the total number of man-hours worked in the year. The "trend productivity" for a year is estimated as the average percentage change in this figure computed over the preceding five years.

No one can seriously argue against using a period longer than a year to compute productivity changes, but the methods of the advisers smack of outright bad faith. The 1966 *Report*

[4] *Economic Report of the President* (1966), p. 91.

gives as its estimate of trend productivity for the current year the figure of 3.6 per cent—but then sets the "guidepost" at only 3.2 per cent, less even than the trend figures (3.4 per cent) for the preceding two years! To justify this odd procedure they suddenly advance the claim that five years is too short a time to establish a meaningful trend, and that the "true" long-term productivity increase is no more than 3 per cent!

In reality, the advisers' statistical manipulations are profoundly mendacious, and in two distinct ways: both their very *definition* of "productivity" and their concept of "trend" are highly biased so as to minimize the actual productivity changes now occurring.

In the first place, they define "labor productivity" in the private economy as total output divided by total labor input (in man-hours). What is ignored here is that "labor input" in reality is not homogeneous but consists of *two* distinct types: workers whose employment *increases* the material output of the firm ("production" or "productive" workers) and those who have no share in producing physical output (sales, clerical, and administrative, or "nonproductive," workers). In neglecting this dichotomy, the advisers willfully conceal a crucial fact: the steady decrease in the percentage of the labor force actually engaged in "productive" work. According to the 1958 Census of Manufacturers (the most recent) this percentage declined from 83.5 in 1947 to 75.2 in 1958. The decline has since persisted at least as strongly. Consequently, the productivity trend as estimated is too low by a full 1 per cent per year!

The second bias is even more flagrant. It assumes that the exceptionally rapid productivity increases of the past five years cannot be sustained. This merely ignores the rapidly accelerating industrial revolution known as "cybernation," the introduction of completely automated computer-directed production processes. This revolution began in 1960 and is only now reaching significant scope: but if one trend is sure, it is that more and more sophisticated computers will be put into use on a dramatically increasing scale (the 1960 computers are already obsolete!). This trend can only serve to speed—probably drastically—the pace of productivity increase.

In sum then, a government policy that allowed the division of income between labor and capital to remain constant would have to envisage annual wage increases at a rate of at least double the 3.2 per cent guidepost.

The foregoing analysis has been mainly theoretical; but it is far from an exaggeration of the pro-business bias in the guideposts. On August 25, 1966, President Johnson pointed with pride to the fact that during the current expansion money wages (wages uncorrected for price increases) had increased by 17 per cent, the price level had gone up "only" 10 per cent, while *profits* had gone up by 83 per cent!

This record makes it obvious why labor leaders have expressed increasing resentment against the guideposts. But what is really noteworthy is the impotence of most of the labor movement to do anything beyond talking. Some unions have succeeded in gaining increases at a 4-5 per cent rate: but there can be little doubt that these increases would have been larger, and more easily won, in the absence of government pressure (indeed, it was always plain that the airline mechanics would have gained a larger increase without a strike if not for the guideposts). However, such "successes" have affected only a minority of labor (in fact, the most privileged groups—such as the construction workers). The great mass-production unions confront the current inflation tied to long-term contracts negotiated under White House pressure. During the relative price stability of the early sixties many unions had surrendered the "cost-of-living" escalator clauses of earlier contracts and accepted "guidepost" limited wage increases. Not until mid-1967 or later will the auto, steel, electrical, and rubber workers have a chance to try to catch up. Meanwhile, prices will continue their ascent; while the bargaining situation will be most unfavorable under the pressures of war hysteria or recession—or even a combination of the two.

The airline strike and the steel price increases of August, 1966, caused some speculation that the guideposts would in effect be abandoned. This is most unlikely: as we have seen, their impact has largely been felt by labor, and they have proven such an effective instrument of pressure that some form will certainly remain in use under all conditions except a major recession. True, the 3.2 per cent figure will have to be raised, since no union can accept a wage increase *lower* than the rate of price increases—but this "flexibility" is likely to be only enough to prevent a break between Johnson and Meany: and that doesn't have to be very much.[5]

In conclusion, we must recognize that the guideposts have "succeeded"—succeeded, that is, in blocking significant wage increases and thus causing spectacular profit gains. There is, however, more to this policy than "capitalist greed." Wage restraint has a direct impeding effect on technological change because by keeping down the cost of human labor, it reduces the savings obtainable from automation. This is desired by the "Great Society" for two reasons:

1. By indirectly reducing business capital investment it avoids a drain on the sophisticated machines and skilled labor required to maintain and escalate the slaughter in Vietnam.

2. Every diversion of resources from productive investment postpones the inevitable day of reckoning, the day when the economy reaches such a peak of cybernation that its only choices will be acceptance of mass nonemployment (with the deeply radical social changes that will entail) or else literally suffocation under smog, sewage, and the vast mass of useless products that a "fully employed" cybernated economy would inflict on us.

[5] In fact, specific guidelines were abandoned by the Johnson Administration in its 1967 *Economic Report of the President*. It urged that "producers absorb cost increases to the maximum extent feasible" (p. 133) and that labor exercise "restraint." Defining the latter, the Council of Economic Advisers stated "it surely must mean wage advances which are substantially less than the productivity trend plus the recent rise in consumer prices" (p. 129).—Eds.

HOW THE GREAT SOCIETY
SOLVES THE SERVANT PROBLEM *

At the fringes of society, both on the left and on the right, there exist a large number of publications that differ substantially from the *New York Times, Newsweek,* and *Life.* One of the more interesting of these is a newsletter put out by Jack Minnis of Atlanta, Georgia. Mr. Minnis is a member of the Student Non-Violent Coordinating Committee (SNCC).

On February 1, Lyndon announced that he was launching yet another battle in the war on poverty. He said he had instructed his Secretary of Labor to use existing funds and laws for what he called his Job Development Program. Lyndon said that there is a labor shortage in employment areas such as domestic service, and he wanted Secretary Wirtz to do something to provide more trained servants for families which don't like to do their dirty work for themselves.

The *Washington Post* calls the new program "dignifying the service jobs that are necessary to running a modern home and meeting the needs of family life today." The *Post* did not explain just how you could inject dignity of any kind into a relationship which requires that one person, in order to live, bind himself to the personal service of another. Nor did the *Post* explain what's to become of those families that can't afford to hire someone to run "a modern home" for them. But the *Post*

* From *Life with Lyndon in the Great Society* (Newsletter), Vol. I, No. 6.

did describe one of Lyndon's Job Development Programs which is underway in LaGrange, Georgia.

Lyndon's Office of Manpower and Training (OMAT) got together with a retired schoolteacher, Emmy Murray, in La-Grange. OMAT put up the money to redecorate an old road-house, and to equip it with various household appliances. Emmy is now teaching prospective household servants "cleanliness and work discipline," which is to say she's teaching Negro women how to address Miss Anne and Mr. Charlie with the proper degree of deference, teaching them how to shuffle their feet and tug their forelocks and convince the white folks of their profound satisfaction with a life of servitude.

The top wage available to the best-trained household servants in LaGrange—that is, the top graduates of Emmy's careful instruction—is $4 per day. If the servant works every day of the year (and this is usually the case) she makes $1,460 per year. This is just half of what Lyndon says (out of the other side of his mouth) is necessary for a minimum subsistence, and about one-fourth of what is really necessary for a decent standard of living. And this is being done with federal tax money from Lyndon, the Second Great Emancipator of Black America.

There are two kinds of people in LaGrange who will be employing Emmy's graduates. The first kind is represented by the Callaway family. They own Callaway Mills, a textile manufacturer which is LaGrange's largest employer, employing more than 3,000 persons in a town of 23,000. The Callaway family owns the mills in a peculiar way. They don't own the stock of the corporation personally. Rather they control tax-exempt foundations, which, in turn, own the stock. In this way dividends paid by the mills to the foundations are free of federal income tax.

Callaway Mills received more than $600,000 of federal money last year as part of Lyndon's program of subsidizing the textile manufacturers. If they used all this to employ household servants for the various branches of the family, they'd be able to hire about 410 servants at the going wage. Thus the Callaways could use the money Lyndon gave them, which is tax free, to employ more servants than an Oriental Potentate, the servants having been trained to the peak of servile perfection with money supplied by Lyndon from the federal taxes from which the Callaways are exempt.

The second kind of prospective employers for Emmy's graduates are the workers in the Callaway Mills. Diane McKaig, who works in the Atlanta office of Lyndon's Labor Department, explains that these Callaway employees don't make much money (she doesn't explain why, nor does she compare the amount they make with the amount the Callaways make), so the servants—she calls them "homemaking aides," a bit of double-talk worthy of Lyndon himself—have to be "taught to make low-cost dishes, including surplus foods." She doesn't say whether the servants will be preparing surplus foods for themselves, or for the Callaway employees—perhaps both, considering the general level of wages.

The white female Callaway employees, of course, can't work in the mills unless they can find Negroes to care for their children and homes while they're at the mills. Since the Callaways don't pay their workers much, the workers can't pay their Negro servants much. So the upshot of Lyndon's new job program, is to provide cheap and well-trained servants for the Callaway employees, at a price the employees can afford to pay without requiring a raise from the Callaways.

The Callaways exploit their white workers at low wages, and the white workers exploit their Negro servants at even lower wages. Lyndon lavishes hundreds of thousands a year on the Callaways, in the form of textile subsidies, and provides federal money with which to train Negro servants for the Callaways and their white mill employees.

It takes the guts of a burglar to call a sewer like this the Great Society. But, whatever he's short of, Lyndon's always been long on guts.

PART IV

POVERTY AND WELFARE

INTRODUCTION

Until the heralded official discovery of poverty in the 1960s, the mere suggestion that there was such a phenomenon in affluent America was either laughed down or brushed off as a local problem not demanding any national solution.[1] Economists generally were glorifying the "income revolution" that had taken place since the 1930s,[2] and popular books expounding the thesis that capitalism had finally eradicated mass poverty were enthusiastically received.[3]

The mood has changed. Government officials now concede that there are thirty million poor in the United States, and the "War on Poverty" has become the most highly publicized component of Lyndon Johnson's Great Society program. What accounts for the change?

Three major interpretations have been suggested. First, there is the suggestion that the poverty war is just a fraud. Besides its simplicity, this view has much to commend it. If the amount of funds allocated is the criterion, then what has been called a "war" is in fact a minor skirmish. The total appropriation for the first year was three-quarters of a billion dollars, less than 10 per cent of the annual cost of the war in Vietnam. Subsequent increases in appropriations for the Office of Economic Opportunity do not change this picture.[4] But the prominent position

---

[1] It is true that Professor John Kenneth Galbraith (*The Affluent Society* [Boston, 1958], Chapt. XXIII) called attention to the disgrace of poverty amid affluence, but he argued that it was confined to relatively few unfortunate individuals, and regionally located in such exceptional areas as Appalachia.

[2] See the discussion of this in the introduction to Part III of this book, pp. 115-23, and note the literature there cited.

[3] A classic of this genre was *Fortune* magazine's *U.S.A.: The Permanent Revolution* (Garden City, N.Y., 1951).

[4] Total obligations of the OEO for fiscal 1965 were $765 million; for 1966 (estimated), $1,509 million; for 1967 (estimated), $1,745 million. The expected cost of Vietnam during fiscal 1967 was $10.3 billion, as

of the War on Poverty in the rhetoric of Johnson's Great Society points to a deeper significance for the program.

A second interpretation ascribes the assault on poverty to the good will of public servants in government. Daniel Patrick Moynihan, former Assistant Secretary of Labor, expresses this view. "The war on poverty began," he wrote, ". . . at a moment when the prospects for an immense expansion in national wealth had never been better. Nor did the war on poverty come about because of any great surge of popular demand. . . . The origins of this effort simply cannot be explained in deterministic terms. It was more a rational than a political event. Men at the center of the government perceived the fact . . . that ugliness, like poverty, is all around them and that the powers of government might eliminate it." [5] The key moments in this modern enactment of the traditional melodrama of "the discovery of poverty" [6] were John Kennedy's personal confrontation with the poor of Appalachia during the West Virginia primary of 1960, the appearance of Michael Harrington's eloquent *The Other America* (New York, 1962), and Dwight MacDonald's essay on poverty in such an unlikely place as *The New Yorker* (January 19, 1963).[7]

The main difficulty with Moynihan's explanation, stressing the voluntary benevolence of professionals, is its failure to explain why the flowering of altruism took place precisely when it did. Certainly the return of the Democrats after the Eisenhower

---

estimated in the budget. Gross National Product for 1966 will exceed $700 billion.

[5] Moynihan, "Three Problems in Combating Poverty," in Margaret S. Gordon (ed.), *Poverty in America: Proceedings of a National Conference held at the University of California, Berkeley, February 26-28, 1965* (San Francisco, 1965), pp. 41-42.

[6] An earlier episode of this sort is analyzed in Robert H. Bremner's skillful discussion of the growing social awareness of certain American humanitarians in the late nineteenth century, *From the Depths: The Discovery of Poverty in the United States* (New York, 1956), and viewed from a different perspective in Marvin E. Gettleman, "Charity and Social Classes in the United States, 1874-1900," *The American Journal of Economics and Sociology*, XXII (April-July, 1963), pp. 313-29, 417-26.

[7] Underlying both of these popular accounts was the early study prepared for the Joint House-Senate Economic Committee by economist Robert Lampman, *The Low Income Population and Economic Growth* [Study Paper #12] (Washington, D.C., December, 1959).

interlude is no answer. New Frontiersmen were long settled in Washington, and some of them were already leaving, when Johnson launched the War on Poverty.

A third, alternative explanation suggests that the government reformers who designed the poverty program were responding to the resurgence of American idealism and radicalism that was being revealed in the 1960s. The Negro freedom movement created an explosive—possibly revolutionary—situation that could not be allayed by more of the usual civil rights legislation. A need was felt for special programs to divert this potential radicalism into controllable channels. The Peace Corps and the poverty program fulfilled this need. As Elinor Graham puts it in her searching exploration of the genesis of the latter: the poverty program ". . . redefine[d] civil rights in a manner that secures the power positions of white public leaders and places them in control. . . ." (See reading 18, below.)

Once adopted by the Johnson Administration, the poverty program had to be fit into bureaucratic concepts, and to be assigned official meanings. The first problem, of course, was to define poverty. Such a definition had to include an element of arbitrariness. At one end of the spectrum of calculations is Rose Friedman's estimation that an urban family of four is no longer in poverty when its annual income reaches $2,195.[8] The estimates of the Bureau of Labor Statistics are much higher. A "modest but adequate" budget, based on the Bureau's estimate of "the total cost of a representative list of goods and services considered necessary by four-person city families," varied between $6,567 in Chicago and $5,370 in Houston, Texas.[9] The Council of Economic Advisers,[10] using unsophisticated calculations, arrived at a much lower figure of $3,000, as the demarcation line between poor and adequately situated families. For

[8] Friedman, *Poverty—Definition and Perspective* (Washington, D.C., 1965), pp. 24-25. Her calculations are based on 1962 prices. It should be added that she does not include any cost of shelter or clothing in her calculation of the cost of necessities.

[9] Louis A. Ferman, Joyce L. Kornbluth, and Alan Haber, eds., *Poverty in America* (Ann Arbor, Mich., 1965), p. 41. The bureau used 1959 figures in this estimate. Updating this research by using 1962 figures, Leon Keyserling (*Progress or Poverty* [Washington, D. C., 1964]) finds the total number of persons living on *less* than the equivalent of the bureau's budget to be 66 million, or 35.5 per cent of the population.

[10] For the status and personnel of this group, see above, p. 153.

single people the line was $1,500. Both these figures have acquired semi-official status.[11]

Any quantitative interpretation of poverty obscures what is socially and personally destructive about being poor. Statistics do not reveal the genuinely novel features of mid-twentieth century American poverty. Michael Harrington describes this novelty in *The Other America*.

If a group has internal vitality, a will—if it has aspiration— it may live in dilapidated housing, it may eat an inadequate diet, and it may suffer poverty, but it is not impoverished. So it was in those ethnic slums of the immigrants that played such a dramatic role in the unfolding of the American dream. The people found themselves in slums, but they were not slum dwellers.

But the new poverty is constructed so as to destroy aspiration; it is a system designed to be impervious to hope. The other America does not contain the adventurous seeking a new life and land. It is populated by the failures, by those driven from the land and bewildered by the city, by old people suddenly confronted with the torments of loneliness and poverty, and by minorities facing a wall of prejudice (p. 10).

The Johnson Administration has proposed—and in an amazingly large number of cases, obtained—a variety of legislative weapons to fight the war on poverty. The most important of these is the Economic Opportunity Act of 1964.[12] President Johnson's description of this measure appears below, along

[11] See the *Economic Report of the President* (1964), pp. 57-62. Later the council adopted a more refined analysis, charted by Mollie Orshansky of the Department of Health, Education, and Welfare, which adjusts for various factors such as family size, age, and rural residency. She concludes that for a family of four, an adequate diet can be purchased daily for $.70 per person, while $1.40 per person can provide for all other needs, including shelter, transportation, clothing, and medical expenses. (Her article in the *Social Security Bulletin* [January, 1965] is reprinted in Ferman, Kornbluth, and Haber, *Poverty in America*, pp. 42-81). Using the Orshansky calculations, the Council of Economic Advisers estimates (*Economic Report of the President* [1966], p. 111) that 34.1 million people are poor in America.

[12] Other Johnsonian poverty measures include: the Elementary and Secondary Education Act of 1965; the Civil Rights Act of 1964; and the Appalachian Regional Development Act of 1965. Carryovers from the Kennedy Administration include the Area Redevelopment Act of 1961 and The Manpower Development and Training Act of 1962.

with the testimony of Sargent Shriver, head of the poverty program (readings 14 and 17). Daniel Patrick Moynihan, who helped draft the legislation, notes the traditional nature of most of the specific suggestions, as well as one "new departure."

Most of the program items, for the greater part in terms of budget allocations, consisted of activities that had been operated either in large scale or in prototype at some point in the past, as for example, the youth employment programs; or which had direct analogies in ongoing programs, such as VISTA and the Peace Corps. For the most distinctive of these, in terms of a new departure in public policy and program, is the Community Action Program, provided by Title II of the bill.[13]

It may have been the need to make some official gesture in the direction of the "participatory democracy" preached by young radicals that prompted the "Community Action Program" component of the poverty program. It was under CAP that the poor were given the chance to shape their own communities. The anomalies of this program were evident. Sociologist Nathan Glazer viewed CAP against the background of previous government benevolence, and concluded that it amounted to the state financing "guerilla warfare" against itself.[14] Conflict with established agencies and programs could be expected to generate opposition. Local politicians feared that if the poor were given a significant voice in community affairs, their own power might thereby be diminished. How the convergence of these hostile pressures brought about the emasculation of the Community Action Program is the subject of the article below (reading 19) by David Stoloff.

Aside from the eclipse of CAP, and the overshadowing of poverty allocations by war expenditures, the war on poverty suffers from other problems. There is the reluctance to run what Paul Jacobs has called "public relations risks."[15] This tendency has been widely noted.

President Johnson, two other knowledgeable writers observe, has "demanded that the War on Poverty evince early success.

[13] Moynihan, "Three Problems in Combatting Poverty," in Gordon, *Poverty in America*, p. 43.

[14] Glazer, "The Grand Design of the Poverty Program," *New York Times Magazine* (February 27, 1966), pp. 72-73.

[15] Comments delivered at a conference at the University of California, Berkeley, in Gordon, *Poverty in America*, p. 413.

Consequently, the pressure will be to cream, to select those youth who are most likely to 'achieve' through these programs and, indeed, might have achieved without them! The Job Corps will not accept youth with physical handicaps or with serious delinquency records regardless of when the delinquencies were committed." [16] With these problems and limitations the prospects for the War on Poverty are difficult to evaluate. Project Headstart (discussed below, reading 15) will not reveal its results for many years. Whole groups of poor people—the sick, the handicapped, the retarded, the families that have been abandoned by a wage-earning father, the aged, and those employed at low wages—are untouched by the poverty program.[17]

Various factors combine to inhibit a more effective war on poverty. It is obvious that the United States can simply abolish the worst poverty by assigning as little as one quarter of the annual *increase* in goods and services (about $11 billion) to the poor. But such direct subsidies—except where they are reserved for industry—violate the traditional American ideological commitment to self-help and individualism.[18] The his-

[16] S. M. Miller and Martin Rein, "The War on Poverty: Perspectives and Prospects," in Ben B. Seligman (ed.), *Poverty as a Public Issue* (New York, 1965), p. 294.

[17] Mollie Orshansky has pointed out that the heads of almost 30 per cent of all poor families (according to her calculations—see note 11, above) held a full time job through the year studied—1963. Ferman, Kornbluth, and Haber, *Poverty in America*, pp. 45, 71-76.

[18] The distinguished conservative economist, and Goldwater supporter in 1964, Professor Milton Friedman of the University of Chicago, has proposed a form of subsidy, the "negative income tax." This plan has much to commend it. It eliminates the degrading paternalism ("welfare colonialism" is a widely used term) that characterizes so many aid programs. On the other hand, the Friedman plan wipes out all other payments in favor of the "negative tax." Since this negative tax will be legislatively determined, it is conceivable that it might be based on an average budget of $1,000, leaving the poor in worse condition. Friedman himself seems to prefer a higher sum, but his whole method of analysis excludes consideration of *who* will determine policy, and in whose interest these policies will be pursued. See Milton Friedman, *Capitalism and Freedom* (Chicago, 1962), pp. 190-95.

It is worth noting that the Ad Hoc Committee on the Triple Revolution, consisting of such luminaries as Gunnar Myrdal, Linus Pauling, H. Stuart Hughes, Gerard Piel, Robert Theobald, and others, have taken the final step implied by Friedman's negative income tax and proposed that the income-through-jobs link be broken altogether. An excerpt from their statement is reprinted below, p. 221.—Eds.

torical and social nature of poverty poses problems for an Administration pledged to eradicate it. The Council of Economic Advisers in 1964 defined poverty in terms of peoples' "needs." [19] These needs are not simply caloric quantities, but are determined also by the surrounding society. It is therefore only in the context of the wealth, power, and available opportunity of the contemporary United States that the condition of "the other America" can be understood. Poverty is most fruitfully seen as a function of social structure, but the system of distribution of wealth and power, far more than the ideology that sustains it, resists change. Yet without such change, the promise to eliminate poverty cannot be fulfilled.

Thus, it is possible, even likely, that the dramatic promise to effect a "total victory" over poverty[20] will be sacrificed to the other less laudable motives that were woven into the poverty program from its inception. If the aim of blunting radicalism is effective, then potential indigenous leaders will be identified, and co-opted into the official program. A most effective tool for absorption and neutralization will have been applied. In a deeper sense the poverty program has what one perceptive observer saw as a "fundamentally conservative" content. By concentrating on "education, training, and character building," government assumes "that the poor are poor not because the economy is mismanaged but because the poor themselves have something wrong with them." [21] Thus the introduction of a program aimed at the radical goal of eliminating poverty, ultimately sustains the very system and ideology responsible for that poverty.

[19] *Economic Report of the President* (1964), p. 57.
[20] See President Johnson's declaration, reading 14, below.
[21] Christopher Jencks, "Johnson *vs.* Poverty," *New Republic* (March 28, 1964).

 THE GOVERNMENT'S PACIFICATION PROGRAM OF THE COUNTRYSIDE HAS THUS FAR FAILED TO PACIFY THE COUNTRYSIDE.

 EXTREMISM, VIOLENCE AND ANTI-AMERICANISM ARE ON THE RISE IN THOSE VERY AREAS INTO WHICH WE ARE POURING OUR VALUABLE PACIFICATION MONEY.

 MUCH OF THIS AID MONEY IS BEING DIVERTED INTO THE POCKETS OF GREEDY AND CORRUPT LAND OWNERS AND LOCAL OFFICIALS.

 OTHER AID MONEY IS FALLING INTO THE HANDS OF OUR ENEMIES WHO USE IT FOR PURPOSES OF DISAFFECTION AND AGITATION—

 SO THAT ONCE OUR SUPERVISORY PERSONNEL ARE TRANSFERRED OUT OF A PACIFIED AREA WE ARE OFTEN UNABLE TO RETAIN CONTROL OVER ITS LOYALTY.

 THAT CONCLUDES MY REMARKS ON THE WAR ON POVERTY. NOW, AS TO VIETNAM—

TOTAL VICTORY OVER POVERTY*

In his 1964 State of the Union Message, President Johnson called for an "unconditional war on poverty." Soon thereafter (March 16, 1964) he sent to Congress his poverty message and before the summer was over, the Economic Opportunity Act of 1964 became law. The message of March 16 gives the President's reasons why legislation was needed and a brief description of the programs involved. Excerpts from that message follow.

We are citizens of the richest and most fortunate nation in the history of the world. One hundred and eighty years ago we were a small country struggling for survival on the margin of a hostile land. Today we have established a civilization of free men which spans an entire continent. . . .

The path forward has not been an easy one. But we have never lost sight of our goal—an America in which every citizen shares all the opportunities of his society, in which every man has a chance to advance his welfare to the limit of his capacities.

We have come a long way toward this goal. We still have a long way to go. The distance which remains is the measure of the great unfinished work of our society. To finish that work I have called for a national war on poverty. Our objective: total victory. There are millions of Americans—one-fifth of our people—who have not shared in the abundance which has been granted to most of us, and on whom the gates of opportunity have been closed.

* Reprinted from *The War on Poverty: The Economic Opportunity Act of 1964*, Senate Document No. 86 (Washington, D. C., 1964).

What does this poverty mean to those who endure it? It means a daily struggle to secure the necessities for even a meager existence. It means that the abundance, the comforts, the opportunities they see all around them are beyond their grasp. Worst of all, it means hopelessness for the young. The young man or woman who grows up without a decent education, in a broken home, in a hostile and squalid environment, in ill health or in the face of racial injustice—that young man or woman is often trapped in a life of poverty. He does not have the skills demanded by a complex society. He does not know how to acquire those skills. He faces a mounting sense of despair which drains initiative and ambition and energy.

Our tax cut will create millions of new jobs—new exits from poverty. But we must also strike down all the barriers which keep many from using those exits. The war on poverty is not a struggle simply to support people, to make them dependent on the generosity of others. It is a struggle to give people a chance. It is an effort to allow them to develop and use their capacities, as we have been allowed to develop and use ours, so that they can share, as others share, in the promise of this nation. . . .

Because it is right, because it is wise, and because, for the first time in our history, it is possible to conquer poverty, I submit, for the consideration of the Congress and the country, the Economic Opportunity Act of 1964. The act does not merely expand old programs or improve what is already being done. It charts a new course. It strikes at the causes, not just the consequences of poverty. It can be a milestone in our 180-year search for a better life for our people.

This act provides five basic opportunities:

It will give almost half a million underprivileged young Americans the opportunity to develop skills, continue education, and find useful work.

It will give every American community the opportunity to develop a comprehensive plan to fight its own poverty—and help them to carry out their plans.

It will give dedicated Americans the opportunity to enlist as volunteers in the war against poverty.

It will give many workers and farmers the opportunity to break through particular barriers which bar their escape from poverty.

It will give the entire nation the opportunity for a concerted attack on poverty through the establishment, under my direction, of the Office of Economic Opportunity, a national headquarters for the war against poverty.

This is how we propose to create these opportunities. *First,* we will give high priority to helping young Americans who lack skills, who have not completed their education or who cannot complete it because they are too poor. The years of high school and college age are the most critical stage of a young person's life. If they are not helped then, many will be condemned to a life of poverty which they, in turn, will pass on to their children.

I therefore recommend the creation of a Job Corps, a work-training program, and a work-study program. A new national Job Corps will build toward an enlistment of 100,000 young men. They will be drawn from those whose background, health, and education make them least fit for useful work.[1] Those who volunteer will enter more than one hundred camps and centers around the country. Half of these young men will work, in the first year, on special conservation projects to give them education, useful work experience, and to enrich the natural resources of the country. Half of these young men will receive, in the first year, a blend of training, basic education, and work experience in job training centers. These are not simply camps for the underprivileged. They are new educational institutions, comparable in innovation to the land-grant colleges. Those who enter them will emerge better qualified to play a productive role in American society.

A new national work-training program operated by the Department of Labor will provide work and training for 200,000 American men and women between the ages of sixteen and twenty-one. This will be developed through state and local governments and nonprofit agencies. Hundreds of thousands of young Americans badly need the experience, the income, and the sense of purpose which useful full or part-time work can bring. For them such work may mean the difference between finishing school or dropping out. Vital community activities

[1] Oddly enough, the Job Corps does not accept the physically handicapped or youth with serious delinquency records. For a further discussion of "creaming," that is, the selection of the least disadvantaged, as it applies to the War on Poverty, see S. M. Miller and Martin Rein, "The War on Poverty: Perspectives and Prospects" in *Poverty as a Public Issue,* edited by Ben B. Seligman (New York, 1965).—Eds.

from hospitals and playgrounds to libraries and settlement houses are suffering because there are not enough people to staff them. We are simply bringing these needs together.

A new national work-study program operated by the Department of Health, Education, and Welfare will provide federal funds for part-time jobs for 140,000 young Americans who do not go to college because they cannot afford it. There is no more senseless waste than the waste of the brainpower and skill of those who are kept from college by economic circumstance. Under this program they will, in a great American tradition, be able to work their way through school. They and the country will be richer for it.

Second, through a new community action program we intend to strike at poverty at its source—in the streets of our cities and on the farms of our countryside among the very young and the impoverished old. This program asks men and women throughout the country to prepare long-range plans for the attack on poverty in their own local communities. These are not plans prepared in Washington and imposed upon hundreds of different situations. They are based on the fact that local citizens best understand their own problems, and know best how to deal with those problems. These plans will be local plans striking at the many unfilled needs which underlie poverty in each community, not just one or two. Their components and emphasis will differ as needs differ. These plans will be local plans calling upon all the resources available to the community—federal and state, local and private, human and material. And when these plans are approved by the Office of Economic Opportunity, the federal government will finance up to 90 per cent of the additional cost for the first two years. . . .

Third, I ask for the authority to recruit and train skilled volunteers for the war against poverty. . . . If the state requests them, if the community needs and will use them, we will recruit and train them and give them the chance to serve.

Fourth, we intend to create new opportunities for certain hard-hit groups to break out of the pattern of poverty. Through a new program of loans and guarantees we can provide incentives to those who will employ the unemployed. Through programs of work and retraining for unemployed fathers and mothers we can help them support their families in dignity while preparing themselves for new work. Through funds to purchase needed land, organize cooperatives, and create new and adequate family farms we can help those whose life on the land has been a struggle without hope.

Fifth, I do not intend that the war against poverty become a series of uncoordinated and unrelated efforts—that it perish for lack of leadership and direction. Therefore this bill creates, in the Executive Office of the President, a new Office of Economic Opportunity. Its director will be my personal chief of staff for the war against poverty. I intend to appoint Sargent Shriver to this post. He will be directly responsible for these new programs. He will work with and through existing agencies of the government. This program—the Economic Opportunity Act—is the foundation of our war against poverty. . . .

And this program is much more than a beginning. Rather it is a commitment. It is a total commitment by this President, and this Congress, and this nation, to pursue victory over the most ancient of mankind's enemies. On many historic occasions the President has requested from Congress the authority to move against forces which were endangering the well-being of our country. This is such an occasion.

On similar occasions in the past we have often been called upon to wage war against foreign enemies which threatened our freedom. Today we are asked to declare war on a domestic enemy which threatens the strength of our nation and the welfare of our people. If we now move forward against this enemy —if we can bring to the challenges of peace the same determination and strength which has brought us victory in war— then this day and this Congress will have won a secure and honorable place in the history of the nation, and the enduring gratitude of generations of Americans yet to come.

FULL EDUCATIONAL OPPORTUNITY
(JANUARY 12, 1965)*

Social scientists and perceptive observers have long recognized the key role that education has played in the American dream of success and upward mobility. One eloquent spokesman for this dream at the turn of the century was confident that there was no need to contemplate schemes of economic redistribution as long as an egalitarian educational system assures "to rich and poor alike a competence in those things which are the real riches of a human being." [1] Educational avenues remained open in America long after other opportunities for social advancement had become sealed off; the public schools, particularly, offered the poor a means of access to the better life.[2]

Recent data suggests that this is less and less the case. In her brilliant study *Education and Income* (New York, 1964), Dr. Patricia Cayo Sexton shows that rather than serving as equalizer, the public schools now reinforce inequalities. In the area of science education, for example, she found substandard facilities, or *no* facilities, in 47 per cent of the schools that serve the poor. By contrast, in those for the children of the well-to-do, only 2 per cent had substandard facilities (p. 125). No wonder that Kenneth B. Clark, in his foreword to Dr. Sexton's book, was moved to conclude: "She has presented concrete evidence

* *Public Papers of the Presidents, Lyndon B. Johnson, 1965,* I, pp. 25-33.
[1] Undated speech of John H. Finley, president of the College of the City of New York, Finley Papers, New York Public Library.
[2] See Robin M. Williams, Jr., *American Society: A Sociological Interpretation* (New York, 1951), pp. 280-83.

which demonstrates beyond doubt that our public school system has rejected its role of facilitating social mobility and has become in fact an instrument of social and economic class distinctions in American society."

President Johnson's message to Congress on education, printed below, was in part a response to the situation so graphically portrayed by Sexton. He ends with a peroration on "the American dream," and an expression of faith that it can remain a real hope. The program he outlined to Congress was intended to do this. As the Great Society unfolds, it will be instructive to see whether the growing gap between the educations offered to different socioeconomic classes can be narrowed by federally aided programs.

◇◇◇

In 1787, the Continental Congress declared in the Northwest Ordinance: "schools and the means of education shall forever be encouraged."

America is strong and prosperous and free because for 178 years we have honored that commitment.

In the United States today:

—One-quarter of all Americans are in the nation's classrooms.

—High school attendance has grown 18-fold since the turn of the century—six times as fast as the population.

—College enrollment has advanced 80-fold. Americans today support a fourth of the world's institutions of higher learning and a third of its professors and college students.

In the life of the individual, education is always an unfinished task.

And in the life of this nation, the advancement of education is a continuing challenge.

There is a darker side to education in America:

—One student out of every three now in the fifth grade will drop out before finishing high school—if the present rate continues.

—Almost a million young people will continue to quit school each year—if our schools fail to stimulate their desire to learn.

—Over one hundred thousand of our brightest high school

graduates each year will not go to college—and many others will leave college—if the opportunity for higher education is not expanded.

The cost of this neglect runs high—both for the youth and the nation.

—Unemployment of young people with an eighth grade education or less is four times the national average.

—Jobs filled by high school graduates rose by 40 per cent in the last ten years. Jobs for those with less schooling decreased by nearly 10 per cent.

We can measure the cost in even starker terms. We now spend about $450 a year per child in our public schools. But we spend $1,800 a year to keep a delinquent youth in a detention home, $2,500 a year for a family on relief, $3,500 a year for a criminal in state prison.

The growing numbers of young people reaching school age demand that we move swiftly even to stand still.

—Attendance in elementary and secondary schools will increase by four million in the next five years. Four hundred thousand new classrooms will be needed to meet this growth. But almost a half million of the nation's existing classrooms are already more than thirty years old.

—The post-World War II boom in babies has now reached college age. And by 1970, our colleges must be prepared to add 50 per cent more enrollment to their presently overcrowded facilities.

In the past, Congress has supported an increasing commitment to education in America. Last year, I signed historic measures passed by the Eighty-eighth Congress to provide:

—facilities badly needed by universities, colleges and community colleges:

—major new resources for vocational training;

—more loans and fellowships for students enrolled in higher education;

—enlarged and improved training for physicians, dentists and nurses.

I propose that the Eighty-ninth Congress join me in extending the commitment still further. I propose that we declare a national goal of *Full Educational Opportunity*.

Every child must be encouraged to get as much education as he has the ability to take.

We want this not only for his sake, but for the nation's sake.

Nothing matters more to the future of our country: not our military preparedness—for armed might is worthless if we lack the brain power to build a world of peace; not our productive economy—for we cannot sustain growth without trained manpower; not our democratic system of government—for freedom is fragile if citizens are ignorant. . . .

Specifically, four major tasks confront us:

—To bring better education to millions of disadvantaged youth who need it most;

—To put the best educational equipment and ideas and innovations within reach of all students;

—To advance the technology of teaching and the training of teachers;

—To provide incentives for those who wish to learn at every stage along the road to learning. . . .

I urge that we now push ahead with the number one business of the American people: the education of our youth in pre-schools, elementary and secondary schools, and in the colleges and universities.

I. Pre-school program

My budget will include up to $150 million for pre-school projects under the Community Action Program of the Economic Opportunity Act.

Education must begin with the very young. The child from the urban or rural slum frequently misses his chance even before he begins school. Tests show that he is usually a year behind in academic attainment by the time he reaches third grade —and up to three years behind *if* he reaches the eighth grade. By then the handicap has grown too great for many children. Their horizons have narrowed; their prospects for lifetimes of failure have hardened. A large percentage of our young people whose family incomes are less than $2,000 do not go beyond the eighth grade.

Pre-school programs have demonstrated marked success in overcoming this initial handicap. In New York City, children from slum neighborhoods who attended nursery school have performed better when tested in the third and fourth grades than those who did not attend. In Baltimore, children with language and cultural handicaps are being helped greatly by a pre-school program. According to preliminary reports, ⅔ of them are in the top 50 per cent of their kindergarten and first grade classes on a citywide measure; ⅙ of them are in the top quarter.

But today, almost half of our school districts conduct no kindergarten classes. Public nursery schools are found in only about 100 of our 26,000 school districts. We must expand our pre-school program in order to reach disadvantaged children early.

Action on a wide front will begin this summer through a special "Headstart" program for children who are scheduled to begin school next fall. In addition, funds for low-income schools, regional education laboratories, and supplementary educational centers and services (recommended below) will be devoted to these vital pre-school programs.

II. Elementary and secondary schools

Elementary and secondary schools are the foundation of our education system. Forty-eight million students are now in our grade and high schools. Seventy-one per cent of the nation's expenditures for education are spent on elementary and secondary schooling.

If these schools are to do their job properly, they need help and they need it now. I propose that we give first priority to a program of:

A. AID TO LOW-INCOME SCHOOL DISTRICTS

I recommend that legislation be enacted to authorize a major program of assistance to public elementary and secondary schools serving children of low-income families. My budget for fiscal year 1966 will request $1 billion for this new program.

One hundred years ago, a man with six or seven years of schooling stood well above the average. His chances to get ahead were as good as the next man's. But today, lack of formal education is likely to mean low wages, frequent unemployment, and a home in an urban or rural slum.

Poverty has many roots, but the tap root is ignorance. Poverty is the lot of two-thirds of the families in which the family head has had eight years or less of schooling. Twenty per cent of the youth age 18-24 with an eighth grade education or less are unemployed—four times the national average.

Just as ignorance breeds poverty, poverty all too often breeds ignorance in the next generation. Nearly half the youths rejected by Selective Service for educational deficiency have fathers who are unemployed or else working in unskilled and low-income jobs. Fathers of more than one-half of the draft rejectees did not complete the eighth grade.

The burden on the nation's schools is not evenly distributed. Low-income families are heavily concentrated in particular urban neighborhoods or rural areas. Faced with the largest educational needs, many of these school districts have inadequate financial resources. This imbalance has been increased by the movement of high-income families from the center of cities to the suburbs, and their replacement by low-income families from rural areas.

—The five states with the lowest incomes spend only an average of $276 per pupil, less than half the average of the five highest-income states.

—Despite a massive effort, our big cities generally spend only about two-thirds as much per pupil as their adjacent suburbs.

—In our fifteen largest cities, 60 per cent of the tenth-grade students from poverty neighborhoods drop out before finishing high school.

This is a national problem. Federal action is needed to assist the states and localities in bringing the full benefits of education to children of low-income families.

Assistance will be provided:

—On the basis of census data showing the distribution of low-income families among the counties or school districts within states;

—Through payments made to states for distribution to school districts;

—With the assurance that the funds will be used for improving the quality of education in schools serving low-income areas;

—On the condition that federal funds will not be used to reduce state and local fiscal efforts;

—For the benefit of all children within the area served, including those who participate in shared services or other special educational projects.

B. SCHOOL LIBRARY RESOURCES
AND INSTRUCTIONAL MATERIALS

I recommend legislation to authorize federal grants to states to assist in the purchase of books for school libraries and for student use, to be made available to children in public and private nonprofit elementary and secondary schools.

Thomas Carlyle once said, "All that mankind has done, thought, gained or been: it is lying as in magic preservation in the pages of books." Yet our school libraries are limping along. Almost 70 per cent of the public elementary schools have no libraries. Eighty-four per cent lack librarians to teach children the value of learning through good books. Many schools have an average of less than ½ book per child. To meet the accepted standards for library materials would require a fourfold increase in current expenditures in our major cities.

The explosion of knowledge and the rapid revision of curricula in the schools have created new demands for school textbooks. The obsolete text can suffocate the learning process. Yet the cost of purchasing textbooks at increasing prices puts a major obstacle in the path of education—an obstacle that can and must be eliminated.

C. SUPPLEMENTARY EDUCATIONAL
CENTERS AND SERVICES

I recommend a program of federal grants for supplementary education centers and services within the community.

We think of schools as places where youth learns, but our schools also need to learn.

The educational gap we face is one of *quality* as well as *quantity*.

Exciting experiments in education are underway, supported by the National Science Foundation, by the Office of Education and other government agencies, and by private philanthropic foundations. Many of our children have studied the "new math." There are highly effective ways of teaching high school physics, biology, chemistry, and foreign languages.

We need to take full advantage of these and other innovations. Specialists can spark the interest of disadvantaged students. Remedial reading courses open up new vistas for slow learners. Gifted students can be brought along at a faster pace.

Yet such special educational services are not available in many communities. A limited local tax base cannot stand the expense. Most individual schools are not large enough to justify the services.

The supplementary center can provide such services as:

—Special courses in science, foreign languages, literature, music, and art;

—Programs for the physically handicapped and mentally retarded;

—Instruction in the sciences and humanities during the summer for economically and culturally deprived children;

—Special assistance after regular school hours:

—Common facilities that can be maintained more efficiently for a group of schools than for a single school—laboratories, libraries, auditoriums, and theaters;

—A system by which gifted persons can teach part-time to provide scarce talents;

—A means of introducing into the school system new courses, instructional materials, and teaching practices;

—A way of tapping the community's extracurricular resources for the benefit of students—museums, concert and lecture programs, and industrial laboratories.

Within each community, public and private nonprofit schools and agencies will cooperate to devise the plan and administer the program for these supplementary centers. Their services should be adapted to meet the pressing needs of each locality.

D. REGIONAL EDUCATION LABORATORIES

I recommend the establishment under the Cooperative Research Act of regional educational laboratories which will undertake research, train teachers, and implement tested research findings.

I further recommend amendments to the act to:

—*Broaden the types of research organizations now eligible for educational projects;*

—*Train educational research personnel;*

—*Provide grants for research, development of new curricula, dissemination of information, and implementation of educational innovations;*

—*Support construction of research facilities and the purchase of research equipment.*

Under auspices of the National Science Foundation, educators have worked with scientists—including Nobel laureates—to develop courses which capture the excitement of contemporary science. They have prepared totally new instructional materials—laboratory equipment, textbooks, teachers' guides, films, supplementary reading and examinations. After testing, they are made available to public and private schools.

We need to extend our research and development—to history, literature, and economics; to art and music; to reading, writing, and speaking; to occupational, vocational, and technical education. We need to extend it to all stages of learning—pre-school, elementary and secondary schools, college and graduate-training.

Regional laboratories for education offer great promise. They draw equally upon educators and the practitioners in all fields of learning—mathematicians, scientists, social scientists, linguists, musicians, artists, and writers. They help both to improve curricula and to train teachers.

E. STRENGTHENING STATE EDUCATIONAL AGENCIES

I recommend a program of grants to state educational agencies.

State leadership becomes increasingly important as we seek to improve the quality of elementary and secondary education.

We should assist the states by strengthening state departments of education in their efforts to:

—Provide consultative and technical assistance for local school districts and local school leadership;

—Formulate long-range plans;

—Expand educational research and development;

—Improve local and state information about education;

—Identify emerging educational problems;

—Provide for the training of state and local education personnel;

—Conduct periodic evaluation of educational programs;

—Promote teacher improvement courses.

These new programs will substantially augment community resources in the war against poverty. As provided by sections 611 and 612 of the Economic Opportunity Act of 1964, I will see that the new efforts are kept in step with our other antipoverty efforts.

In those localities where the community has undertaken a Community Action Program under the Economic Opportunity Act, the community agency should participate in the planning of these new educational programs and in their coordination with on-going and developing antipoverty efforts.

Enactment of these proposals for elementary and secondary education is of utmost urgency. I urge early and favorable consideration by the Congress.

III. Higher education

Higher education is no longer a luxury, but a necessity.

Programs enacted by Congress in the past have contributed greatly to strengthening our colleges and universities. These will be carried forward under my 1966 budget, which includes:

—An additional $179 million to assist construction of college classrooms, libraries and laboratories;

—An additional $25 million for 4,500 more graduate fellowships to overcome college teaching shortages;

—An additional $110 million to further basic research in the universities, to provide science fellowships, and to promote science education.

But we need to do more:

—To extend the opportunity for higher education more broadly among lower- and middle-income families;

—To help small and less well developed colleges improve their programs;

—To enrich the library resources of colleges and universities;

—To draw upon the unique and invaluable resources of our great universities to deal with national problems of poverty and community development.

A. ASSISTANCE TO STUDENTS

1. *Scholarships.* *I recommend a program of scholarships for needy and qualified high school graduates to enable them to enter and to continue in college.*

Loans authorized by the National Defense Education Act currently assist nearly 300,000 college students. Still the following conditions exist:

—Each year an estimated 100,000 young people of demonstrated ability fail to go on to college because of lack of money. Many thousands more from low-income families must borrow heavily to meet college costs;

—Only one out of three young people from *low*-income families attend college compared with four out of five from *high*-income families.

For many young people from poor families loans are not enough to open the way to higher education.

Under this program, a special effort will be made to identify needy students of promise early in their high school careers. The scholarship will serve as a building block, to be augmented by work-study and other support, so that the needy student can chart his own course in higher studies. . . .

[In this lengthy message the President went on to call for expanded "work–study" programs, more easily available federally guaranteed loans, aid to colleges, and support of library expansion and extension courses.—Eds.]

Conclusion

In 1838 Mirabeau B. Lamar, the second President of the Republic of Texas and the father of Texas education, declared: "The cultivated mind is the guardian genius of democracy. It is the only dictator that free man acknowledges. It is the only security that free man desires."

Throughout the history of our nation, the United States has recognized this truth. But during the periods when the country has been most astir with creative activity, when it most keenly sensed the sturdiness of the old reaching out for the vigor of the new, it has given special attention to its educational system.

This was true in the expansive 1820s and 30s, when the American people acted decisively to build a public school system for the lower grades. It was no less true at the vigorous turn of the twentieth century, when high schools were developed for the millions. Again, during the questing 1930s, fresh ideas stirred the traditions of the ruler and blackboard.

We are now embarked on another venture to put the American dream to work in meeting the new demands of a new day. Once again we must start where men who would improve their society have always known they must begin—with an educational system restudied, reinforced, and revitalized.

MEDICARE: THE
DEFERRED COMMITMENT
(JULY 30, 1965)*

With a rare sense of political theatrics, President Johnson chose the Truman Library in Independence, Missouri, as the scene for the signing of the Medicare Bill of 1965. In some ways this was appropriate. Truman, at 81 years of age, was undeniably one of that group called in America "senior citizens," and the bill was aimed at them. It was Truman in 1945 who proposed a comprehensive program of health insurance, more elaborate than Johnson's later proposals, under the Social Security program.[1]

No one disturbed the proceedings at Independence to point out that the Truman Fair Deal health program was far more comprehensive than the Medicare. Neither was it mentioned that a Congressman from Texas named Lyndon Johnson had *opposed* Truman's policy. He said in 1948: "I want no part of socialized medicine. I have fought against the Wagner-Murray-Dingell Bill. The Democratic answer to this form of socialism is more hospitals, more doctors, more nurses; and the county courthouse can't build hospitals, nor can the sheriff's office be used for an operating room." [2] But, by the time he became President

---

* *Public Papers of the Presidents, Lyndon B. Johnson, 1965,* II, pp. 811-14.

[1] See Barton J. Bernstein and Allen J. Matusow, *The Truman Administration: A Documentary History* (New York, 1966), pp. 114-18.

[2] Quoted by Ronnie Dugger in *Texas Observer* (June 10, 1960).

himself, Johnson had swung around in support of government-sponsored health insurance.

◇ ◇ ◇

PRESIDENT TRUMAN: Thank you very much. I am glad you like the President. I like him too. He is one of the finest men I ever ran across.

Mr. President, Mrs. Johnson, distinguished guests: You have done me a great honor in coming here today, and you have made me a very, very happy man.

This is an important hour for the nation, for those of our citizens who have completed their tour of duty and have moved to the sidelines. These are the days that we are trying to celebrate for them. These people are our prideful responsibility and they are entitled, among other benefits, to the best medical protection available.

Not one of these, our citizens, should ever be abandoned to the indignity of charity. Charity is indignity when you have to have it. But we don't want these people to have anything to do with charity and we don't want them to have any idea of hopeless despair.

Mr. President, I am glad to have lived this long and to witness today the signing of the Medicare bill which puts this Nation right where it needs to be, to be right. Your inspired leadership and a responsive forward-looking Congress have made it historically possible for this day to come about.

Thank all of you most highly for coming here. It is an honor I haven't had for, well, quite awhile, I'll say that to you, but here it is:

Ladies and gentlemen, the President of the United States.

PRESIDENT JOHNSON: The people of the United States love and voted for Harry Truman, not because he gave them hell—but because he gave them hope.

I believe today that all America shares my joy that he is present now when the hope that he offered becomes a reality for millions of our fellow citizens.

I am so proud that this has come to pass in the Johnson Administration. But it was really Harry Truman of Missouri who planted the seeds of compassion and duty which have today flowered into care for the sick, and serenity for the fearful.

Many men can make many proposals. Many men can draft

many laws. But few have the piercing and humane eye which can see beyond the words to the people that they touch. Few can see past the speeches and the political battles to the doctor over there that is tending the infirm, and to the hospital that is receiving those in anguish, or feel in their heart painful wrath at the injustice which denies the miracle of healing to the old and to the poor. And fewer still have the courage to stake reputation, and position, and the effort of a lifetime upon such a cause when there are so few that share it.

But it is just such men who illuminate the life and the history of a nation. And so, President Harry Truman, it is in tribute not to you, but to the America that you represent, that we have come here to pay our love and our respects to you today. For a country can be known by the quality of the men it honors. By praising you, and by carrying forward your dreams, we really reaffirm the greatness of America.

It was a generation ago that Harry Truman said, and I quote him: "Millions of our citizens do not now have a full measure of opportunity to achieve and to enjoy good health. Millions do not now have protection or security against the economic effects of sickness. And the time has now arrived for action to help them attain that opportunity and to help them get that protection."

Well, today, Mr. President, and my fellow Americans, we are taking such action—twenty years later. And we are doing that under the great leadership of men like John McCormack, our speaker; Carl Albert, our majority leader; our very able and beloved majority leader of the Senate, Mike Mansfield; and distinguished members of the Ways and Means and Finance Committees of the House and Senate—of both parties, Democratic and Republican.

Because the need for this action is plain; and it is so clear indeed that we marvel not simply at the passage of this bill, but what we marvel at is that it took so many years to pass it. And I am so glad that Aime Forand is here to see it finally passed and signed—one of the first authors.

There are more than 18 million Americans over the age of sixty-five. Most of them have low incomes. Most of them are threatened by illness and medical expenses that they cannot afford.

And through this new law, Mr. President, every citizen will

be able, in his productive years when he is earning, to insure himself against the ravages of illness in his old age.

This insurance will help pay for care in hospitals, in skilled nursing homes, or in the home. And under a separate plan it will help meet the fees of the doctors.

Now here is how the plan will affect you.

During your working years, the people of America—you—will contribute through the Social Security program a small amount each payday for hospital insurance protection. For example, the average worker in 1966 will contribute about $1.50 per month. The employer will contribute a similar amount. And this will provide the funds to pay up to 90 days of hospital care for each illness, plus diagnostic care, and up to 100 home health visits after you are sixty-five. And beginning in 1967, you will also be covered for up to 100 days of care in a skilled nursing home after a period of hospital care.

And under a separate plan, when you are 65—that the Congress originated itself, in its own good judgment—you may be covered for medical and surgical fees whether you are in or out of the hospital. You will pay $3 per month after you are 65 and your government will contribute an equal amount.

The benefits under the law are as varied and broad as the marvelous modern medicine itself. If it has a few defects—such as the method of payment of certain specialists—then I am confident those can be quickly remedied and I hope they will be.

No longer will older Americans be denied the healing miracle of modern medicine. No longer will illness crush and destroy the savings that they have so carefully put away over a lifetime so that they might enjoy dignity in their later years. No longer will young families see their own incomes, and their own hopes, eaten away simply because they are carrying out their deep moral obligations to their parents, and to their uncles, and their aunts.

And no longer will this nation refuse the hand of justice to those who have given a lifetime of service and wisdom and labor to the progress of this progressive country.

And this bill, Mr. President, is even broader than that. It will increase social security benefits for all of our older Americans. It will improve a wide range of health and medical services for Americans of all ages.

In 1935, when the man that both of us loved so much, Franklin Delano Roosevelt, signed the Social Security Act, he said it was, and I quote him, "a cornerstone in a structure which is being built but it is by no means complete."

Well, perhaps no single act in the entire Administration of the beloved Franklin D. Roosevelt really did more to win him the illustrious place in history that he has as did the laying of that cornerstone. And I am so happy that his oldest son Jimmy could be here to share with us the joy that is ours today. And those who share this day will also be remembered for making the most important addition to that structure, and you are making it in this bill, the most important addition that has been made in three decades. . . .

President Harry Truman, as any President must, made many decisions of great moment; although he always made them frankly and with a courage and a clarity that few men have ever shared. The immense and the intricate questions of freedom and survival were caught up many times in the web of Harry Truman's judgment. And this is in the tradition of leadership.

But there is another tradition that we share today. It calls upon us never to be indifferent toward despair. It commands us never to turn away from helplessness. It directs us never to ignore or to spurn those who suffer untended in a land that is bursting with abundance.

I said to Senator [George A.] Smathers [of Florida], the whip of the Democrats in the Senate, who worked with us in the Finance Committee on this legislation—I said, the highest traditions of the medical profession are really directed to the ends that we are trying to serve. And it was only yesterday, at the request of some of my friends, I met with the leaders of the American Medical Association to seek their assistance in advancing the cause of one of the greatest professions of all—the medical profession—in helping us to maintain and to improve the health of all Americans.

And this is not just our tradition—or the tradition of the Democratic Party—or even the tradition of the nation. It is as old as the day it was first commanded: "Thou shalt open thine hand wide unto thy brother, to thy poor, to thy needy, in thy land."

And just think, Mr. President, because of this document—and the long years of struggle which so many have put into creating it—in this town, and a thousand other towns like it, there are men and women in pain who will now find ease. There are those, alone in suffering, who will now hear the sound of some approaching footsteps coming to help. There are those fearing the terrible darkness of despairing poverty—despite their long years of labor and expectation—who will now look up to see the light of hope and realization.

There just can be no satisfaction, nor any act of leadership, that gives greater satisfaction than this.

And perhaps you alone, President Truman, perhaps you alone can fully know just how grateful I am for this day.

THE WAR ON POVERTY
IS A MOVEMENT OF CONSCIENCE
(APRIL 12, 1965)*

During the spring of 1965, the Ad Hoc (House) Sub-committee on the War on Poverty, under the chairman-ship of Adam Clayton Powell, held hearings to examine the unfolding antipoverty program. The first witness was the director of the Office of Economic Opportunity, Sargent Shriver, the one remaining member of the Kennedy family still closely associated with the Johnson Administration.

As is usually the case, the hearings were conducted in a friendly manner, though Shriver's cross-examination by Republican Representative Albert H. Quie, of Minnesota, was sharp and quite critical. Excerpts from Shriver's opening statement and the colloquy with Congressman Quie are reprinted below.

One year later, Sargent Shriver's "testimony" before a very different audience received somewhat less than an enthusiastic reception:

Sargent Shriver, director of the drive against poverty, was booed, jostled and almost hooted down today while defending his program at a "poor people's convention." Mr. Shriver plunged on with his speech despite the up-roar and shouts of "You're lying" and "Stop listening to him" from a rebel group that moved up near the stage.

* Reprinted from *Examination of the War on Poverty Program, Hear-ings, Subcommittee on the War on Poverty Program,* House Committee on Education and Labor (April, 1965), pp. 16-18, 23-28.

The director of the Office of Economic Opportunity, look-ing strained and upset, was hustled from the International Inn immediately after his speech despite pleas to remain for questions. "I will not participate in a riot," he de-clared. The meeting of the Citizen's Crusade Against Pov-erty, the biggest and most broadly based such conference since Mr. Shriver's agency was set up in 1964, disinte-grated shortly afterward into chaotic anger and frustra-tion.[1]

◇ ◇ ◇

First, the war on poverty is an attempt to help individuals—35 million of them—get out of poverty. But it is not just aimed at individuals. It embraces entire neighborhoods, communities, cities, and states. It is an attempt to change institutions as well as people. It must deal with the culture of poverty as well as the individual victims. Second, the war on poverty embraces a cluster of government programs. But it is not just a governmen-tal effort. It involves and must involve all sectors of the econ-omy and all the American people. Third, it is a program, which must and will produce results—quantifiable results—numerical results. But it is not simply a series of numerical results. It is also a process—of arousing, of mobilizing, of harnessing the moral energies of the American people.

Let's take one at a time. . . . The war on poverty starts with individuals—with a man, a woman, a child—taking them one by one. But it does not stop there, because poverty is not just an individual affair. It is also a condition, a relationship to soci-ety, and to all the institutions which comprise society. Poverty is need. It is lack of opportunity. But it is also helplessness to cope with hostile or uncaring or exploitive institutions. It is lack of dignity. And it is vulnerability to injustice. The treatment the poor get, at the hands of bureaucrats and politicians, at the hands of private industry, at the hands of landlords and mer-chants and agriculturists—this treatment is more than the sum of the individuals involved. It is a pattern of response, a way of reacting to and treating the poor that has become entrenched, and institutionalized.

Poverty is personal. But it is also a terrifying impersonal and dehumanizing condition, imposed on 35 million Americans.

[1] *New York Times* (April 15, 1966).

Both dimensions of poverty come through in this statement by Mrs. Janice Bradshaw, of Pueblo, Colorado. It says a whole lot:

"Poverty is a personal thing! Poverty is taking your children to the hospital and spending the whole day waiting with no one even taking your name—and then coming back the next day, and the next, until they finally get around to you. . . .

"Poverty is having the welfare investigators break in at four o'clock in the morning and cut off your welfare check without an explanation—and then when you go down and ask, they tell you it is because they found a pair of men's house slippers in the attic, where your brother left them when he visited a month ago.

"Poverty is having a child with glaucoma and watching that eye condition grow worse every day, while the welfare officials send you to the private agencies, and the private agencies send you back to the welfare, and when you ask the welfare officials to refer you to this special hospital, they say they can't—and then when you say it is prejudice because you are a Negro, they deny it flatly—and they shout at you: 'Name one white child we have referred there.' And when you name twenty-five, they sit down—and they shut up—and they finally refer you but it is too late then, because your child has permanently lost 80 per cent of his vision—and you are told that if only they had caught it a month earlier, when you first made inquiry about the film over his eyes, they could have preserved his vision." . . .

Our general counsel would tell you that the war on poverty —or at least the community action phase of it—is a program where an entire city, or neighborhood, or county, or state enters into a binding agreement to pull itself up by its bootstraps. In effect, it means that communities are applying to us for a new type of corporate charter. They are incorporating themselves as a new enterprise—a new business—the business of creating opportunity for the very poor. This job can't be done piecemeal. This new enterprise—the community action program—will have to design and tool up for a new model: Opportunity—1965 style.

Each of the component parts—education and training, experience and motivation, confidence and health, hope and self-reliance—each of these has to be designed afresh. We have to go back to the drawing boards because for 35 million Americans, the old product has not been selling. It isn't reaching the consumer—the poor themselves. And so, we have to engage in a new kind of market research. We have to find out why the old product didn't appeal to the consumer—to one-fifth of the market. And only the poor—the consumer—can tell us.

In short, the war on poverty is not a handout program—or an individual casework program. It is a part of that effort to fashion a world where, in President Johnson's words, "the meaning of man's life matches the marvels of man's labors." . . .

But the point needs to be made—over and over again—that these programs, including the many other federal programs which help the poor—that all of the programs taken together are not the war on poverty. If the war on poverty were just a governmental program, it would be doomed. Because no matter how big the federal payroll or budget may become, it can't get big enough to reach out to all the poor and to enlist all America in a war which will determine the future and share of our society. And perhaps one of the most important and exciting things about the war on poverty is that all America is joining in. Religious groups, professional groups, labor groups, civic and patriotic groups are all rallying to the call. . . .

And this brings me to my last point about what the war on poverty is. It is a set of production goals, a series of specific target goals and production quotas. . . . But beyond these specific results, these particular numerical target figures, the war on poverty is a catalytic force And the effectiveness of the programs you have been asked to continue and enlarge must be judged, not only in terms of their specific, tangible results—but equally, in terms of their catalytic effect. For we are beginning to find out—that the processes we set in motion are at least as important as the direct results we achieve; the energies we release are at least as important as the specific production goals we attain; the attitudes we affect, the concerns we generate, the myths we destroy are at least as important as the number of salaries we pay, directly or indirectly.

Let me be even more specific—because this applies on every level. There are five-year-olds who don't even know how to hold a book or how to listen to a sentence with more than two or three words. When we teach him those things, we aren't making him "employable." But we will have begun to supply the missing ingredient—the catalyst—so that our regular school system won't lose that child along the way. And with that child, that five-year-old, we will have set in motion a process, a possibility, a chance which in our time, in our generation, can spell the end of poverty.

The same is true when we train a teenager in one of our Job Corps centers. Suppose we teach him how to repair a car engine—or operate a tool-cutting machine We can't guarantee that next year's cars won't change to turbine engines—or that that particular machine will always be in use. But we can say that that boy will feel different about himself and about work. He'll have a new sense of dignity, of self-confidence—because for what may be the first time in his life, he'll have proven that he can learn, and that he can succeed. That's a form of "poverty proofing" that won't wear off.

And this catalytic effect works on communities as well as individuals. When we fund a local antipoverty program—like the one here in Washington—UPO[1]—or in Chicago or St. Louis, or Detroit, or Atlanta—there may be about fifteen or twenty or thirty parts—prekindergarten classes, literacy classes, consumer education, job training, counseling, placement, legal services, health services. We don't know and they don't know if every single one of those programs will work. Or if that particular assortment of programs is exactly the right combination to eliminate poverty today, or tomorrow, or the next day.

What counts, what really counts, is that there is an organization like UPO—that for the first time, an entire community has pulled together to worry about the poor, and to find out about the causes of poverty; that for the first time government has pooled resources with private agencies in a special kind of partnership; and that for the first time, the poor have a forum in which they are represented, in which their voice will be heard.

And this perhaps is the final lesson—and the ultimate dimension of the war on poverty—the spiritual dimension. Because for us—for all America—the war on poverty is a movement of conscience—a national act of expiation, of humbling and prostrating ourselves before our Creator. And when all is said and

[1] United Poverty Office.—Eds.

done, what the war on poverty will have achieved—is to have gained for an entire people an appreciation of those words attributed to St. Vincent de Paul: "Before you go out and help the poor, you must first beg their pardon." And that is what the war on poverty is really all about. . . .

[The formal part of Mr. Shriver's testimony completed, he was then questioned by members of the committee.]

MR. SHRIVER. I would like just to comment too about minority representations on those councils I will give you some from the South. I think that this minority representation on community action councils and planning committees in the South is unprecedented in the history of this country. Huntsville, Ala., out of 16 people on the committee, 4 are Negroes. Chattanooga, 25 people on the committee, 6 Negroes. Albemarle, N. C., 17 people on the committee, 4 Negroes. Tuskegee, Ala., 6 people on the committee, 4 are Negroes.

MR. QUIE. Are these poor Negroes or is it just that they are Negroes and are representative of the poor?

MR. SHRIVER. That is a very good point. As we say on page 85 of our presentation, the bottom of the page, if you will look, just because you are Negro does not mean you are poor, and just because you are poor does not mean you are a Negro. Right, Mr. Chairman?

CHAIRMAN POWELL. Thank you, sir.

MR. QUIE. Negroes on the board does not mean that they are poor Negroes, is that it?

MR. SHRIVER. I was not addressing myself to the question of involvement of the poor. I was addressing myself to minority representation as an aspect of broad communitywide representation in, and support of, community action programs Some of them, however, probably are poor or have recently been poor and know what it is. . . .

MR. QUIE. The indications that I read of the reports of the Southern task forces is that the percentage of Negroes runs as high as 50 per cent of the people who are poor. Yet when there are only one or two Negroes on a council it is pretty small representation

MR. SHRIVER. Let me agree with you, one or two, although I did not cite any case of one and only two cases of two, but cited the many cases of three, four, five, six, and seven. That may be small. The problem is not to say whether it is small or large, but it is how do you get more?

MINORITY REPRESENTATION ON CAP [2]
GOVERNING BOARDS

Community	Number of persons on governing body	Minority group members on governing body	Per cent of population that is nonwhite	Per cent of families with incomes under $3,000 that is nonwhite
Birmingham, Ala.	20	5	35	63
Huntsville, Ala.	16	4	16	40
Tuskegee, Ala.	6	4	84	°
Miami, Fla.	28	6	14	27
St. Petersburg, Fla.	13	3	13	15
Atlanta, Ga.	13	2	38	61
Savannah, Ga.	15	3	40	64
Lafayette, La.	12	2	25	47
New Orleans, La.	48	7	36	57
Albermarle, N. C.	17	4	40	°
Durham, N. C.	48	12	36	62
Chattanooga, Tenn.	25	6	20	49
Knoxville, Tenn.	23	6	9	28
Nashville, Tenn.	42	9	19	50
San Antonio, Tex.	66	17	50	13

° Not available.

MR. QUIE. I can cite some where there are one or two.

MR. SHRIVER. You can. I said I did not cite any. In those cases where you cite one or two, you will probably find it is maybe the first time there has been one or two. I am not saying one or two is ideal, and I don't want to be misinterpreted on that. I am not saying that this record is perfect. All I am saying is that it is unprecedented.

You say how do you get more. The lady who was put on the Community Action Program Committee in Cleveland is a good example of what happens if you just enlist a person and put him or her on the committee and say, "You are the poor repre-

[2] Community Action Program.—Eds.

sentative." What do they do? They get off the committee. Why? Obviously, they don't want to be labeled as poor. And that lady did not like the publicity she got. She did not like it because of the way it identified her as being the representative of the poor.

You have to get people trained so that they can fulfill these responsibilities. . . .

Another thing that is funny about people is that, as soon as somebody gets on the committee, they no longer represent the poor, in the opinion of the people who were left off the committee.

Frequently, Mr. Chairman, as soon as the minority group member is put on the committee, he becomes an "Uncle Tom." He was not before he got on.

CHAIRMAN POWELL. In most instances it is true.

MR. SHRIVER. Perhaps it is. But it is a funny thing about the fact as soon as someone joins the committee they become unqualified thereafter to speak for the people who are not selected.

CHAIRMAN POWELL. I disagree with you on that.

MR. SHRIVER. Sometimes it happens.

CHAIRMAN POWELL. The person is proud to represent them. But you may pick someone who is not representative of the people.

MR. QUIE. Speaking of representatives, those of us sitting here are Representatives, and if somebody in our district had selected us, the people of our district would feel we did not represent them. But because they selected us they feel that.

From my conversations with the poor they have rather the same attitude. When the people—as they call them, the power structure in the community—selected somebody who was poor, they did not necessarily feel that they represented them anymore.

But they wanted to get the organization—to get the people together. They said, "Through some democratic process we ought to be able to pick them."

In Detroit they have done a much better job of including representatives of the other communities we have looked at. However, it is interesting to note that in both of these communities they started planning with their own money. They planned before the bill was ever passed. These representatives of the poor are now going to their first meeting. You say the war on poverty has been operating 182 days, or really got started, you say, after the election. I wonder why they could not have found somebody to represent the poor to work on the planning until this time, rather than having to wait until there is some pressure before they include some poor representatives on the council.

MR. SHRIVER. I think the answer is quite obvious, and as well known to you as to me, and that is that the local government varies across the country in its capacity to respond quickly and to initiate new programs. In the case of Detroit, it did it; and in the case of Cleveland, I gather from your evidence, they did not. But that is to say why is not Cleveland as good in this respect as Detroit, and that is something I am not qualified to answer.

CHAIRMAN POWELL. In Cleveland, the mayor appointed the first board there, as you know, of 22 people, and he appointed 15 people from outside of Cleveland, who lived in the suburbs. I'll refer you to the same phrase I have been using repeatedly: "The people who have kept the poor impoverished" were appointed, from Shaker Heights, and from wealthy suburbia of Cleveland and to direct the war on poverty program. As you know, and as I have repeated and repeated, this must be changed.

18 / ELINOR GRAHAM

THE POLITICS OF POVERTY*

Ever since Lyndon Johnson popularized the issue of poverty by his dramatic declaration of war, an almost endless flood of literature on the subject has splashed forth. Almost all of it, in the dubious tradition of pragmatic American scholarship, is concerned with the enumeration and location of the poor as well as the degree of success possible in the various programs. Few have attempted a serious essay on why such a program arose in the first place. Elinor Graham's article, which attempts to explain the motivations of those in power, is a rare exception. A student of political science at Antioch College, Miss Graham wrote the paper while at the Institute for Policy Studies in Washington, D. C.

In January, 1964, a man familiar to congressional surroundings delivered his first address to a joint session of Congress in his new role as President of the United States. As he presented his presidential program to Congress, Lyndon Johnson called for an "unconditional war on poverty," a government commitment "not only to relieve the symptoms of poverty, but to cure it; and above all, to prevent it."

The complex of ideological themes and political programs officially recognized and initiated by this address—all under the slogan of a War on Poverty—is the topic of this paper. The analysis developed here views this "war" as a key ingredient in

* Reprinted with permission of the Free Press from *Poverty as a Public Issue*, edited by Ben B. Seligman (New York, 1965), pp. 231-50. Copyright © 1965 by the Free Press, a division of the Macmillan Company.

the social and political ideology embraced by President Johnson, his administrative officials, and his advisers. As part of an ideology, it is designed to motivate elements in the society to political action. The language of the War on Poverty and the form of its accompanying social welfare programs are set within the boundaries of traditional social beliefs, arise from the pressure of political needs, and are molded by the nature of those groups seeking action, as well as by the official bodies from which they must receive approval.

Poverty, consequently, is now a major preoccupation of hundreds of public officials, statisticians and social planners across the nation. In less than a year it has been thrust dramatically into the center of governmental programing on local, regional, and national levels. President Johnson has called for "total victory" in a national War on Poverty—"a total commitment by the President, and this Congress, and this nation, to pursue victory over the most ancient of mankind's enemies."[1] Joining the Administration forces and local and state governments, private social welfare organizations and institutions normally engaged in nonwelfare activities have increasingly indicated an awareness of possibilities, and a willingness, to engage their organizational resources in "extra-institutional" activities aimed at the alleviation of poverty. Colleges, churches, and corporations have plunged into a potpourri of activities designed to provide "opportunities" for deserving members of low-income groups, in forms and to an extent that welfare workers could previously conceive only in their wildest dreams.

Given an "understanding of the enemy" which emphasizes the special characteristics of certain low-income groups that cannot easily be integrated into the market economy, what "strategy of attack" is advocated by the national policy makers? The War on Poverty proposed in 1964 consisted of a ten-point attack which strikingly resembled the President's entire domestic program: income-tax cuts, a civil rights bill, Appalachian regional development, urban and rural community rehabilitation, youth programs, teenage and adult vocational training and basic educational programs, and hospital insurance for the aged. A special "antipoverty package" was introduced—the Economic Opportunity Act of 1964. The Office of Economic

[1] President's Message on Poverty to the Congress, March 16, 1964. See reading 14.—Eds.

Opportunity created by this legislation was to be the headquarters for the new "war."

Administration of the Economic Opportunity Act and supporting programs, as well as plans for future expansion, indicate that the War on Poverty seeks to mobilize the social services of the nation along three major lines: youth education and employment programs, planned regional and community redevelopment, and vocational training and retraining under the beginnings of a national manpower policy.

Under this "strategy of attack," aid to the poor is, in theory, provided in the nature of a new and expanded "opportunity environment." Such aid is primarily directed toward the youth and employable heads of poor families; it will not reach the really critical poverty categories—the aged female heads of families and poor farm families—except in the form of improvements in the surrounding physical and economic environments or the administration of welfare and health services. As the Council of Economic Advisers noted in their 1964 report, the proposed programs are designed "to equip and to permit the poor of the nation to produce and to earn . . . the American standard of living by their own efforts and contributions." Those Americans who are not in a physical or family position which allows them to earn their way out of poverty will not be immediately aided by the programs under the War on Poverty. This situation simply illustrates the difference between social needs defined in a statistical manner and a political designation of poverty. It does not indicate that the War on Poverty is a political hoax or a hollow slogan to attract votes; on the contrary, its ideology and programs respond to social and political needs of a very real, although very different nature than those of poverty per se.

The sociology of poverty programs

It is useful to locate welfare-state programs on two scales, vertically and horizontally, in order to visualize the range and nature of programs open to government planners in formulating the War on Poverty and to understand the implications of the particular path chosen. The vertical scale of our imaginary axes indicates at one end whether the poverty-stricken are singled out of the total society as objects for special aid or, at the opposite pole, social services and income payments are provided to all as a right of citizenship. The latter method is followed in most of the Swedish welfare programs. Family payments, old-age pensions, and health services are provided for all members of the society regardless of their financial position. Most United States welfare programs, including those proposed under the War on Poverty, are located at the opposite pole: programs are focused at a particular low-income category and need must be proven in order to receive aid. The second (and horizontal) scale indicates at one end that aid may be provided in the form of direct income payments and at the other extreme through social services. The major portion of the welfare activities in the United States, and particularly those connected with the War on Poverty, are found in the service category, even though . . . the nature of American poverty in the sixties indicates an urgent need for consideration of direct income payments to critical poverty-stricken groups.

Certain important implications follow from the need-based and service-oriented nature of the War on Poverty programs. First, separation of the poor from the rest of the society by means of need requirements increases the visibility of the low-income earners. This is a "war" *on poverty*—the very nature of such a proposal requires an exposure of "the enemy" in its human form. In addition, separation of the poor creates a donor-donee relationship whether it exists between the income-tax-paying middle and upper classes and the low-income earners, or the social worker and his client. In the context of American social philosophy, such a situation enhances the self-image of the well-to-do and places a stigma of failure and dependency upon aid recipients. Above all, it is "the American way" to approach social-welfare issues, for it places the burden of responsibility upon the individual and not upon the socio-economic system. Social services are preferred to income payments in an ideological atmosphere which abhors "handouts."

Second, a focus upon *poverty* allows for a redefinition of the racial clash into the politically understandable and useful terms of a conflict between the "haves" and the "have-nots." The donor-donee relationship, sharply cast into relief by the poverty label, reasserts and stabilizes the power of the political elite, whose positions have been threatened by enfranchisement of the Negro.

Third, the social-service orientation, particularly the stress upon the "reorganization" and "total mobilization" of existing programs, is strongly supported by the nature of the experimental programs started during the Kennedy years. These programs and, of more importance, the ideas and "method of attack" which they initiated, are vigorously advocated by a well-organized and sophisticated lobby within the administrative branch.

Fourth, the social-service orientation of the War on Poverty is *activity-* and *job-*creating for the middle and upper classes. Provision of social services, as opposed to income payments, requires the formation of new organizations and institutions which in turn are the source of activities and income-paying roles for the nation's expanding number of college-educated individuals. The War on Poverty, its programs and ideology, are a response to the demands of an educated "new class": it provides a legitimate outlet for the energies of a group that poses a greater threat to the political system and moral fabric of the society than the inadequately educated poor who are the official objects of aid.

Ideology and poverty

A nation which confidently points to its unparalleled level of wealth, the "magnificent abundance" of the American way of life, has been suddenly and surprisingly engaged in the public unveiling of the impoverished degradation of one-fifth of its population. Affluence and poverty confront each other, and the shock of the encounter is reflected in the phrase that acknowledges the "stranger's" presence: a "paradox"—the "paradox of poverty in the midst of plenty." This mysterious stranger is apparently inconsistent with the nation's vision of itself and particularly with its moral notions of equality.

One supposes that there is an element of honest surprise and, with many, disbelief, for they *know* that if you work hard and take advantage of all of the opportunities available, you *can* climb out of poverty and reach the top—well, perhaps not *the* top, but certainly a comfortable level of living. It is axiomatic. Numerous individuals will tediously cite their own life experiences as examples of this general law of dynamics of American society. The following account was provided by a retired educator who sought to establish his qualification to talk about poverty in the sixties:

. . . I was born in a homestead on the lowland swamps of Louisiana. There were no schools. We lived off the land. And, since I have viewed the very sections of the underprivileged and poor people in the Appalachian highland, I decided I must have been very poor, because those children there have much more than I had. We lived from game, and we had no electric lights. We got food if there were plenty of ducks and geese and rabbits. . . . I was a drop-in at school when they finally got a little one- or two-room school. I mean, I dropped in when there were no potatoes to plant or corn to pull, or something of that sort. I have three college degrees from standard universities, and I never spent a day on a college campus during regular session. I belong to the old school. I took correspondence; I did some summer terms, and I did extension work, traveling sometimes a hundred miles each weekend to take it. So I think I know what it means to get an education the hard way. . . . I understand the phrase in our help to the underprivileged.[2]

Everyone who is over thirty will say that they know what it is like to be poor because they lived during the Great Depression; that is taken as automatic qualification. When attacked by his Democratic "brethren" for a lack of understanding of the complexities of the problem, Representative Griffin (R.-Mich.) responded with: "My father worked most of his life in a plant; and I worked my way through school, and I believe I do know a little bit about poverty." [3] Without denying the achievements of the poor boy from the swamps of Louisiana who is now a distinguished educator, or the son of a worker holding the office of U. S. Congressman, such accounts and their implications for the "struggling young men" from present-day poor families reflect a general confusion of the income and social-class mobility of an individual with a rising national standard of living. The American dream is substituted for the American

[2] House Hearings, Economic Opportunity Act of 1964, Subcommittee on the War on Poverty Program of the Committee on Education and Labor, House of Representatives, 88th Congress, 2nd Session, part II, pp. 1120-21, "Statement of Joseph J. Vincent, Superintendent of Schools, South Park Independent School District, Beaumont, Texas."

[3] Ibid., pp. 854-55.

reality and evidence drawn from the second is said to be proof
of the first.

President Johnson intertwined the two concepts when he declared in his 1964 War on Poverty message that:

*With the growth of our country has come opportunity for our
people—opportunity to educate our children, to use our energies in productive work, to increase our leisure—opportunity
for almost every American to hope that through work and
talent he could create a better life for himself and his family.*[4]

Traditional themes of the bright boy attaining entrance to the
world of wealth through "work and talent" are intermingled
with the profit figures of economic growth. In suggesting that
the benefits of a rising standard of living include increased opportunity for bettering income and even social-class position,
two distinct and different concepts are equated for ideological
purposes.

Fusion of dream and actuality in the national vision has been
strongly influenced by the American business creed and its
image of the relationship between the economic system and the
individual. Benefits derived from the economic growth of the
nation are not conceived as social products. The idealized "free-
enterprise" system produces the national wealth through the
efforts of atomized individuals operating within a "free competitive market system with individual freedom." A guarantee of
the rights of the individual to insure his freedom and free opportunity are thus essential. Since mythology need not correspond to reality (particularly if believed in strongly enough),
equality of opportunity is assumed and is "proved" through the
individual success stories which abound in the popular literature. Such "proof" is, however, subject to a great deal of doubt.
Citing several sociological studies, the authors of *The American
Business Creed* observe that a survey of the overall statistical
situation "might well lead to more tempered conclusions about
American freedom of opportunity." [5]

With an image of itself that denies the possibility of widespread poverty, a nation bent on "recognizing realities" must

[4] Special Message on Poverty to the United States Congress, March
16, 1964. [See reading 14.—Eds.]

[5] F. X. Sutton, et al., *The American Business Creed* (Cambridge,
Mass., 1956), p. 26.

squeeze the poor in through the basement window. We are told that we are not faced with extensive conditions of poverty (as are other less fortunate nations). Poverty in the United States is "grinding poverty," found only in "pockets of poverty," and has defied all laws of genetics to acquire an hereditary quality exhibited in the "ruthless pattern" and "cycle of poverty." This is not a case of good old-fashioned poverty, it is a special and uniquely American 1964 brand.

A particularly vivid exposition of this version of poverty can be found in the explanation of the Economic Opportunity Act prepared by Sargent Shriver's office for the first congressional hearings.[6] Much of the credit for the modern version of poverty expounded within its covers must go to the influence of John Kenneth Galbraith's writings. He broke the poor into two groups—those afflicted with *case* poverty and those who are victims of *insular* poverty. Characteristics of the individual afflicted with case poverty prevent him from mastering his environment, while the environment proves to be the handicapping factor for those living in "islands of poverty." In both situations a hereditary factor is introduced either in fact (as a physical tendency toward poor health or mental deficiency) or in effect through the deficiencies of the social environment (as with poor schools, lack of job opportunities, lack of motivation and direction from parents).[7] Whether or not such a view corresponds to reality, it should be recognized that when one maintains that the society is affluent, poverty can hardly be tolerated as a widespread phenomenon and must be of a very special and individual variety. With such a thesis, one is not likely to observe that an average American family with an income of $5,665—the median for all families in 1960—may not feel particularly affluent at this "modest but adequate" level.

Where, then, are the roots of poverty in an affluent society? Few combatants in the war of ideologies argue that the fault underlies the American landscape and may be lodged in the economic system. The principle according to which the wealth of the society is divided is left unscathed. On official levels, voices do not openly suggest that a system which distributes

[6] *The War on Poverty, A Congressional Presentation,* Office of Economic Opportunity, March 17, 1964.

[7] John Kenneth Galbraith, *The Affluent Society* (Boston, 1958), pp. 251ff.

economic goods solely upon the basis of the individual's present or past functional role within the economy may be at the source of American poverty now and increasingly so in the future. Although not reflecting official opinion, the statement of the Ad Hoc Committee on the Triple Revolution was a notable exception. This group of distinguished educators, labor leaders, economists, and critics suggested in part that:

The economy of abundance can sustain all citizens in comfort and economic security whether or not they engage in what is commonly reckoned as work. . . . We urge, therefore, that society through its appropriate legal and governmental institutions undertake an unqualified commitment to provide every individual in every family with an adequate income as a matter of right.[8]

Right-wing reaction is clear and quite predictable when the legitimacy of the American economic system is questioned in any context. There was no doubt in the mind of Representative Martin (R.-Neb.) that the suggestions of the committee were of "the same kind of plan worked out in Communist nations."[9] Such a reaction hardly leaves room for political debate.

Where questions regarding "the system" are taboo, those focusing upon the individual are welcome and quite comprehensible to the political protagonists. In acceptable political circles, the causes of poverty are sought in the process through which individuals acquire qualities enabling them to succeed and share in the national wealth. Conservatives argue that the fault lies with the poor for being lazy or stupid and not taking advantage of opportunities to obtain education, good health, a marketable skill, and a stable family life. "The fact is that most people who have no skill, have had no education for the same reason—low intelligence or low ambition!" says Barry Goldwater.[10] On the other hand, liberals maintain that something is wrong with the present means provided for individuals to obtain these desirable attributes—in short, the society is at fault: the poor are the "have-not people of America. They are denied, deprived, disadvantaged, and they are discriminated against,"

[8] *Report of the Ad Hoc Committee on the Triple Revolution* (April, 1964).

[9] House Hearings, *op. cit.,* p. 747.

[10] *New York Times* (January 16, 1964).

argues Walter Reuther of the United Auto Workers.[11] President Johnson and Sargent Shriver, commander of the poverty forces, bow to both groups. They maintain that it is first necessary to change the attitudes of the poor—to give them achievement motivations by changing "indifference to interest, ignorance to awareness, resignation to ambition, and an attitude of withdrawal to one of participation." [12] At the same time, present education, social welfare, and job-training programs sponsored at all levels of government and in both the public and private sectors of society, must be coordinated, consolidated and expanded to provide a new "opportunity environment" for the poor.

The emphasis is upon the process by which Americans attain the attributes necessary to achieve economic success rather than the legitimacy of the system to distribute the national wealth. This view is enhanced by the assumption that Americans, and poor Americans in particular, must earn and "want to earn" any social or economic benefits they receive. In our society, states former Senator Goldwater, one receives rewards by "merit and not by fiat"—essentially, you earn your keep or you get out (or stay out):

I strongly believe that all people are entitled to an opportunity . . . to get an education and to earn a living in keeping with the value of their work [emphasis supplied]. . . . But I do not believe that the mere fact of having little money entitles everybody, regardless of circumstance, to be permanently maintained by the taxpayers at an average or comfortable standard of living.[13]

Conservatives make no effort to conceal their reliance on this basic assumption; they quite frankly do not want to change the present distribution of wealth, or potential advantages they may have in gaining a greater future share. They are successful because they deserve to be successful, while others are poor because they are innately incapable of doing any better. This assumption about human nature is an integral part of the business creed, for the idealized economic system is dependent upon the "achievement motivations" of the individual. These

11 House Hearings, *op. cit.*, part I, p. 429.
12 *The War on Poverty, A Congressional Presentation, op. cit.*, p. 43.
13 *New York Times* (January 16, 1964).

crucial motivations could easily be destroyed if people became dependent upon government doles. If this happened, the greatest welfare system of all, the "free-enterprise system," would be destroyed. As the witness from the Chamber of Commerce explained to Representative Edith Green during the House antipoverty hearings, the chamber does not support "programs for people" because:

> . . . *economic measures to improve the efficiency of production and thus to get a larger output for our people from the same input of materials and manpower and capital goods is one of the greatest contributions to wealth that has ever been discovered in the history of mankind and the United States excels among all nations of the world in providing this kind of welfare.*[14]

Despite conservative denunciations, President Johnson eagerly reserves a benevolent role for the federal government, and particularly on an ideological level. He counters conservative views by adding a second act to the drama of the poor struggling young man working his way to the top in the "free-enterprise system." A magnanimous millionaire, glowing with compassion and wisdom, stretches out a benevolent helping hand to enable "Ragged Dick" to make good in the final panel of the American dream. Evoking an image of a goddess of peace and plenty rather than lanky Uncle Sam, Johnson declares that both at home and abroad, "We will extend the helping hand of a just nation to the poor and helpless and the oppressed."[15] In the American reality, however, "we" take care to see that the "helping hand" doesn't contain money or tangible goods—just opportunities to earn a better way of life and opportunities *to learn* to "want to earn" in the American way.

Such a sense of *noblesse oblige* is not inherent in the actual programs and techniques proposed in the War on Poverty, but it plays a part in the language which is inevitably used to describe them (and which is perhaps latent within our "progressive" attitudes toward social welfare). It is also the result of the effective control and administration of the government by the affluent and educated classes. In short, the official government attitude toward poverty should be expected to reflect the views

[14] House Hearings, *op. cit.,* part I, p. 707.
[15] *New York Times* (September 23, 1964).

arising from the life-situations of those who have formulated it. In speaking of poverty, no one bothers to deny or to hide the fact that the federal government is an instrumentality of the successful classes. This is assumed. The poor are recognized as not having a significant political voice. The entire War on Poverty was created, inspired, and will be carried out by the affluent. Action by the upper classes and all superior groups is urged on moral grounds, because it is right, because, as Senator Robert Kennedy stated simply, "those of us who are better off, who do not have that problem, have a responsibility to our fellow citizens who do." [16]

Without an economic crisis which affects the upper-income groups as well as the poor, the social philosophy of the federal antipoverty programs will necessarily contain this strong moral emphasis. Caught between the language of American social mythology and the attitudes generated by the existing social and political realities of a wealthy nation ruled by a distinct class of successful men, the public debate generated by the proposed "war" can only reveal our poverty of ideology. Conservatives balk at action because the poor are "getting what they deserve," and liberals cannot seem to act without assuming the "white man's burden." The militants of the new "war" look for the enemy and find him all too often in the personal attributes of the poor. The remedy offered for poverty amounts to a middle-class success formula (and, perhaps it *is* the route to success in American society): education, a stable family life, and above all, the proper attitudes. In short, there appears to be justification for the charge that the War on Poverty can be more accurately characterized as a "war on the poor." [17]

The politics of poverty and race

Confronted with a social ideology which easily obscures the existence of poverty, and lacking a thunderous economic crisis that directly threatens the middle and upper classes, the public concern with poverty of a traditionally reactive government is most remarkable. Why did poverty become a politically important issue in 1964?

[16] House Hearings, *op. cit.*, p. 330.
[17] Christopher Jencks, "Johnson *vs.* Poverty," *New Republic* (March 28, 1964).

When asked the reasons for a War on Poverty, President Johnson and Sargent Shriver presented themselves as puppets of the American people who "are interested in the government and in themselves making a focused or concentrated effort to attack poverty."[18] A public demand for the elimination of poverty did not, however, exist before it was deliberately made into an issue by the Johnson Administration in 1964. Government programs were not a response to public protests against conditions of poverty for one-fifth of a nation. (An exception to this was perhaps the March on Washington in the summer of 1963, which came close to protesting poverty directly with demands for more jobs; but the publicity impact of this event was channeled into exclusive concern with civil rights.)

After President Johnson announced his War on Poverty in his State of the Union address on January 8, 1964, the nation was deluged with vivid descriptions of the life of the poor, statistical accounts of their number and characteristics, and details of their geographic location. Poverty became such a "problem" that by the time Shriver testified at the congressional hearings, there was a degree of truth to his statement. The power of the presidency to stimulate the news media into undertaking a massive effort to increase public awareness, if not to generate actual demands for government action, was dramatically demonstrated. This achievement should not, however, obscure the fact that demands for action directly focused upon poverty did not exist prior to the time that the Administration began to produce its new policy line.

Political power-needs, rather than an articulated public demand, were at the source of the sudden resolution to recognize poverty in 1964. Briefly, the most plausible occasion for the urgency and publicity devoted to poverty by the Executive Office can be found in the political and emotionally disrupting effects of the civil rights movement, especially in regard to white morality and the white power structure. Emotionally, the nation needed to redefine the racial conflict as a conflict between the "haves" and the "have-nots." Politically, a transmutation of the civil rights movement secured the threatened power position of whites as whites, and further eased the agonies of the slow political death of the South. The latter, with its implications for the composition of the national political parties, has held spe-

[18] House Hearings, *op. cit.*, p. 99.

cial meaning for Johnson in his struggle to unify the Democratic Party and attain congressional compliance with presidential programs. In practical terms, the War on Poverty and its implications for opening a new field of jobs and social status, is the means by which American society will expand to accommodate the Negroes' demands for integration.

For over four years, white America has been forced into a state of acute consciousness of its prejudices and unexamined beliefs. In a white man's world, however, Negroes from the time of their early years live with a racial awareness. They must know and understand this world in a very practical sense in order to survive. But whites "experience race" at a more mature age—they are not "born" with it—and in the past they gained their experience somewhat at their own convenience. Suddenly in the sixties, the Negro has become a political power; he has become a "new" Negro who won't fit into the old images. This forced racial confrontation has caught the white off-guard. He does not possess a cultural reservoir that would allow him to interact—or avoid interaction—easily and unemotionally. Political protests, in short, have resulted in a social dislocation of the Negro and have created a necessity for both races to become aware of themselves and their inter-projective images. Politically, this awareness and the knowledge it can bring, is both necessary and beneficial. But this is an inconvenience for the white, an inconvenience requiring extra effort that may result in heightened tension as well as awareness.

The task of knowing is greatly simplified for the white American if he substitutes "poverty" for "race." He can more easily understand the frustrations of job hunting or unemployment than what it means to possess a black skin. "Poverty" has a comfortable sound to it, it makes "sense" and is not emotionally upsetting. Politically speaking, to redefine race and civil rights as a manifestation of conditions of poverty, opens a path for action. Where race and nationalism are vivid, emotion-based issues, not easily resolved through reason and logic, conflict between the "haves" and the "have-nots" is well understood. The western world has a supply of practical tools and intellectual theories with which this persistent enemy can be explained and controlled. Marxian ideology, liberal benevolence, or a religious morality all allow for practical political action that is denied when confronted by race in and of itself. Whether or not the civil rights movement dramatized existing conditions of poverty, white Americans had to raise the poverty issue to relieve the emotional tension and political impasse created by the racial confrontation. The dollar costs of a War on Poverty are exchanged for the high emotional price-tag attached to race.

Aside from this exchange of emotion for practicality, poverty redefines civil rights in a manner that secures the power positions of white public leaders and places them in control of a movement which frequently has attempted to exclude them, on racial grounds, from exercising a directing influence. Three groups are the principal beneficiaries of this effect: the white liberal "sympathetic" to the Negro cause, public officials in the large urban centers, and the Southern politician.

The white liberal has found himself increasingly excluded from policy-making positions in the civil rights movement. He has been told that he could contribute his warm body and little else in a revolution which was felt to express legitimately only the suffering of the American Negro. However, when the "movement" is placed in the context of a battle between the wealthy and the poor, between the "power-lords" and the "exploited underdog," it is possible to carve out a legitimate place for whites within a dynamic and powerful social movement. Such a recasting of the Negro struggle cuts across racial boundaries to transform it into a fight for "all humanity." A new struggle is created which has a great potential for rallying sustained activities within accepted political channels. But, also, it may push the Negro to the background once again, for he does not have the same priority for a leading role in the new antipoverty struggle. Professional and respectable social revolutionaries assume directing positions in a poverty war whereas indigenous leadership was beginning to develop out of the civil rights struggle.

Public officials in the large urban centers have also found their authority threatened and severely shaken by a ground swell which they had to appease in order to survive. Something had to be offered the angry Negro segment of the populace. They couldn't offer to make a Negro white, or at least they couldn't overtly approach the racial question in this manner, although such an objective may underlie the antipoverty programs offered the Negro, with their emphasis upon instilling white middle-class motivations and values. They could, however, offer to train him, to educate him, and perhaps give him a little more *hope* of obtaining solid employment. In other words, the Negro must be viewed as "poor," as deprived of services which the government apparatus can provide, in order to engage him in political bargaining. The demonstrators are taken off the streets and placed in the hands of the welfare bureaucracies and the new "antipoverty" programs which can placate demands more quickly than the courts. (And, hopefully, in a more substantial and lasting manner.) This need exists on the national level, but in its War on Poverty the federal government has left the distribution of public goods and services to the local political leaders, whose positions are most immediately threatened by the volatile protest and developing political power of the Negro.

Reaction to the race riots of previous summers provides ample illustration of the ideological function of an antipoverty slogan and the practical role of its accompanying programs. Immediately after the 1964 riots in New York City, [Mayor Robert] Wagner made a special trip to Washington to see if more antipoverty projects and other federal money could be directed toward the slum areas of the city. As the *New York Times* interpreted the visit:

It would be highly surprising if Mr. Wagner—mayor of the city where the present epidemic of racial disturbances began —did not mean, as part of his mission, to remind members of the House of the intimate connection between the battle against poverty and the battle against riots. . . . The antipoverty bill, in the new perspective given by the disturbances of this long, hot summer, is also an anti-riot bill. The members of the House of Representatives will do well to bear that in mind when the time comes for a vote.[19]

The fact that Wagner's trip produced few promises for programs and less cash was not as important as the public assurance that something could and would be done. Fortunately, the city had initiated its own antipoverty planning in the spring and could point to several programs already underway. Both large federal juvenile-delinquency programs, Mobilization for Youth and Haryou-Act, as well as the city's own program, Job

---

[19] Editorial, "Riots and Poverty," *New York Times* (August 4, 1964).

Opportunities in Neighborhoods, were paraded before public view. In addition, the city signed a contract providing a $223,-225 grant for Youth in Action, Inc., to develop an antipoverty program for youth in Brooklyn's Bedford–Stuyvesant area. A job-finding project for semi-skilled and unskilled youngsters was accelerated. Programs of training and basic education conducted under MDTA[20] received personal inspections from the mayor, with attendant publicity.

Not only has the President's War on Poverty provided evidence of sincere efforts to alleviate some of the needs of the low-income Negro ghettos, but it also provided white society with a defense against charges of overt racism. Poverty and racism have joined hands to create the Negro's hell—the effects of one cannot be separated easily from the other. When given the choice, however, white society prefers to attribute the source of Negro resentment and protests to poverty. The *New York Times* employed this defense when it maintained that the race riots were "as much demonstrations against Negro poverty as against discrimination and what some call 'police brutality.'"[21] In this respect, we should note the extent to which right-wing politicians ignore the racial aspect of the Negro protest and refer to it almost exclusively as a conflict between the "haves" and the "have-nots." They simply make it clear that they are on the side of the "haves." Morally there may be something wrong with denying privileges on the basis of race, but within the right-wing ideology, there is "nothing wrong" with defending your own property and privileges from someone who is not as successful.

For reasons of a less than morally commendable nature, white America has responded to the Negroes' demands for an integrated society with an antipoverty movement: a response slow in coming and pitifully inadequate at first, but still a response. In terms of realistic social dynamics, integration is not, and will not be, an interpenetration of the old by the new, but will be a process of *expansion* and then assimilation. Societies expand and contract; they do not bend except with passing of generations, and that cannot even be predicted with assurance. Those who are within the socio-economic structure will not give up their positions to Negroes seeking entrance. New roles must be

[20] Manpower Development and Training Act of 1962.—Eds.
[21] Editorial, "Riots and Poverty," *New York Times* (August 4, 1964).

added to the job structure and new status rungs created in the social ladder.

Such is the function of the War on Poverty. As was pointed out, it is a service-oriented welfare measure. The activity- and job-creating nature of its programs is presently opening and shaping new fields in the social services, a process that is certain to increase its range in the future. New professional positions in community organization and social planning, as well as the clerical and blue-collar jobs created to staff the research institutions and service organizations of the "antipoverty" projects, are particularly accessible to the Negro. This is true, above all, for the now small but increasing ranks of the college-educated and professionally trained Negro. The politically dangerous energies of the Negro elite can be molded into socially legitimate channels through the creation of roles in an entirely new area of the nation's job structure.

The Negro asks for integration and receives a War on Poverty: it is perhaps not exactly what he ordered nor in the form he imagined, but it is the first step American society is capable of providing. And it is a step that can lead potentially through jobs and social status toward the dignity and justice he desires.

THE SHORT UNHAPPY HISTORY
OF COMMUNITY ACTION PROGRAMS

Under Title I B of the Economic Opportunity Act of 1964, the Neighborhood Job Corps was formed to provide training and work experience for youths between the ages of sixteen and twenty-one. One Lucky New York City enrollee was Lyman Thompson, age twenty-one. "I'm working down here at the Newark City Museum and I like it very much but however when I first came here I was told about reptiles and there was certain kinds I didn't like. . . . One kind especially that I didn't like was snakes. . . . But I can manage along with them now. I really do like my work and I'm proud of it and I'm proud to be here. . . . We feed them, we clean their cages and kids come from different schools and so on. It's a lot of fun in the reptile corner." [1]

Aside from the fact that learning how to handle snakes may be more interesting than useful, the real issue of the poverty program concerns the goal of "maximum feasible participation" of the poor. At a recent conference in Washington (see introductory note to reading 17), which included both the poor and Washington officials, the following took place:

In committee meetings the poor talked of "organizing against the political and economic structure" that has

---

[1] Office of Economic Opportunity, *Congressional Presentation* (Washington, D. C., April, 1965), Vol. I, p. 25.

denied them control over antipoverty expenditures. There was talk of "political assassination" to oust office holders accused of "keeping us down." Mrs. Unita Blackwell of the Mississippi Freedom Democratic Party declared: "The federal government ought to be ashamed of itself. The same men who pay us $3 a day and are bent on putting people off the land—that's the men who are on the poverty committee. You just come up with the resources, and we'll show you what we can do with the money." Carl Johnson of Harlan County, Ky., said his area was no better off despite $1 million in poverty funds.[2]

In the article that follows, David Stoloff traces the origins of the Community Action Programs and raises serious questions about the efficacy of the training programs and the role the poor are to play in Johnson's War on Poverty.

Mr. Stoloff received an M.A. in Planning from the University of Chicago. He is Director of the Commission on Community Interrelations of the American Jewish Congress. He is also a consultant on planning and housing for HARYOU-ACT, Inc., and teaches urban planning at Hunter College. His article was written specifically for inclusion in this book.

◇ ◇ ◇

The War on Poverty began with the introduction of a bold new concept in social welfare—the Community Action Program.

. . . through a new community action program we intend to strike at poverty at its source. . . . This program asks men and women throughout the country to prepare long-range plans for the attack on poverty in their own local communities. These are not plans prepared in Washington and imposed upon hundreds of different situations. They are based on the fact that local citizens best understand their own problems, and know best how to deal with those problems. These plans will be local plans striking at the many unfilled needs which underlie poverty in each community, not just one or two. Their components and emphasis will differ as needs differ.

[2] *Time* (April 22, 1966), p. 21.

So said President Johnson in his message on poverty delivered to the Congress on March 16, 1964.[3]

But while the concept is bold, the implementation has been timid. At the first sign of opposition, the antipoverty generals have made a strategic retreat, abandoning the community action program to the enemy.

The place of community action in the Economic Opportunity Act of 1964

The legislation that gave expression to the community action concept was Title II of the Economic Opportunity Act of 1964, entitled Community Action Programs (CAP). It provided that a "community action program means a program which . . . is developed, conducted, and administered with the maximum feasible participation of residents of the areas and members of the groups served." [4] The first year of the program $340 million was authorized, and $850 million in the second year.[5] The funds were to be given to local groups—either private non-profit or public—to engage in a wide range of innovative activities dealing with the recognized conditions of poverty, i.e., unemployment, poor health, poor housing, and inadequate education. While the program was aimed at both urban and rural communities, virtually all grants have been to urban agencies.

CAP was the heart of the Administration's War on Poverty. The other programs included in the Economic Opportunity Act were an unconnected series of traditionally conceived and oriented programs. The Job Corps, Neighborhood Youth Corps, Special Loan Program, Work Experience Program, and VISTA are either extensions, renewals, or variations of programs with which there has been considerable experience. Essentially, these are either work-relief or job-training programs and thus

[3] Excerpts from this message are reprinted in this volume, reading 14. —Eds.

[4] *Economic Opportunity Act of 1964* (U.S. Government Printing Office, Washington, D. C.).

[5] Since this article was first prepared, figures released by the Office of Economic Opportunity show that only $666 million of the authorized $850 million was actually spent. Of this, $395 million went to the locally planned CAP groups rather than to the "packaged" programs described later in this article.

are extensions of the old centrally administered, "supplier oriented" approaches to the problems of the poor. That is, they reflect the attitudes of the professional and bureaucratic suppliers of the services as to the nature of the problems, and the appropriate solutions.

It is precisely these "supplier oriented" programs that have proven inadequate and inappropriate for the chronically poor. Such programs have no real impact on the aged poor, dependent children, welfare mothers, alcoholics, dope addicts, or on the alienated and culturally deprived youth and adults of the nation's ethnic ghettoes. Studies by Michael Harrington[6] and others dramatized this need for a fresh approach to poverty and helped set the stage for the War on Poverty.

The important feature of the CAP is that it opens the possibility for the development of "user-" or "client-oriented" approaches to poverty. Programs developed, conducted, and administered with the active participation of the poor are bound to operate with more sensitivity to the felt needs of the poor. In addition, the very process of developing and operating programs is instructive and beneficial. The chronically poor have not only been excluded from the world of work, they have been excluded from decision making, program development, fiscal management, personnel management, and other processes that are the stuff of productive activity. CAP gave promise of providing such experiences—experiences that might well lead to new confidence and self-respect among the poor.

The struggle for control of CAP

Immediately after the passage of the Economic Opportunity Act, a number of communities began to organize antipoverty councils to draw up plans for Community Action Programs. These councils were by and large made up of upper-middle-class charity and social work professionals with a number of elected and appointed city officials thrown in. Sometimes "representatives" of the poor were added as well, but not frequently—and always upon recommendation of the mayor or other official. The many neighborhood organizations and other "grass roots" groups that were by-passed in this process began to voice their protests. It seemed to them that no attempt was

[6] *The Other America* (New York, 1962).

being made to meet the intent of the law, the mandate that programs be conducted with "maximum feasible participation" of the poor.

A three-way struggle for control of the local groups resulted —between the local political interests, the established welfare agencies, and those who sought substantial representation for the poor. It quickly became apparent that the Johnson Administration had neither the will nor the ability to resist the co-option of the CAP groups by local political organizations or to ensure any substantial participation of the poor—at least any participation in deciding how the money was to be spent. As early as January 1965, Saul Alinsky,[7] nationally known advocate of community action, was pointing out in detail how local politicos were manipulating the program to create patronage and prevent any but token participation of the people who were supposed to be served.

The Administration made some early attempts to prevent this from occurring. During the first year, the OEO tried to cajole cities into structuring more satisfactory councils. But hearings before the House Committee on Education and Labor during the summer of 1965, when the program was a year old, brought out what little effect they had had. Citizen delegations from New York, Cleveland, Philadelphia, Chicago, and elsewhere protested what was going on. Under this pressure, the Administration threatened to withhold funds unless the poor gained more representation in CAP agencies.

These threats turned out to be hollow: it seems a Democratic Administration has a difficult time withholding appropriated funds from Democratic city organizations. It is true that the Office of Economic Opportunity established certain guidelines about representation of the poor. A number of cities even seemed to allow the poor to elect their own representatives to the local antipoverty councils. But the guidelines demanded very little and the councils were restructured to prevent the elected poor from achieving real control over the antipoverty funds. In Chicago, twelve out of a sixty-member council are ostensibly representatives from six poverty areas—they are selected by the politically appointed administrators of "service centers" in the six areas! In New York, the city government

---

[7] Saul D. Alinsky, "The War on Poverty—Political Pornography," *Journal of Social Issues* (January 1965), pp. 41-47.

finally agreed that the Council Against Poverty would be one-third poor. However, the city declared it illegal for the council to receive funds, so an office called the Economic Opportunity Committee, with no poor representation, was set up as the program's fiscal agent. In Los Angeles, Mayor Yorty refused to worry about the problem, and, like many such problems, it simply went away—that is, the Administration never withheld a penny because of lack of representation of the poor. In Newark, somehow the local Democratic machine allowed the local antipoverty council to omit them from membership. When the council, the United Community Corporation, refused to repair this oversight, the city council in turn refused to put up their share, 10 per cent, of the cost of the proposed program—which has embarrassed the OEO and stymied the program. These are but a few examples.

The Newark situation referred to above had another outgrowth, which confirmed a fear harbored by every mayor of a city with an antipoverty program. Kenneth Gibson, a vice-president of United Community Corporation, with a campaign based on issues raised by the antipoverty program, ran for mayor in the Democratic primary [spring, 1966] and captured enough votes to force a run-off election between the two major candidates. From the beginning of the Community Action Programs, it was clear to any alert politician that "community action" and "citizen participation" imply direct confrontation with established systems of political power and social control.[8]

[8] The theoretical basis for the Community Action Programs is to be found in the results of a series of thirteen experimental antidelinquency projects conducted during the period 1961-64 by the President's Committee on Juvenile Delinquency and Youth Crime. During the second year of the antipoverty program, the Office of Economic Opportunity agreed to accept responsibility for all projects originally funded by the President's Committee. Two of these projects, HARYOU and Mobilization for Youth—both in New York City—developed highly structured theoretical program frameworks which included strong "community action" and community self-determination components. They postulated that delinquency is the result of both lack of opportunity and the sense of powerlessness over one's life and environment that pervades slum culture. The remedy must include transferring some measure of political and economic power into the hands of the poor. For more detail on the HARYOU and MFY program rationale, see HARYOU's *Youth in the Ghetto: A Study of the Consequences of Powerlessness and a Blueprint for Change* (New York, 1964); MFY's *A Proposal for the Prevention and Control of Delinquency by Expanding Opportunities* (New York,

To create new organizations that control money and jobs and that operate programs that directly affect people in the street, is to create new bases for political power. The easiest way to prevent this is to have the old systems run the new programs: and this is the pattern that pervades CAP around the nation.

The advent of the packaged programs

Perhaps because of these difficulties, but in direct opposition to the intent of the legislation and President Johnson's antipoverty message quoted earlier, the Office of Economic Opportunity is moving rapidly to usurp nearly all local initiative in the planning of Community Action Program activities.

Beginning last summer, OEO began to develop a series of "prepackaged" programs to be administered by the local CAP groups. The first and most successful of these was the Headstart program. Headstart, which provides intensive preschool training for children from poor families, is administered by CAP agencies and local school districts. Headstart is now the largest single Title II program and will likely account for more than 40 per cent of Title II monies next year.[9]

Another such package is the "Nelson Amendment" program, which permits cities to put actual or potential welfare recipients to work on beautification projects.[10] This program might absorb more than 10 per cent of Title II funds next year.

The "Foster Grandparents" program—which puts elderly poor into children's institutions to act as substitute parents—is another such program just now being promoted by OEO.

Legal services programs are another prepackaged item that will be paid for out of CAP funds but will not be administered by local CAP agencies. The Office of Economic Opportunity refused to fund legal aid components of local CAP groups be-

---

1961); and Richard A. Cloward and Lloyd E. Ohlin, *Delinquency and Opportunity* (Glencoe, Ill., 1960).

[9] *Economic Opportunity Amendments of 1966*, House of Representatives, 89th Congress, 2nd Session, Report No. 1568 (Washington, D.C.).

[10] The "Nelson Amendment" was sponsored by Senator Gaylord Nelson of Wisconsin. The amendment authorized the Director of OEO to make grants for special projects ". . . directed to the needs of those chronically unemployed poor who have poor employment prospects and are unable, because of age or otherwise, to secure appropriate employment or training assistance under other programs. . . ."

cause of the complaints of legal professional groups who feared "socialized" law. The compromise here was to fund separately organized legal assistance projects that would set up neighborhood legal offices controlled by the local bar associations.

The Title II demonstration program is also being diverted from its original purposes. The demonstration program was supposed to explore new ways of organizing and carrying out Community Action Programs. However, the amendments to the Economic Opportunity Act now before Congress would earmark nearly half of the demonstration funds for experimental narcotics programs.

Clearly the packaged programs have usurped local initiative and reduced the possibilities for innovation at the local level. Carried to the extreme, as seems to be the trend, the local CAP agencies will be reduced to mere administrative arms of national programs aimed at limited groups of people. The planning and program development functions of local CAP agencies, as mandated by the EOA, can now be performed in only limited ways.[11]

. . .

The great promise of the antipoverty program was embodied in its community action component. This was the one program that seemed to approach the problems of poverty in a truly unique and potentially meaningful manner. Visions of impoverished communities organizing to help themselves, encouraged to think through their own problems and come up with programmatic solutions, were created by the legislation. And it seems reasonable to believe that that is just what the framers of the legislation had in mind.

But CAP is dead for all real purposes. It died, not because of the invalidity of the concept, but because the Administration had little interest in fighting for it in the local political arenas. It turns out that the poor are powerless after all. When the mayors of major cities decided that antipoverty was important

[11] Since this article was first drafted, the Economic Opportunity Act of 1966 and its related appropriations bill were passed by Congress. Funds for "un-packaged" Title II programs were authorized at $323 million, but the appropriations provide for only $200 million (compared to the $395 million spent last year). Headstart ended up with 50 per cent of the appropriated funds, $352 million. The Nelson Amendment program (now combined with another work-training program) was provided with $73 million and other packaged programs with the remaining $98 million.

political business, replete with patronage and potentially threatening to their political power, they grabbed it and met with little effective resistance. The OEO put up a little fight, but in the end has responded by becoming overly specific about how antipoverty funds can be spent.

Yet, the problems of the poor remain unsolved. If the experimental programs that formed the basis for CAP were correct in their diagnosis—that the poor must be involved if real solutions to their problems are to be found—then we are not yet on the right road. Current programs add up to more of the same welfare-dole and work-relief approach to the poor, and will leave the chronically impoverished as trapped as they have been for generations.

PART V

THE BLACK MAN IN THE GREAT SOCIETY

INTRODUCTION

The deepening radicalism of the civil rights movement in mid-twentieth-century America poses a challenge to the existing structure of power in the United States. It also poses a challenge to our understanding of the actual context of Negro life. The long-established view, enshrined in such works as Gunnar Myrdal's *An American Dilemma* (2 vols., New York, 1944), begins with the assumption that American society has from the outset been consecrated to the achievement of freedom and equality. Oppression of black men and women is viewed as an unfortunate and irrational detour from this benign main path, and progress is seen as steady, since the Civil War.

Historical scholarship no longer supports this view. As our understanding of slavery grows, it appears that the "peculiar institution" was no foreign excrescence on the American social order, but an intimate part of its economics and political life.[1] The allied idea that "the Negro problem" is a sectional aberration affecting only that benighted region south of Mason and Dixon's line, has also fallen before the onslaughts of scholars,[2] as have the notions of gradual and steady improvement in the condition of the Negro since at least the beginning of the twentieth century. Instead of uniform progress, there has been definite retrogression in the position of the Negro after Reconstruc-

---

[1] See on this Eugene D. Genovese, *The Political Economy of Slavery: Studies in the Economy and Society of the Slave South* (New York, 1965); Staughton Lynd, "On Turner, Beard and Slavery," *The Journal of Negro History,* XLVIII (October 1963), pp. 235-50; Lynd, "The Compromise of 1787," *Political Science Quarterly,* LXXXI (June 1966), pp. 225-50; etc. Compare, however, with Kenneth M. Stampp, *The Peculiar Institution: Slavery in the Ante-Bellum South* (New York, 1956).

[2] Especially Leon Litwack, whose *North of Slavery: The Negro in the Free States, 1790-1860* (Chicago, 1961) clearly demonstrates the unwillingness of white America in the North to accord the blacks anything approaching equal status.

tion and after the Populist period of the 1890s.[3] The central government in Washington was a major instrument of white domination, enforcing segregation through all three divisions—the courts, the Congress, and the executive branch. Only in the 1940s, with the concessions wrested from the Roosevelt and Truman Administrations, did the tide begin to turn and white America begin to pay attention to the accumulating grievances of the black population in its midst.

The process of awakening white America is agonizingly slow. The school segregation cases of 1954 and 1955 were the product of one long legal battle, and the beginning of another. The court victories, real and substantial though they were, contributed to the illusion that through gradual and orderly steps the "Negro problem" would solve itself, without unduly disturbing people. But in the early 1960s the movement turned to more radical tactics to end discrimination and bring about equality—the tactics of mass action and civil disobedience.

These events burst in on the consciousness of white Americans with an explosive force, posing a fundamental challenge to the nation: does the American dream of freedom and equality mean "for Caucasians only"? The Negro revolt has obliged well-intentioned citizens to contemplate the grim reality of black life in the United States. Instead of steady progress in such areas as equal employment, the reality is substantial deterioration. Unemployment rates for Negroes have always been higher than for whites, but since the early postwar years the gap has widened for both males and females. The ratio of total nonwhite unemployment to that of whites in 1949, for example, was 8.9 to 5.6, or 1.59 to 1. This means that nonwhite unemployment was nearly 60 per cent higher. In 1965 it was 2.1 times white unemployment: nonwhite unemployment had risen in sixteen years to more than twice that of whites. Among male youth between the ages of fourteen and nineteen the differences are dramatically sharp, especially when traced over time. In 1948 there was *less* nonwhite unemployment in this age group than white. In the period from 1949 to 1954 unemployment rates for black youth never exceeded those of whites by more than 30 per cent, and in one year (1952) they were

---

[3] See, for example, C. Vann Woodward, *The Strange Career of Jim Crow* (rev. ed., New York, 1965), and Rayford W. Logan, *The Negro in American Life and Thought: The Nadir, 1877-1901* (New York, 1954).

almost identical. By 1965 the economic conditions had so deteriorated for Negro teenagers that their unemployment rate was over 90 per cent higher than whites (22.6 per cent to 11.8 per cent)! [4] The significance of these figures seems to be that while our society is undergoing rapid technological changes that bring prosperity to many Americans, these changes have eliminated jobs traditionally held by young Negroes.

Income statistics, too, bring into question the doctrine of steady progress in race relations: Census Bureau economist Herman P. Miller has found the median pay of black workers to be only 55 per cent of that enjoyed by whites. Nor has he found any change in this ratio over the preceding decade.[5] It is astounding to learn that the lifetime earnings of an average male Negro college graduate are actually lower than what a white man with an eighth grade education can earn.[6]

In addition, discrimination and deprivation take a physical toll, literally condemning black people to premature death. The table on the next page taken from the *Economic Report of the President* (1966), p. 101, graphically presents the evidence.

When one looks at education from a national perspective rather than generalizing from the situation of a few middle-class Negroes, the situation is no better. Integrated, quality education is one obvious necessity, but such education is simply not available. Reading 23, below, shows how the Washington authorities have evaded their responsibilities under the school segregation decisions of the Supreme Court and under congressional legislation to wipe out separate and unequal

[4] US Department of Labor, *Manpower Report of the President* (Washington, D.C., March, 1966), pp. 166, 168.

[5] *New York Times* (August 12, 1963). See, also, US Department of Labor, *Manpower Report of the President* (Washington, D.C., March, 1964), p. 275.

[6] *Employment and Earnings,* Bureau of Labor Statistics (February, 1964). Comparison of white–nonwhite earnings, when educational achievements are roughly similar, shows nonwhites to earn less than 80 per cent of their white counterparts in such occupations as carpenters, painters, plumbers, and a host of others. See *Manpower Report* (1964), p. 276. To be sure, part of the differential may be "explained" by the geographical factor of Negroes being located, not of course by accident, in the South, traditionally a low-wage region. Offsetting this is the fact that black–white income differentials are understated by comparisons of earnings *within* selected occupations since the occupational distribution of jobs still confines the black man to the relatively low–paying occupations. For evidence on this, see *Manpower Report* (1963), 274.

HEALTH INDICATORS, SELECTED YEARS 1940-64

Indicator	1940	1950	1960	1964
	Years			
Life expectancy*				
At birth	63.6	68.1	69.7	70.2
White	64.9	69.0	70.6	71.0
Nonwhite	53.9**	60.7	63.6	64.1
At age 45	26.9	28.5	29.4	29.7
White	27.3	28.9	29.7	30.1
Nonwhite	22.8**	24.8	26.2	26.6
	Deaths per 1,000 live births			
Infant mortality rate				
Total	47.0	29.2	26.0	24.8
White	43.2	26.8	22.9	21.6
Nonwhite	73.8	44.5	43.2	41.1
	Deaths per 10,000 live births			
Maternal mortality rate				
Total	37.6	8.3	3.7	3.3
White	32.0	6.1	2.6	2.2
Nonwhite	77.4	22.2	9.8	9.0

* Life expectancy figures in first two columns are for 1939-41 and 1949-51, respectively.
** Negroes only.

schools. Available data clearly reveals that school systems in the North remain segregated. In Chicago, for example, 87 per cent of Negro elementary school children go to all-Negro schools. The picture is substantially similar in the other large cities of the North.[7] It hardly needs to be mentioned that progress toward school integration in the South is virtually nonexistent because of the effectiveness of the delaying tactics used by local school boards and because of the reluctance of the central government to exercise its duly authorized powers.

As for housing: Black Americans remain trapped in overcrowded ghettos, while whites take flight to the suburbs or are driven to send their children to private schools. The *New York Times,* in late 1964, reported the results of a study based on census data that showed that "with some notable exceptions,

[7] Tom Kahn, *The Economics of Equality* (New York, 1964), p. 31.

racial segregation, far from disappearing, is on the increase in the United States." [8]

What all this adds up to is a convincing demonstration that American liberalism has utterly failed to provide an answer to the sickness of racism. Black Americans are offered the grim equality of fighting and dying in Vietnam, where their bodies are found useful in the defense of what political leaders are pleased to call the "free world."

But what of the future? A state apparatus determined to use its economic resources and its police power—force, in other words—to end discrimination and achieve equality would, in time, be likely to succeed. But no such apparatus exists, nor will it exist as long as power is exercised according to rules set up by the prevailing political parties. A recent essay argues that at least five major white groups

benefit from the existence of a Negro subproletariat. (a) Employers benefit from divisions in the labor force which enable them to play one group off against another, thus weakening all. Historically, for example, no small amount of Negro migration was in direct response to the recruiting of strikebreakers. (b) Owners of ghetto real estate are able to overcrowd and overcharge. (c) Middle and upper income groups benefit from having at their disposal a large supply of cheap domestic labor. (d) Many small marginal businesses, especially in the service trades, can operate profitably only if cheap labor is available to them. (e) White workers benefit by being protected from Negro competition for the more desirable and higher paying jobs.[9]

To be sure, concessions are made. "World opinion"—especially in the nonwhite world of Africa, Asia, and Latin America —requires American politicians to make some efforts toward ending racial discrimination that appear to go beyond mere lip service. But the rhetoric that accompanies federal actions should never be confused with the reality. Black people have a vivid sense of the gap between the two. In a white world that does not want Negroes, except as menials and cannon fodder, it

---

[8] November 26, 1964.

[9] Paul A. Baran and Paul M. Sweezy, *Monopoly Capital: An Essay on the American Economic and Social Order* (New York and London, 1966), pp. 263-64.

was inevitable that a section of the black movement would reject the kind of "coalition strategy" that ties the Negro even more closely to the Johnson Administration and official liberalism. (For an authoritative statement of this strategy, see the piece by Bayard Rustin, reading 21, below). The threat this strategy poses for the integrity and independence of Negro radicalism is forcefully demonstrated by Ronald Radosh (reading 22, below).

The alternate strategy, "Black Power," has electrified many in the civil rights movement. While enemies mischievously label it "racism in reverse" or willfully confuse it with separatism, it is clear that its proponents use it to mean black control over their struggle for freedom. But even more significantly, it symbolizes for them real and meaningful political representation for black people, who previously were not allowed to vote, or when allowed, were intimidated or hoodwinked into voting for persons who did not respond to their needs. For Stokely Carmichael, former chairman of the Student Non-Violent Coordinating Committee: "It does not mean merely putting black faces into office. . . . Most of the black politicians we see around the country are not what SNCC means by black power. The power must be that of a community, and emanate from there." [10]

One historian of the South has given his assessment of black nationalism against a backdrop that includes the emasculating effects of slavery and the inevitability that most of our major cities will contain black majorities within a few decades.

Black nationalism, in its various manifestations, constitutes a necessary response on the part of the black masses. The Muslims, for example, have understood the inner needs of the working-class blacks, who have filled their ranks and have understood the futility—for these people at least—of integrationist hopes. Their insistence on the forcible assertion of a dignified, disciplined, collectively responsible black community represents a rational response to a harsh reality. . . . Such ownership [of business in Harlem] will do little toward the creation of a black economy, but many of its advocates are easily bright enough to know as much. The point is that it may,

[10] "What We Want," *New York Review of Books* (September 22, 1966), p. 5. See also *Black Power: The Politics of Liberation in America,* by Stokely Carmichael and Charles Hamilton (New York, 1967).

*as Malcolm X suggested, play a decisive role in the establish-
ment of community stability and self-respect. . . . The assertion of black hegemony in specific cities and districts—nationalism, if you will—offers the only politically realistic hope of
transcending the slave heritage. First, it seems the only way for
black communities to police themselves, to curb antisocial elements, and to enforce adequate health and housing standards,
and yet break with paternalism and instill pride and a sense of
worth. Second, it seems the best way to build a position of
strength from which to fight for a proper share of jobs and federal funds as a matter of right not privilege. Black nationalism
may yet prove to be the only force capable of restraining the
impulse to violence, of disciplining black rebelliousness, and of
absorbing the nihilistic tradition into a socially constructive
movement. . . . Notwithstanding some offensive and preten-
tious rhetoric, the advocates of "Black Power" have judged their
position correctly. They are determined to win control of the
ghettos, and we would be foolish not to bet on them. The
use to which they put that power, however, depends not on
our good wishes or on their good intentions, but on what they
are offered as a* quid pro quo. *For American socialism the
black revolt opens an opportunity for relevance that has been
missing for decades.*[11]

Farfetched? Perhaps, but if housing integration is blocked, as
it is in Chicago by masses of whites wearing swastikas; if liberal Senators like Mansfield conclude, because of pressures
from their constituency, that civil rights is moving "too fast,"
when the facts show it to be moving at a snail's pace, if at
all—then can we doubt a growing black discontent with the
"liberalism" of the Great Society? Or if the polarization process
continues, might it not grow to the point where even the stability of the American corporate order itself is threatened?

Carmichael's concluding words in "What We Want" are certainly worth pondering:

*As for white America, perhaps it can stop crying out against
"black supremacy," "black nationalism," "racism in reverse,"
and begin facing reality. The reality is that this nation, from*

---

[11] Eugene D. Genovese, in a paper originally given at the second annual Socialist Scholars Conference and printed in *Studies on the Left,*
VI (November-December, 1966).

top to bottom, is racist; that racism is not primarily a problem of "human relations" but of an exploitation maintained—either actively or through silence—by the society as a whole. Camus and Sartre have asked, can a man condemn himself? Can whites, particularly liberal whites, condemn themselves? Can they stop blaming us, and blame their own system? Are they capable of the shame which might become a revolutionary emotion?

We have found that they usually cannot condemn themselves, and so we have done it. But the rebuilding of this society, if at all possible, is basically the responsibility of whites—not blacks. We won't fight to save the present society, in Vietnam or anywhere else. We are just going to work, in the way we see fit, and on goals we define, not for civil rights but for all our human rights.[12]

[12] *New York Review of Books* (September 22, 1966), p. 8.

TO FULFILL THESE RIGHTS

(JUNE 4, 1965)*

During his early political career, Lyndon Johnson, no different from other Southern politicians, was committed to "the status quo of racial inequality." He spoke out vigorously against Civil Rights legislation before entering the Senate (see above, p. 5), and afterward was frequently heard to complain that his liberal colleagues in the upper house were excessively concerned about the "Nigras." In the course of discovering his *national* political ambitions, Johnson found it necessary to shake off his regional identification and embrace the cause of civil rights. (See on this Rowland Evans and Robert Novak, *Lyndon B. Johnson: The Exercise of Power* [New York, 1967], Chapt. VII.) No other explanation than political expediency has been seriously offered to account for this switch.

But once the change was made, Johnson became an active verbal supporter of the cause of Negro freedom and equality. In the summer of 1964 he signed into law a dramatic Civil Rights Act that Congress had passed in large measure under his prompting. (See Evans and Novak, *Johnson*, pp. 376-80.) Less than a year later, at predominantly Negro Howard University in Washington, D.C., President Johnson gave the passionate and eloquent speech (written by Richard Goodwin and Daniel P. Moynihan) reprinted below. A reporter described him as "working up a head of oratorical steam. Apparently losing

* *Public Papers of the Presidents, Lyndon B. Johnson, 1965*, II, pp. 635-40.

himself in enthusiasm, he said he would include 'Negro leaders of both races.' " [1]

The substantive proposals advanced at Howard University derived in large measure from ideas developed by "professional reformers" in government service such as Daniel Patrick Moynihan. (See reading 33, below.) As Assistant Secretary of Labor for Policy Planning and Research, Moynihan prepared a report on *The Negro Family: The Case for National Action* (Washington, D.C., March, 1965). This report was, in its author's words, "the original precipitant of the Howard speech." The aim was to get the federal government behind a massive effort to solve the "Negro problem" by upgrading the Negro family. The structure of American society as presently constituted was accepted as a "given" (after all, this was a *government* document), and Negroes were to be made "competitive" within that structure by untangling the "pathology" of their family life. It was tacitly assumed that there was no "white problem" to speak of, and Negroes were urged to look for improvement through the efforts of a benevolent government.

Moynihan could not hide the resentment he felt at the ingratitude of the Negroes (though he was careful to make certain white radicals his main targets), who rejected his strategy.[2] The civil rights movement was entering a more militant phase, unwilling to admit that the plight of the black man in America was a "Negro problem" quite in the way that Moynihan suggested it was. And there was no longer any widespread sympathy for the "coalition strategy" (see readings 21 and 22, below) that was implicit in the report, and in the Howard University speech. Ironically, at the very White House conference called in June, 1966, "To Fulfill These Rights," Moynihan's proposals were repudiated. His disappointment over this reveals more than anything else the distance that separates the professional reformers from a

---

[1] *New York Times* (June 5, 1965).

[2] Moynihan, "The President and the Negro: The Moment Lost," *Commentary*, XLIII (February, 1967), pp. 31–45. See also Lee Rainwater and William L. Yancey, *The Moynihan Report and the Politics of Controversy* (Cambridge, Mass., 1967).

movement that is discovering for itself deeper and more radical goals than those supplied by benevolent white liberals.

◇◇◇

I am delighted at the chance to speak at this important and this historic institution. Howard has long been an outstanding center for the education of Negro Americans. Its students are of every race and color and they come from many countries of the world. It is truly a working example of democratic excellence.

Our earth is the home of revolution. In every corner of every continent men charged with hope contend with ancient ways in the pursuit of justice. They reach for the newest of weapons to realize the oldest of dreams, that each may walk in freedom and pride, stretching his talents, enjoying the fruits of the earth.

Our enemies may occasionally seize the day of change, but it is the banner of our revolution they take. And our own future is linked to this process of swift and turbulent change in many lands in the world. But nothing in any country touches us more profoundly, and nothing is more freighted with meaning for our own destiny than the revolution of the Negro American.

In far too many ways American Negroes have been another nation; deprived of freedom, crippled by hatred, the doors of opportunity closed to hope.

In our time change has come to this nation, too. The American Negro, acting with impressive restraint, has peacefully protested and marched, entered the courtrooms and the seats of government, demanding a justice that has long been denied. The voice of the Negro was the call to action. But it is a tribute to America that, once aroused, the courts and the Congress, the President and most of the people, have been the allies of progress.

Thus we have seen the high court of the country declare that discrimination based on race was repugnant to the Constitution, and therefore void. We have seen in 1957, and 1960, and again in 1964, the first civil rights legislation in this nation in almost an entire century.

As majority leader of the United States Senate, I helped to guide two of these bills through the Senate. And, as your President, I was proud to sign the third. And now very soon we will have the fourth—a new law guaranteeing every American the right to vote.

No act of my entire administration will give me greater satisfaction than the day when my signature makes this bill, too, the law of this land.[3]

The voting rights bill will be the latest, and among the most important, in a long series of victories. But this victory—as Winston Churchill said of another triumph for freedom—"is not the end. It is not even the beginning of the end. But it is, perhaps, the end of the beginning."

That beginning is freedom; and the barriers to that freedom are tumbling down. Freedom is the right to share, share fully and equally, in American society—to vote, to hold a job, to enter a public place, to go to school. It is the right to be treated in every part of our national life as a person equal in dignity and promise to all others.

But freedom is not enough. You do not wipe away the scars of centuries by saying: Now you are free to go where you want, and do as you desire, and choose the leaders you please.

You do not take a person who for years has been hobbled by chains and liberate him, bring him up to the starting line of a race and then say, "you are free to compete with all the others," and still justly believe that you have been completely fair.

Thus it is not enough just to open the gates of opportunity. All our citizens must have the ability to walk through those gates.

This is the next and the more profound stage of the battle for civil rights. We seek not just freedom but opportunity. We seek not just legal equity but human ability, not just equality as a right and a theory but equality as a fact and equality as a result.

For the task is to give 20 million Negroes the same chance as every other American to learn and grow, to work and share in society, to develop their abilities—physical, mental and spiritual, and to pursue their individual happiness.

To this end equal opportunity is essential, but not enough, not enough. Men and women of all races are born with the same range of abilities. But ability is not just the product of

[3] On August 6, 1965, the President signed the Voting Rights Act into law.—Eds.

birth. Ability is stretched or stunted by the family that you live with, and the neighborhood you live in—by the school you go to and the poverty or the richness of your surroundings. It is the product of a hundred unseen forces playing upon the little infant, the child, and finally the man.

This graduating class at Howard University is witness to the indomitable determination of the Negro American to win his way in American life.

The number of Negroes in schools of higher learning has almost doubled in fifteen years. The number of nonwhite professional workers has more than doubled in ten years. The median income of Negro college women tonight exceeds that of white college women. And there are also the enormous accomplishments of distinguished individual Negroes—many of them graduates of this institution, and one of them the first lady ambassador in the history of the United States.

These are proud and impressive achievements. But they tell only the story of a growing middle class minority, steadily narrowing the gap between them and their white counterparts.

But for the great majority of Negro Americans—the poor, the unemployed, the uprooted, and the dispossessed—there is a much grimmer story. They still, as we meet here tonight, are another nation. Despite the court orders and the laws, despite the legislative victories and the speeches, for them the walls are rising and the gulf is widening.

Here are some of the facts of this American failure.

Thirty-five years ago the rate of unemployment for Negroes and whites was about the same. Tonight the Negro rate is twice as high.

In 1948 the 8 per cent unemployment rate for Negro teenage boys was actually less than that of whites. By last year that rate had grown to 23 per cent, as against 13 per cent for whites unemployed.

Between 1949 and 1959, the income of Negro men relative to white men declined in every section of this country. From 1952 to 1963 the median income of Negro families compared to white actually dropped from 57 per cent to 53 per cent.

In the years 1955 through 1957, 22 per cent of experienced Negro workers were out of work at some time during the year. In 1961 through 1963 that proportion had soared to 29 per cent.

Since 1947 the number of white families living in poverty has decreased 27 per cent, while the number of poorer nonwhite families decreased only 3 per cent.

The infant mortality of nonwhites in 1940 was 70 per cent greater than whites. Twenty-two years later it was 90 per cent greater.

Moreover, the isolation of Negro from white communities is increasing, rather than decreasing, as Negroes crowd into the central cities and become a city within a city.

Of course Negro Americans as well as white Americans have shared in our rising national abundance. But the harsh fact of the matter is that in the battle for true equality too many—far too many—are losing ground every day.

We are not completely sure why this is. We know the causes are complex and subtle. But we do know the two broad basic reasons. And we do know that we have to act.

First, Negroes are trapped—as many whites are trapped—in inherited, gateless poverty. They lack training and skills. They are shut in, in slums, without decent medical care. Private and public poverty combine to cripple their capacities.

We are trying to attack these evils through our poverty program, through our education program, through our medical care and our other health programs, and a dozen more of the Great Society programs that are aimed at the root causes of this poverty.

We will increase, and we will accelerate, and we will broaden this attack in years to come until this most enduring of foes finally yields to our unyielding will.

But there is a second cause—much more difficult to explain, more deeply grounded, more desperate in its force. It is the devastating heritage of long years of slavery; and a century of oppression, hatred, and injustice.

For Negro poverty is not white poverty. Many of its causes and many of its cures are the same. But there are differences— deep, corrosive, obstinate differences—radiating painful roots into the community, and into the family, and the nature of the individual.

These differences are not racial differences. They are solely and simply the consequence of ancient brutality, past injustice, and present prejudice. They are anguishing to observe. For the Negro they are a constant reminder of oppression. For the white they are a constant reminder of guilt. But they must be faced and they must be dealt with and they must be overcome, if we are ever to reach the time when the only difference between Negroes and whites is the color of their skin.

Nor can we find a complete answer in the experience of other American minorities. They made a valiant and a largely successful effort to emerge from poverty and prejudice.

The Negro, like these others, will have to rely mostly upon his own efforts. But he just cannot do it alone. For they did not have the heritage of centuries to overcome, and they did not have a cultural tradition which had been twisted and battered by endless years of hatred and hopelessness, nor were they excluded—these others—because of race or color—a feeling whose dark intensity is matched by no other prejudice in our society.

Nor can these differences be understood as isolated infirmities. They are a seamless web. They cause each other. They result from each other. They reinforce each other.

Much of the Negro community is buried under a blanket of history and circumstance. It is not a lasting solution to lift just one corner of that blanket. We must stand on all sides and we must raise the entire cover if we are to liberate our fellow citizens.

One of the differences is the increased concentration of Negroes in our cities. More than 73 per cent of all Negroes live in urban areas compared with less than 70 per cent of the whites. Most of these Negroes live in slums. Most of these Negroes live together—a separated people.

Men are shaped by their world. When it is a world of decay, ringed by an invisible wall, when escape is arduous and uncertain, and the saving pressures of a more hopeful society are unknown, it can cripple the youth and it can desolate the men.

There is also the burden that a dark skin can add to the search for a productive place in our society. Unemployment strikes most swiftly and broadly at the Negro, and this burden erodes hope. Blighted hope breeds despair. Despair brings indifferences to the learning which offers a way out. And despair, coupled with indifferences, is often the source of destructive rebellion against the fabric of society.

There is also the lacerating hurt of early collision with white hatred or prejudice, distaste or condescension. Other groups have felt similar intolerance. But success and achievement could wipe it away. They do not change the color of a man's skin. I have seen this uncomprehending pain in the eyes of the little, young Mexican-American schoolchildren that I taught many years ago. But it can be overcome. But, for many, the wounds are always open.

Perhaps most important—its influence radiating to every part of life—is the breakdown of the Negro family structure. For this, most of all, white America must accept responsibility. It flows from centuries of oppression and persecution of the Negro man. It flows from the long years of degradation and discrimination, which have attacked his dignity and assaulted his ability to produce for his family.

This, too, is not pleasant to look upon. But it must be faced by those whose serious intent is to improve the life of all Americans.

Only a minority—less than half—of all Negro children reach the age of 18 having lived all their lives with both of their parents. At this moment, tonight, little less than two-thirds are at home with both of their parents. Probably a majority of all Negro children receive federally-aided public assistance sometime during their childhood.

The family is the cornerstone of our society. More than any other force it shapes the attitude, the hopes, the ambitions, and the values of the child. And when the family collapses it is the children that are usually damaged. When it happens on a massive scale the community itself is crippled.

So, unless we work to strengthen the family, to create conditions under which most parents will stay together—all the rest: schools, and playgrounds, and public assistance, and private concern, will never be enough to cut completely the circle of despair and deprivation.

There is no single easy answer to all of these problems.

Jobs are part of the answer. They bring the income which permits a man to provide for his family.

Decent homes in decent surroundings and a chance to learn —an equal chance to learn—are part of the answer.

Welfare and social programs better designed to hold families together are part of the answer.

Care for the sick is part of the answer.

An understanding heart by all Americans is another big part of the answer.

And to all of these fronts—and a dozen more—I will dedicate the expanding efforts of the Johnson Administration.

But there are other answers that are still to be found. Nor do we fully understand even all of the problems. Therefore, I want to announce tonight that this fall I intend to call a White House conference of scholars, and experts, and outstanding Negro leaders—men of both races—and officials of government at every level.

This White House conference's theme and title will be "To Fulfill These Rights."

Its object will be to help the American Negro fulfill the rights which, after the long time of injustice, he is finally about to secure.

To move beyond opportunity to achievement.

To shatter forever not only the barriers of law and public practice, but the walls which bound the condition of man by the color of his skin.

To dissolve, as best we can, the antique enmities of the heart which diminish the holder, divide the great democracy, and do wrong—great wrong—to the children of God.

And I pledge you tonight that this will be a chief goal of my Administration, and of my program next year, and in the years to come. And I hope, and I pray, and I believe, it will be a part of the program of all America.

For what is justice?

It is to fulfill the fair expectations of man.

Thus, American justice is a very special thing. For, from the first, this has been a land of towering expectations. It was to be a nation where each man could be ruled by the common consent of all—enshrined in law, given life by institutions, guided by men themselves subject to its rule. And all—all of every station and origin—would be touched equally in obligation and in liberty.

Beyond the law lay the land. It was a rich land, glowing with more abundant promise than man had ever seen. Here, unlike any place yet known, all were to share the harvest.

And beyond this was the dignity of man. Each could become whatever his qualities of mind and spirit would permit—to strive, to seek, and, if he could, to find his happiness.

This is American justice. We have pursued it faithfully to the edge of our imperfections, and we have failed to find it for the American Negro.

So, it is the glorious opportunity of this generation to end the one huge wrong of the American nation and, in so doing, to find America for ourselves, with the same immense thrill of discovery which gripped those who first began to realize that here, at last, was a home for freedom.

All it will take is for all of us to understand what this country is and what this country must become.

The Scripture promises: "I shall light a candle of understanding in thine heart, which shall not be put out."

Together, and with millions more, we can light that candle of understanding in the heart of all America.

And, once lit, it will never again go out.

FROM PROTEST TO COALITION POLITICS*

In the two articles that follow, sharply clashing views are aired on the future tactics to be employed by the civil rights movement. The first is by Bayard Rustin, the organizer of the 1963 March on Washington and a close associate of Martin Luther King. Among black people, the contrast between Rustin, who advocates a coalition within the Democratic Party, and the murdered Malcolm X, who rejected it, could scarcely be greater. Malcolm said:

> *If Johnson had been running all by himself, he would not have been acceptable to anyone. The only thing that made him acceptable to the world was that the shrewd capitalists, the shrewd imperialists, knew that the only way people would run toward the fox would be if you showed them a wolf. So they created a ghastly alternative. And it had the whole world—including people who call themselves Marxists—hoping that Johnson would beat Goldwater.*
> *I have to say this: Those who claim to be enemies of the system were on their hands and knees waiting for Johnson to get elected—because he is supposed to be a man of peace. And* at that moment *he had troops invading the Congo and South Vietnam! He even has troops in*

* Reprinted from *Commentary* (February 1965, pp. 25-31), by permission; copyright © 1965 by the American Jewish Committee.

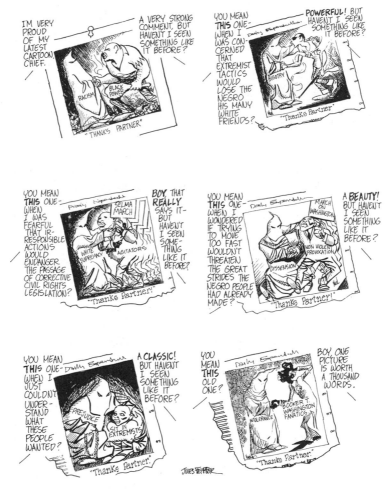

areas where other imperialists have already withdrawn. Peace Corps to Nigeria, mercenaries to the Congo! [1]

◇ ◇ ◇

I

The decade spanned by the 1954 Supreme Court decision on school desegregation and the Civil Rights Act of 1964 will undoubtedly be recorded as the period in which the legal foundations of racism in America were destroyed. To be sure, pockets of resistance remain; but it would be hard to quarrel with the assertion that the elaborate legal structure of segregation and discrimination, particularly in relation to public accommodations, has virtually collapsed. On the other hand, without making light of the human sacrifices involved in the direct-action tactics (sit-ins, freedom rides, and the rest) that were so instrumental to this achievement, we must recognize that in desegregating public accommodations, we affected institutions which are relatively peripheral both to the American socio-economic order and to the fundamental conditions of life of the Negro people. In a highly industrialized, twentieth-century civilization, we hit Jim Crow precisely where it was most anachronistic, dispensable, and vulnerable—in hotels, lunch counters, terminals, libraries, swimming pools, and the like. For in these forms, Jim Crow does impede the flow of commerce in the broadest sense: it is a nuisance in a society on the move (and on the make). Not surprisingly, therefore, it was the most mobility-conscious and relatively liberated groups in the Negro community—lower-middle-class college students—who launched the attack that brought down this imposing but hollow structure.

The term "classical" appears especially apt for this phase of the civil rights movement. But in the few years that have passed since the first flush of sit-ins, several developments have taken place that have complicated matters enormously. One is the shifting focus of the movement in the South, symbolized by Birmingham; another is the spread of the revolution to the North; and the third, common to the other two, is the expansion of the movement's base in the Negro community. To attempt to disentangle these three strands is to do violence to reality. David Danzig's perceptive article, "The Meaning of

[1] *Malcolm X Speaks* (New York, 1965), pp. 217-18.—Eds.

Negro Strategy," [2] correctly saw in the Birmingham events the victory of the concept of collective struggle over individual achievement as the road to Negro freedom. And Birmingham remains the unmatched symbol of grass-roots protest involving all strata of the black community. It was also in this most industrialized of Southern cities that the single-issue demands of the movement's classical stage gave way to the "package deal." No longer were Negroes satisfied with integrating lunch counters. They now sought advances in employment, housing, school integration, police protection, and so forth.

Thus, the movement in the South began to attack areas of discrimination which were not so remote from the Northern experience as were Jim Crow lunch counters. At the same time, the interrelationship of these apparently distinct areas became increasingly evident. What is the value of winning access to public accommodations for those who lack money to use them? The minute the movement faced this question, it was compelled to expand its vision beyond race relations to economic relations, including the role of education in modern society. And what also became clear is that all these interrelated problems, by their very nature, are not soluble by private, voluntary efforts but require government action—or politics. Already Southern demonstrators had recognized that the most effective way to strike at the police brutality they suffered from was by getting rid of the local sheriff—and that meant political action, which in turn meant, and still means, political action within the Democratic party where the only meaningful primary contests in the South are fought.

And so, in Mississippi, thanks largely to the leadership of Bob Moses,[3] a turn toward political action has been taken. More than voter registration is involved here. A conscious bid for *political power* is being made, and in the course of that effort a tactical shift is being effected: direct-action techniques are being subordinated to a strategy calling for the building of community institutions or power bases. Clearly, the implications of this shift reach far beyond Mississippi. What began as a protest movement is being challenged to translate itself into a political movement. Is this the right course? And if it is, can the transformation be accomplished?

[2] *Commentary* (February 1964).
[3] Now called Robert Parris.—Eds.

II

The very decade which has witnessed the decline of legal
Jim Crow has also seen the rise of *de facto* segregation in our
most fundamental socio-economic institutions. More Negroes
are unemployed today than in 1954, and the unemployment
gap between the races is wider. The median income of Negroes
has dropped from 57 per cent to 54 per cent of that of whites. A
higher percentage of Negro workers is now concentrated in
jobs vulnerable to automation than was the case ten years ago.
More Negroes attend *de facto* segregated schools today than
when the Supreme Court handed down its famous decision;
while school integration proceeds at a snail's pace in the South,
the number of Northern schools with an excessive proportion of
minority youth proliferates. And behind this is the continuing
growth of racial slums, spreading over our central cities and
trapping Negro youth in a milieu which, whatever its legal
definition, sows an unimaginable demoralization. Again, legal
niceties aside, a resident of a racial ghetto lives in segregated
housing, and more Negroes fall into this category than ever
before.

These are the facts of life which generate frustration in the
Negro community and challenge the civil rights movement. At
issue, after all, is not *civil rights*, strictly speaking, but social
and economic conditions. Last summer's riots were not race
riots; they were outbursts of class aggression in a society where
class and color definitions are converging disastrously. How
can the (perhaps misnamed) civil rights movement deal with
this problem?

Before trying to answer, let me first insist that the task of the
movement is vastly complicated by the failure of many whites
of good will to understand the nature of our problem. There is
a widespread assumption that the removal of artificial racial
barriers should result in the automatic integration of the Negro
into all aspects of American life. This myth is fostered by facile
analogies with the experience of various ethnic immigrant
groups, particularly the Jews. But the analogies with the Jews
do not hold for three simple but profound reasons. First, Jews
have a long history as a literate people, a resource which has
afforded them opportunities to advance in the academic and

professional worlds, to achieve intellectual status even in the midst of economic hardship, and to evolve sustaining value systems in the context of ghetto life. Negroes, for the greater part of their presence in this country, were forbidden by law to read or write. Second, Jews have a long history of family stability, the importance of which in terms of aspiration and self-image is obvious. The Negro family structure was totally destroyed by slavery and with it the possibility of cultural transmission (the right of Negroes to marry and rear children is barely a century old). Third, Jews are white and have the *option* of relinquishing their cultural-religious identity, intermarrying, passing, etc. Negroes, or at least the overwhelming majority of them, do not have this option. There is also a fourth, vulgar reason. If the Jewish and Negro communities are not comparable in terms of education, family structure, and color, it is also true that their respective economic roles bear little resemblance.

This matter of economic role brings us to the greater problem—the fact that we are moving into an era in which the natural functioning of the market does not by itself ensure every man with will and ambition a place in the productive process. The immigrant who came to this country during the late nineteenth and early twentieth centuries entered a society which was expanding territorially and/or economically. It was then possible to start at the bottom, as an unskilled or semi-skilled worker, and move up the ladder, acquiring new skills along the way. Especially was this true when industrial unionism was burgeoning, giving new dignity and higher wages to organized workers. Today the situation has changed. We are not expanding territorially, the western frontier is settled, labor organizing has leveled off, our rate of economic growth has been stagnant for a decade. And we are in the midst of a technological revolution which is altering the fundamental structure of the labor force, destroying unskilled and semi-skilled jobs—jobs in which Negroes are disproportionately concentrated.

Whatever the pace of this technological revolution may be, the *direction* is clear: the lower rungs of the economic ladder are being lopped off. This means that an individual will no longer be able to start at the bottom and work his way up; he will have to start in the middle or on top, and hold on tight. It will not even be enough to have certain specific skills, for many skilled jobs are also vulnerable to automation. A broad educational background, permitting vocational adaptability and flexibility, seems more imperative than ever. We live in a society where, as Secretary of Labor Willard Wirtz puts it, machines have the equivalent of a high school diploma. Yet the average educational attainment of American Negroes is 8.2 years.

Negroes, of course, are not the only people being affected by these developments. It is reported that there are now 50 per cent fewer unskilled and semi-skilled jobs than there are high school dropouts. Almost one-third of the 26 million young people entering the labor market in the 1960s will be dropouts. But the percentage of Negro dropouts nationally is 57 per cent, and in New York City, among Negroes 25 years of age or over, it is 68 per cent. They are without a future.

To what extent can the kind of self-help campaign recently prescribed by Eric Hoffer in the *New York Times Magazine* cope with such a situation? I would advise those who think that self-help is the answer to familiarize themselves with the long history of such efforts in the Negro community, and to consider why so many foundered on the shoals of ghetto life. It goes without saying that any effort to combat demoralization and apathy is desirable, but we must understand that demoralization in the Negro community is largely a common-sense response to an objective reality. Negro youths have no need of statistics to perceive, fairly accurately, what their odds are in American society. Indeed, from the point of view of motivation, some of the healthiest Negro youngsters I know are juvenile delinquents: vigorously pursuing the American Dream of material acquisition and status, yet finding the conventional means of attaining it blocked off, they do not yield to defeatism but resort to illegal (and often ingenious) methods. They are not alien to American culture. They are, in Gunnar Myrdal's phrase, "exaggerated Americans." To want a Cadillac is not un-American; to push a cart in the garment center is. If Negroes are to be persuaded that the conventional path (school, work, etc.) is superior, we had better provide evidence which is now sorely lacking. It is a double cruelty to harangue Negro youth about education and training when we do not know what jobs will be available for them. When a Negro youth can reasonably foresee a future free of slums, when the prospect of gainful employment is realistic, we will see motivation and self-help in abundant enough quantities.

Meanwhile, there is an ironic similarity between the self-help advocated by many liberals and the doctrines of the Black Muslims. Professional sociologists, psychiatrists, and social workers have expressed amazement at the Muslims' success in transforming prostitutes and dope addicts into respectable citizens. But every prostitute the Muslims convert to a model of Calvinist virtue is replaced by the ghetto with two more. Dedicated as they are to maintenance of the ghetto, the Muslims are powerless to affect substantial moral reform. So too with every other group or program which is not aimed at the destruction of slums, their causes and effects. Self-help efforts, directly or indirectly, must be geared to mobilizing people into power units capable of effecting social change. That is, their goal must be genuine self-help, not merely self-improvement. Obviously, where self-improvement activities succeed in imparting to their participants a feeling of some control over their environment, those involved may find their appetites for change whetted; they may move into the political arena.

III

Let me sum up what I have thus far been trying to say: the civil rights movement is evolving from a protest movement into a full-fledged *social movement*—an evolution calling its very name into question. It is now concerned not merely with removing the barriers to full *opportunity* but with achieving the fact of *equality*. From sit-ins and freedom rides we have gone into rent strikes, boycotts, community organization, and political action. As a consequence of this natural evolution, the Negro today finds himself stymied by obstacles of far greater magnitude than the legal barriers he was attacking before: automation, urban decay, *de facto* school segregation. These are problems which, while conditioned by Jim Crow, do not vanish upon its demise. They are more deeply rooted in our socio-economic order; they are the result of the total society's failure to meet not only the Negro's needs, but human needs generally.

These propositions have won increasing recognition and acceptance, but with a curious twist. They have formed the common premise of two apparently contradictory lines of thought which simultaneously nourish and antagonize each other. On the one hand, there is the reasoning of the *New York Times* moderate who says that the problems are so enormous and complicated that Negro militancy is a futile irritation, and that the need is for "intelligent moderation." Thus, during the first New York school boycott, the *Times* editorialized that Negro demands, while abstractly just, would necessitate massive reforms, the funds for which could not realistically be anticipated; therefore the just demands were also foolish demands and would only antagonize white people. Moderates of this stripe are often correct in perceiving the difficulty or impossibility of racial progress in the context of present social and economic policies. But they accept the context as fixed. They ignore (or perhaps see all too well) the potentialities inherent in linking Negro demands to broader pressures for radical revision of existing policies. They apparently see nothing strange in the fact that in the last twenty-five years we have spent nearly a trillion dollars fighting or preparing for wars, yet throw up our hands before the need for overhauling our schools, clearing the slums, and really abolishing poverty. My quarrel with these moderates is that they do not even envision radical changes; their admonitions of moderation are, for all practical purposes, admonitions to the Negro to adjust to the status quo, and are therefore immoral.

The more effectively the moderates argue their case, the more they convince Negroes that American society will not or cannot be reorganized for full racial equality. Michael Harrington has said that a successful war on poverty might well require the expenditure of $100 billion. Where, the Negro wonders, are the forces now in motion to compel such a commitment? If the voices of the moderates were raised in an insistence upon a reallocation of national resources at levels that could not be confused with tokenism (that is, if the moderates stopped being moderates), Negroes would have greater grounds for hope. Meanwhile, the Negro movement cannot escape a sense of isolation.

It is precisely this sense of isolation that gives rise to the second line of thought I want to examine—the tendency within the civil rights movement which, despite its militancy, pursues what I call a "no-win" policy. Sharing with many moderates a recognition of the magnitude of the obstacles to freedom, spokesmen for this tendency survey the American scene and find no forces prepared to move toward radical solutions. From this they conclude that the only viable strategy is shock; above all, the hypocrisy of white liberals must be exposed. These spokesmen are often described as the radicals of the movement, but they are really its moralists. They seek to change white hearts—by traumatizing them. Frequently abetted by white self-flagellants, they may gleefully applaud (though not really agreeing with) Malcolm X because, while they admit he has no program, they think he can frighten white people into doing the right thing. To believe this, of course, you must be convinced, even if unconsciously, that at the core of the white man's heart lies a buried affection for Negroes—a proposition one may be permitted to doubt. But in any case, hearts are not relevant to the issue; neither racial affinities nor racial hostilities are rooted there. It is institutions—social, political, and economic institutions—which are the ultimate molders of collective sentiments. Let these institutions be reconstructed *today*, and let the ineluctable gradualism of history govern the formation of a new psychology.

My quarrel with the "no-win" tendency in the civil rights movement (and the reason I have so designated it) parallels my quarrel with the moderates outside the movement. As the latter lack the vision or will for fundamental change, the former lack a realistic strategy for achieving it. For such a strategy they substitute militancy. But militancy is a matter of posture and volume and not of effect.

I believe that the Negro's struggle for equality in America is essentially revolutionary. While most Negroes—in their hearts —unquestionably seek only to enjoy the fruits of American society as it now exists, their quest cannot *objectively* be satisfied within the framework of existing political and economic relations. The young Negro who would demonstrate his way into the labor market may be motivated by a thoroughly bourgeois ambition and thoroughly "capitalist" considerations, but he will end up having to favor a great expansion of the public sector of the economy. At any rate, that is the position the movement will be forced to take as it looks at the number of jobs being generated by the private economy, and if it is to remain true to the masses of Negroes.

The revolutionary character of the Negro's struggle is manifest in the fact that this struggle may have done more to democratize life for whites than for Negroes. Clearly, it was the

sit-in movement of young Southern Negroes which, as it galva-
nized white students, banished the ugliest features of McCarthyism from the American campus and resurrected political
debate. It was not until Negroes assaulted *de facto* school segregation in the urban centers that the issue of quality education
for *all* children stirred into motion. Finally, it seems reasonably
clear that the civil rights movement, directly and through the
resurgence of social conscience it kindled, did more to initiate
the war on poverty than any other single force.

It will be—it has been—argued that these by-products of the
Negro struggle are not revolutionary. But the term revolutionary, as I am using it, does not connote violence; it refers to the
qualitative transformation of fundamental institutions, more or
less rapidly, to the point where the social and economic structure which they comprised can no longer be said to be the
same. The Negro struggle has hardly run its course; and it will
not stop moving until it has been utterly defeated or won substantial equality. But I fail to see how the movement can be
victorious in the absence of radical programs for full employment, abolition of slums, the reconstruction of our educational
system, new definitions of work and leisure. Adding up the cost
of such programs, we can only conclude that we are talking
about a refashioning of our political economy. It has been estimated, for example, that the price of replacing New York City's
slums with public housing would be $17 billion. Again, a multi-
billion dollar federal public-works program, dwarfing the currently proposed $2 billion program, is required to reabsorb un-
skilled and semi-skilled workers into the labor market—and
this must be done if Negro workers in these categories are to be
employed. "Preferential treatment" cannot help them.

I am not trying here to delineate a total program, only to suggest the scope of economic reforms which are most immediately related to the plight of the Negro community. One could
speculate on their political implications—whether, for example,
they do not indicate the obsolescence of state government and
the superiority of regional structures as viable units of planning.
Such speculations aside, it is clear that Negro needs cannot be
satisfied unless we go beyond what has so far been placed on
the agenda. How are these radical objectives to be achieved?
The answer is simple, deceptively so: *through political power.*

There is a strong moralistic strain in the civil rights movement which would remind us that power corrupts, forgetting that the absence of power also corrupts. But this is not the view I want to debate here, for it is waning. Our problem is posed by those who accept the need for political power but do not understand the nature of the object and therefore lack sound strategies for achieving it; they tend to confuse political institutions with lunch counters.

A handful of Negroes, acting alone, could integrate a lunch counter by strategically locating their bodies so as *directly* to interrupt the operation of the proprietor's will; their numbers were relatively unimportant. In politics, however, such a confrontation is difficult because the interests involved are merely *represented.* In the execution of a political decision a direct confrontation may ensue (as when federal marshals escorted James Meredith into the University of Mississippi—to turn from an example of nonviolent coercion to one of force backed up with the threat of violence). But in arriving at a political decision, numbers and organizations are crucial, especially for the economically disenfranchised. (Needless to say, I am assuming that the forms of political democracy exist in America, however imperfectly, that they are valued, and that elitist or putschist conceptions of exercising power are beyond the pale of discussion for the civil rights movement.)

Neither that movement nor the country's twenty million black people can win political power alone. We need allies. The future of the Negro struggle depends on whether the contradictions of this society can be resolved by a coalition of progressive forces which becomes the *effective* political majority in the United States. I speak of the coalition which staged the March on Washington, passed the Civil Rights Act, and laid the basis for the Johnson landslide—Negroes, trade unionists, liberals, and religious groups.

There are those who argue that a coalition strategy would force the Negro to surrender his political independence to white liberals, that he would be neutralized, deprived of his cutting edge, absorbed into the Establishment. Some who take this position urged last year that votes be withheld from the Johnson-Humphrey ticket as a demonstration of the Negro's political power. Curiously enough, these people who sought to demonstrate power through the non-exercise of it, also point to the Negro "swing vote" in crucial urban areas as the source of the Negro's independent political power. But here they are closer to being right: the urban Negro vote will grow in importance in the coming years. If there is anything positive in the spread of the ghetto, it is the potential political power base thus created, and to realize this potential is one of the most challenging and urgent tasks before the civil rights movement. If the movement can wrest leadership of the ghetto vote from the machines, it will have acquired an organized constituency such as other major groups in our society now have.

But we must also remember that the effectiveness of a swing vote depends solely on "other" votes. It derives its power from them. In that sense, it can never be "independent," but must opt for one candidate or the other, even if by default. Thus coalitions are inescapable, however tentative they may be. And this is the case in all but those few situations in which Negroes running on an independent ticket might conceivably win. "Independence," in other words, is not a value in itself. The issue is which coalition to join and how to make it responsive to your program. Necessarily there will be compromise. But the difference between expediency and morality in politics is the difference between selling out a principle and making smaller concessions to win larger ones. The leader who shrinks from this task reveals not his purity but his lack of political sense.

The task of molding a political movement out of the March on Washington coalition is not simple, but no alternatives have been advanced. We need to choose our allies on the basis of common political objectives. It has become fashionable in some no-win Negro circles to decry the white liberal as the main enemy (his hypocrisy is what sustains racism); by virtue of this reverse recitation of the reactionary's litany (liberalism leads to socialism, which leads to Communism) the Negro is left in majestic isolation, except for a tiny band of fervent white initiates. But the objective fact is that *Eastland and Goldwater* are the main enemies—they and the opponents of civil rights, of the war on poverty, of medicare, of social security, of federal aid to education, of unions, and so forth. The labor movement, despite its obvious faults, has been the largest single organized force in this country pushing for progressive social legislation. And where the Negro–labor–liberal axis is weak, as in the farm belt, it was the religious groups that were most influential in rallying support for the Civil Rights Bill.

The durability of the coalition was interestingly tested during the election. I do not believe that the Johnson landslide proved the "white backlash" to be a myth. It proved, rather, that economic interests are more fundamental than prejudice: the backlashers decided that loss of Social Security was, after all, too high a price to pay for a slap at the Negro. This lesson was a valuable first step in re-educating such people, and it must be kept alive, for the civil rights movement will be advanced only to the degree that social and economic welfare gets to be inextricably entangled with civil rights.

The 1964 elections marked a turning point in American politics. The Democratic landslide was not merely the result of a negative reaction to Goldwaterism; it was also the expression of a majority liberal consensus. The near unanimity with which Negro voters joined in that expression was, I am convinced, a vindication of the July 25th statement by Negro leaders calling for a strategic turn toward political action and a temporary curtailment of mass demonstrations. Despite the controversy surrounding the statement, the instinctive response it met with in the community is suggested by the fact that demonstrations were down 75 per cent as compared with the same period in 1963. But should so high a percentage of Negro voters have gone to Johnson, or should they have held back to narrow his margin of victory and thus give greater visibility to our swing vote? How has our loyalty changed things? Certainly the Negro vote had higher visibility in 1960, when a switch of only 7 per cent from the Republican column of 1956 elected President Kennedy. But the slimness of Kennedy's victory—of his "mandate"—dictated a go-slow approach on civil rights, at least until the Birmingham upheaval.

Although Johnson's popular majority was so large that he could have won without such overwhelming Negro support, that support was important from several angles. Beyond adding to Johnson's total national margin, it was specifically responsible for his victories in Virginia, Florida, Tennessee, and Arkansas. Goldwater took only those states where fewer than 45 per cent of eligible Negroes were registered. That Johnson would have won those states had Negro voting rights been enforced is a lesson not likely to be lost on a man who would have been happy with a unanimous electoral college. In any case, the 1.6 million Southern Negroes who voted have had a shattering impact on the Southern political party structure, as illustrated in the changed composition of the Southern congressional delegation. The "backlash" gave the Republicans five House seats in Alabama, one in Georgia, and one in Mississippi. But on the Democratic side, seven segregationists were defeated while all nine Southerners who voted for the Civil Rights Act were re-elected. It may be premature to predict a Southern Democratic party of Negroes and white moderates and a Republican Party of refugee racists and economic conservatives, but there certainly is a strong tendency toward such a realignment; and an additional 3.6 million Negroes of voting age in the eleven Southern states are still to be heard from. Even the *tendency* toward disintegration of the Democratic party's racist wing defines a new context for presidential and liberal strategy in the congressional battles ahead. Thus the Negro vote (North as well as South), while not *decisive* in the presidential race, was enormously effective. It was a dramatic element of a historic mandate which contains vast possibilities and dangers that will fundamentally affect the future course of the civil rights movement.

The liberal congressional sweep raises hope for an assault on the seniority system, Rule Twenty-two, and other citadels of Dixiecrat–Republican power. The overwhelming of this conservative coalition should also mean progress on much bottlenecked legislation of profound interest to the movement (e.g., bills by Senators Clark and Nelson on planning, manpower, and employment). Moreover, the irrelevance of the South to Johnson's victory gives the President more freedom to act than his predecessor had and more leverage to the movement to pressure for executive action in Mississippi and other racist strongholds.

None of this *guarantees* vigorous executive or legislative action, for the other side of the Johnson landslide is that it has a Gaullist quality. Goldwater's capture of the Republican party forced into the Democratic camp many disparate elements which do not belong there, Big Business being the major example.[4] Johnson, who wants to be President "of all people," may try to keep his new coalition together by sticking close to the political center. But if he decides to do this, it is unlikely that even his political genius will be able to hold together a coali-

[4] Compare reading 11, above.—Eds.

tion so inherently unstable and rife with contradictions. It must come apart. Should it do so while Johnson is pursuing a centrist course, then the mandate will have been wastefully dissipated. However, if the mandate is seized upon to set fundamental changes in motion, then the basis can be laid for a new mandate, a new coalition including hitherto inert and dispossessed strata of the population.

Here is where the cutting edge of the civil rights movement can be applied. We must see to it that the reorganization of the "consensus party" proceeds along lines which will make it an effective vehicle for social reconstruction, a role it cannot play so long as it furnishes Southern racism with its national political power. (One of Barry Goldwater's few attractive ideas was that the Dixiecrats belong with him in the same party.) And nowhere has the civil rights movement's political cutting edge been more magnificently demonstrated than at Atlantic City, where the Mississippi Freedom Democratic Party not only secured recognition as a bona fide component of the national party, but in the process routed the representatives of the most rabid racists—the white Mississippi and Alabama delegations. While I still believe that the FDP made a tactical error in spurning the compromise, there is no question that they launched a political revolution whose logic is the displacement of Dixiecrat power. They launched that revolution within a major political institution and as part of a coalitional effort.

The role of the civil rights movement in the reorganization of American political life is programmatic as well as strategic. We are challenged now to broaden our social vision, to develop functional programs with concrete objectives. We need to propose alternatives to technological unemployment, urban decay, and the rest. We need to be calling for public works and training, for national economic planning, for federal aid to education, for attractive public housing—all this on a sufficiently massive scale to make a difference. We need to protest the notion that our integration into American life, so long delayed, must now proceed in an atmosphere of competitive scarcity instead of in the security of abundance which technology makes possible. We cannot claim to have answers to all the complex problems of modern society. That is too much to ask of a movement still battling barbarism in Mississippi. But we can agitate the right questions by probing at the contradictions which still stand in the way of the "Great Society." The questions having been asked, motion must begin in the larger society, for there is a limit to what Negroes can do alone.

FROM PROTEST TO BLACK POWER:
THE FAILURE OF COALITION POLITICS

The previous reading, by Bayard Rustin, attempted to persuade activists in the civil rights movement to "see to it that the reorganization of the 'consensus party' proceeds along lines which will make it an effective vehicle for social reconstruction. . . ." Underlying Rustin's formulation is a series of assumptions concerning the nature of American society that are widely shared. On the other hand, these assumptions have been challenged by spokesmen for SNCC and CORE, Stokely Carmichael and Floyd McKissick, respectively. In this volume, Ronald Radosh gives a careful critique of the Rustin approach and finds that it "has actually directed one segment of the movement into co-operation with the dominant system of oppression. . . ."

Dr. Radosh is Assistant Professor of History at Queensborough Community College of the City University of New York and an associate editor of *Studies on the Left*. He is the author of "John Spargo and Wilson's Russian Policy, 1920" (*Journal of American History*, LII [December, 1965], pp. 548-65), as well as other articles and reviews. His book, *Teach-ins USA* (New York, 1967), was co-edited with Louis Menashe. The essay printed below was written specifically for inclusion in the present volume.

◇ ◇ ◇

The strategy outlined by Bayard Rustin[1] has succeeded in doing what its author predicted—it has opened him to the

[1] See reading 21.

charge of trying to deprive the civil rights movement of its cutting edge by becoming absorbed in the Establishment. Beneath Rustin's seemingly radical rhetoric is revealed an outlook that is indistinguishable from that of the corporate liberals who rule America.

Rustin begins with the valid observation that the broad range of problems that confront the Negro cannot be solved solely by a call for civil rights, nor by the Negro alone. He is satisfied that the existing system of power contains all necessary avenues for the realizations of the movement's ideals. Rustin would have the movement believe that coalition inside the Democratic Party is more desirable than independent action outside it. Rustin explains that President Johnson is pursuing a "centrist course," trying to hold both the Negro and big business as part of his consensus. He therefore urges that the electoral mandate received by the President be seized by the mythical coalition to set fundamental changes in motion, so that reorganization of the consensus party can take place to make it a vehicle for social reconstruction. But if the Democrats are assured of the unequivocal support of the Negro population, those in the center will not have to respond to the desires of those on the left. Having been guaranteed the backing of the Negro vote, the center will have to cater only to those on the right—which the experience of the past two years has shown to be the exact course taken by President Johnson!

Unlike Rustin, the radical black leadership does not seek a position within the Democratic Party as the proper forum for the Negro dispossessed. It is unfair of Rustin to accuse these leaders of substituting a posture of militancy for a strategy. The black militants, centered in the rural South and the big city all-black ghettos, advance their concept of "black power" as a result of their understanding that most of the protest groups that whites see as allies of the Negro are so integrated into the existing system that they function as enemies of social change. The black radicals maintain that the goals of the Negro cannot be realized within American society as it now exists—that a society that proposes to "help" poor Negroes by drafting 40,000 of them into the army where they will fight Vietnamese revolutionaries, is no longer capable of creating worthwhile avenues of liberation for the Negro. Logic, they assert, dictates that the Negro rebellion must evolve to a revolutionary position.

Their view, as James Boggs explains, is that centers of black political power should be developed from which Negroes will use their strength not to "put white men in office, to whom they can go and ask for things, but rather to develop their own power" [2] to determine such things. The movement toward black political power differs sharply from Rustin's tactical path, though the proclaimed goal of both is to achieve a fundamental reconstruction of the entire society. Actually, the "realignment" Rustin proposes can only occur if the Negro uses his power to develop an independent base from which he can force real alternatives on the major parties—particularly by threatening to withdraw an automatic endorsement usually given to the Democratic Party. An independent and politically alert constituency that stated its own desires and grievances would be effective precisely because it is not tied to the mechanism of the Establishment.

The presidential consensus, Rustin believes, is made up of contradictory elements and should be ruptured. Rustin's approach leads in a direction quite the opposite of that which he says is desirable. The depths to which the movement would descend if it followed Rustin's advice is illustrated by the lesson of the Atlantic City Democratic Convention of 1964. Supposedly the Freedom Democratic Party was organized in order to break the Southern Democrats' stranglehold on the party, so that it would then become an organ of progress responsive to "coalition" forces. The Administration did not support the FDP challenge. Rustin's desire to effect a compromise meant that he was asking the FDP to give up its very reason for existence— since the Freedom Party intended from the beginning to cause a walkout of white Southern Democrats and thus bring about a truer representation of Mississippi Democrats at the Convention. As the FDP explained:

The compromise was an effort by the Administration, led by President Johnson, to prevent a floor fight on the issue at the convention. The compromise was not designed to deal with the issues raised by the FDP in challenging the regular delegation. The FDP delegation came to Atlantic City to raise the issue of racism, not simply to demand recognition. It could

[2] James Boggs, "Black Political Power," *Monthly Review*, IV (March, 1963), p. 639.

*not accept a token decision which had as its goal the avoidance
of the question of racism.*[3]

As SNCC Chairman Stokely Carmichael has pointed out, the
FDP came pledged to support the Democratic platform and
the Democrats' chosen candidates. The white Mississippi delegation came supporting Goldwater, and pledging to continue
oppression of Mississippi Negroes. And yet the Administration
told the FDP it would have "to seat the white guys," but would
allow "two of you to go with them." As Carmichael indicated,
the FDP members "didn't want any part of that."

Yet Bayard Rustin was asking the FDP to accept precisely
such an unacceptable alternative. Rustin recoiled lest the FDP
policy lead to the very result the civil rights movement was
trying to achieve. Rustin ended up joining Walter Reuther and
Joseph Rauh in urging a "back of the bus" settlement. Accommodation to liberalism led to uncritical support of traditional
Democratic Party politics, and also to the disavowal of Rustin's
own concept of realignment. The Rustin fiasco at Atlantic City
was the first bit of evidence that his path meant subordination
of the movement to the political interests of the liberal Establishment.

Another pre-election example of the Rustin strategy was the
call by a former CORE official, Norman Hill, for a temporary
moratorium on all demonstrations by the movement, on the
ground that the "labor–liberal–Negro coalition" would be
harmed since demonstrations would antagonize whites and
send them into the Goldwater camp. Hill favored only voter
registration rallies, marches to the polls, and activity on behalf
of Johnson's campaign. The result was the spectacle of "Negro
leaders" calling for the temporary dissolution of the rights
movement itself—an effect that even the victory of Barry Goldwater would not have achieved! It is true that the movement
needs a political and economic program, and that concentration on demonstrations alone is a grave weakness. What is
needed is the creation of a political constituency in the black
community that does not hesitate to raise demands of a radical
nature, and that does not operate within the framework of the
corporation-dominated liberal consensus. The alternatives proposed by Rustin and Hill would not advance such a solution—

[3] Quoted in *Freedom North*, I:1 (1965).

but would make all activity subordinate to the development of a broad coalition. Any demonstrations are stopped out of fear that a backlash will develop and harm the growth of a coalition. One can only wonder at the worth of a coalition whose members hesitate to join when the Negro "partners" demand their rights!

Rustin's desire for a coalition politics dovetails exactly with the Administration's plan for keeping the Negro movement tied to the corporate system. An important but neglected news story in the August 10, 1965, *New York Times*[4] revealed the Administration's plans for revamping of the Democratic Party in Mississippi—plans necessitated by fears of the Mississippi Negroes' response to the campaign efforts of the Freedom Democratic Party. In order to head off the threat to the Democratic Party presented by independent political action by Mississippi Negroes, the Administration gave "unmistakable encouragement" to the Mississippi Democratic Conference, organized on July 18 of 1965 by leaders of organized labor, the NAACP and a group of white moderates including Hodding Carter III, Claude Ramsay, president of the Mississippi Labor Council, Aaron Henry and Charles Evers of the NAACP, and Robert Oswald, a lawyer who heads the Jackson County Democratic executive committee and who is chairman of the conference.

The hope is that after Negro registration takes place, possibly in time for the 1968 election, the new moderate party would have enough votes committed to outvote the old conservative Mississippi Party. The old Democrats had all announced their decision to support Goldwater before the 1964 election— hence the talk of rebuilding the Democratic Party around the conference group. One aim of the new moderate party, the *Times* reported, is to "squeeze out the Freedom Democratic Party," because of a "growing fear among Democratic loyalists" that the "radical group might end up with national Democratic Party credentials"—a step that the Administration does not desire. Because the Democratic convention had declared that future Mississippi delegations had to be integrated, the Democratic Conference was formed to prevent national party recognition going by default to the Freedom Party, and FDP

[4] "Democrats Seek Mississippi Peace," *New York Times* (August 10, 1965), p. 14.

leaders were purposefully kept out of the conference's organizational meeting.

Most interesting about the Democratic Conference and its liberal–labor–Negro coalition gambit, is that the proposed coalition includes none other than the most powerful Southern racist official, Senator James Eastland of Mississippi. The manager for Johnson's presidential campaign in Mississippi was Douglas Wynn, a Lake Tindall lawyer who is also a close friend of Senator Eastland. Wynn, the story explained, "is known to feel that any loyalist organization should include the Senator and his friends." While the suggestion might "sound preposterous in the North," the *Times* writes, "where Senator Eastland is known only as a diehard segregationist . . . it sounds less so in Mississippi," since the Senator "is a power in his home state and he is one of the few friends President Johnson has there." As with all coalitions, once the assumption is made of the need to defeat the great Goldwater threat on the right, a diehard of a year ago becomes depicted as a moderate, and the prospectus is announced of "Senator Eastland in the same organization with the state president of the N.A.A.C.P." The problem is that while most of the Democratic Conference leaders did not desire his entrance, without Eastland's participation the conference would "risk losing the favor of President Johnson." Again: in practice, acceptance of coalition leads to strengthening of the consensus and a shift to the Right—evidenced by the Administration's naming of racist judges to sit in federal benches in Mississippi, and the pronounced failure to use the federal registrars provided for in the 1964 Civil Rights Act in sufficient numbers to effect a difference.

When it comes to economics, Rustin again uses faulty arguments. He contends that a Negro cannot be given preference over a white if no job exists for either of them; a call for hiring more Negroes is based on the illusion that Negroes can make progress in a declining economy. The fact is, however, that while the unemployment rate declined for the general population in the past few years, it rose substantially for Negroes. Moreover, demonstrations demanding that Negroes be hired in proportion to their number in the population have often succeeded. Under Rustin's theory, no victories would be won because a fight would never be waged. Rustin actually implies that Negroes should cease demands for an end to employment discrimination until a full-employment economy exists. The irony is that war production has sustained the economy and led to employment for whites—while unskilled black laborers find their employment as cannon fodder in the infantry.

Most ironic is the development of what Bayard Rustin has opposed for years—a new Socialist–Communist informal united front. Rustin's theoretical approach is precisely that offered by the Communist Party from the 1940s through the '60s. The Communists had become so absorbed in the New Deal that they opposed all militant action for civil rights—a tactic persistently criticized by Rustin's colleagues in the Socialist Party. The Communist Party had opposed A. Philip Randolph's wartime "March on Washington" in 1941 because they argued that the war against fascism necessitated halting the struggle for Negro rights at home. Raising this issue, the party believed, endangered unity around the Roosevelt Administration and might lead to lack of unity with the Negro's "natural allies" who were fighting fascism.

Today the same fallacious reasoning is used by Rustin—who talks of the need to unite with liberals, and who opposes activity independent of the Establishment on the grounds that it would result in loss of allies and lead to success of a rightist movement. Unless Rustin is willing to say that his former critique of the Communists was incorrect and that Randolph's militant wartime policy was also wrong, he has no basis for gaining adherents in his present campaign to curb independent action, until whites in the "coalition" accept their Negro "allies."

The final test by which one can evaluate the cogency of Rustin's approach is by analyzing the stance of the Johnson Administration vis-à-vis civil rights and the Negro in 1965 and 1966. Nineteen sixty-five saw the highly praised March on Selma, Alabama, in which leaders of organized labor, church dignitaries, and white liberals joined the entire spectrum of Negro leadership in marching on the Alabama capital and demanding the guarantee of civil rights in that state. Called as a response to the massive brutality of Alabama troopers toward Negro demonstrators, the march was held against a background of serious tension between Martin Luther King and the young Negro radicals in SNCC. Many interpreted the march as evidence that King and the Southern Christian Leadership Conference were stepping in after months of careful and sustained labor by

SNCC—a group that was emphasizing independent politics opposed by both the Administration and King.

Selma did lead to new rights legislation in Congress, and to the famous Johnson speech at Howard University[5]—in which the President sought to co-opt the rights movement by praising the Negro leadership for taking to the streets and pointing out to the entire country what deficiencies had to be rectified. Truly, it seemed to be a victory for the Rustin analysis—the President was sounding like a leader of the movement.

But by 1966, the true nature of the presidential rights campaign was sorely exposed. The war in Vietnam was steadily emerging as the key issue in the nation. The younger Negro militants began to voice their concern that this war was a classic case of a fight being fought by the very black dispossessed who had no democracy in their own homeland. Despite the Johnson rhetoric at Howard, high unemployment among Negroes continued—and from Harlem in 1964 to Watts in 1965 and Omaha and Philadelphia and Chicago in 1966, black ghettos throughout America erupted in mass violence—and the desperation and alienation of the Negro masses was symbolized in the highly publicized phrase, "Burn, baby, burn."

Two different responses emerged in the Negro community. One was the new approach taken by SNCC—and its decision to build the all-Negro Lowndes County Freedom Organization (commonly misnamed the Black Panther Party) in Alabama as a base for Negro power in the South. White liberals expressed immediate dissatisfaction with this course, attacking SNCC for turning to "black racism" and anti-white black nationalism. The reality was that SNCC realized that in an area such as Lowndes County, Alabama, where Negroes composed 80 per cent of the population, any entrance into the Democratic Party would have meant giving support to the one political organization totally responsible for the oppression of Negroes. They realized that if they organized on a local, county basis, Negroes elected to the office of tax assessor, for example, would be able to tax equitably and use funds to build roads and schools to serve the otherwise-neglected Negro community. It would mean, as Stokely Carmichael explained, proper representation for the Negro and sharing of control. SNCC understood "black power" to be a means of forming power bases from which Ne-

[5] Reprinted in this volume, reading 20.—Eds.

groes could make changes in their daily lives on a local level and then attempt to change nationwide patterns of oppression by negotiation from a position of strength.

As for coalitions, SNCC argued that no political alliances with the white community were feasible until the Negro had his own, independent sources of strength, and *until whites were organized in groups with which Negroes could form coalitions.* SNCC is not opposed to working with whites in a coalition for radical social change. Their point is that no such coalition can now exist since there are no parallel radical white groups with which to join forces—and that the Negro will continue to be viewed as a junior partner until he asserts his own independent strength.

The other response was that of Bayard Rustin, the national leadership of the N.A.A.C.P., and the Administration. Their campaign for civil rights culminated in the White House Conference on Civil Rights, prepared one year in advance and finally held in the first week of June 1966. Boycotted by SNCC, on the grounds that an Administration that was obliterating human rights in Vietnam could not further them within the United States, and attacked internally by the leaders of CORE, the conference was supported only by the Administration, the N.A.A.C.P. and the Urban League, and professional social workers. As John Herbers pointed out in the *New York Times* on June 4, the conference was "President Johnson's show all the way." The chairman was Ben W. Heineman, head of the Chicago and Northwestern Railway, and he led the careful screening of delegates "to keep out potential troublemakers."

The announced purpose was to gain a large, nationwide constituency behind legislative proposals that would emerge from the conference, and be submitted to Congress.[6] But the report that came from the conference fell far short of meeting the needs of the black community. Police relations in the ghetto, for example, received conventional treatment, calling merely for federal assistance in training, hiring, and setting standards for policemen.

Martin Luther King, who had been close to the Administra-

[6] Two excellent appraisals of the conference and its failure are: Andrew Kopkind, "No Fire This Time," *New Republic* (June 18, 1966), pp. 15-16; and Robert G. Sherrill, "Bubble of Unreality," *The Nation* (June 2, 1966), pp. 734-37. These reports have been used as a basis for this discussion.

tion when John F. Kennedy was President, either stayed closeted in his hotel room or was not even in Washington. Dr. King had taken a stand on the immorality of the war in Vietnam, a stand that put him outside the consensus. James Nabrit, chairman of a major committee at the conference and a Johnson appointee to the United Nations delegation, dismissed the attempt of Floyd McKissick of CORE to pass an anti-war resolution as an "albatross" around the Negro's neck. Actually, the war was a relevant fact that the Administration chose not to have discussed. Leslie Dunbar of the Field Foundation pointed out at the conference that the housing proposals advanced by the conference calling for 2 million new housing units a year, half for low-income occupancy, required redirection of funds from the war; and that unless the conference faced that problem, "everything else is unreal."

It was precisely failure to face real problems that characterized the conference. Delegates called for reforms that the civil rights movement had spoken of for ten previous years.

SNCC militants pointed out, contrary to the position of the White House Conference, that a new Civil Rights Act was not really a necessity. All the government had to do was enforce laws already on the books. In the area of school integration, it was explained that less than 1 per cent of Negro pupils in Mississippi and Alabama go to integrated schools; those who do are often isolated and even beaten by their white schoolmates.[7] (Yet SNCC's desire to concentrate on building quality Negro education is attacked as "racism.") The federal government does not use its control over school funds to help the Negro. Lawrence Guyot, chairman of the Mississippi Freedom Democratic Party, told how even after passage of the Voting Rights Act, candidates are threatened and MFDP activists shot at. One Congressional candidate in the fourth district, Rev. Clinton Collier, was repeatedly arrested by Sheriff Rainey and was beaten in Neshoba County. Men like Guyot know that the Fifteenth Amendment and the equal-protection clause of the Fourteenth are meant to protect the Negro against such harassment—yet the Justice Department offers no real protection.

Another area in which rights are denied are economic—and the federal Department of Agriculture sides with large plantation owners in their effort to crush Negro sharecroppers. One

[7] See the SNCC report, reprinted in this section, reading 23.—Eds.

cropper, James Robertson, explained that he worked five years cropping seventy-one acres, for which he received $8,600 while earning $51,000 for the owner. Yet he was chased off his farm after enrolling his children in a white school, and he has been unable to get a loan from the Farmers Home Administration to buy his own place. Instead of helping Negro farmers to get loans with reasonable interest rates, the Department of Agriculture instituted a new law allowing the landowner to charge any interest rate he wants on cash advances—further impoverishing the sharecropper.

The White House Conference, in its total effect, failed "to shatter forever not only the barriers of law and public practice, but the walls which bound the condition of man by the color of his skin," to quote from the President's Howard University speech in 1965. The delegates assumed that all that was needed to "fulfill these rights" was political dealing and education, exampled by the invitations offered to businessmen, segregationist politicians like Governor Paul Johnson of Mississippi, and regular influential citizens. Yet the situation in Watts and Harlem, in the cities of the urban North and in the rural South, reveals that the country at large is not allocating the necessary resources to make a difference in the lives of the black poor. In this respect, the conference and its proposals did not help. Changes occur only as a response to power exercised in the Negro community, and, as Kopkind wrote, while "the Conference confirmed the existence of that power, it cannot extend it. The next phase of the movement seems to be in the hands of those who weren't there." [8]

Events during the weeks that immediately followed the conference provide substantiation of Kopkind's judgment and final evidence of the failure of Rustin's coalition approach. After James Meredith was shot by a segregationist (despite the presence of FBI and Justice Department officials) during his projected one-man protest walk from Memphis to Jackson, Mississippi, in June 1966, his march was immediately carried on by King's SCLC and the militants of SNCC and CORE. With this "Meredith march" the civil rights movement gained back a vitality that had been lost in the previous year—and the crisis within the movement caused by the two different approaches became openly visible. The Selma march of 1965 saw support

[8] Kopkind, *New Republic* (June 18, 1966), p. 16.

by every rights organization, by the Administration, and by white liberals such as trade union leaders who walked during the last day of the March and who returned to defend segregated unions at home. But the March in 1966 became a grassroots action in which militant Negroes showed their solidarity with those still fearful of registering and voting, and it evoked a demand that the nation act to protect the hopes of those Negroes who wanted to use their power to vote.

The March leaders issued a broad Manifesto proclaiming the March to be "a massive public indictment and protest of the failure of American society, the government of the United States and the state of Mississippi to 'Fulfill These Rights.'" The March manifesto demanded that the President send federal voting registrars into all of the six hundred Southern communities to register disenfranchised Negroes, and that the President order federal law-enforcement agencies to "actively enforce existing federal laws." More important, the March partially fulfilled its goals. The Marchers registered about 4,000 Negroes whom it might have taken three to four years to reach. An estimated 10,000 turned out to greet the marchers at various points through the rural Mississippi towns, and close to 50,000 attended the final rally at the Mississippi capitol.

The Black Establishment, which had supported the ineffectual White House Conference, opposed the Meredith action, his call for self-defense by the Negro community when attacked, and the militant March Manifesto. Roy Wilkins, the N.A.A.C.P. chairman, refused to support the march because he did not wish to "endanger" the chance for passage of new civil rights legislation by alienating certain crucial white Congressmen. Bayard Rustin refused when asked by Dr. Martin Luther King to help arrange the logistics of the Meredith March—a task for which Rustin, who had led the March on Washington, would have been eminently suited.

By the stand they took in this event, the Rustin group showed their total opposition to meaningful social change as well as to grass-roots demands for federal action to enforce the Negro's rights. Fearing that the militancy of the marchers and the forthright manifesto would embarrass the Administration, these so-called civil rights organizations and leaders opposed the most massive rights movement to develop since 1965. Most offensive to them was the tone of the march—set by SNCC

Chairman Stokely Carmichael—who brought out the response and mood of the rural community by urging them to "stop begging and take power—black power."

The Meredith march revealed that the Negro community could be mobilized by and would respond to:

1. A program based on black power—the building of an independent Negro political base reflecting all the aspirations and demands of the oppressed Negro community;

2. A proud espousal of black consciousness and an affirmation of the great heritage of black people and their culture— one that promotes a race pride so long denied to the American Negro;

3. A program that declares that the war in Vietnam is of crucial importance to the black community—and that the Negro at home must see himself as part of a worldwide rebellion against colonialism and imperialism. As CORE leader Lincoln Lynch explained, to support the war so "suffused with conscious racism, is to support the racism on which it feeds," and to support the use of Negro taxpayers' money "to destroy and subjugate other poor colored folk." Rather than being an "albatross" around the neck of the rights movement, as Mr. Nabrit claimed, it is the war that brings death to the Negro who must fight in it. To the non-Establishment figures, the struggle to end the war is regarded as an integral part of the struggle for civil rights.

The plans of the Lowndes County Freedom Organization and SNCC to organize Negroes in the ghettos and the rural South as an independent force, and the program of the Mississippi Freedom Democratic Party to run candidates against the Democratic Party's segregationist ticket, are examples of the response to the failure of the Johnson consensus. The development of black political blocs that wield power by which the Negro would gain an influence over the course of his own life, is the sole avenue of advance for the Negro—until such time as white radicals build their own movement with which the Negro can align to change America.

This process would be severely hindered, and perhaps totally set back, if the civil rights movement were to give up its independence and allow itself to become absorbed into the Johnson Administration—much as the old Socialist and Communist movements allowed themselves to be destroyed by absorption into Franklin Roosevelt's New Deal. Such absorption and subsequent permeation will occur, however, if the liberal ideology, which puts coalition ahead of independent action, becomes the movement's basic strategy. Fortunately, the recent events in the Negro ghettos and the growing militancy of the young rights activists offer hope that coalition strategy has been rejected. Bayard Rustin will no doubt continue to prescribe a strategy that attacks radical black action as racist, and that seeks to limit the change from protest to radical politics—but he will become the theoretician not of the Negro movement, but of the moderate white liberals who fear radical change and of the Administration that continues to play politics at home and wage war abroad—and that leads in the drive to contain the black movement within "safe" channels. Rustin's role and use is therefore not at an end. He is an able spokesman for the White House. He may trust, however, that fewer and fewer Negro activists in the movement for human rights will be looking to him for counsel or advice.

[The above article was written in the summer of 1966. Events since then have led Dr. Radosh to reformulate his argument, below. He still holds that independent political action is a necessity if freedom is to be obtained, but he confesses to having been overoptimistic in his appraisal of its potential. Rustin's approach, not SNCC's, has triumphed in the South and Radosh views this as a sharp setback to the Negro freedom movement.—Eds.]

Events occurring since this article was composed, particularly the 1966 elections, reveal the difficulties and dilemmas facing the Negro movement. The third and most advanced stage of the Movement, that depicted by independent political action, has almost completely collapsed.[9] County branches of the MFDP are almost all dead. SNCC has but a few workers in two or three widely scattered counties, and the Lowndes County Freedom Organization was badly defeated in the November county elections. Whether the result of fears arising out of the potential loss of one's job if votes were cast for black

[9] See Robert Gabriner, "The Deferred Moment," *Connections,* Madison, Wis., March 16-31, 1967.

candidates, or of a conservative sense that gains would materialize only within the system, the electoral defeat ruined SNCC's strategy for independent political action in the rural South.

Essentially the Johnson's strategy of getting Negro voters to support moderate Democrats is succeeding. The new movement is being led not by black radicals, but by ambitious young white politicians "who are seeking allies from among the more comfortable black community and former civil rights activists." Richmond Flowers is typical of this style politician. Over 200,-000 Negroes are registered in Alabama, 150,000 in Mississippi, and a large percentage elsewhere in the South. In these conditions racist demagogy is diminishing and the politicos are changing their style. New young white Mississippians pledged to integration in a middle-class Democratic Party are replacing the overtly racist politicians of the Bilbo-Eastland era. The Negro will move to attain freedom in politics, but through the mechanism of the reconstructed Democratic Party in the South. Federal money in the South, via such agencies as VISTA and Headstart, will be used to give jobs to former movement Negroes—as the case with the 3,000 on the payroll of the Child Development Group. This policy motivates Negroes to give their allegiance to traditional channels for change.

The major dilemma is that the pronounced program of the Great Society, and Negro freedom, cannot be won within the context of the existing political-economic system. Fundamental problems will not be alleviated by a larger Democratic Party vote. In Tennessee, Gabriner reports, former movement people have attached themselves to the liberal wing of the state Demmocratic Party. Although they have pressured the state to hire more Negro employees in the state capital and elected a few Negroes to the legislature, the life situation of the Negro in rural west Tennessee is the same, and the counties rank among the poorest Negro areas in the nation. Yet the Negro voter feels he is participating in civic events, and has rejected SNCC attempts at organizational independence.

What has occurred is a dialectical irony. The Negro movement created political action, but the politicians of the Democratic Party have co-opted the Negroes and used sentiment and the vote to reinforce the predominance of the Washington consensus. Only the future can tell how many years it will take for a movement of liberation to develop, that will see the Negroes of the South moving away from Washington and developing their own black and radical consciousness.

ENFORCEMENT OF THE EDUCATIONAL PROVISION OF THE CIVIL RIGHTS ACT OF 1964 *

In February, 1960, four Negro students sat down at a white lunch counter in Greensboro, North Carolina, and refused to leave until served. This first sit-in had an electrifying effect and in its wake followed countless new sit-ins, freedom rides, and economic boycotts. New civil rights organizations sprang up, among them the Student Non-Violent Coordinating Committee. The courage of these young people, subject to brutal beatings, jail, and even murder, won the admiration of the nation. The Mississippi Summer Project of 1964, forever memorialized in American history by the tragic deaths of Schwerner, Chaney, and Goodman, was the high point in public acceptance of SNCC. Since then, SNCC has moved steadily to the left, as experience has dampened whatever hope they had had that meaningful gains could be won by operating within the accepted political structure.

Many informed Americans will be surprised to read SNCC's evaluation of the educational provision of the 1964 Civil Rights Act (reprinted below). Not only is it well documented and a scholarly effort of the first order; it shows that as recently as 1965, SNCC felt integration of the schools to be absolutely essential. If SNCC now

* This report, with portions omitted, was prepared by SNCC field secretary, Betty Garman, and Marion Barry, Jr., in 1965. By permission.

chooses to see the situation as one in which black people must unite politically to win further gains, and in which the drive toward integration is less urgent, their new ideology grew out of the bitter experience of enforced segregation.

◇ ◇ ◇

The Civil Rights Act became law in July, 1964. Title VI prohibited discrimination in federally assisted programs . . . under it, each department was to draw up regulations for ensuring compliance with the Civil Rights Act of 1964. . . . Yet the seven-page "rules, regulations, or orders of general applicability" to implement Section 602 were not printed in the Federal Register until December 4, 1964, five months after the bill became law, and exactly one month after the presidential election. . . . Not until April 29 did the commissioner and his office make public any information that clarified the "Instructions," although March 4 was set as the suggested date for compliance with Title VI. . . .

Slow pace

With over 2,000 school districts required to submit plans, only 352 had been approved by June 31. This slow pace continued, and as late as July 19, only 466 plans had been approved, although 1,839 districts in the seventeen Southern and border states had sent their plans to Washington by that date.

With less than six weeks to go before school opened, everybody began to scream—the President, the school boards, Congressmen, and parents. As a result, emphasis was increasingly placed on getting out as many plans per day as possible rather than on plans which would assure compliance with Title VI. EEOP[1] published a daily check sheet during the summer showing "progress" in terms of the number of plans submitted to date, the number of plans approved, and the number of plans still under negotiation.

The rush was on. Many plans slid through without even meeting the minimum guidelines.

For example, the General Statement of Policies indicated that if a school system desegregated fewer than twelve grades this year, it had to "sustain the burden of justifying the delay"

[1] Equal Education Opportunities Program.—Eds.

but must make a "substantial good faith start"—defined as at least four grades in 1965. Since many school districts were willing to meet only the minimum requirements, most submitted four-grade-a-year free choice plans. In many instances, the Office of Education accepted these without question and made little or no effort to require justifications for four instead of twelve grades. If the school districts, by some chance, tried to justify four grades a year, the justifications went something like this:

The emotional atmosphere of our patrons requires that we not go faster than the majority of our neighboring districts (Clarendon, Arkansas School District). . . .

In Mississippi, where some two-grades-a-year plans were accepted, several indicated overcrowding as the reason. But every free-choice plan submitted had a built-in overcrowding clause, which usually read: "In cases of overcrowding, students will be assigned on the basis of proximity of residence."

And, given the history of the effect of "freedom of choice" plans in producing "tokenism," there was no excuse for accepting four-grades-a-year plans. "Freedom of choice" for fewer than twelve grades also breaks up families where parents would rather have all children in the same school. In addition, the moral support of a brother or sister helps in adjusting to a possibly hostile school environment. (To make certain that these plans were no exception, we examined over 100 four-grades-a-year plans. The same pattern prevailed throughout.)

Bumbling, bungling, and white rights

Given the disorganized nature of the plan-approval operation, it was inevitable that bungling and bumbling would soon rear their ugly heads. But our survey of over 100 plans approved by the US Office of Education produced another unexpected and alarming discovery—protection of white rights instead of enforcement of Title VI.

[Below is one example.]

. . .

Gould, Arkansas. *This "freedom of choice" plan provided for choice in grades 1-12 but the School Board could refuse Ne-*

gro transfers in grades 5, 10, and 11 because of overcrowding. The Office of Education accepted a provision that white high school students would be accepted from Wells Bayou School District.

Here is a case where the Office of Education accepted a plan which restricts the choice of Negro students and gives first preference to whites outside the district. Thirty Negro students were, in fact, refused the right to transfer in grades 5, 10, and 11.

. . .

Clearly, Commissioner [Francis] Keppel and the Office of Education were willing to accept tokenism as the definition of compliance with Title VI of the Civil Rights Act of 1964.

Court orders

Every school district that submitted a court order as its plan for desegregation was considered to be in compliance with Title VI (at least we found no evidence to suggest otherwise). . . . There was no wording in Title VI that stated that court orders had to be accepted. . . .

The majority of the court orders say nothing about teacher desegregation, teacher dismissal, desegregation of school facilities and activities, or community preparation. Registration procedures are very seldom spelled out and provisions for public notice are nonexistent. . . . In Bullock County, Alabama, a district desegregating under court order, the school board said that it would admit only 15 Negro students to white schools. In later court action, the board was directed to admit 14 of the remaining 26 Negro students who had applied for transfer. The district has 3,078 Negro students. Thus, less than 1 per cent are enrolled in white schools after two years of desegregation. . . .

Given these and other examples we submit that *most court orders do not even meet the provisions in the guidelines.* The "General Statement of Policies" provides that court orders will not be accepted by the US Office of Education if they "otherwise fail to require the elimination of the dual or segregated system of schools based on race, color, or national origin." . . .

Finally, another problem with court orders is that they have to be policed by the courts or by the Justice Department and not by the US Office of Education. There are two problems to this. First, to the extent that school board actions in neighboring counties have an effect on each other, it is important to apply a consistent desegregation standard. Once county officials see that the court desegregation rulings do nothing to endanger their federal funds and require less than the US Office of Education, they will be eager to find a local Negro who will file a desegregation suit.

Secondly, the remedy for bad court decisions is more drawn-out litigation and not the enforcement of Title VI. And, in most cases, the burden of appealing court rulings will fall to the Negro families who initiated the action—an often difficult process considering the time involved and the small number of lawyers in Southern states committed to desegregation.

Freedom of choice

Many of the so-called "freedom of choice" plans accepted by Commissioner Keppel, although seemingly workable on paper, are in fact a farce. They offer no meaningful choice and certainly no "freedom of choice." How can a choice be free when often it is a choice between a student's parents' losing their jobs or transferring their child to a white school?

We are sure that Commissioner Keppel knew about the failure of "freedom of choice"—as applied in Prince George, Dorchester, and other Eastern and Southern Maryland counties for the past nine years—to bring about any meaningful desegregation. Yet, after the Lauderdale County, Alabama, "freedom of choice" plan was accepted on May 5, Commissioner Keppel and the Office of Education actively promoted "freedom of choice." . . .

Since "freedom of choice" required only minimum compliance and because the Office of Education made it easy for districts to have their "free choice" plans accepted, over 90 per cent of those districts in the eleven Southern states submitting voluntary plans used the "freedom of choice" principle. . . .

In a June 4 letter to Commissioner Keppel, Galen Martin, Executive Director of the Kentucky Commission on Human Relations, partly stated the case against freedom of choice:

. . . Turning to the matter of so-called "free choice" plans, as applied to Kentucky situations, the Office of Education is approving plans for continuation of very small schools for Negroes that may not even meet the test of separate but equal under Plessy v. Ferguson, *1896, much less the principles of the Civil Rights Act of 1964. . . .*

There are at least three additional arguments against "freedom of choice."

1. "FREEDOM OF CHOICE" PLANS PUT
THE BURDEN OF RESPONSIBILITY FOR
DESEGREGATION ON NEGRO
CHILDREN AND THEIR PARENTS RATHER
THAN ON THE SCHOOL BOARD

The . . . incidents listed below are only a few examples of what happens when Negro parents choose to send their children to white schools. Each incident would be multiplied a hundred times if all instances of harassment and intimidation were reported. . . .

In Aberdeen, Mississippi, thirty-two shots were fired into the home of the Walker family, one of the two Negro families which registered children for the second grade in a white school. . . .

Willie Lemon, a Negro from Camilla, Georgia, was brutally beaten by the deputy sheriff after he registered his three daughters in the white school.

Baker County, Georgia: not only have many people lost their jobs, one Negro family with six children was threatened by Mrs. Elma Andrews, the local welfare agent, with loss of welfare for requesting transfer of their children to a white school.

In Holmes County, Mississippi, Negro elementary school students going to Goodman schools have to ride the bus with Holmes Junior College and high school students. The white teenagers slap, kick, shove, and curse the young Negro children.

In the following counties or school districts, there are no Negro students going to white schools. The total Negro enrollment in the district is in parentheses. This is only a partial list.

ALABAMA: Chambers (137); Franklin (38); Houston (1,760); Lee (2,114).

ARKANSAS: Carthage in Dallas County (198); Aubrey (345); Guernsey (85); Hermitage (474); New Edinburg (132); Patmos (44); Village (95); Washington (440).

GEORGIA: Brooks (2,376); Jones (1,426); Crawford (1,079); Pulaski (757); Buford (344); Cook (1,155); Hawkinsville (1,189); Lanier (499); Miller (667).

MISSISSIPPI: East Jasper (2,041); Scott County (1,959); Attala County (1,551); Simpson County (2,410); Perry (547); Monroe (300); Lafayette (2,649).

According to the Arkansas newspaper, a spokesman for the US Office of Education said his office would not be concerned if no Negroes chose to attend formerly all-white schools in districts with accepted "freedom of choice" plans. The newspaper was reporting on a telephone conversation between the Office of Education and a school official in Monticello, Arkansas. This attitude is incredible. We also suspect that little or no effort will be made by the Office of Education to find out what actually happened in those counties where no Negro students applied for transfer. In most counties where no Negroes have applied for transfer to white schools *we know that fear of retaliation was the reason.*

Because of this, we feel that *the Office of Education has a responsibility to conduct thorough investigations in every county where no Negro students are enrolled in formerly all-white schools.*

2. "FREEDOM OF CHOICE" ENCOURAGES AND PRODUCES TOKENISM

. . .

The statewide enrollment figures for September, 1965,[2] speak better than words.

[2] From 1964-65 enrollment figures from *Southern School News* (December, 1964.)

Enrollment

State	White	Negro	Negroes enrolled with whites	Per cent
ALABAMA				
1964-65	549,543	293,476	94	0.032
1965-66	575,000	300,000	1,500	0.5
GEORGIA				
1964-65	752,620	354,850	1,337	0.377
1965-66	900,000	375,000	6,000	1.5
LOUISIANA				
1964-65	489,000	321,000	3,581	1.12
1965-66	506,000	331,000	1,850	0.6
MISSISSIPPI				
1964-65	308,409	295,962	58	0.020
1965-66	350,000*	325,000	1,500	0.5
NORTH CAROLINA				
1964-65	828,638	349,282	4,918	1.41
1965-66	900,000	375,000*	8,000*	2.2
SOUTH CAROLINA				
1964-65	371,921	260,667	260	0.10
1965-66	383,902	272,000	3,500	1.3

* Estimates.

3. "FREEDOM OF CHOICE" PROMOTES NONCOMPLIANCE

One of the easiest ways for school boards to comply with Title VI and yet "not comply" is to adopt a so-called "freedom of choice" plan. The method is simple—submit a free choice plan, get a few Negroes to sign up to attend white schools, and then let the local citizens "encourage" them to withdraw their applications. An even better way is to reject all Negro applicants because of overcrowding, bad character, improper registration, or any other excuses the school board wants to use. But, if by chance a few Negroes slip through—go directly to the parents' employers or to the local welfare agent.

By using evasion, dishonesty, and duplicity, school boards have successfully maintained "separate but unequal" schools. Similar tactics were used to "hoodwink" the US Office of Education. Below are . . . representative examples of devices used to keep Negro children from going to white schools.[3]

. . .

Perry County, Alabama. Parents were told on the first day of school to take their children back to the Negro school and to come back in ten days to fill out transfer forms. When the ten days were up, several parents tried to register their children in the white schools and were not allowed to do so.

Baldwin County, Alabama. The letters informing parents of the "free choice" plan arrived two days before the close of registration. A few selected Negro families received letters a number of days earlier. . . .

Lafayette County, Mississippi. School officials first said that only Negro children who had A averages could transfer to white schools. Later they limited acceptance to the daughter of a wealthy Negro in town. He refused to send his daughter alone; therefore, no Negroes are enrolled.

Benton County, Mississippi (under court order). Registration for transfer to the white schools was held on two different days. Registration for the Negro schools was open for at least thirty days. Some registration-for-transfer periods were as short as four hours on one day, i.e., 8 AM to 12 noon. . . .

. . .

Marks, Mississippi. A father and his daughter went to register for the white school. The superintendent told them that he wouldn't enroll anyone in the white school who had been on split session because they would be two months ahead of the white students. The father asked if he could wait two months and then enroll his daughter. The answer was no.

Compliance after plans are approved

Commissioner Keppel and EEOP Acting Director [David] Seeley must have known that paper plans for desegregation

[3] On March 10, 1967, US Assistant Attorney General John Doar in hearings before the Fifth Circuit Court of Appeals admitted that the court-sanctioned free-choice pupil assignment plans had failed to eliminate dual racial systems. See the *New York Times,* March 30, 1967, p. 37.—Eds.

submitted by racist Southern school boards and superintendents would not be enough to ensure compliance with Title VI. *Yet little or no effort was made to have a compliance section functioning by the opening of the 1965–66 school year.*

We submit that it is absolutely essential for any civil rights compliance section in the government to establish and maintain communication with active civil rights groups and local movements in every county. Some small attempts to establish these contacts have been made—but, because federal agency policy is to work primarily through local and state governments, it will be difficult for the EEOP compliance staff to develop a meaningful program along these lines. Government officials in Washington *must learn,* however, that compliance with civil rights legislation can only become more than token if voluntary organizations are closely involved in the process. And this work cannot be done from a desk in the capital city. More emphasis must be placed on finding competent field investigators.

The final problem in assuring compliance is the most crucial. Federal funds which are supposed to be held back if a district does not comply with Title VI have already been released to the state departments of education. And once a district had its plan approved, the state was free to release money to it. Already hundreds of thousands of dollars have been distributed to school districts which have only superficially complied with Title VI. *Federal money is again being used to continue segregation in Southern classrooms, and to deny Negro students equal educational opportunities.*

Hearings

Those school districts that did not send in desegregation plans will be brought to a hearing in the middle of October. . . . There are two important things to be said about these hearings. First, they are only a preliminary step toward actually cutting off federal funds. Judicial review is available to any district which is cited for noncompliance with Title VI. Second, it appears that every effort is being made by the commissioner, President Johnson, and others to allow districts as much leeway as possible to "comply" before the hearings are held. We expect that the hearings will be postponed again and that pressure will be exerted on the 103 counties to submit some kind of plan which meets the minimum requirements.[4] This would be a great "victory" for the President—100 per cent of the school districts required to submit plans in "compliance." But the proof of compliance is not found in the plan, as written; rather it must be seen through the actual process of desegregation. . . .

In several Alabama counties where plans had been submitted but not yet approved, official intimidation occurred. For instance, in Greene County, Alabama, Negro students went to the white high school on opening day in an effort to register. State troopers, local police, and white students with arms had surrounded the school. The Negro students left. Now one Negro girl is enrolled. The registration and transfer procedures were nonexistent. There was no "free choice" involved. Yet Greene County's "free choice" plan is under "negotiation." The Office of Education will require that the Greene County school board hold another registration period when the plan is accepted. This could be in the middle of the semester. What student will transfer then? Greene County will not be required to hold another registration period until the fall of 1966. But, Greene County will have its federal money. Any school districts wishing to circumvent compliance could do what Greene County did—submit a bad plan just before the "deadline," which would necessitate numerous discussions with the Washington "plan-approvers." The idea is to continually include provisions which will have to be deleted, cling obstinately to some of them, but always express a desire to comply. . . .

Conclusion

On the basis of the information contained in this report, we conclude that Commissioner Keppel and Acting Director of

[4] These hearings were held as scheduled but knowledgeable Washington insiders report that the Office of Education softened their criteria of acceptability. As a result only 50 school districts ultimately had funds withheld from them, according to data provided by the Office of Education. Segregation has therefore been maintained. As an indication of this, see the decision of the Court of Appeals for the Fifth Circuit that six Southern states must integrate their segregated public schools from kindergarten up, as reported in the *New York Times,* March 30, 1967, p. 1.—Eds.

EEOP David Seeley were more concerned about facilitating the flow of federal funds to racist school boards than in ensuring equal educational opportunities for all. We do not absolve the President of his responsibility in this matter either. We are certain that our chief executive contributed to the pressure placed on the Equal Education Opportunities Program staff to approve plans as quickly as possible. We are certain, too, that he could have played a greater part in the early months after the passage of the Civil Rights Act in making certain that an adequate program for enforcing Title VI in federally assisted educational programs was developed. It is ultimately the responsibility of the President to administer cabinet departments and to ensure that legislation is adequately enforced. . . .

JUSTICE IN THESE UNITED STATES*

The United States Commission on Civil Rights is an independent executive agency, established by Congress under the Civil Rights Acts of 1957, 1960 and 1964. The commission operates under elaborate procedures to ensure that no witness may be defamed, degraded, or incriminated. The first witness in the February, 1965, hearings was the Hon. Paul B. Johnson, Governor of Mississippi, who apologized for the earlier hostility shown to the commission. "The responsible people of the state, the leaders in business, the leaders in politics or government, have boycotted or refrained from attending the hearings [in the past]. As a result, we have permitted every type of person known to man to go into these hearings and tell every type of falsehood about the State of Mississippi without anyone in the state rebutting it." [1] Governor Johnson encouraged "responsible" leaders to come forward before the commission and testify that Mississippi is "the State of Law and Order."

◇ ◇ ◇

* *Hearings Before the United States Commission on Civil Rights . . . Jackson, Mississippi, February 16-20, 1965, Vol. II: Administration of Justice*, pp. 5-10, 12, 14-15, 23-26, 30-31, 46-63.

[1] *Hearings Before the United States Commission on Civil Rights, Vol. I: Voting*, pp. 1-8.

Willie Dillon's home is bombed

MR. TAYLOR.[2] Mr. Dillon, will you give us for the record your full name and address, and your occupation?

MR. DILLON. My full name is Willie J. Dillon. McComb, Miss., Route 1, Box 17.

MR. TAYLOR. How long have you lived in Mississippi?

MR. DILLON. I have lived in Mississippi all my life.

MR. TAYLOR. And in Pike County?

MR. DILLON. I was born in Pike County.

MR. TAYLOR. Would you state your occupation for the record?

MR. DILLON. I am a mechanic by trade.

MR. TAYLOR. Have you or your wife ever been involved in civil rights activities?

MR. DILLON. Well, I haven't. My wife, she goes to the meetings at the COFO [3] office, and my kids went to COFO school.

MR. TAYLOR. Have you ever attempted to register to vote?

MR. DILLON. I haven't, but my wife have.

MR. TAYLOR. I understand that dynamite was thrown at your home on the evening of August 28, 1964. Can you tell us about that?

MR. DILLON. It were. I always work in my yard, you know, at night, on a car or something like that. Somebody come by— and one of the COFO cars came by; his car wouldn't crank and he asked me, reckon I could make it crank? And I told him I thought I could. Well, he left the car, and during the week I worked on the automobile. And so it took me about two or three nights, you know, working it part-time when I come from my regular job. And so on the third night, well, I put another battery in the car and run it some, to see would it crank when it got hot.

Well, I worked, and guys come by and talked. But anyways, it was around 12 or 12:30 that night when I quit working on it. I went in to take a bath and shave. I got through shaving and went to step in the bathtub, and I heard the explosion go off.

[2] William L. Taylor, general counsel of the commission.—Eds.

[3] COFO are the initials of the Council of Federated Organizations, a church-sponsored civil rights group that carried out various educational projects throughout the south in 1964 and 1965.—Eds.

My wife was in the bed and she jumped up and asked me what happened, or what was it. I told her I didn't know, and we ran to the window and looked. We couldn't see anything but smoke on the outside.

So I put my clothes back on and went running out on the porch. The neighbors were beginning to come out and nobody knows what happened, and they seen a lot of smoke. So the people come and we looked to see what happened, where it was at, and so we didn't find anything. So after about five minutes, some other guy came and he walked over nine sticks of dynamite in my front yard.

My wife went to the telephone next door and called FBI men. They came and about that time all the officers in Mc-Comb and the sheriff and all was there around the same time. Well, they went to asking questions. Why was it put at my house. I told them I didn't know anything, why it was put there, who put it there, anything like that. Well, they questioned and questioned. Well, they asked me, you know, about anything I was involved in, about COFO. Well, I told them I didn't belong to anything; that my wife, she participated in it. Well, they questioned her, and then told us that we knowed something about who was putting the dynamite out and things like that.

Mr. Taylor. Who told you?

Mr. Dillon. The law officer.

Mr. Taylor. Do you know which law officer?

Willie Dillon is arrested

Mr. Dillon. Well, the sheriff and, well, most all of them. I didn't know, you know, all the law officers. I didn't know about them. But anyway, they all questioned me and questioned my wife and some of them questioned my kids and, well, told us we knowed about who was bombing, that the Negroes was bombing and saying the white people was doing it. And so they kept up the questioning. I said, "Well, the only reason I could see that anybody would bomb at my house was because I worked on a COFO car." So then they went to the COFO car and they searched it and said it had been run. I told them, "Yes, it had been run because I had been working on it trying to see would it start." And so they searched and searched. I had to hang a light in a chinaball tree in the yard from my electric line coming into the house. They looked and seen that there and they said, "Well, we're going to take you to jail." And I said, "For what?" And they said, "For stealing electricity and running a garage without a license." I said, "I don't have a garage. If this chinaball tree is a garage, well I guess I'm running one." And they told me, "Well, we're going to take you to jail."

Well, they told me to go in and get my shoes and hat. Well, I went on and got it. They told me to go to the car, and I went in. I went and got in the car. Well, they taken me to the nearby overnight service station. Then they questioned me some more about it, said I knowed something I wasn't telling them. "You know who's doing the bombing," or something like that, and I said, "I don't know anything about any bombs."

MR. TAYLOR. Who took you to the service station?

MR. DILLON. I was in the car with the sheriff and a deputy, I reckon. I don't know who it was.

MR. TAYLOR. About what time of night was this?

MR. DILLON. —It had to be about 2 or 3. It was beginning to be morning then. Well, they taken me on from the overnight station to the county jail at Magnolia and turned me over to the jailer.

Well, I stayed in jail until the next morning, and then, well someone come to question me again. I had told them what I knowed. They questioned me and told me that I was lying and things like that, and I told them, "Well, I told you what I knowed about it: nothing. I didn't see anyone put it there, so I don't know anything about who's bombing."

So I was questioned and jailed and stayed there a month. I was fined three months and $100 for stealing electricity and five months and $500 for operating a garage without a license.

MR. TAYLOR. You said you were in jail for a month. When were you first taken before a justice of the peace?

MR. DILLON. I was taken—that happened on a—let's see; I can't think of the date.

MR. TAYLOR. Was it the day after you were arrested?

MR. DILLON. I was taken that next day after the bomb was put in my yard, that next evening between 2 and 3, to the justice of the peace. And so they read off the charge, what they had me in there for. So they asked did I have a lawyer, and I replied back "no." And he said, "Well, if you had a lawyer, why, it wouldn't do any good. It would be the same if you had a lawyer or if you didn't have one."

MR. TAYLOR. When you were taken before the justice of the peace, you were asked if you had a lawyer at that time?

MR. DILLON. At that time.

MR. TAYLOR. Had you been asked at any time previously if you wanted to see a lawyer?

MR. DILLON. I hadn't.

MR. TAYLOR. Had you been asked to see if you wanted to see any member of your family or a friend?

MR. DILLON. I wasn't asked anything about did I want to see anyone, because I was expecting, you know, someone to come. But my wife said she came and they wouldn't let her see me, so I didn't know anything, only I was in jail.

MR. TAYLOR. And when you came before the justice of the peace, you did not have a lawyer and you pleaded guilty?

MR. DILLON. I pleaded guilty because I had no other choice but to plead guilty. I had no lawyer. And in the jail in Mc-Comb, whatever the law said, that's what it is. Nobody said I wasn't guilty; nobody said anything, the way I see it. That's the way it always has been.

CHAIRMAN HANNAH.[4] Would you speak a little louder?

MR. DILLON. I said I didn't have a lawyer and I didn't know to ask for one, because I figured I hadn't done any crime to have a lawyer, so I figured I'd just plead guilty and pay a fine. But I was sentenced to eight months and $800.

MR. TAYLOR. I would just like to note for the record at this point that Mr. Dillon's sentence was appealed for a trial de nova. The case was removed to a federal court where the appeal bond was reduced to $500, and the case then remanded to the state court. The remand order was appealed and on January 18 Mr. Dillon paid court costs of $42.60 and the case was dropped. I have no further questions at this point.

CHAIRMAN HANNAH. Mrs. Freeman?

COMMISSIONER FREEMAN.[5] Mr. Dillon, you are an automobile mechanic, are you not? How long have you been an automobile mechanic?

[4] John A. Hannah, president of Michigan State University.—Eds.
[5] Mrs. Frankie Muse Freeman, associate general counsel of the St. Louis, Missouri, Housing and Land Clearance Authorities.—Eds.

MR. DILLON. Well, I have been a mechanic mostly all my life.

COMMISSIONER FREEMAN. You have been working as a mechanic in the same place in McComb all the time?

MR. DILLON. Well, for different jobs. Not at the same place all the time.

COMMISSIONER FREEMAN. How long have you been self-employed?

MR. DILLON. I haven't been self-employed. I always worked for other people all the time.

COMMISSIONER FREEMAN. Have you ever repaired cars for your friends before?

MR. DILLON. All the time. I have friends and they, you know, would ask me to repair them. Some of them I didn't have no tools, you know, to repair with, of my own. I just have a few tools. But just minor little things I do to them on my own.

COMMISSIONER FREEMAN. Had you had occasion to know the sheriff before?

MR. DILLON. I hadn't, no.

COMMISSIONER FREEMAN. You knew who he was though?

MR. DILLON. I knew who he was when I seen him. I didn't know him before.

COMMISSIONER FREEMAN. You were never charged with operating a garage?

MR. DILLON. I never had a garage. I would just—maybe someone come by and ask me to make their car run or something like that; that would be all. I didn't run a garage.

COMMISSIONER FREEMAN. There is no garage on your property?

MR. DILLON. No garage on my property at all.

COMMISSIONER FREEMAN. When the sheriff saw the dynamite and the place where there had been an explosion, did he look to see whether there had been any damage before he started charging you?

MR. DILLON. He looked to see if there was any damage. There was no damage done because it was maybe ten feet from my porch.

COMMISSIONER FREEMAN. Do you know if he did anything to try to find out who did this?

MR. DILLON. I didn't hear anything.

CHAIRMAN HANNAH. Dean Griswold?

COMMISSIONER GRISWOLD.[6] Mr. Dillon, do you know whether the sheriff undertook to see if there were any fingerprints on the dynamite which was found?

MR. DILLON. I wouldn't know that, because they took the dynamite.

COMMISSIONER GRISWOLD. Did you see him pick up the dynamite?

MR. DILLON. I didn't see them pick it up because I was in the house being questioned when the dynamite was picked up, I think.

COMMISSIONER GRISWOLD. How long have you lived in this present house?

MR. DILLON. I lived in that house about twelve years.

COMMISSIONER GRISWOLD. And during those twelve years, have you from time to time repaired friends' automobiles as they were brought there?

MR. DILLON. Well, there were occasions. Well, I—I guess I have all my life. I couldn't say, you know, over a period of time. But I work, anyway, on my spare time.

COMMISSIONER GRISWOLD. Have there been several automobiles parked on your grounds from time to time during that period of twelve years?

MR. DILLON. I have three myself.

COMMISSIONER GRISWOLD. Have there been automobiles of other persons parked on your grounds awaiting repairs during this period of twelve years?

MR. DILLON. Well, maybe one car, waiting for repairs. Maybe somebody will bring one by and it won't run and he will leave it sitting by the road, because I don't have much ground to park one on.

COMMISSIONER GRISWOLD. Had the sheriff or any of his deputies or anyone else ever talked with you before about operating a garage without a permit?

MR. DILLON. Well, they hadn't, because I didn't run any garage.

COMMISSIONER GRISWOLD. Were you doing anything different on the evening of August 28, before the bomb explosion, with respect to other persons' automobiles than you had been doing

[6] Dean Erwin N. Griswold, dean of the Harvard University Law School.—Eds.

during the preceding twelve years?

MR. DILLON. No.

COMMISSIONER GRISWOLD. And you had not received any arrest or complaint prior to this evening?

MR. DILLON. No, not about running no garage; no.

COMMISSIONER GRISWOLD. What you were doing with auomobiles on your premises was not concealed in any way? I take it you worked in the front, visible from the street?

MR. DILLON. It was in my front yard, right on the street.

COMMSSIONER GRISWOLD. And you had no shed or other building there?

MR. DILLON. I haven't anything there but a chinaball tree.

COMMISSIONER GRISWOLD. Thank you. . . .

The FBI

MR. ROGERSON.[7] Did you say, Mr. Dillon, that the FBI did come to your house the night of the bombing?

MR. DILLON. They did come.

MR. ROGERSON. About the same time as the sheriff?

MR. DILLON. Well, I don't think they got there the same time because it was I think another incident had happened before it happened. They was out somewhere else and they came shortly afterward, from what I can recall.

MR. ROGERSON. Did the FBI agent interview you at your home?

MR. DILLON. They did.

MR. ROGERSON. Did the FBI ever interview you after you were taken to jail?

MR. DILLON. No.

MR. ROGERSON. Was the last time that you saw an FBI agent at your house?

MR. DILLON. That was the last time I saw one. . . .

The sheriff of Pike County, Mississippi

MR. TAYLOR. Sheriff Warren, will you state your name and your residence and your occupation for the record?

[7] Howard W. Rogerson, acting staff director of the Civil Rights Commission.—Eds.

MR. WARREN. My name is Robert R. Warren. I live just out of McComb on the west side Highway 24. I am sheriff of Pike County.

MR. TAYLOR. How long have you held that office?

MR. WARREN. Since the 6th of January, 1964.

MR. TAYLOR. Prior to that time, what training had you received in law enforcement?

MR. WARREN. I was trained in the Mississippi Highway Patrol some twenty years before that, and worked for the Mississippi Highway Patrol for six years. This was prior to being elected sheriff.

MR. TAYLOR. What is the nature of your enforcement duties as sheriff of Pike County?

MR. WARREN. Well, it covers quite a territory under the sheriff's duties, which is law enforcement, collecting taxes, selling tags—it covers quite a territory.

MR. TAYLOR. Does it include keeping the peace and good order of the community?

MR. WARREN. Yes, sir; it sure does.

MR. TAYLOR. How many men do you have on your force?

MR. WARREN. I have, I believe, ten deputies.

MR. TAYLOR. Do you have any auxiliaries in addition to the deputies?

MR. WARREN. No, sir; I do not.

MR. TAYLOR. Are any of the deputies or any of the men on your force detectives or trained as detectives?

MR. WARREN. Most of the men have gone through some type of training school. Most of them also have been officers for as long as ten and fifteen years.

MR. TAYLOR. Do you have any Negroes on your force?

MR. WARREN. No. sir; I do not. . . .[8]

COMMISSIONER HESBURGH.[9] I just would like to refresh my memory. In the case of Willie Dillon, he spent, I believe, a month in jail; is that correct?

MR. WARREN. Yes, sir. But I would like to clarify that, if I might.

COMMISSIONER HESBURGH. Go ahead.

[8] About 40 per cent of the population in Pike County, in Southern Mississippi, on the Louisiana Border, are Negro.—Eds.
[9] The Reverend Theodore M. Hesburgh, president of Notre Dame University.—Eds.

MR. WARREN. This was after Willie Dillon had been sentenced by the court. Now Willie Dillon was arrested at 3:30 or 4 o'clock on that morning and at 1 o'clock that same day—not the following day—he was carried into court and advised that he could have an attorney, which he said he didn't want an attorney, didn't have an attorney. He was sentenced at this time. Now this was after he had been sentenced that he spent this time in jail.

Willie Dillon's case in comparative perspective

COMMISSIONER HESBURGH. I mean he was actually sentenced five months on one term and three on another. Now, in contrast to that, the gentlemen who were apprehended for the bombings and burnings,[10] how long were they sentenced to spend in jail?

MR. WARREN. Well, before the pleading of guilty, they spent some forty days in jail. And I wouldn't like to be held accountable for this, but they were held incommunicado, some of them for seventy-two hours before we got the confession. They spent forty days in jail, though, before court came up.

COMMISSIONER HESBURGH. Then after the sentence, they didn't spend any more time in jail?

MR. WARREN. No, sir. As I said, that is where my authority ends, at the court.

COMMISSIONER HESBURGH. I understand.

MR. WARREN. And I don't have anything to do with the sentence or what might happen on it.

COMMISSIONER HESBURGH. No, I wasn't trying to relate this to your office. I was merely trying to get the fact that Mr. Dillon, whose house was bombed, spent this time in jail, and the people who admitted to many of these bombings, after their trial spent no time in jail.

MR. WARREN. Yes. . . .

---

[10] White youths who had bombed Negro churches and burned meeting places in the vicinity of McComb were dismissed by a local judge after a verbal reprimand.—Eds.

Reporting complaints in Pike County

COMMISSIONER GRISWOLD. Sheriff, as I recall your testimony, you said that reports on many of these events were not made to you, but were made to the FBI, and that you heard about it indirectly. Was that correct?

MR. WARREN. That is true, sir.

COMMISSIONER GRISWOLD. Do you have any idea why that was the situation?

MR. WARREN. Well, no actual proof. I was told that COFO people probably told the Negroes to call the FBI and not to have anything to do with the local law enforcement.

COMMISSIONER GRISWOLD. You think they had any reason for such advice if they gave it?

MR. WARREN. I don't see why they would have because we made every investigation regardless of whether they called us or not. I mean when we finally did get the word, we made the investigation.

COMMISSIONER GRISWOLD. Do you think what happened to Willie Dillon had anything to do with such advice?

MR. WARREN. I don't believe I quite get you there, sir.

COMMISSIONER GRISWOLD. Mrs. Dillon reported to the FBI that a bomb had gone off in their front yard.

MR. WARREN. Yes, sir.

COMMISSIONER GRISWOLD. And you came and promptly arrested Mr. Dillon on two charges and took him off to jail. He was tried without a lawyer and kept in jail for thirty days. Finally, through the aid of a lawyer and removal to the federal courts, his problems were solved. Do you think that many people were likely to report to you thereafter about bombs going off in their yard?

MR. WARREN. Do you mind if I explain that just a little?

COMMISSIONER GRISWOLD. I would be glad to hear it.

MR. WARREN. In the first place, we didn't arrest Willie Dillon promptly. We made an investigation. There was in that yard what looked like a dynamite cap had gone off and on the edge of the hole, possibly within six inches of this hole, lay nine sticks of dynamite.

We don't believe that that dynamite was laying there when that cap went off, because we think it would have exploded.

We did quite a bit of investigating. In fact, we arrived at Willie Dillon's house somewhere around 1 o'clock and I believe Willie was arrested about 3 or 3:30 that same morning.

Now, during the investigation these violations came up which naturally I am sworn to uphold the law in the county that I am sheriff in. We had worked possibly two hours and a half on the investigation before Dillon was arrested.

COMMISSIONER GRISWOLD. What evidence did you feel you had that Mr. Dillon was operating a garage on his premises?

MR. WARREN. Well, there was three or four cars there. He admitted to us that night that he was working on this automobile, and that he had commonly worked on people's automobiles for hire. So that gave us the right to make a charge against him for operating without a license.

COMMISSIONER GRISWOLD. Does working on a person's automobile constitute operating a garage, even when there is no equipment . . . ?

MR. WARREN. Well, in Mississippi, we think if a person is under a shade tree working on automobiles for hire, he is operating a garage. If he is working on these automobiles for hire, which he admitted that night to be doing, I could do nothing else than arrest him.

COMMISSIONER GRISWOLD. Did you ever arrest any other person for operating a garage when he was repairing automobiles on his personal premises under a shade tree?

MR. WARREN. No, sir; I haven't. But none of them admitted they were working on them for hire.

COMMISSIONER GRISWOLD. You still think that what happened to Willie Dillon has nothing to do with the Negroes' reluctance to report violations to your office?

MR. WARREN. Yes, sir. I feel like they should be reported to my office. I don't think that—

COMMISSIONER GRISWOLD. That wasn't my question.

MR. WARREN. I don't think it should have anything—

COMMISSIONER GRISWOLD. My question was whether people are afraid to report incidents to your office because they encounter what seems to them to be arbitrary enforcement of the law if they make reports to your office.

MR. WARREN. Not unless they are violating the law, and which I say that Willie Dillon was violating a law.

COMMISSIONER GRISWOLD. I think we can leave the record as it stands.

Testimony of Robert W. Brumfield, Esq., Pike County, Mississippi

MR. TAYLOR. Mr. Brumfield, would you please give your full name, your residence, and your occupation for the record?

MR. BRUMFIELD. Robert W. Brumfield. I am a resident of McComb, Miss., and I am an attorney.

MR. TAYLOR. How long have you lived in McComb?

MR. BRUMFIELD. All of my life, with the exception of when I was away at college and some six months in California.

MR. TAYLOR. Have you held public office in Pike County or McComb?

MR. BRUMFIELD. Yes; I have. I was police judge or city judge from 1955 to the latter part of 1962.

MR. TAYLOR. With what community organizations are you affiliated?

MR. BRUMFIELD. Well, during 1964 I was president of the McComb Chamber of Commerce. I am a member of the McComb Lions Club and past president of that organization, and a member or affiliated with a number of other clubs there in town.

MR. TAYLOR. We understand that a group of white people in McComb became concerned about the incidents of racial violence which we heard testimony about yesterday. Can you tell us what they did about it?

MR. BRUMFIELD. Well, sir, we became greatly disturbed about the incidents there in McComb and formed a group to try to determine what, if anything, we could or should do to help solve the problems. We started having meetings the latter part of October, and in November came out with a statement of principles that we felt embodied the ideas that would help solve the problems that we had in particular in McComb.

And Mr. Taylor, if you would like, I have brought for the benefit of the commission the advertisement setting forth that statement of principles which I would like to present. This was published in the *McComb Enterprise Journal* in its edition of November 17, 1964. . . .

MR. TAYLOR. Mr. Brumfield, the statement isn't very long. Would you care to read it or summarize its major points for the commission?

MR. BRUMFIELD. Yes, I will be glad to.

The great majority of our citizens believe in law and order and are against violence of any kind. In spite of this, acts of terrorism have been committed numerous times against citizens both Negro and white.

We believe the time has come for responsible people to speak out for what is right and against what is wrong. For too long we have let the extremists on both sides bring our community close to chaos.

There is only one responsible stance we can take: And that is for equal treatment under the law for all citizens regardless of race, creed, position or wealth; for making our protests within the framework of the law; and for obeying the laws of the land regardless of our personal feelings. Certain of these laws may be contrary to our traditions, customs, or beliefs, but as God-fearing men and women, and as citizens of these United States, we see no other honorable course to follow.

To these ends and for the purpose of restoring peace, tranquillity, and progress to our area, we respectfully urge the following:

1. Order and respect for law must be reestablished and maintained.

(a) Law officers should make only lawful arrests. "Harassment" arrests, no matter what the provocation, are not consonant with impartiality of the law.

(b) To insure the confidence of the people in their officials, we insist that no man is entitled to serve in a public office, elective or appointive, who is a member of any organization declared to be subversive by the Senate Internal Security Subcommittee or the U.S. Army, Navy, or Air Force, or to take any obligation upon himself in conflict with his oath of office.

2. Economic threats and sanctions against people of both races must be ended. They only bring harm to both races.

3. We urge citizens of both races to establish avenues of communication and understanding. In addition, it is urged that the Negro leadership cooperate with local officials.

4. *We urge widest possible use of our citizenship in the selection of juries. We further urge that men called for jury duty not be excused except for the most compelling reasons.*

5. *We urge our fellow citizens to take a greater interest in public affairs, in the selection of candidates, and in the support and/or constructive criticism of public servants.*

6. *We urge all of our people to approach the future with a renewed dedication and to reflect an attitude of optimism about our county.*

This statement was signed, as of 7 p.m., approximately three days after its original circulation, by over 650 people, and the names are attached to this list.

MR. TAYLOR. What would you say has been the effect of the Citizens for Progress?

MR. BRUMFIELD. Well, I think the effect has been very good. Now, unquestionably, the court in our county, getting a plea of guilty in these bombing cases and putting these men on probation, had a great deal of effect in calming the situation in our town and in our county. We also feel that our statement of principles has had some effect toward calming our people and toward trying to make everyone understand that we are part of the United States, these are the laws of the United States, and that we have to live with them as best we can. . . .

COMMISSIONER HESBURGH. Mr. Brumfield, that is a fine statement of principles, and I am sure I speak for many people when I say that we welcome it. Is it possible to get what you have done extended throughout the state to other counties where we have had difficulty?

MR. BRUMFIELD. Well, sir, the Mississippi Economic Council, the Mississippi Manufacturers Association, I noticed in the paper this morning, the Mississippi Association of Supervisors, the Mississippi Sheriffs Association have adopted statements very similar to the statement of principles that we formulated there in McComb. There is a little difference in the wording. There are a few items we have in our statement that are not in theirs. But as I understand, they are going to try to circulate this statement that the Mississippi Economic Council has formulated throughout the state.

COMMISSIONER HESBURGH. Mr. Brumfield, does part of one of

the points in your statement indicate that a State official should not be able to belong to the Ku Klux Klan?

MR. BRUMFIELD. Well, sir, I won't name any organization. I will say that if the Ku Klux Klan is on the subversive list,[11] that it certainly would be included.

COMMISSIONER HESBURGH. I just wasn't sure. And the last question I had is that it has seemed to me, at least listening to the testimony the last few days, that at one time in McComb there seemed to be a breakdown of confidence in the law, so to speak, or in the protection of homes and life under the law. Do you think that can be rebuilt?

MR. BRUMFIELD. Yes. We—now when I say "we" I speak primarily for white people—now we did not have any lack of confidence in our law enforcement officials there. It did appear that law and order at times was breaking down in our county. We believe that the lack of cooperation that has been brought out by previous witnesses in this hearing yesterday has been resolved by the sheriff and the other parties.

COMMISSIONER HESBURGH. When I said that the confidence had broken down, I probably should have been more specific. The confidence of the Negro community was broken down to the extent that Negroes were reluctant to call the law when they had difficulty because it often involved further difficulty.

MR. BRUMFIELD. Well, I don't believe that you could say that the confidence of the majority of the Negro community was broken down, because of course there were just a small portion of our colored population that was involved in these activities. I am sure that while these acts were going on and were being committed, that they were meeting other law violations that were being prosecuted in the courts where the complaining witnesses were colored people or where the defendants were colored people.

COMMISSIONER HESBURGH. Well, I was very happy to see as part of your statement that there should be an end to arrests that simply involve harassment. I think that is a very good statement.

MR. BRUMFIELD. Thank you, sir. . . .

COMMISSIONER GRISWOLD. Mr. Brumfield, I want to make it plain that I welcome and applaud this statement and your part

[11] It is.—Eds.

in attaining it. There are some facts about it that I would like to ascertain. Are there any Negro signers to this statement?

Mr. Brumfield. No, sir. To my knowledge we didn't ask any to sign. We didn't ask any public officials to sign this statement.

Commissioner Griswold. Why did you not ask any Negroes to sign?

Mr. Brumfield. Well, we just didn't. Why, I don't know. We just didn't. . . .

Willie Dillon's case

Commissioner Griswold. Now let me turn to another matter. You are a lawyer in McComb and a former police judge. We had as a witness here yesterday, Willie Dillon, who was arrested at 3 or 4 a.m. one day last August and by 3 p.m. of the same day was arraigned in your local court. I assume you were not the judge at that time?

Mr. Brumfield. No, sir; that was the justice of the peace court, which is a county court. I was police justice. I had the same subject jurisdiction as the justice of the peace, only my territorial jurisdiction was confined to the city limits.

Commissioner Griswold. According to the evidence before us, he was arraigned at 3 o'clock the afternoon of the same day, having been in jail all of the interval from his arrest to the arraignment without any counsel. He pleaded guilty to two charges. With respect to at least one of these, operating of a garage without a license, would appear to me to be at least a substantial question whether his acts constituted that offense. He received a substantial sentence; both a substantial fine and a period in jail. Is this the customary way, the ordinary way, in which offenses of this kind are handled in McComb?

Mr. Brumfield. Well, now, I don't know what you mean by "Is this the ordinary way?" Do you mean the speed with which it was handled, or what?

Commissioner Griswold. I mean the speed and the lack of counsel and the substantial penalty.

Mr. Brumfield. Well, Dean Griswold, of course I am not familiar with that case other than what I heard testified to here yesterday and other than what I read through the newspaper. Now the only thing I can tell you is the experience that I had in the seven or eight years that I was the judge there in McComb.

We held court every morning at 8 o'clock, and people that had committed an offense in the preceding twenty-four hours were brought before me and were arraigned and either tried at that time, or their case was set for a later date. Now, the justice courts operate a little bit different. They do not have regularly scheduled criminal terms of court. Generally speaking, in the justice court, the criminal hearing would be held just about any time the defendant was brought before the justice.

As to the matter of fines, I can't comment one way or the other on that. I was city judge in McComb when we had the original racial trouble in 1961, and our fines, the fines that I imposed, where there was a plea of guilty, were $100 and thirty-day jail sentence suspended pending good behavior. Where the plea was not guilty and there was a conviction, I believe the sentence was $100 fine and thirty days in jail with no suspension.

COMMISSIONER GRISWOLD. When, in this case, after the substantial sentence was imposed, counsel was obtained, he was from Jackson. Do you have any idea why they would go to Jackson to get a lawyer in such case?

MR. BRUMFIELD. No sir; I don't. Mr. Wiltshire, who represented Chief Guy here yesterday, is president of our local bar association. The state bar and the local bar association decided that they would handle these cases. I personally could not handle them, because I am a law partner of Mr. Reeves, the county prosecuting attorney, and, of course, I would have been barred from appearing in criminal court.

COMMISSIONER GRISWOLD. I want to make it plain, I am not seeking to be critical of you in any way.

MR. BRUMFIELD. Yes.

COMMISSIONER GRISWOLD. On the contrary, I greatly admire what you have done. I am just trying to find the situation, the atmosphere in McComb. Are there any Negro lawyers in McComb?

MR. BRUMFIELD. No, sir.

COMMISSIONER GRISWOLD. Is it the practice in McComb that substantial jail sentences are imposed in the local courts without counsel for the defendants?

MR. BRUMFIELD. No, sir; no, sir; there again, as I say, I am barred from practicing in the criminal courts. The only thing I can tell you is the experience that I had while I was city judge.

Now, take, for instance, public drunkenness. The fine was $22.50. That applied regardless of whether they were colored or whether they were white. Assault and battery, minor assault and battery would run around that. Fines in the city court would run anywhere from around $12.50 on a simple speeding charge to as much as $100 on a driving while under the influence of intoxicating liquor charge.

COMMISSIONER GRISWOLD. These were all fines and not jail sentences?

MR. BRUMFIELD. That's right, they were all fines.

COMMISSIONER GRISWOLD. In this case I find myself still rather startled not merely by the arrests under the circumstances, but also by the three-month and five-month jail sentences on these charges.

MR. BRUMFIELD. I myself have placed jail sentences on defendants and did place jail sentences on defendants in racial cases, in 1961, where they pled not guilty and were convicted. That involved white and colored.

COMMISSIONER GRISWOLD. Do you think there should be a heavier sentence imposed when there is a plea of not guilty?

MR. BRUMFIELD. Well, to my knowledge, that is more or less the procedure of courts. Where there is an admission of guilt or recognition of the fact that one has broken the law. I think the courts are generally inclined to be a little bit more lenient than they are when one just denies guilt and is later convicted.

COMMISSIONER GRISWOLD. In this case, the defendant did plead guilty. He got an aggregate of eight months for rather trivial offenses. Isn't that a little steep on the basis of your experience?

MR. BRUMFIELD. Well, I think the steepest jail sentence I imposed was approximately three months while I was there.

COMMISSIONER GRISWOLD. Thank you. . . .

The economic interest

COMMISSIONER RANKIN.[12] This statement that you gave us has helped McComb a lot, hasn't it?

MR. BRUMFIELD. Yes, it has helped. There is no question it has helped. . . . But . . . I don't want to sit up here and tell

[12] Robert S. Rankin, professor of political science, Duke University. —Eds.

you that this statement of principles alone is what calmed the situation in McComb. . . .

COMMISSIONER RANKIN. But McComb has prospered since then, hasn't it? Didn't you say a few minutes ago that it hasn't hurt them economically?

MR. BRUMFIELD. That is true.

COMMISSIONER RANKIN. And a few minutes ago you also made the statement that the Civil Rights Act of 1964 was of no particular economic benefit to the area; that it in itself would not bring prosperity.

MR. BRUMFIELD. That's right.

COMMISSIONER RANKIN. Don't you think it would help? That is my point. I have before me Frank Morgan's article in the *Wall Street Journal* for February 2, 1965, which he calls, "The Price of Strife." He goes into it and shows what a heavy price that you pay. Conformity to the Civil Rights Act might after all be the means whereby you might secure economic advantage.

MR. BRUMFIELD. Well, it could possibly, Mr. Rankin, but of course, if you have a hundred jobs in the community, a possible redistribution of those jobs on different racial lines in effect would not benefit your community economically.

COMMISSIONER RANKIN. Well, now, wait just a minute. If it were known that there was no racial strife in McComb and that there was labor in McComb, would not new industries come in? Wouldn't this be a place where they would want to locate? Couldn't that bring them?

MR. BRUMFIELD. Well, yes, sir.

COMMISSIONER RANKIN. Why, sure. Therefore, as it says in this article, "The Price of Strife," maybe, after all, complying with the Civil Rights Act of 1964 might be an instrument for improving economic conditions?

MR. BRUMFIELD. That's right. . . .

Calm in McComb

VICE CHAIRMAN PATTERSON.[13] Mr. Brumfield, we have had some witnesses here at this hearing who questioned whether words about change mean anything, whether deeds will follow in Mississippi. You state that following the breaking of the

[13] Eugene Patterson, editor of the *Atlanta* (Georgia) *Constitution.* —Eds.

bombing case in McComb, plus the issuance of this statement of principles by your business leadership, some things did change. Is that an accurate assessment of what you said?

MR. BRUMFIELD. Well, it certainly appeared [that] . . . after the solving of these cases, and the matters that took place subsequent to that, the calm was restored to the community.

VICE CHAIRMAN PATTERSON. This strikes me as a very dramatic thing. McComb and Pike County were nationally publicized as a hotbed of trouble in Mississippi for a long time. All of a sudden, after a case was cracked and after the business community issued its statement of principles, tranquillity was restored and has been maintained to this day, has it not?

MR. BRUMFIELD. Yes, sir.

VICE CHAIRMAN PATTERSON. Would you say to any troubled community in the South that this is the proper way to restore tranquillity to a community?

MR. BRUMFIELD. I think vigorous law enforcement and unified effort by all of the citizens of the community to maintain law and order is very definitely what is needed. And we had vigorous law enforcement. I couldn't help admiring Sheriff Warren yesterday. And, of course, I am sure you gentlemen are familiar with this. Assisting Sheriff Warren in this investigation were some twenty-five or thirty Federal Bureau of Investigation agents working on these cases, and some ten or fifteen more Mississippi State Highway Patrol specially trained investigators. These fellows worked round the clock and they solved these cases about as quickly as they could have been solved. And in fact, it is possible that their haste in solving them may be the reason some of the evidence would not have been admissible.

VICE CHAIRMAN PATTERSON. Mr. Brumfield, Sheriff Warren also mentioned in his testimony that his job of law enforcement became a lot easier when the business and professional power structure of McComb got behind him and issued its statement of principles. As a member of that power structure, would you have any advice for other communities in Mississippi?

MR. BRUMFIELD. Well, I certainly think that as problems like this confront other communities, that they need to have unified leadership to try to cope with them. Through perhaps unified leadership and asking the people to abide by the laws, they would not get themselves involved in difficulty. . . .

Jessie Lee Harris, SNCC worker

MR. TAYLOR. Mr. Harris, would you please give us your full name, your address, and your occupation?

MR. HARRIS. Jessie Lee Harris, 702 Wall Street, McComb, Miss. I am a field worker for the Student Nonviolent Coordinating Committee.

MR. TAYLOR. How long have you live in Mississippi?

MR. HARRIS. All my life.

MR. TAYLOR. How long have you been active in the civil rights movement?

MR. HARRIS. Ever since 1961 when I was arrested here in Jackson for breach of the peace when I went into the Trailway bus station. Since then I have been active in voter registration in Mississippi. . . .

When ten of us went into McComb to set up a voter registration project, we mostly expected to be arrested, you might say be beaten, or even killed. We knowed that we was going into an area where voter registration or activities had never got really off the ground before. We also knew of the atmosphere that was created down there for the last, you might say, four or five years or so, so we was afraid to go in there. And after we went in there, it was pretty much true. We went in and bought a house in the city—well, you might say leased a house for a year or two. We was followed by highway patrolmen all the way from Crystal Spring into McComb. When we got into Mc-Comb we were stopped by the highway patrol and taken to the nearest town somewhere in Lincoln County for investigation. We were questioned. This was practically the same pattern which we always expected—we would be stopped, you know.

When we got into McComb, we were stopped by some deputies and we were asked our names and where we were from and what we was doing there, and we was released without charge.

And I might say we went in—it is kind of hard to really explain the whole line of fear, not only among us but among the people we worked with.

MR. TAYLOR. Were there many arrests during the course of the summer of people in your organization?

MR. HARRIS. Well, we had quite a few. I think after we arrived in McComb about two weeks—about four days after that, after our house was bombed—I knows in the last part of June and about a week after we arrived in McComb, we were stopped by highway patrolmens, and we was given tickets and so forth. At one time I was picked up and taken down to the jail for speeding. Most of all the staff there in McComb was arrested for food handling without securing a permit. We was arrested in October at the county courthouse for trespassing. We were stopped many times for investigation during the bombings and so forth.

MR. TAYLOR. Were there also incidents of violence in connection with your project?

MR. HARRIS. What do you mean when you say "incidents of violence"?

MR. TAYLOR. Incidents of violence directed at the place where you conducted your project?

MR. HARRIS. Well, sixteen bombings took place in McComb, and we really feel that the reason for these sixteen bombings, was because of our activities there in McComb. I spoke at Society Hill, tried to ask them to let us use the church for voter-registration class, and about two days after that the church was bombed.

MR. TAYLOR. I mean particularly with respect to the place where you conducted your business, the Freedom House.

MR. HARRIS. Well, the Freedom House was bombed.

MR. TAYLOR. Do you think that the situation is improving now?

MR. HARRIS. No; I don't think so. I have listened to the testimony of the last person who testified. He mentioned something about the 650 people who signed the statement of principles. He also mentioned that no Negroes was asked to sign the statement.[14] I think that I can speak for the majority of the peoples who live in Pike County, or McComb, that the statement of principles to them really don't solve their problems. We think that the statement of principles in McComb—came out in Mc-Comb, you might say, was another trick to stop all the attention that was focused on McComb during the summer.

As I mentioned before, before we went into McComb, there was about two or three bombings had already occurred and there was some shooting up and down one of the main streets

[14] See pp. 318-22 above.

there and there were many cases where people that came into McComb and were practically ran out of town because they were from outside of the state. When we got to McComb I think that you might say that we was a threat. We was a threat not only to the white community, but we was a threat to the power structure there.

After all the bombing that took place there, and because of our presence, because we wanted to use churches to set up classes and because we wanted to teach Negroes how to fill out the registration card and to participate in the government, and because we wanted to teach other subjects, like in Freedom School where we teach students courses that they never get in high school, and we want to get them involved in community organization, I think that this is a threat to the power structure there. And so I think that this is just another trick, you might say, to focus all the attention off of McComb. And you know, it really don't solve any of the problems. . . .

Can black and white get together?

COMMISSIONER HESBURGH. Mr. Harris, your main purpose in McComb was to get people registered. How many did you get registered?

MR. HARRIS. Well, we don't know. We can't tell, because we have tried many times to contact the registrar, you know, and he refused to give us this type of information.

COMMISSIONER HESBURGH. Well, let me put it differently. How many persons did you train who tried to register?

MR. HARRIS. I don't know. I think it is close to 200 people that went through the process of these classes that we set up. And we have taken down maybe 125 people.

COMMISSIONER HESBURGH. So you trained about 125, and they in turn have gone to register?

MR. HARRIS. Right.

COMMISSIONER HESBURGH. Now you don't have any information on any of these 125?

MR. HARRIS. No, we don't have any information, because when they go down to the courthouse, they take the test and the registrar will tell them to come back in thirty days to check to see did they pass or not. And in many cases these people are afraid to go back by themselves and check.

COMMISSIONER HESBURGH. Haven't they gone back to check whether or not they are registered?

MR. HARRIS. Most of them have went back and most of them failed.

COMMISSIONER HESBURGH. You say most of those who went back found they failed?

MR. HARRIS. Right.

COMMISSIONER HESBURGH. So really the net result after this long hot summer is that not many people were registered?

MR. HARRIS. That's right.

COMMISSIONER HESBURGH. Mr. Harris, I appreciate the anguish that you and your fellow workers went through to try to get more people registered in a place—in a county where only 2.1 per cent of the Negro population is registered. But don't you think that both sides, the white and the Negro side, would have to look forward to some kind of a break to calm down this climate and make it more constructive . . . ?

Now wouldn't it be better—and I'm just making this as a supposition—wouldn't it be better if your group assumed that the white group which signed this statement was serious about it and meant to do these things? Wouldn't it be better to assume these people meant to get rid of harassment, that they meant to get rid of public officials who were trying to hurt other people, that they are trying to get responsible law, that they are trying to get fair jury trial?

These are all rather clear public statements. Wouldn't it be a good thing, now, if your group in response to that would come out with the things that you think ought to happen, maybe some of the same things and maybe some other things, and then possibly get the two groups together and discuss what are the two goals of the community called McComb? Wouldn't this be better than the first time they came out—and this is probably the first time they ever came out with such a statement—to say "I don't believe them, it is just another trick." If every time either side makes a move it is looked on as a trick, if your coming in to register people is looked on as a trick by the white people, if their statement that they want a better community is looked on as a trick by the colored people, then we never get anywhere. But somewhere along in the middle of this bad situation we have to get both sides together and we have to communicate. That was one of the points, that there has to be better communication.

Now I grant you may feel badly if they independently get out their statement, but you independently could get out your statement, and then the two groups could get together. I think if they could get together and find that they want the same kind of things and same kind of community, perhaps the immediate prize that you are looking for, that these people who are qualified get registered, could be realized sooner. I'm sure there are a lot of white people in town who can see that they do get registered.

Mr. HARRIS. Well, as I mentioned before, mainly we are working in voter education where we set up classes and talk about politics.

COMMISSIONER HESBURGH. Yes.

Mr. HARRIS. You know, we mainly get people to express themselves, what they feel about the situation which they live in, what they think. Do they think that they are the cause of the trouble or are the people across the track the cause of the trouble? I think everyone agrees that the white community and the Negro community have to get together in order to solve some of the problems. But here, in Mississippi, where I have lived all of my life, I think that this is one of the problems, that the Negro and the white community have to get together. I think in McComb you have a power structure which is very strong there, and where it is kind of hard for the Negro community and the white community to get together. . . .

COMMISSIONER HESBURGH. What I am really saying, Mr. Harris, is something President Kennedy said once, looking at the bad situation in the whole world. He said, "Let us begin." Now how do you make a beginning? I would assume as an outsider that the white people are trying to make a beginning and the violence has stopped. Now suppose your group, which has a legitimate job to do, to train people to be able to register and vote and take part in the political life of your community, put down the things that you would like, and maybe you find that these things coincide with what the white group wants. You say you can't talk to the white community. I say talk to Mr. Brumfield. He started this on the white side, and you started some of this from the colored side. Why don't you talk to him and then you get something started. And then maybe you could have a get-together periodically and you say this and this and this happened which seems against your statement of principles, and he could say this and this and this happened which seems against your statement of principles. You could then talk it out. But somehow a conversation has to get started, somehow a beginning has to be made to get from what was admittedly a very bad situation all summer to what I think most reasonable citizens would like to see as a good community. Does that sound reasonable?

MR. HARRIS. Well, it sounds beautiful, you know. But working in Mississippi, you might say, anywhere, that, you know—back to what I said before—that we think that we have certain things on our mind, most of us, as you know; that is, from our side of the state. And we don't go into a community, you might say, with this type of idea or with this purpose in mind. We go into a community just to talk to people and to listen to them; we don't get the impression that we have to go and talk to Mr. Brumfield, because we know that these people that live in Mississippi, you know, and they know Mr. Brumfield, and they know—you know, all the peoples like Mr. Brumfield. They know the response they are going to get, because they work for him every day and because they associates with him downtown, you know, and so forth. They know these people. They already talked to him, you know, and in other words, they are afraid to talk to him because they know him and so forth. . . .

PART VI

AMERICA'S GREAT SOCIETY IN A REVOLUTIONARY WORLD

INTRODUCTION

Since the defeat of the Axis powers in 1945 the United States has been involved in a Cold War that has developed in at least two distinct but overlapping phases. The first originated in the Eastern European settlement of 1945-48 in which Western and Soviet aims sharply clashed. The precise nature of this clash is still bitterly disputed by rival schools of scholarship. On the American side, the official conviction remains that Stalin's dogmatic determination to spread Russian control as far westward as possible is sufficient to explain the origin of the Cold War.[1] For their part, the Soviets argued that growing Communist power in Eastern Europe meant merely that the indigenous populations were recognizing the Communists, who had struggled bravely against fascism, as bearers of freedom. Anyway, Russian national interest demanded friendly regimes on its western borders.[2]

Trying to free Cold War scholarship from the passions that surround the events themselves, a third group of scholars[3] has resisted both official views. They reject the notion that because events developed the way they did, this development was inevitable. Instead they explore the way in which toughening US

[1] A sophisticated statement of this argument appears in W. W. Rostow, *The United States in the World Arena: An Essay in Recent History* (New York, 1960), Chaps. 19-25.

[2] This was Stalin's position, as revealed in *Pravda* (March 14, 1946), reprinted in Robert H. McNeal, ed., *Lenin, Stalin, Khrushchev: Voices of Bolshevism* (Englewood Cliffs, N.J., 1963), pp. 120-23. We are grateful to our colleague Dr. Louis Menashe for bringing this item to our attention.

[3] Gar Alperovitz, *Atomic Diplomacy: Hiroshima and Potsdam* (New York, 1965); David Horowitz, *The Free World Colossus: A Critique of American Foreign Policy in the Cold War* (New York, 1965); Frederick L. Schuman, *The Cold War: Retrospect and Prospect* (Baton Rouge, La., 1962); D. F. Fleming, *The Cold War and Its Origins, 1917-1960* (2 vols., Garden City, N.Y., 1961).

and Soviet attitudes mutually reinforced each other, eventually bringing about the phenomenon we call the Cold War.

Whatever the verdict of history on the origins and course of the Cold War, its outbreak triggered in the United States that whole range of fears and passions that are the traditional American reactions to threats from abroad, real or fancied. In the 1940s and 50s we seemed to feel obliged, because of this interpretation of events, to assume the burden of defense of the "free world." In the course of its response to the threat of Communist expansion—presumed to be directed by Moscow—the United States began to pick up the pieces, one by one, of the former colonial empires that were crumbling rapidly after the end of the Second World War. Speaking in Canberra, Australia, President Johnson gave his own view of this process:

My countrymen have lived so long with crises and danger that we accept almost if it were inevitable, the assumption of American concern for disorders that threaten the peace in other parts of the world.

We accepted this responsibility, first, because at one time no other nation could do it. For the last twenty years, only under the shadow of our strength could our good friends keep their freedom.

Second, we have learned, at painful costs, that aggression and upheaval in any part of the world carry the seeds of destruction to free men everywhere.

Finally, since the end of World War II we have assumed this responsibility for a reason that is often difficult for others to understand. We have accepted responsibility because we have believed it to be right that we should.[4]

This assumption of responsibility set the stage for the Cold War's second phase.

Our survey of recent American Cold War policy, and its historical and even metaphysical roots, is not intended to be a comprehensive view. The readings in this section deal mostly with the crisis areas of Vietnam and Santo Domingo (see below, readings 28-32). Some material on the Alliance for Progress (readings 26 and 27) is also included, to illustrate developments in a key area of American interest that is not prom-

[4] Speech delivered at the Parliament House, Canberra, October 21, 1966; *New York Times* (October 21, 1966), p. 16.

inent in the headlines. Although many other "trouble spots," such as the Middle East, may dominate the news, the choice of Vietnam and Santo Domingo as the main foci of this section can be justified on other grounds than mere space limitations: it is our judgment that the crises in these areas are just the most visible, virulent manifestations of deep contradictions in American foreign policy generally, and in American society as well. We cannot accept any interpretation that would dismiss the suppression of revolution in the Caribbean and the attempt to crush insurgency in Southeast Asia as mere exceptions to what would otherwise be pictured as a benign, generous unfolding of American virtue and power. These policies, as John McDermott points out with specific reference to Vietnam (see reading 32, below), are not exceptions or mistakes, but the essence of a conscious strategy adopted by American policy makers in the present phase of the Cold War.

The first Cold War has ended with the stabilization of a variety of national communisms in Eastern Europe and a seeming *détente* between the Soviet Union and the United States. The arena of the second Cold War has been the underdeveloped "third world," in which new nations, not formally aligned with either the East or West, are trying to shake off the crippling legacy of colonialism.[5] Only rudimentary ties bind these nations to each other. They draw whatever unity they display from the common experience of poverty and exploitation, as well as a consequent tendency toward "disorders" of the kind that attracts the attention of the US government.

In part, this attention consists of vast programs of foreign aid. Despite the huge sums involved,[6] these programs do not provide unambiguous evidence of the essential altruism of American foreign policy. A large amount of what the United States spends abroad is, in fact, for military aid, dictated by military and geopolitical imperatives. Between 1958 and 1962,

[5] We use the term "third world" merely as a convenient phrase, and because there is no generally agreed-upon substitute. No implication that these underdeveloped countries are genuinely independent of the capitalist world is intended. Their feeble efforts to build up a "neutralist bloc" should not be overestimated. These nations, sunk in poverty, play a generally subordinate role, as suppliers of raw materials and as objects for outside investment. As such they are *in* the capitalist world system, but not *of* it.

[6] In 1965, $7 billion. *Economic Report of the President* (1967), p. 310.

for example, over 30 per cent of all US foreign assistance was direct military aid.[7] But even this may be an understatement. A Presidential committee recently considering the overall relation of the foreign assistance program to "the economic and political stability of the free world" revealed the official view of what even nonmilitary spending is supposed to accomplish. The Clay Committee found that 72 per cent of the total appropriation for foreign aid went to countries on the periphery of the "Communist bloc," and that "dollar for dollar, these programs contribute more to the security of the free world than corresponding expenditures in our defense appropriations." [8]

Even more explicit appraisal of American purposes was forthcoming from a distinguished economist, who advises many governments and served on the Clay Committee. It is doubtful, wrote Harvard Professor Edward S. Mason, "that humanitarianism (a desire to improve the living conditions and opportunities of people abroad without regard to the security or economic prosperity of the United States) can be considered important either in explaining the actions of this country since 1947 or in laying the basis for a reasonable expectation of future action. Government aid programs are devised and promoted in an administrative and political setting that is not very amenable to humanitarian considerations. The agencies of government responsible for the initiation and administration of these programs have annually to justify them before a Congress concerned with demonstrating to its voting constituencies that their interests are being served. An administration unable to show that taxes for foreign aid programs have some fairly direct relations to the economic interests of important political groups or to the safety of the state will have difficulty in continuing these programs—and, probably, continuing in power." [9] In such a statement reverberate the authentic tones of Washington decision-makers.

[7] US Department of State, Agency for International Development, *U.S. Foreign Assistance and Assistance from International Organizations* (April, 1963).

[8] Report of the committee appointed by President Kennedy (December 10, 1962), under the chairmanship of General Lucius D. Clay, in Gustav Ranis, ed., *The United States and the Developing Economies* (New York, 1964), pp. 71, 75.

[9] Mason, "United States Interests in Foreign Economic Assistance," in *ibid.*, pp. 14-15.

Most Americans would prefer to avert their eyes from the harshness of such *Realpolitik*[10] and dwell instead upon the benevolence of the American purpose—especially when compared with the evil intentions of whoever is considered the enemy. The determination to hold fast to an immaculate conception of US foreign policy is deeply rooted in the American past and leads many liberal critics to do little beyond lamenting the ineptitude of the State Department and the rigidity of the Joint Chiefs of Staff.[11]

In many other parts of the globe, where faith in American rectitude is not automatic, the US is perceived as a great counterrevolutionary power that uses its might to forestall and extinguish popular insurgency movements.[12] Among the insurgents themselves, the US is usually cast as the enemy, operating directly or through puppet regimes that are prepared to carry out America's will.

Washington spokesmen solemnly declare that they have no desire to police the third world or to crush popular insurrections.[13] Yet the US government has initiated a broad range of repressive activities against insurgent movements on the grounds that these movements represent unwarranted "promotion of the Communist world revolution." [14] The Johnson Administration's policy toward the Dominican revolution of 1965 is a clear example of this process, though it should be remembered that the commitment to the use of force to suppress revolution in Latin America had been a traditional part of US policy before Johnson became President. The official

[10] See on this tendency, Gabriel Almond, *The American People and Foreign Policy* (New York, 1950).

[11] This line of argument is taken by Arthur Schlesinger, Jr. (see reading 31, below), and others. See John Kenneth Galbraith, "An Agenda for American liberals," *Commentary*, XLI (June, 1966), pp. 33-34, and John McDermott, "Welfare Imperialism in Vietnam," *The Nation* (July 25, 1966). But see McDermott's subsequent article, reprinted below, reading 32.

[12] See, for example, the judgment of the distinguished British historian, Arnold Toynbee, "The Failure of American Foreign Policy," *Fact,* II (September/October, 1965), pp. 3-7.

[13] See for example, Secretary of State Dean Rusk's testimony in William J. Fulbright, ed., *The Vietnam Hearings* (New York, 1966), pp. 228-29.

[14] Dean Rusk, address to the American Society of International Law (April 23, 1965), in Marvin E. Gettleman, ed., *Vietnam: History, Documents and Opinions* . . . (New York, 1965), p. 330.

justification of the Dominican repression (see reading 28, below) contrasts sharply with the reports of many American newsmen and scholars. (See James Petras' account, reading 29, below.)

The official Washington views and those of critics have diverged even more sharply in the case of Vietnam. The Administration and its supporters have repeatedly referred to our commitment to combat Communist insurgency there as the inevitable consequence of US treaty obligations, our "honor," and the irascible evil of the other side.[15] Arguments such as these have been subjected to merciless criticism. At teach-in after teach-in and in the increasing literature on the subject, the indigenous nature of the insurrection in South Vietnam has been stressed and the legal—not to say moral—justification for American involvement has been questioned tellingly.[16] The widespread distrust of the official rhetoric emanating from Washington on Vietnam has resulted in a "credibility gap"[17] of serious magnitude. James Reston, the distinguished *New York Times* Washington correspondent, has revealed this problem with biting insight.

The Johnson Administration [writes Reston] may finally get over its agony in Vietnam—it may even achieve its military objective in the end—but it will probably never regain the confidence it has lost in its judgment and veracity.

With the bombing of targets on the outskirts of Hanoi and Haiphong it has now done almost everything it said or indicated it would not do except bomb China, and the end of this melancholy chapter in American history is not yet.

The Johnson Administration said it was not seeking a military solution to the war, and it is now obviously seeking precisely that. It said it was there merely to help a legitimate government defend itself, and it has ended up by supporting a military clique that is not a government, not legitimate and is not really defending itself.

Even when allowances are made for the uncertainties and

[15] See readings 25 and 30 below, and Johnson's Johns Hopkins University address (April 7, 1965), in Gettleman, *Vietnam*, pp. 323-26.

[16] These issues are fully explored in Louis Menashe and Ronald Radosh, *Teach-ins USA* (New York, 1967).

[17] See Philip Geyelin, *Lyndon B. Johnson and The World* (New York and Washington, 1966), pp. 220-21.

moral ambiguities of warfare, the guile of this Administration, exercised in the name of high and even noble principle, is hard to match. It was not going beyond the Seventeenth Parallel in Vietnam, but went beyond. It was merely going to respond to enemy attacks on its bases, but it went over to the offensive. It was not going to get involved in a major war on the Asian land mass, but it did.

The President was not even faithful to his bad resolves: He said he would not negotiate, but then offered to do so, and spoiled that by refusing to negotiate with the major elements of the enemy he faces. He has not misled merely his enemies, but his friends. His old colleagues in the Congress have not forgiven him yet for tricking them into support of a blank check defense of all of Southeast Asia under circumstances they could not possibly oppose.[18]

What is the Johnson Administration hiding from the American people? Is it, for example, a policy of imperialism? Few Americans would easily assent to the suggestion that their nation follows an imperialist policy, except for the unfortunate "aberration" of 1898. Authoritative spokesmen for the government continue to assure us that the US "is not imperialist in design, in fact, or in temper." They point to the obvious fact that American control of Samoa, Okinawa, and the Virgin Islands simply does not amount to a substantial territorial empire.[19] But this merely confuses imperialism with one of its

[18] Reston, "Johnson and the Larger Crisis," *New York Times* (July 1, 1966). Reston refers to the Senate resolution passed at the time of the Tonkin Gulf incident of the summer of 1964. For analysis of this episode, see Franz Schurmann, Peter Dale Scott and Reginald Zelnik, *The Politics of Escalation in Vietnam* (New York, 1966), Chapt. III; and George McTurnan Kahin and John W. Lewis, *The United States in Vietnam* (New York, 1967), pp. 156-59.

[19] See, for an example, Herbert Feis, "Is The United States Imperialist?" *Yale Review*, XLI (Autumn, 1951), pp. 13-24. The phrase cited is from p. 13. Feis, a distinguished diplomatic and economic historian, was a long-time State Department official. His fervent belief in essential American rectitude leads him in this *Yale Review* article to certain indefensible positions. For example, he refers to the American acceptance of the U.N. Charter, which binds signatories to eschew force in settling disputes, and obliges them to respect the integrity and independence of all nations. "What use would a country with imperialist tendencies have for such a code?" Feis asks rhetorically (p. 18). Yet it is a fact that the Soviet Union (a country that Feis believes *is* imperialist) is also a signatory of that code.

historic forms—nineteenth-century colonialism. The twentieth-century American world empire of formally independent states, bound into a global network in which the United States dictates the terms of the alliance, presents a vastly different appearance from the pre-World War II British or French empires. The American variant, in which local native elites do covertly much of what the colonial governors used to do, has significant advantages. It enables economic and political penetration to proceed while avoiding the disadvantages of governing colonies directly and the necessity of acknowledging imperial control.[20] Without such an acknowledgment it becomes easy for Americans of many degrees of sophistication to dismiss the very notion of empire as a cranky heresy.[21]

The argument that the virtue of US aims precludes an imperialistic role may be easily dismissed as a naïve bit of parochialism. Another objection is more serious, however. Whatever may be the case in Latin America, US investments in Vietnam on the eve of escalation were too insubstantial to be the primary explanation of the deepening involvement.

But even if there were no substantial investment in Southeast Asia able to explain US policy there, it should be observed that total US foreign investment all over the world *is* quite large, and that Vietnam might just be that distant rampart chosen by American decision-makers to hold back the revolutionary tide threatening to engulf capitalism. Such a hypothesis would help explain the stepped-up vigilance of the US since the early 1950s, when direct investment abroad was only $11.8 billion. Now it is $49.2 billion, of which 30 per cent ($14.9 billion) is in the uneasy regions of Asia, Africa, and Latin America.[22] American businessmen are increasingly allured by the profits

[20] This line of argument is set forth in greater detail in Conor Cruise O'Brien, "Modern Forms of Imperialism," *Studies on The Left,* V (Fall, 1965), pp. 13-26; Kwame Nkrumah, *Neo-Colonialism: The Last Stage of Imperialism* (New York, 1966), and Paul Baran, *The Political Economy of Growth* (New York, 1957).

[21] Some foreign observers, not laboring under such constraints, are willing to talk of the reality behind the anti-imperialist façade. See, for example, Henry Fairlie, "A Cheer for American Imperialism," *New York Times Magazine* (July 11, 1965). Fairlie gaily concedes the existence of a US empire, and then goes on to praise it as being good, benevolent, etc.

[22] US Department of Commerce, *Survey of Current Business* (August, 1964), p. 10; (September, 1966), p. 34.

of foreign investment and ". . . increasingly are deciding
that markets abroad—not those in this country—offer the
biggest potential for future growth. The feeling grows that the
US market, while huge, is relatively 'saturated.'"[23] On this
basis it can be argued that the expansion abroad (that is, the
very existence) of the American corporate order is threatened
by revolutions in the third world,[24] and that the determination
to crush these revolutions is a rational response.

But the very premises of this line of argument may be challenged. There is much reason to suppose that the essential structure of world capitalism will survive even if revolutions spread
in the third world.[25] It is easy to conceive of a profitable trade
being carried on with a Communist China, as well as a Communist Russia, Vietnam, Cuba, or Dominican Republic. Lenin himself once announced to the capitalist world that Soviet Russia
would be a profitable trading partner and investment opportunity. This view is the economic counterpart of the doctrine of
peaceful coexistence, which thoughtful defenders of American

[23] *U.S. News and World Report* (June 1, 1964), quoted in Paul Baran
and Paul M. Sweezy, *Monopoly Capital: An Essay on the American
Economic and Social Order* (New York and London, 1966), p. 198.

[24] Overall figures tend to obscure the crucial role of leading US corporations, who have a high proportion of their capital tied up in specific
countries in the third world. Little research has been done on this problem, but the inquiries of Paul Baran and Paul Sweezy into Standard Oil
(New Jersey) holdings provide a strong indication of what further research will show. Using company figures, they find that Standard Oil's
profit rates in underdeveloped regions are greater than those in the developed countries. The percentage distribution of assets and profits by
region is as follows:

	Assets	Profits
United States and Canada	67	34
Latin America	20	39
Eastern Hemisphere	13	27
	100	100

(*Monopoly Capital*, p. 194, where the bases for these calculations are
reviewed.) To directors of such companies as Standard Oil, whose influence on the decisions taken in Washington is far greater than the ordinary citizen's, nationalization of their property is more than merely an
outrage; it is a matter of vast immediate and long-range interest.

[25] In offering the following arguments we wish to acknowledge (without fixing responsibility) helpful conversations with our colleagues, Professors Shane Mage and Louis Menashe. See also Robert Wolfe, "Imperialism and the Peace Movement," and Ronald Aronson, "Socialism:
The Sustaining Menace," *Studies on the Left*, VI (May-June, 1966),
pp. 28-61.

capitalism have sought since the early years of the Cold War.[26]

The belief that capitalist America can inhabit the same shrinking planet with Communist nations in Eastern Europe and in the third world not only accords with the simple human instincts for survival; it contains strong elements of self-interest for capitalist powers. In addition to prospects of profitable trade, normal relations with Communist nations can reduce the fervor of their commitment to worldwide revolution and bring them closer to the capitalist fold. Evidence for the possibility of taming radical revolutions is available; besides the examples of the Soviet Union and other Eastern European countries, there is the case of Mexico, whose revolution in 1910 did not prevent it from evolving into a thoroughly manageable American ally in the Western Hemisphere.[27] Thus, as a global strategy for the long-term defeat of Communism, peaceful coexistence has much to commend it.

Then why has the United States not adopted this policy at least in Asia, Africa, and Latin America? Why has another global strategy, that of relentless counterrevolutionary pressure, been maintained by the Johnson Administration? What conclusions can one draw about the rationality of American foreign policy and the ability to change that policy?

No definite answers to these questions can be given. But when they are, it will be necessary to recognize a large irrational component. This irrationality is evident in a number of areas. First, there is the persistent belief that the US is struggling against a unified world-conspiratorial movement aimed at overthrowing capitalism. Washington policy makers do have a vivid appreciation of the extent of disunity in the socialist camp, and they often act tactically on the basis of this disunity. But on the deepest level American strategy is aimed at opposing a monolithic, unified, global Communist movement that no

---

[26] See for examples, Walter Lippmann, *The Cold War: A Study in U.S. Foreign Policy* (New York, 1947); Lippmann, *The Communist World and Ours* (Boston, 1959); James P. Warburg, *Germany: Bridge or Battle Ground* (New York, 1947); Warburg, *Faith, Purpose and Power: A Plea for a Positive Policy* (New York, 1950); Warburg, *Agenda for Action: Toward Peace Through Disengagement* (New York, 1957); George F. Kennan, *On Dealing with the Communist World* (New York, 1964).

[27] See Stanley R. Ross ed., *Is the Mexican Revolution Dead?* (New York, 1966).

longer exists.[28] Furthermore, to the extent that US policy is supported by a popular consensus, the belief in the monolithic evil of world Communism shared by most Americans helps to sustain such international adventures as the attempt to stamp out the Communist-led revolution in Vietnam.

In the United States government's policy toward China this irrationality—and others[29]—are clearly revealed. The lack of any real substance in the notion of a world Communist conspiracy is even more evident if Peking rather than Moscow is seen as its hypothetical center. Certainly the People's Republic of China has declared its support for insurgent movements in Southeast Asia, most notably Vietnam; but very little more than verbal endorsement has been forthcoming. No responsible scholar has ever demonstrated that these Asian revolutionaries are controlled by Peking. The power play in Eastern Europe, where Communist regimes were brutally installed with the same Red Army bayonets used to defeat Hitler, finds no coun-

[28] No serious student of Communism would argue that after the 1920s the actual Communist International (COMINTERN) was a genuine force for spreading the proletarian world revolution. On this matter see Helmut Gruber, *International Communism in the Age of Lenin* (Ithaca and New York, 1967). On the thinking of US policy makers, see Arthur M. Schlesinger, Jr., *A Thousand Days* (Boston, 1965), *passim;* and Edmund Stillman and William Pfaff, *The New Politics: America and the End of the Postwar World* (New York, 1962), pp. 73-74.

[29] Including, of course, irrationality on the part of political leaders of mainland China itself. Discussion of this latter phenomenon falls outside of the scope of this present volume. But see on this Professor John K. Fairbanks' testimony in *U.S. Policy With Respect to Mainland China* [Hearings Before the Committee on Foreign Relations, United States Senate, 89th Congress, 2d Session] (March, 1966), pp. 98 ff.

[30] The apparent exception, Tibet, does not really weaken this generalization. The Chinese republican government succeeded in 1914 in getting formal recognition from the British (who had been encouraging Tibetan separatism for decades) of Chinese suzerainty there, and during the Second World War the validity of Chinese claims to Tibet was conceded by the allied powers. It is true, however, that until 1950 no Chinese government was able to *exercise* its formal sovereignty over Tibet. But in that year the Chinese Red army occupied the region, and the Communist government in Peking entered into an agreement (May 23, 1951 —see Chanakaya Sen, ed., *Tibet Disappears: A Documentary History* . . . [London, 1960], pp. 78-81) which provided for local autonomy and the indefinite postponement of the communization of Tibet. Thereafter, the Peking authorities introduced schools where none existed, brought the Marxist message, and thereby undermined the feudal, theo-

terpart in the Asian region.[30] There, successful Communist movements established themselves largely on their own resources, and often *despite* the wishes of Moscow.[31]

A characteristic American response to the post-World War Asian revolution is to assume that once the Communists achieve power in one place, neighboring regions will of necessity succumb to the power of Peking. This is the essence of the celebrated "dominoes theory," first enunciated by President Eisenhower in 1954.[32] Its logical corollary is that when insurrections are crushed in one place, they will be less likely to appear in another. When subject to logical and empirical scrutiny, the irrationality of the dominoes theory becomes evident. First, as we have seen, the evidence is that Communist insurgency in Asia is not the result simply, or even mainly, of Peking's initiatives. Secondly, if the dominoes theory has any validity, it must (according to the canons of logic)[33] be capable of being proven false by contrary evidence. Thus the defeat of Communist insurgency in Malaya and the Philippines in the 1950s[34] should have forestalled the development of an insurrection in Vietnam. But, of course, it did not. The desperation with which

cratic system of Lamaism. The traditionalist supporters of the Dalai Lama, with the aid of the government of India, sought to end this slow whittling away of their power, and in 1959 staged a full-scale separatist revolt. The uprising was crushed by the Chinese Red Army, and Tibet finally had to bow to the central power. Through minimization of India's role in the 1959 uprising, these events are used as illustrations of "Chinese imperialism" in such works as Frank Moraes, *The Revolt in Tibet* (New York, 1960), Chapt. III, and A. Doak Barnett, *Communist China and Asia: Challenge to American Policy* (Vintage ed., New York, 1961), *passim*. For a more balanced account, see Edgar Snow, *The Other Side of the River: Red China Today* (New York, 1961), Chapt. 77.

[31] On this, see Robert C. North, *Moscow and Chinese Communism* (2nd ed., Stanford, Calif., 1963). Without an understanding of the disputes of the 1920s and 1930s, the current stage of Moscow–Peking hostilities must remain incomprehensible.

[32] See his press conference remarks of April 7, 1954 in William A. Williams ed., *The Shaping of American Diplomacy* (Chicago, 1956), p. 1119.

[33] See Morris R. Cohen and Ernest Nagel, *An Introduction to Logic and the Scientific Method* (New York, 1934), Chapt. XIX.

[34] Lucian W. Pye, *Guerilla Communism in Malaya: Its Social and Political Meaning* (Princeton, N.J., 1956); David Wurfel, "The Philippines," in George M. Kahin (ed.), *Government and Politics of Southeast Asia* (2nd ed., Ithaca, N.Y., 1964), pp. 698-702.

the United States government holds to this discredited dominoes theory is testimony to a deep irrational strain in American policy.

It may be that this particular element of irrationality may be the result of the necessity of justifying an inherently unpopular war to the American people. It is difficult to develop wide enthusiasm for the notions of "counter-insurgency," and "limited war." These concepts are the stock-in-trade of military intellectuals and the eager consumers of their ideas in the Pentagon.[35] Whether from a deliberate attempt to deceive the citizenry, or because policy makers themselves share the more primitive notions, the US government has tacitly allowed irrational, even paranoid, doctrines to represent justifications of American actions.

Conditioned as they are to these irrationalities by twenty years of Cold War propaganda, Americans can easily overlook the prima facie reality in present-day Southeast Asia. That is, it is American troops, not Chinese, who are fighting Orientals in the jungles of South Vietnam, and it is American planes, not Chinese, that are daily dropping their cargoes of destruction on North Vietnam. In the light of these realities, it should be no surprise if increasing numbers of independent Asians conclude that there is infinitely greater danger in American presence now, than in any risk of theoretical Chinese takeover in the future. Such a realization has already come to Cambodia.[36] If it were to spread, then US policy would have the dubious distinction of bringing about that very expansion of Chinese influence it is hoping to combat.

Yet all these irrationalities inherent in American policy toward China are as nothing beside the danger of increasing racial enmity by engaging as an adversary the most populous non-white nation of the globe. The escalation of the struggle in Southeast Asia toward possible nuclear war with China is an imminent reality. In an age of vast destructive potential, when

[35] See on this, Irving Louis Horowitz, *The War Game: Studies of the New Civilian Militarists* (New York, 1963), and Sol Stern, "The Defense Intellectuals," *Ramparts* (February, 1967), pp. 31-40.

[36] See Roger Smith, *Cambodia's Foreign Policy* (Ithaca, N.Y., 1965); Robert Scheer, "A View From Southeast Asia: Phnom Penh," *Ramparts* (July, 1965), reprinted in *Ramparts Vietnam Primer* (San Francisco, 1966), pp. 37-49.

the concept of "victory" itself has become obsolete, what rational goal can conceivably be pursued by a policy that recklessly risks nuclear holocaust?

We argue that there is in fact little rationality in such a policy, and that irrational currents are evident not only on the lunatic fringe, but right in the mainstream of American foreign policy. Some of the implications of this view are developed elsewhere in this volume.[37]

However irrational American foreign policy may be when viewed from the interests of humanity at large, the current international orientation of the US may have a high degree of rationality in the eyes of those who have far-flung investments to defend. If this is true, then irrationality and rationality have to be distinguished. First, there would be the nonexistent case of a totally irrational policy that is in no one's interest. Second, there is the cold calculation in purely monetary terms by interested groups within the American corporate complex (including labor groups). From the point of view of these people, the Cold War (as long as it could be contained within manageable bounds), could be considered something of a small insurance charge to protect the high profitability of foreign investment. In recent years, as costs have mounted, it is possible that the class interests of the owners of corporate America may be better served by the alternative strategy of "peaceful coexistence." On the basis of this notion of interest, then, it may in fact be financially rational, as we have suggested,[38] to call off the Cold War and exploit the lucrative trade and investment opportunities that would then follow.

Nonetheless, this course of action is not likely to be adopted; to comprehend why is to understand the broad psychological motivations of policy makers which go beyond mere profit maximization. Such an understanding would have to take into account the larger pattern of how the corporate elite holds and wields power. Calling off the Cold War would mean that US policy makers would have to learn to tolerate left-wing revolutions in the third world and do business with their leaders. They would have to face the fact that dispatching American boys to fight in Asian jungles was no longer available as a sub-

[37] See our introduction to Part VII, below.
[38] See above, pp. 343-44.

stitute for full employment and equal opportunity at home.[39] Without war as a spur to the economy, a rational reorganization of industry would be a necessity. Massive, planned diversion of productive capacity from military to peaceful uses would have to be accomplished. A shift in priorities to meet the new domestic needs more vast than anything dreamed of in Lyndon Johnson's Great Society would have to be brought about.[40]

Bringing about these changes would involve at least a relative loss of power for those groups and individuals that wield power and have the greatest stake in the present order. They would possibly, in the long run, benefit financially, but the uncertainty of this eventual outcome measured against the profitability of the present short-run course will decide the matter. Men who are not only accustomed to exercising power, but to exercising it in traditional ways over subordinate peoples at home and abroad, will not easily give it up. Or they may have to have power taken from them. Until this is done, the likelihood is that the present form of corporate leadership will commit the nation to more and more desperate attempts to beat back the rising tide of revolution. Continuing the anti-Communist crusade will reinforce the authority of this leadership,[41] and deepen the social divisions and exacerbate the unsolved problems of contemporary America.

[39] The explicitness with which members of the liberal establishment are now willing to adopt militaristic solutions to social problems is little short of astounding. Daniel P. Moynihan's "Who Gets in the Army?" (*New Republic*, CLV [November 5, 1966], pp. 19-22) must be read to be believed. Arguing for Secretary of Defense McNamara's plan to use the army as a tool in the war on poverty, Moynihan never bothers to spell out the implications of "socializing" society's dropouts by enrolling them in the nation's armed forces. Presumably there would always have to be a threat to American security to justify maintaining a military establishment (with its built-in "rehabilitation center" as a by-product).

[40] Some of the problems involved in the transformation of the American economy to a peacetime basis have recently been explored in *The National Priorities Problem: Choices and Consequences, Papers Presented to a Meeting at Columbia University, September 30-October 1, 1966.* See also, p. 48, note 17.

[41] There is little evidence that the corporate elite will somehow fade away in the United States, to be replaced by some sort of technological or managerial elite, even when presented in skillful argument by Robert L. Heilbroner in *The Limits of American Capitalism* (New York, 1966).

AMERICAN STRATEGY
ON THE WORLD SCENE*

A writer in the *New York Times Magazine* (October 24, 1965) recently observed that the liberal intellectuals "are off in full pursuit of the President for his 'provocative' foreign policy. Indeed, never in my memory has the intellectual community been so bitterly anti-Administration." Two exceptions to this judgment immediately come to mind. John P. Roche, former Professor of Political Science at Brandeis, and once National Chairman of Americans for Democratic Action (ADA), is one. (The *Times* article mentioned above, entitled "A Professor Votes for Mr. Johnson," was written by Roche. Subsequent to the appearance of this piece, Roche was appointed Special Assistant to the President, where he is a kind of White House "intellectual in residence.")

The second example of an establishment intellectual is Walt Whitman Rostow, former Professor at the Massachusetts Institute of Technology. "He is one of the most original thinkers that I know of," President Johnson said on March 31 when he announced that Mr. Rostow would come to the White House as his Special Assistant. "I shall look to him," the President added, "as a catalyst for ideas and programs on the various continents of the world." [1]

* From W. W. Rostow, *View From the Seventh Floor* (New York, 1964), pp. 20-33. By permission of the publishers, Harper and Row.

[1] Announcement in *The U.S. Department of State Bulletin*, LIV (May 23, 1966), p. 803.

The predominating news which comes to us from day to day —in the newspapers, over television and radio—is the news of crises: Berlin and the Congo; Laos and Vietnam; and all the others. These crises are very much part of the reality we face. But our strategy goes beyond the crises that are forced upon us. We have a clear and constructive strategy. This strategy goes forward in quiet ways which do not make exciting news. Nor is this forward movement always easy to measure.

My main purpose here is to try to explain what it is that we are trying to achieve on the world scene as a nation—positively and constructively—and what our prospects appear to be.

When the Kennedy Administration came to responsibility it confronted situations of acute crisis in Southeast Asia, in the Congo, in Cuba, as well as the threat which has overhung Berlin since 1958—Mr. Khrushchev's threat that he would make a separate German treaty which, in his view, would extinguish Western rights in West Berlin. These were by no means the first crises of the postwar years. Such crises have been the lot of all who have borne responsibility in Washington since 1945.

Why is it that we appear to be living in a sea of troubles? What is it that determines the chronic recurrence of crises in our environment?

Leaving aside the direct intrusions of Communist military power in the postwar years—symbolized, for example, by the blockade of Berlin in 1948-49, the invasion of South Korea in 1950, and the periodic attacks on the offshore islands—postwar crises have been of three kinds, usually in some sort of combination: international crises arising from internal struggles for power, reflecting the inevitable political and social strains of modernization going forward in the underdeveloped areas; colonial or postcolonial conflicts involving European nations on the one hand and the nations and territories of the southern continents on the other; and the Communist efforts systematically to exploit the opportunities offered by these two inherent types of trouble. Think back and you will, I think, agree: Indochina, Suez, Iraq, Cuba, Algeria, the Congo, Bizerte, Goa, West New Guinea, the Dominican Republic. They were all compounded of some combination of these three elements, and they all arose in what we call the underdeveloped areas.

In Stalin's time the main thrust of Communist policy was

fairly direct and military; but in the last decade the Communists have worked systematically to make the most of the inevitable turbulence of the modernization process on the one hand and of the North–South conflicts on the other—using that shorthand geographical designation to represent the approximate fact that the industrial revolution came first to the northern portions of the world and is only now gathering strength to the south.

For example, in order to maximize the chance that Indonesia would go to war in order to acquire the Dutch-held territory of West New Guinea, the Communists advanced credits of about a billion dollars to Djakarta, just as, starting in 1955, they granted substantial arms credits in the Middle East to disrupt this area and to align themselves and the local Communist parties with issues that had strong national appeal.

Communist activity is global and is not, of course, confined to arms deals. There is almost literally no nation in Asia, the Middle East, Africa, and Latin America in which the Communists are not investing significant resources in order to organize individuals and groups for the purpose of overthrowing the existing governments and supplanting them with Communist regimes; and they look quite openly to what they call wars of national liberation—that is, to systematic subversion building up to urban insurrection or guerrilla warfare—as a way of bringing communism to the underdeveloped areas. Khrushchev has stated that he regards it as legitimate for Communist regimes to support such insurrection, which we can see in full cry in South Vietnam—a guerrilla war instigated, supplied, and guided from outside the country. In a speech of December 2, 1961, Castro spoke of guerrilla warfare as the match to be thrown into the haystack, and noted that many Latin American countries were ready for such treatment.

It is not difficult to see why the Communists look on the underdeveloped areas as an arena of opportunity. The process of modernization involves radical change not merely in the economy of underdeveloped nations but in their social structure and political life. We live, quite literally, in a revolutionary time. We must expect over the next decade recurrent turbulence in these areas; we must expect systematic efforts by the Communists to exploit this turbulence; we must expect from time to time that crises will occur; and a great deal of skill, courage, and insight will be required to handle them in ways which do not damage—and if possible promote—the interests of the free world.

But our strategy is not built on a merely defensive reaction to these turbulent situations and the Communist effort to exploit them. We are, I think, learning better how to anticipate crises; and we are working with our friends in the free world to head off or to deal with Communist efforts to exploit them. But we are doing more than that, and we intend to do more. We are working to a positive strategy which takes into account the forces at work in our environment and seeks to shape them constructively to our own purposes and interests—as a nation and as members of a community committed to the principles of national independence and human freedom.

What are these fundamental forces which we confront and which we must shape?

—The revolution in military technology, yielding an uncontrolled competitive arms race and, at present, an imbalance of the offensive over the defensive in the field of nuclear weapons.

—The revolution of modernization in Latin America, Africa, Asia, and the Middle East, including the modernization going forward in underdeveloped areas under Communist control.

—The revival of economic momentum and political strength in Western Europe and Japan.

—The revolution in science and technology, notably in international communications.

—The political revolution, marked simultaneously by proliferation of ardent new nations and an intensified interdependence which requires the individual nation-state to cooperate increasingly with others in order to provide for its security and economic welfare.

Taken together, these forces decree a world setting where power and influence are being progressively diffused within, as well as without, the Communist bloc; where strong inhibitions exist against all-out use of military force; where the interaction of societies and sovereign nations becomes progressively more intimate.

In the light of this view of what we confront in the world around us, our strategy has five dimensions.

First, we are strengthening the bonds of association among the more industrialized nations which lie mainly in the northern portion of the free world: Western Europe, Canada, and Japan.

Western Europe and Japan have been caught up in a remarkable phase of postwar recovery and economic growth. During that period they were protected by American military strength and supported in many ways by American economic resources. Although they must still rely on the deterrent power of American nuclear resources, they are evidently entering a phase where they wish to play a larger role on the world scene and have the resources to do so. We are in the midst of an exciting and complicated process of working out new terms of partnership with Western Europe in every dimension.

The European role in nuclear affairs is expanding in the light of Soviet possession of nuclear weapons and missiles, and Moscow's recurrent threat that Western Europe is "hostage" to its missiles.

New patterns of trade are being worked out within Europe, between Europe and the United States, between the whole Atlantic Community and the rest of the world.

Our policies with respect to economic growth and currency reserves are being discussed and aligned in the Organization for Economic Cooperation and Development; and we are moving into a new partnership in the business of aid to the underdeveloped areas.

Although Japan stands in a somewhat different relation to us than does Europe with respect to military affairs, in each of the other dimensions of alliance policy—trade, reserves, and aid—it is moving into a role of partnership with the industrialized north. And bilaterally we have moved closer to Japan, with the visits to Washington of Prime Minister Ikeda, Attorney General Kennedy's visit to Japan, and the meetings of the Joint Committee of Cabinet Ministers of the two nations.

The constructive steps that mark this process of mobilizing strength and resources of the advanced nations of the free world for global tasks do not usually make headlines unless—as is inevitable—there are phases of disagreement along the way; but it is a rapidly developing piece of history which will give to the cause of freedom a new strength, a new bone structure. The Trade Expansion Act of 1962 is both a symbol of what we are trying to create and a crucial element in its architecture.

The second dimension of our strategy concerns our posture

toward the revolution of modernization going forward in Latin America, Africa, Asia, and the Middle East.

What we sometimes call underdeveloped nations represent a wide spectrum with different problems marking each stage along the road to self-sustained growth. Some of these nations are well along the road; others are just beginning. And in the end, each nation, like each individual, is, in an important sense, unique. What is common throughout these regions is that men and women are determined to bring to bear what modern science and technology can afford in order to elevate the standards of life of their peoples and to provide a firm basis for positions of national dignity and independence on the world scene.

The United States is firmly committed to support this effort. We look forward to the emergence of strong assertive nations which, out of their own traditions and aspirations, create their own forms of modern society. We take it as our duty—and our interest—to help maintain the integrity and the independence of this vast modernization process—insofar as our resources and our ability to influence the course of events permit.

In 1961 the Executive Branch and the Congress collaborated to launch a new program[2] which would grant aid increasingly on the basis of each nation's effort to mobilize its own resources. This approach to the development problem—which looks to the creation of long-term national development programs—is beginning to take hold. We are in the midst of a complex turn-around—affecting both our own policy and that of many other nations.

National development plans cannot be made effective by writing them down in government offices; they require effective administration and the mobilization of millions of men and women.

New roads and dams, schools and factories require feasibility studies and blueprints if they are to be built—not merely listing

---

[2] Rostow is apparently referring to the New Frontier departure from the previous Republican policy of "massive retaliation," popularized by President Eisenhower's Secretary of State, John Foster Dulles. The new policy had two aspects. First, the U.S. as defender of the "free world" would extend its flexibility and range of military alternatives to include greater "limited" and non-nuclear capabilities. Second, it would involve the sorts of foreign aid proposals that Rostow mentions. Vietnam was a major test of the new strategies. See readings 31 and 32, below.—Eds.

in hopeful government documents. This turn-around process will, therefore, take time; but from one end of the underdeveloped regions to the other it is actively under way.

More than that, it is now clear that the United States is positively aligned with those men and women who do not merely talk about economic development and the modernization of their societies, but who really mean it and are prepared to dedicate their lives to its achievement.

It is no accident that President Kennedy spoke of a "decade of development." We are up against a longer and tougher job than the Marshall Plan. But we have already begun to create a new basis of partnership not merely between ourselves and the underdeveloped areas, but between the whole industrialized northern part of the free world and its less developed regions.

Our objective is to see emerge a new relation of cooperation among self-respecting sovereign nations to supplant the old colonial ties which are gone or fast disappearing from the world scene. While the headlines have been filled with the residual colonial problems—and they are very real—quiet but real progress has been made in fashioning new links between the more developed and the less developed areas.

The building of this new North-South tie is the third major dimension of our strategy on the world scene. It goes forward in the Alliance for Progress; in our relations with the new African nations; in the meetings of the Development Assistance Committee of the OECD in Paris; in the consortium arrangements of the International Bank for Reconstruction and Development; in the transformed relations of the British Commonwealth and the French Community; in the enlarging contribution of Germany, Japan, and other nations to economic development. And, above all, it goes forward in the minds of citizens in both the North and the South who are gradually coming to perceive that—however painful the memories of the colonial past may be—major and abiding areas of common interest are emerging between nations at different stages of the growth process, nations that are authentically committed to the goals of national independence and human freedom.

The fourth dimension of our strategy is military. There is much for us to build within the free world; but we must protect what we are building, or there will be no freedom.

A persistent characteristic of Communist strategy has been

its searching attention to specific gaps—regional and technical —in the defenses of the free world. It has been, thus far, an evident purpose of Communist strategy to avoid a direct confrontation not only with United States main strength, but with positions of relative strength within the free world.

Soviet policy appears to be based on sustained and sophisticated study of particular areas of vulnerability (e.g., northern Azerbaijan, Greece, Berlin, Indochina, South Korea) and particular types of vulnerability (e.g., the geographical position of Berlin, the shortage of local defenses against guerrilla warfare in Laos and South Vietnam).

We cannot rule out that in the future the Communists will be prepared to assault directly the United States or other positions of evident strength within the free community. Therefore, it is a first charge on United States military policy to make such direct assault grossly unattractive and unprofitable. But a major lesson of postwar history is that United States and Allied policy must achieve, to the maximum degree possible, a closing off of areas of vulnerability, if we wish to minimize the number and effectiveness of Communist probes. It is this lesson which requires that the United States and its allies develop a full spectrum of military strength, under sensitive and flexible control, capable of covering all regions of the free world, if we are to create a stable military environment and minimize the opportunity for Communist intrusions.

It is toward this objective that we have been working over the past three years. We have been building American military forces over the whole range from virtually unattackable Polaris submarines to the training of our own men and the soldiers of our allies to deter or to defeat guerrilla warfare.

We have made it clear to those who might attack that a nuclear assault on ourselves or our allies would bring in return nuclear disaster. We have made it clear that we would use all the force at our disposal if we or our allies are attacked massively by other means; but we require also the kinds of force that would permit us to deter or deal with limited Communist attack without having to choose between nuclear war and surrender.

At the same time we recognize that the arms race is an unsatisfactory way to provide national security in a nuclear age. We are prepared to take either limited or radical evenhanded

measures to reduce the risks of war and the burden of armaments, so long as we are confident that these measures can be
verified and controlled by effective measures of inspection.
This has been the burden of our position at the Geneva Disarmament Conference.

Our approach to problems of arms control and disarmament
is not in terms of propaganda; it is a soberly weighed aspect of
national security policy. We are in deadly earnest. But no
amount of United States staff work or seriousness of intent can
substitute for the essential missing ingredient: a Soviet willingness to acknowledge and to act on the simple fact that an end
to the arms race requires a progressive opening of societies to
mutual inspection.

The fifth element in our strategy concerns our posture toward the nations now under Communist rule. We have made it
clear that we do not intend to initiate nuclear war to destroy
the Communist world. The question then arises: Are we content merely to fend off Communist intrusion, military and subversive? What are our hopes and our prospects with respect to
the Communist world? Are we reconciled to a planet that shall,
at best, be forever split?

We are engaged in an historic test of strength—not merely of
military strength but of our capacity to understand and to deal
with the forces at work in the world about us. The ultimate
question at issue is whether this small planet is to be organized
on the principles of the Communist bloc or on the principles
of voluntary cooperation among independent nation-states
dedicated to human freedom. If we succeed in defending the
present frontiers of freedom, the outcome of that test of
strength will be determined by slow-moving forces of history.
It will be determined by whether the elements in the world
environment, which I listed earlier, are more successfully
gripped and organized by ourselves and our friends than by the
Communists.

The question then becomes: How is history moving? Are
these underlying forces now working for us or against us?

I would put it to you strongly that they are working our way,
if we have the wit to work with them.

First, in the more industrialized North we have seen in the
postwar years a remarkable demonstration which has had a
more profound effect on Communist thought than is generally

understood. Until very recently the Communists believed that the United States was something of a special case. We were viewed as the fortunate democratic island-continent with much land and few people, permitted to enjoy—at least for a time—a special favored destiny. They looked to Europe and Japan as more vulnerable regions subject to Communist takeover in the fairly near future. What has been demonstrated in the past decade is that advanced democratic societies have learned to avoid protracted phases of severe unemployment and that the American pattern of development—our standard of living and the provision of high standards of consumption to the mass of the people—is the general pattern. The trend toward the Americanization of standards of living in Western Europe and Japan, and the vitality of democratic capitalism in the past decade, is a major setback to the Communist image of history, to their ideology, and to their working plans.

Partly because of this setback they have looked with increasing hope and enterprise to the underdeveloped areas. There they thought the Communist methods of organization and the Communist example in China, North Vietnam, and elsewhere —as a means of moving an underdeveloped country forward rapidly toward modern status—would draw others to the bloc. They turned to a strategy of outflanking and isolating the United States, Europe, and Japan by winning over the underdeveloped areas—by ideological attraction as well as by subversion, aid, and diplomacy.

The returns are not yet in; but a sober and cautious assessment shows this: Where the Communists have had power in underdeveloped areas—in China, North Korea, North Vietnam, and now in Cuba—they have done an unimpressive job technically, quite aside from the inhumanity of a police state. The most striking fact about the mood in Asia, when I went out there with General Taylor in 1961, was the loss by the Communists of their power to attract by example in either North Vietnam or in China. The Communist states are drab and hungry. In particular, the Chinese Communists have demonstrated that the most powerful control machine ever mounted in an underdeveloped country is incapable of forcing men to grow enough food; and their agricultural crisis has compounded into a general crisis of industrial production and foreign exchange.

Meanwhile, India and certain other underdeveloped nations

have begun to demonstrate that real momentum and steady progress can be obtained in an underdeveloped area by mobilizing the energies and loyalties of the people by consent and normal human incentives.

The demonstration in the underdeveloped areas is not yet as definitive a victory for freedom as that in the northern half of the free world. One of the great tasks of this decade is to complete this demonstration. But the lesson of our experience thus far is that we should be confident that in going forward with economic development by the methods of pragmatic planning and individual consent which are natural to us, we are on the right track technically as well as morally; and that the Communist image of the problems of modernization—and Communist techniques for handling them in the underdeveloped areas— are just as archaic as their notions of how one should organize an advanced industrial society.

There is yet another force working our way, and that is the intent of people and governments in the underdeveloped areas to maintain their independence.

The drive for independence is a most powerful force. We can honestly align our policy with this force. In the end the Communists cannot, and this is one fundamental reason why the Communist offensive in the underdeveloped areas will fail.

Finally, the Communist bloc itself is now in the midst of a slow-moving but great historical crisis. This crisis takes the form of the deep dispute between Moscow and Peiping—a dispute which has engaged, in one way or another, Communist parties throughout the world. What lies behind this dispute, among other factors, is the rise of nationalism as a living and growing force within the Communist bloc. It is a force within Russia itself, and it is a growing force in other regions where Communist regimes are in power. Despite the interest of Communists in maintaining their cohesion against the West, the slow fragmentation of the Communist bloc and the diffusion of power within it go forward.

We expect no quick or cheap benefits from this process. In the short run it may present problems to us, as when the Russians and the Chinese compete to exert their influence over the Communist party in Hanoi. But, fundamentally, the assertion of nationalism and national interests within the Communist bloc should tend to produce a more livable world. The diffusion of power, we know, is the basis for human liberty within societies; and on the world scene it is the basis for independent nations.

For example, we have every reason to believe that the limited assistance we have given Yugoslavia and Poland over the years and our willingness to maintain wide human contacts with their citizens have been sound long-run investments in the principle of national independence and human freedom.

We should, therefore, be prepared—as these national interests exert themselves—to find limited areas of overlapping interest with Communist regimes and to work toward a world which increasingly approximates the kind of world we envisaged when the United Nations was set up.

Our strategy is, then, quite simple. We are working from day to day to bind up in closer partnership the industrialized nations of the north, to work with our friends in the North to create a new partnership between the more developed and less developed nations. Recognizing and welcoming the new strength to be found in Western Europe and Japan, recognizing and welcoming the impulse of the southern nations to modernize, we see a path ahead which would reconcile the great interests involved and gradually build a community of free nations.

We intend to defend this community of free nations and to do so in ways which will minimize the possibility that a nuclear war will come about; and we intend—with all the poise and insight we can muster—to draw the nations now under Communist regimes toward the free world community by both ruling out the expansion of communism and exploiting specific areas of overlapping interest which we believe will increasingly emerge as the strength, unity, and effectiveness of the free community is demonstrated. As Secretary Rusk has said: ". . . we should be aware that the concepts of independent nationhood, of national interest and of natural culture, are day to day asserting themselves strongly" within the Communist bloc. We have every reason to be confident that the wave of the future lies with the fundamental principles on which our own society is based and which are rooted also in the United Nations Charter.

It is in this spirit—in terms of these objectives and this intent —that we do our work from day to day in Washington. We know that there will be frustrations and setbacks. We know that we shall have to deal with difficult crises as well as press forward with our work of construction. But, as we go about our business, we are in good heart, and we shall not be deflected. We believe that time is on the side of the things this nation stands for, if we use time well; and we intend to do so.

THE ALLIANCE FOR PROGRESS IS A REVOLUTION AT WORK*

On March 13, 1961, John F. Kennedy asked the nations of the hemisphere to unite "in a new Alliance for Progress, a vast cooperative effort, unparalleled in magnitude and nobility of purpose, to satisfy the basic needs of the American people. . . . Let us once again awaken our American Revolution until it guides the struggle of people everywhere—not with an imperialism of force or fear— but the rule of courage and freedom and hope for the future of man." Five months later, at the Inter-American Conference of Punta del Este, the assembled governments —twenty in all—agreed to establish the Alliance. Two of its major objectives were "to improve and strengthen democratic institutions . . ." and "to encourage, in accordance with the characteristics of each country, programs of comprehensive agrarian reform. . . ." Five years later, speaking at the new headquarters of the Pan American Health Organization, to an audience of Latin American diplomats and alliance officials, President Johnson gave his assessment of the impact of the Alliance for Progress.

◇ ◇ ◇

The health of this hemisphere is the business of the house in which we have assembled this morning to celebrate the fifth anniversary of the Alliance for Progress.

From this building Dr. [Abraham] Horwitz [Director of the Pan American Sanitary Bureau] and his staff reach to the far

* From *Department of State Bulletin* (September 5, 1966).

corners of our continent to combat disease and to minister to the medical needs of people. They know that not only the claims of compassion and personal dignity but the promise of economic prosperity demand sound bodies and healthy environments.

In the field of public health, the Pan American Health Organization was an early forerunner of the Alliance for Progress. Today it is a very integral part.

Five years ago the American governments embarked on this audacious experiment. We were neither cautious in concept nor timid in scope. We knew that our common purpose was to make a new kind of revolution.

The great question of the hemisphere was: Can sweeping change come about peacefully and constructively in freedom, or must it rise from the wreckage of violence and destruction?

Our answer began with the Act of Bogotá in 1960. The Charter of Punta del Este and the progress of five years since then have clearly confirmed that answer. The republics of this hemisphere have shown that deep social change is compatible with peace, is consistent with democracy, and is consonant with individual liberty.

We have sounded a sure and a certain note; namely, that great change can be wrought by reason and not rifles, by builders and not bullets.

The alliance is not a Marshall Plan to rebuild war-torn economies. Nor is it a program of handouts to bolster the status quo. The aim of the alliance is to build new societies. And its method is to build democratically through a partnership of all. Today, the alliance is a revolution at work—it is creating, building, transforming, reaching forward; it is touching the lives of hundreds of millions of our fellow citizens.

We are encouraged today that the average Latin American growth rates are now exceeding the minimum goal of 2½ per cent per capita that was set forth at Punta del Este. But we do know that growth charts and statistics never tell the whole story. The true measure of our work is in its impact upon our peoples.

We see it in the teacher and her pupils as they move into new classrooms in the mountain plateaus of the Andes and the *barrios* of the cities; we see it in the isolated Indians of remote villages that are striving to become part of larger national communities; we see it in the laborers that are carving roads on the eastern slopes of a vast mountain range to open up the heartland of South America; we see it in the farm extension agents and in the *campesino* who for the first time works a farm that he can now call his own. We see it in the workers and the managers that are building new and great and modern industries. We see it in families that are moving from the slums to a new apartment or a new house.

We see it in wholly new institutions such as cooperatives, development banks, and unions and see them unlock the energies and the resources of thousands of people who learn the strength of a common endeavor. And we see it in new legislation to revamp outdated tax structures, to modernize obsolete systems of land tenure, and to renovate archaic institutions of government.

Beyond these visible accomplishments lie very profound changes in attitude from which the future development of this hemisphere will flow. For the alliance has shattered the myths that five years ago threatened its promise.

It has shattered the myth that the status quo will not yield to progressive change as a way of life. It has shattered the myth that the nations of the hemisphere cannot look across national frontiers to their sister nations in the search for common solutions. It has shattered the myth that inflationary spending is the royal road to rapid development. It has shattered the myth that Communism in this hemisphere is the wave of the future. The tragic plight of the Cuban people has shown Communism's writ to be worthless.

The framers of the Charter of Punta del Este labored under no illusions. They know there are no panaceas for progress. And so they charted the right, but hard, course.

They called upon the hemisphere to mobilize public and private resources for diversified investment. They called for governments to modernize public services, taxation, and agriculture. They called for our nations to mount major programs in education, health, and housing. They called for Latin America to move toward economic integration. And they called for better trading conditions and increased external financial and technical cooperation for all of Latin America.

Every man and woman in this room knows that these are not easy tasks. But we also know that the beginning of the beginning is already behind us. And now we must look to what lies ahead of us.

We have only begun to meet the needs of today, and these are but a small fraction of the needs of tomorrow.

If present trends continue, the population of this hemisphere will be almost one billion by the year 2000. Two-thirds, some 625 million, will live in Latin America. Whatever may be done through programs to reduce the rate of population growth, Latin America faces a vast challenge.

Farm production, for instance, should increase by 6 per cent every year, and that will be double the present rate.

At least 140 million new jobs will need to be created.

Over a million new homes should be built each year.

More than 175,000 new doctors need to be trained to meet the very minimum requirements.

Hundreds of thousands of new classrooms should be constructed.

And annual per capita growth rates should increase to the range of 4 to 6 per cent.

These requirements, added to the demands of the present, mean that new sights must be set, that new directions and renewed drive must be found if we are to meet the challenge, if we are to move forward.

In a few months the Presidents of the American republics will meet to establish the priorities for the years that are ahead of us. Our governments are carefully and today thoroughly preparing the agenda for that conference. Some of the areas of very special concern are already emerging.

First among these is the economic integration of Latin America.

The question is whether progress lies ahead in unity or in isolation. Our sister republics in Latin America must decide that question, and they must decide it for themselves. For our part, we deeply believe that effective unity and not separation is vital to the needs of expanding populations.

In the total development of Latin America national and local plans and projects are most important, but regionwide plans and collaboration are absolutely essential. Nineteen fertilizer industries, nineteen steel complexes, nineteen isolated markets, and nineteen different systems of tariffs—these would signify only stagnation and inefficiency, and in many instances pure waste.

We are ready, therefore, to work in close cooperation toward an integrated Latin America. As the other republics are forming their policies to accelerate this movement, at the moment we are now reviewing the opportunities for joint action throughout the hemisphere.

To my fellow Presidents, I pledge: Move boldly along this path and the United States will be by your side.

To all the hemisphere we say: Let the pace be quickened. Time is not our ally.

The path to economic unity and growth is manyfold. We must first concentrate on those assets within our reach that are not being used to full advantage.

For instance, there are lands that are lying fallow or failing to yield their potential at the moment because of inadequate techniques or because there is too little fertilizer or because there is not enough equipment.

There are factories that are standing idle or operating at reduced capacity because production is inefficient. The national market may be too small, or the purchasing power may be too little.

There are human resources that are unused because of the shortage of jobs or the absence of skills.

And while we meet these problems, we must also prepare to conquer the inner frontiers which can provide living room and resources for generations that are yet to come. The eastern slopes of the Andes, the water systems of the Gran Pantanal, River Plate and Orinoco, the barely touched areas of Central America and of Panama—these are just a few of the frontiers which this morning beckon to us.

But not every frontier is geographic. My fellow American Presidents and I will be greatly concerned with the other vistas before us.

For instance, there is education.

The Americas of the seventies and eighties will make large demands for trained men and women—not only for engineers, scientists, and agronomists to guide our paths, not only for electricians, carpenters, and machinists to use our tools, but for poets, artists, and musicians to enrich our lives.

All of us know that education is primarily a national task to be done with local resources. But there are endeavors where more is needed and where the alliance must help: school construction, teacher training, and improved administration. The challenge of vocational and modern higher education is wide open—for management, technical, and administrative skills in government and in private business.

The alliance so far has only scratched a thin mark on the great mass of illiteracy, although Latin America is the only continent in the developing world where the number and percentage of illiterates is decreasing each year.

Education, then, must become the passion of us all. Let us approach this challenge completely dissatisfied with our traditional methods. Let us adapt the modern miracles of science, radio and television, and audio-visual techniques. Let us adapt these to the needs of our children and indeed to the needs of our adults.

The time has also come to develop multinational institutions for advanced training in science and technology. For without these Latin America will suffer the continued "brain drain" of some of its ablest youth.

There is also for us the frontier of agriculture.

For too many years we have acted as if the road to prosperity runs only through the main streets of our large cities. Now we know that national prosperity is closely linked to the land and closely linked to those who cultivate the land.

In most Latin American countries it is in urban areas where poverty and despair catch our eye. But half of the people live in rural Latin America and receive less than a quarter of the national income.

There is no reason why the land of the hemisphere cannot be made to fill the needs of our homes and our factories. There is no reason why rural population should not be full partners in modern economic life. And, looking beyond our hemisphere, there is no reason why the Americas cannot supply a larger share of the growing world market for food and for fiber.

This, of course, will require better planning of crops to fit the soil and to fit the markets available. It will demand better soil and better fertilizer and better water control. It will need a good extension service to educate farmers in new methods. It will require shared mechanization, better credit and markets, and better distribution.

The resources required for these tasks must not be needlessly spent on arms. Military budgets in Latin America are not exceptionally large by the general world standards, but there is a recurrent tendency to seek expensive weapons with little relevance to the real requirements of security. This tendency is often reinforced by competition among the neighboring countries.

And in these Americas, where by solemn treaty and by established practice our governments are bound to resolve disputes by peaceful means, we just must find a way to avoid the cost of procuring and maintaining unnecessary military equipment that will take clothes off the backs and food away from the stomachs and education away from the minds of our children.

Well, these are some of the basic tasks—and only some—which lie before us as we try to fulfill the promise of the modern world in which we are so privileged to live.

These tasks are going to be accomplished by concrete acts and not by rhetoric. We are not interested in the appearance; we are dedicated to the achievement. By specific steps we can strengthen and we can carry forward this great Alliance for Progress that was started five years ago.

This will mean democratic stability in which free men can labor without upheavals and without chaos. This will mean monetary stability so that the savings of the people can work effectively to develop all the resources. This will mean fiscal responsibility—that means an efficient public administration, a sensibly managed public debt, realistic exchange rates, and a market that's unhampered by artificial monopolies. This means progressive leadership—a government wise enough to insist on modernizing reforms and the most effective allocation of public resources.

This means, above all, personal freedom and human dignity. For if men are not truly free, if individuals are not protected against economic and political exploitation, then they do turn to violence and to extremism, whose first victim, then, is progressive reform.

So, as we meet here together this morning, we all recognize that change is everywhere throughout this hemisphere. We shall either shape it or be misshaped by it. And along with change will come contrast and contradiction. One man will be orbiting the earth while below him millions of his fellow men starve. *Campesinos* will be plowing the ground with oxen while a thousand miles away atomic power works its wonders. That is the kind of world in which we are living and this is the world that we are called upon to deal with.

So I say to you this morning, let's go back to the original question, the basic question: Can sweeping change be progressive and be peaceful?

My own country knows of this question. We are going through such a change even as I speak. It began in the 1930s, and it is continuing today. I lived here during the Great Depression. I remember the tattered soldiers going down Pennsylvania Avenue to Anacostia. I remember the poor who went hungry and formed our soup lines and the men and women who searched for work that they could not find.

I remember the loss of confidence and hope, the biting despair and the fear that gripped a whole continent. If ever a great nation was tempted to surrender to authoritarian rule, if ever free people were tempted to barter freedom for bread, we were tempted in the United States in the early 1930s.

Instead, by peaceful although sometimes very controversial means, we rebuilt our society. We shaped laws which preserved the freedom of individuals but protected them against the excesses of extremism. They are all so familiar in my mind. I remember the stock market regulations and the stock exchange and securities act. I remember the Social Security that so many people feared was so socialistic, and federal housing and guaranteed bank deposits, and minimum wages when we voted for 25 cents an hour (many predicted our political defeat), when collective bargaining was insured by law, and when we rescued and saved and brought back to life the Tennessee Valley Authority, the agricultural extension act, and many more.

We gave the lie in those years, and since, to Karl Marx's theory that the rich must get richer and the poor, poorer.

Through a peaceful and a very progressive adventure, the poor have moved on upward, the middle class has broadened enormously, and prosperity has reached so many that we can afford to be concerned not only about quantity but about quality as well—the quality of our children's education, the quality of the medical care for our parents, the quality of our life in the rural and in the urban areas.

Now, I would be the last to indicate that all of our problems are solved. Far, far from it. But with all the world watching us operate in this goldfish bowl, we are continually striving to fulfill our promises, to live up to our expectations.

Throughout the hemisphere this morning I think this same experience is underway. Our chosen instrument is the Alliance for Progress. It is not a recipe for instant utopia, as President Kennedy assured you so many times in his statements about his dreams. Perhaps only our children and theirs will finally know whether the alliance really wins or not. But we do know this much: We are moving! We do know what must be done, and we think we know how to do it.

We do know that social progress and economic change under liberty are the only acceptable roads to national vitality and to individual dignity. We do know that to achieve fulfillment a people must be free. And for people to be free, they must be educated. And to learn, they must have bread.

We know that risk and danger are the marks of our time.

We know that what we do now will shape not only this generation but generations yet unborn.

So I am very proud that you asked me to come here today, and I am so glad that I am privileged to be here with you on this occasion.

A meeting like this, and like the conference of American Presidents that is ahead of us, does not in itself change the conditions in which we live. But if it changes us, if it renews our confidence in one another, if it inspires us and gives us strength to carry on and continue the grueling and challenging work that peaceful change requires, it will have served its purpose and met its responsibilities.

DECLINE OF THE ALLIANCE
FOR PROGRESS *

Shortly after coming to power, Fidel Castro, in a speech in Buenos Aires, suggested that the United States allocate $30 billion of its vast wealth to develop Latin America. Although this suggestion was ridiculed at the time, many today attribute the $20 billion Alliance for Progress, launched only one year later by President Kennedy, to Fidel Castro and the Cuban Revolution. For example, Jerome Slater, writing in the *Yale Review*, states:

Although the extent of rising mass dissatisfaction with the status quo in Latin America had been well known to observers for years, its implications had escaped United States policy makers. But the revolt against Batista sharply dramatized this discontent, making it painfully obvious that rightist dictatorships, through their reactionary social and economic policies and repression of all political opposition, were creating an environment ripe for Communist exploitation. In order, then, to forestall the spread of "Castro Communism," the incoming Kennedy Administration decided to press actively for democracy and modernization in Latin America.

He goes on to pinpoint the differences between the Kennedy and Johnson Administrations. Whereas the former "viewed the threat [of Communism] primarily as long-term in nature, to be met by long-term measures . . . [the

* From "Whatever Happened to Baby *Alianza?*" *New Politics*, IV (Winter, 1965), pp. 90–95. By permission.
1 *Yale Review* (Winter, 1966), p. 172.

latter] is far more preoccupied with the allegedly immediate dangers of Communist subversion, so that cooperation with the 'anti-Communists' of Latin America, *any* anti-
Communists, seems necessary." [2]

In the article that follows, Robert F. Smith challenges
the official evaluation of the Alliance made by the President in reading 26. He asks, was the Baby *Alianza* "strangled in the cradle, or was the creature in the nursery
really grandma dollar diplomacy in disguise?" Dr. Smith
is Professor of History at Rhode Island University and
the author of *The United States and Cuba: Business and
Diplomacy, 1917-1960* (New York, 1960).

The original pronouncements concerning the *Alianza para
Progreso* were filled with the idea that this new program would
enable the countries of Latin America to make a social revolution without violent upheaval. The Charter of Punta del Este
proclaimed the ideals of the *Alianza* in such terms as:

*They [the people of the hemisphere] are determined for them-
selves and their children to have decent and ever more abundant lives, to gain access to knowledge and equal opportunity
for all, to end those conditions which benefit the few at the
expense of the needs and dignity of the many. It is our inescapable task to fulfill these just desires—to demonstrate to
the poor and forsaken of our countries, and of all lands, that
the creative powers of free men hold the key to their progress
and to the progress of future generations.*[3]

The charter also put great emphasis upon providing a more
equitable distribution of national income and rapidly raising
the standard of living of the masses.

Were these statements empty rhetoric or did they reflect a
sincere belief that drastic socio-economic change could come to
Latin America through peaceful, democratic means? This question has been argued with much heat since 1961, but undoubtedly some of the authors of the charter honestly believed in
the latter postulate. Some individuals did question the major

[2] *Ibid.*, p. 179.
[3] Lincoln Gordon, *A New Deal for Latin America* (Cambridge, Mass.,
1963), pp. 118-19.

shift in US policy which the charter and supporting speeches seemed to imply. It just did not appear likely that the United States was planning to give up its basic goal of hemispheric hegemony, but the alliance did seem to promise at least a new approach to dollar diplomacy; an approach more flexible and less committed to the orthodoxies of US capitalism. The alliance seemed to indicate that the United States was prepared to accept, nay even to advocate, drastic changes in the prevailing system of distributing wealth.

In the beginning it was possible to see in the alliance the promise that the United States would encourage the development of a variety of systems in the middle ground between capitalism and complete statism. Such a development would have meant a decided retreat from the traditional position that reforms must not in any way violate the economic concepts of business or step outside of the legal framework of capitalism. In short, the United States government appeared ready to accept rather drastic modifications of the "trickle down" concept of economic distribution based on the "iron law of scarcity."

At least such an impression could be gained from various pronouncements on the Alliance. During the Senate debate on the new program J. William Fulbright declared:

Latin Americans have felt the domination of the United States. They have been on the receiving end of the preachments of the advantages of capitalism and free enterprise. But these words have been at best meaningless to most of them, and at worst in their countries a source of exploitation.

The Senator hammered away at the conservative oligarchies for their failure to do something for the common people, and he warned that the U.S. would help them only if they were "converted to the cause of genuine social reform." [4]

No sooner was the alliance off the drawing boards than vocal opposition rang forth both in Latin America and the United States. Considering the ruling groups in some Latin American countries, statements like those of Senator Fulbright were comparable to lecturing a whorehouse madame on the virtues of celibacy. The same could be said for various elements in the US

[4] Speech of May 9, 1961; *Congressional Record,* 87th Cong., 1st Sess., 1961, Vol. 107, No. 77, pp. 7117-7119.

business community. The editors of *Business Week* magazine declared:

A *US policy of sponsoring revolutionary change in the under-developed countries could well undermine the position of US private investment in many areas. To a considerable degree, the revolution of rising expectations is a revolt against capitalism, or at least against the way it seems to operate in the underdeveloped nations.*[5]

These editors showed an amazing degree of insight in the last sentence. As far as they were concerned freedom and democracy were synonymous with their brand of capitalism. After all, they reported one critic as saying, "It took fifteen years and many billions of US government dollars to rebuild the capitalist world on the Bretton Woods pattern. . . . The Administration will bring the system crashing down, if it isn't careful."

The *Business Week* editors also stated that social reform and economic development were contradictory objectives since reform would involve a redistribution of income and an increase in consumption. The editors quite frankly admitted that the businessman's program for Latin America would not meet the demands of the people or the intellectuals, and would not save every country from "Communist-sponsored revolution." The answer to the latter problem would be militarily intervention against any such revolutions to protect capitalism in the hemisphere.

Similar attacks on the alliance could be heard in Congress and in other segments of the business community. One of the most influential blows, however, came from President Kennedy's

[5] "Keeping Out the Reds by Revolution," *Business Week* (July 5, 1961), pp. 67-69; in an editorial résumé of the article the editors stressed the point that underdeveloped nations must remain "aligned to us economically," even if they were politically neutral, "A Program That Tries to Reach Too Far," *Ibid.*, p. 128. More subtle criticism can be found in the testimony of Rodman C. Rockefeller (International Basic Economy Corp.), Leonard Kamsky (W. R. Grace & Co.), John F. Gallagher (Sears Roebuck & Co.), and William F. Butler (Chase Manhattan Bank) before the Subcommittee on Inter-American Economic Relationships of the Joint Economic Committee (US Congress) in May, 1962; *Economic Developments in South America* (Washington, D.C., 1962), pp. 44-95. See also, Julio E. Nuñez, "The Importance of Latin America's Elite," *Fortune* (January, 1963), pp. 70, 210.

specially selected "Committee to Strengthen the Security of the Free World." This group—better known as the Clay Committee—reflected almost identically the views of *Business Week*. Its report gave much emphasis to denying foreign economic aid to any country which deviated to any extent from private enterprise. Any intention to intervene in such countries to "impose" the US economic system was denied, but several pages later the committee emphatically stated that the US "cannot allow another Castroite-Communist Cuba to come into existence." In other words the Clay Committee was saying that the US should cut off economic assistance to countries which drifted any appreciable distance from private enterprise even if this meant creating "less friendly political climates," but that in Latin America any country which then turned elsewhere for assistance would be prevented from doing so. Clearly, the nonintervention proviso was not to apply in this hemisphere.[6]

In its report on the Alliance for Progress the committee repeatedly emphasized the primacy of private investment and private enterprise. The list of the reforms which the committee stressed are quite illustrative of the basic thinking of the group. Most of the items were part of the canon of orthodox business practices, such as monetary stability, balanced budgets, elimination of subsidies to government enterprises, and stimulation of private investment. The last item on the list was a reference to "better utilization of land" to—among other things—increase the income of the "lower levels of society." In the next paragraph, however, the committee pointedly declared that expropriation or nationalization was completely alien to proper economic development. In addition, Latin American countries were warned that there was no real middle ground between capitalism and state-controlled economies and that accumulation of wealth must precede improvement in the standard of living.

As an interesting second thought, the Clay Committee recommended that economic aid be increasingly funneled through international agencies such as the International Bank and the International Development Association. This would, hopefully,

[6] The Committee to Strengthen the Security of the Free World, *The Scope and Distribution of United States Military and Economic Assistance Programs* (Washington, D.C., March 20, 1963), pp. 5-12; cited as *Clay Comm. Report*.

make the United States less subject to attack when it was necessary to "offend national sensitivities" by imposing conditions to insure "sound" economic practices. United Nations agencies were pointedly excluded from the recommended list.[7]

There was one dissenting voice on the Clay Committee. Mr. George Meany—hardly an economic radical—stated that he could not regard AID and the alliance "as business operations primarily." His major criticism of the report was its concern with institutions rather than people. As he stated: "We cannot expect this vast sector [the workers] to voluntarily enlist in our cause without rights, without freedom, without justice, without bread." [8]

The Meany dissent had much less impact on policy than the majority report. This report was part of a rising tide designed to put the alliance back into the familiar policy ruts. One of the best ways to observe this movement is to compare the reports of the Subcommittee on Inter-American Economic Relations of the Joint Economic Committee (US Congress) for 1962 and 1964. The 1962 report contained some criticism of the alliance, but it also devoted some attention to the need for social reform.[9]

The 1964 report, however, was entirely dedicated to the necessity and the means for bolstering private investment and private enterprise. This congressional committee vigorously criticized the Charter of Punta del Este for its failure to assign a predominant role to private investment. It pointed out that in the 3,000-word section on national development programs, only a ten-word phrase referred to the role of the private sectors.[10] In the opinion of the committee this created a misconception in regard to the real aims of the alliance, and those who fell into this misconception—concerning private investment—"failed to appreciate fully the spirit which prevails in the United States." The committee defined this "spirit" as equating freedom and

[7] *Ibid.*, pp. 15-17.
[8] *Ibid.*, pp. 22-25.
[9] Subcommittee on Inter-American Economic Relationships of the Joint Economic Committee (US Congress), *Economic Developments in South America* (Washington, D.C., 1962); also, *Economic Policies and Programs in South America* (Washington, D.C., 1962).
[10] Subcommittee on Inter-American Economic Relationships of the Joint Economic Committee (US Congress), *Private Investment in Latin America* (Washington, D.C., 1964), pp. 5-6.

democratic institutions with "the system of private enterprise, private investment, and free choice."

The basic theme that emerges from this report is that the Alliance for Progress is a program which depends on a good climate for business. All reform or change must be geared to attracting private investment. Thus, the traditional pattern of distribution of wealth—the trickle-down concept—must not be disturbed since this would pose a threat to immediate profits and hence create a bad climate for business. For all practical purposes the committee defined the Alliance for Progress as another facet of the American business system. In their own words:

We concluded these hearings . . . with the feeling that the virtues of the free enterprise system itself needed to be better understood and more aggressively presented and "sold." Along with certain members of the Commerce Committee for the Alliance for Progress "we are persuaded that the most important way in which the United States can help is by exporting the ideas implicit in a free economy." [11]

This is further illustrated by the committee's denunciation of any expropriation of private property, even for agrarian reform; which had been given a few kind words in the 1962 report. Given the conditions outlined by this group, any restructuring of the distribution system would be well-nigh impossible. The committee even resorted to the traditional nationalization policy of the United States in words that go back to the first social revolution in the hemisphere. Mexicans, Guatemalans, and Cubans have all heard, "Compensation must be prompt and effective"; a phrase meaning "compensation must be made in sound, convertible currencies." [12]

For one who had hoped that the Alliance for Progress reflected at least some wisdom gained from the revolutionary upheavals of the twentieth century, this committee report sounded too much like the Bourbons who never learned and never forgot.

By the end of 1964 it was quite evident that the alliance was hardly more than the dollar diplomacy of the 1930s with a new facade. All of the old vocabulary had reappeared, and all of the

[11] *Ibid.*, p. 6.
[12] *Ibid.*, p. 11.

traditional concepts of business diplomacy had been restated. The business of America was still business; not the restructuring of societies. Alliance for Progress houses were selling for fifteen thousand pesos—seven thousand in cash—in Colombia, and one landless native commented about the program, "It has not touched the poor." [13]

In retrospect, was the alliance ever intended to touch the poor directly, or was the thinking behind it based on the assumption that the fruits of economic expansion automatically trickle down to the lower levels? The chief architects of the alliance were New Deal Democrats who accepted the trickle-down concept of distribution as an article of faith, and who were at heart unable to accept any real restructuring of the socio-economic system. Lincoln Gordon—Ambassador to Brazil and the prime author of the Alliance—has described the program as a "New Deal for Latin America," and has constantly told the Latin Americans to emulate those aspects of the New Deal which stressed expansion over distribution. Gordon separated distributive reformers from expansionist reformers and has written that the "primary emphasis" must be placed on expansion.[14] This downgrading of reform in the system of distribution fits in with the overall emphasis on reinforcing private enterprise capitalism and guiding Latin American development into the international structure of the US business system. This is definitely not social revolution, and is reformist only in the minimal sense that the RFC, FHA, and AAA were in the United States of the 1930s. None of these agencies were especially noted for improving the condition of workers, slum-dwellers, or tenant farmers.

The role of the Alliance for Progress as a new vehicle for US economic expansion has become apparent since 1962. The fact that Adolph A. Berle, Jr. was one of President Kennedy's key advisers indicates that this was at least one important aspect of the original alliance planning. In 1956, Berle called for a broad, new program to use Latin America as "an outlet for our surplus," and thus prevent a business recession in the United States. According to Berle this program would entail an Inter-American Bank, some financing by the US government, and a

[13] John P. Powelson, "The Land-Grabbers of Cali," *The Reporter* (January 16, 1964).
[14] Gordon, *New Deal for Latin America,* pp. 102-07.

major expansion of US business in Latin America. He stated the goal of such an effort in these terms:

Is this "giveaway foreign aid" in new dress? Nothing of the sort. . . . When New York and New England financed the development of industry, transport, and power plants on the US Pacific Coast we did not talk of "giveaway" from New York to Oregon or California. We bought stocks and long-term bonds and knew that we were building a national economy. Now we can tackle the business of building a supranational economy. Whether we know it or not, this is the real basis for the economy of the United States.[15]

These views were certainly embodied in Berle's concept of the alliance, and they have become basic themes in the program.

Thus, from the beginning the alliance has involved an apparent contradiction. The vocabulary was that of social revolution, but the concepts were a mixture of US-oriented capitalism and New Deal economics. This is not to say that some US officials did not want to see reforms in Latin America, but the concept of development underlying the alliance has forced even these officials to steadily dilute the reform element. The US assistance to the literacy program in Guatemala, for example, is scheduled to end in July, 1965, and one authority has written that the reason for this is that "many people in the State Department" view literacy "primarily as a dangerously volatile element extremely difficult to control, and thus, in the interest of stability, to be avoided." [16] This is the process we have been witnessing since the birth of the alliance. The reform programs and the rhetoric of social change have been steadily eliminated since these have appeared to threaten the kind of stability which is based upon private enterprise and the protection of private investments. Today the basic concepts of the founders of the alliance stand forth in pristine simplicity.

This raises a basic question concerning the future of the Alliance and social reform in general. Can the United States government which is basically oriented to the needs of capitalists— both North and South American—really support basic socioeconomic change? Even the hint of such a possibility produced outcries and pressures in the United States and Latin America.

[15] A. A. Berle, Jr., *The Reporter* (June 28, 1956), p. 11.
[16] Alan Howard, *New York Times Magazine* (February 1, 1965), p. 76.

Those officials who were sincere about reform have seen their position evaporate as the US government has increasingly gone out of its way to reassure businessmen that the alliance did not in any way threaten the prevailing system of distribution. The future of peaceful revolution under democratic auspices has been severely shaken by the seven military coups which have taken place since 1961. Most of these have involved resistance to change by groups holding economic power, and in each case the United States has taken the path of least resistance and recognized the new governments after some token demonstrations toward "democracy." The US accommodation to this combination of forces seems to provide a negative answer to the above question.

Today the policy of the United States indicates that the words of warning which Senator J. William Fulbright issued to the Latin American oligarchies in 1961 have been shelved. Now the Latin Americans are told that the freedom, democracy, and economic well-being proclaimed in the Charter of Punta del Este really means the freedom to shop at the supermarket of one's choice. With this reductio ad absurdum it is high time to recall the words of wisdom spoken by Mr. Dooley; "Hunger, Hinnissy, is about th' same thing in a raypublic as in a dispotism. They'se not much choice iv unhappiness between a hungry slave an' a hungry freeman." [17] Senator Fulbright was referring to this idea in 1961 when he warned:

We have now an opportunity—and it may be our last—to put our relationships with Latin America in order. We have now an opportunity to begin a program that will provide things for the people, not for the governments—not for the upper crust.[18]

This was the supposed promise of "Baby *Alianza*." Was the baby strangled in the cradle, or was the creature in the nursery really grandma dollar diplomacy in disguise?

[17] Finley Peter Dunne, "Cuba vs. Beet Sugar," in Louis Filler, ed., *The World of Mr. Dooley* (New York, 1962), p. 168.
[18] Congressional Record (May 9, 1961), pp. 7, 117-119.

THIS IS FOR BACKGROUND ONLY GENTLEMEN.

IT IS NOW POLICY TO NOT ALLOW ANY FURTHER REVOLUTIONS IN LATIN AMERICA WITHOUT PRIOR AMERICAN CLEARANCE.

ALL POTENTIAL REVOLUTIONARIES ARE WARNED THAT IF THEY WISH TO OVERTHROW ENTRENCHED GOVERNMENTS THEY MUST FIRST SUBMIT TO US IN ADVANCE A FULL LIST OF THEIR LEADERSHIP SO WE CAN CHECK THEIR LOYALTY TO THE U.S. GOVERNMENT.

ONCE SUCH A LIST IS CLEARED, A LEGISLATIVE PROGRAM BY THE REVOLUTIONARIES SHOULD BE FORWARDED IN TRIPLICATE TO THE DEPARTMENTS OF STATE, DEFENSE, AND COMMERCE, AS WELL AS TO BOTH HOUSES OF CONGRESS.

IF A CONSENSUS CAN BE ARRIVED AT THE GOVERNMENT OF THE UNITED STATES WILL SO INFORM THE REVOLUTIONARIES -

WHO, AFTER TWENTY ONE DAYS, MAY HAVE THEIR REVOLUTION.

I WILLING.

© 1965 JULES FEIFFER, JUNE 27, 1965.
THE HALL SYNDICATE, INC.

THE DOMINICAN REVOLUTION TOOK A TRAGIC TURN*

On April 24, 1965, military elements sympathetic to Juan Bosch, the former President of the Dominican Republic who had been ousted the previous September in a bloodless military coup, staged an uprising against the ruling junta. Four days later, on President Johnson's instructions, 400 marines were sent to the Dominican Republic; the sole stated purpose at the time was the safeguarding of the lives of American citizens. By May 1, the total number of American troops in the Dominican Republic (or en route) had reached 6,200. The State Department denied at the time that United States troops were taking sides in the conflict. On May 2, the President went before the television cameras to give an accounting to the nation. In his address, reprinted below, President Johnson now declared that the revolution "took a tragic turn" and had been "seized and placed into the hands of a band of Communist conspirators." The best recent account of these events is Tad Szulc, *Dominican Diary* (New York, 1965).

◇ ◇ ◇

I have just come from a meeting with the leaders of both parties in the Congress, which was held in the Cabinet Room of the White House. I briefed them on the facts of the situation in the Dominican Republic. I want to make those same facts known to all the American people and to all the world.

There are times in the affairs of nations when great princi-

* From *Department of State Bulletin* (May 17, 1965), p. 744.

ples are tested in an ordeal of conflict and danger. This is such a time for the American nations.

At stake are the lives of thousands, the liberty of a nation, and the principles and the values of all the American republics.

That is why the hopes and the concern of this entire hemisphere are on this Sabbath Sunday focused on the Dominican Republic.

In the dark mist of conflict and violence, revolution and confusion, it is not easy to find clear and unclouded truths.

But certain things are clear. And they require equally clear action. To understand, I think it is necessary to begin with the events of eight or nine days ago.

Last week our observers warned of an approaching political storm in the Dominican Republic. I immediately asked our Ambassador [W. Tapley Bennett, Jr.] to return to Washington at once so that we might discuss the situation and might plan a course of conduct, but events soon outran our hopes for peace.

Saturday, April 24—eight days ago—while Ambassador Bennett was conferring with the highest officials of your government, revolution erupted in the Dominican Republic. Elements of the military forces of that country overthrew their government. However, the rebels themselves were divided. Some wanted to restore former President Juan Bosch. Others opposed his restoration. President Bosch, elected after the fall of Trujillo and his assassination, had been driven from office by an earlier revolution in the Dominican Republic.

Those who opposed Mr. Bosch's return formed a military committee in an effort to control that country. The others took to the street, and they began to lead a revolt on behalf of President Bosch. Control and effective government dissolved in conflict and confusion.

Meanwhile the United States was making a constant effort to restore peace. From Saturday afternoon onward, our embassy urged a ceasefire, and I and all the officials of the American government worked with every weapon at our command to achieve it.

On Tuesday the situation of turmoil was presented to the Peace Committee of the Organization of American States.

On Wednesday the entire Council of the Organization of American States received a full report from the Dominican ambassador.

Meanwhile, all this time, from Saturday to Wednesday, the danger was mounting. Even though we were deeply saddened by bloodshed and violence in a close and friendly neighbor, we had no desire to interfere in the affairs of a sister republic.

On Wednesday afternoon there was no longer any choice for the man who is your President. I was sitting in my little office reviewing the world situation with Secretary Rusk, Secretary McNamara, and Mr. McGeorge Bundy. Shortly after 3 o'clock I received a cable from our ambassador, and he said that things were in danger; he had been informed the chief of police and governmental authorities could no longer protect us. We immediately started the necessary conference calls to be prepared.

At 5:14, almost two hours later, we received a cable that was labeled "critic," a word that is reserved for only the most urgent and immediate matters of national security.

The cable reported that Dominican law enforcement and military officials had informed our embassy that the situation was completely out of control and that the police and the government could no longer give any guarantee concerning the safety of Americans or any foreign nationals.

Ambassador Bennett, who is one of our most experienced foreign-service officers, went on in that cable to say that only an immediate landing of American forces could safeguard and protect the lives of thousands of Americans and thousands of other citizens of some thirty other countries. Ambassador Bennett urged your President to order an immediate landing.

In this situation hesitation and vacillation could mean death for many of our people, as well as many of the citizens of other lands.

I thought that we could not and we did not hesitate. Our forces, American forces, were ordered in immediately to protect American lives. They have done that. They have attacked no one, and although some of our servicemen gave their lives, not a single American civilian or the civilian of any other nation, as a result of this protection, lost their lives.

There may be those in our own country who say that such action was good but we should have waited, or we should have delayed, or we should have consulted further, or we should have called a meeting. But from the very beginning, the United States, at my instructions, had worked for a ceasefire beginning the Saturday the revolution took place. The matter was before the OAS Peace Committee on Tuesday, at our suggestion. It was before the full council on Wednesday, and when I made my announcement to the American people that evening, I announced then I was notifying the council.

When that cable arrived, when our entire country team in the Dominican Republic, made up of nine men—one from the army, navy, and air force, our ambassador, our AID man, and others—said to your President unanimously: Mr. President, if you do not send forces immediately, men and women—Americans and those of other lands—will die in the streets—well, I knew there was no time to talk, to consult, or to delay. For in this situation delay itself would be decision—the decision to risk and to lose the lives of thousands of Americans and thousands of innocent people from all lands.

I want you to know that it is not a light or an easy matter to send our American boys to another country, but I do not think that the American people expect their President to hesitate or to vacillate in the face of danger, just because the decision is hard when life is in peril.

The revolutionary movement took a tragic turn. Communist leaders, many of them trained in Cuba, seeing a chance to increase disorder, to gain a foothold, joined the revolution. They took increasing control. And what began as a popular democratic revolution, committed to democracy and social justice, very shortly moved and was taken over and really seized and placed into the hands of a band of Communist conspirators.

Many of the original leaders of the rebellion, the followers of President Bosch, took refuge in foreign embassies because they had been superseded by other evil forces, and the Secretary General of the rebel government, Martínez Francisco, appealed for a ceasefire. But he was ignored. The revolution was now in other and dangerous hands.

When these new and ominous developments emerged, the OAS met again, and it met at the request of the United States. I am glad to say they responded wisely and decisively. A five-nation OAS team is now in the Dominican Republic, acting to achieve a ceasefire to insure the safety of innocent people, to restore normal conditions, and to open a path to democratic progress.

That is the situation now.

I plead, therefore, with every person and every country in

this hemisphere that would choose to do so, to contact their ambassador in the Dominican Republic directly and to get first-hand evidence of the horrors and the hardship, the violence and the terror, and the international conspiracy from which United States servicemen have rescued the people of more than thirty nations from that war-torn land.

Earlier today I ordered two additional battalions—2,000 extra men—to proceed immediately to the Dominican Republic. In the meeting I have just concluded with the congressional leaders—following that meeting—I directed the Secretary of Defense and the Chairman of the Joint Chiefs of Staff to issue instructions to land an additional 4,500 men at the earliest possible moment. The distribution of food to people who have not eaten for days, the need of medical supplies and attention for the sick and wounded, the health requirements to avoid an epidemic because there are hundreds that have been dead for days that are now in the streets, and other protection and security of each individual that is caught on that island require the attention of the additional forces which I have ordered to proceed to the Dominican Republic.

In addition, our servicemen have already, since they landed on Wednesday night, evacuated 3,000 persons from 30 countries in the world from this little island. But more than 5,000 people, 1,500 of whom are Americans—the others are foreign nationals—are tonight awaiting evacuation as I speak. We just must get on with that job immediately. . . .

The American nations cannot, must not, and will not permit the establishment of another Communist government in the Western Hemisphere. This was the unanimous view of all the American nations when, in January, 1962, they declared, and I quote: "The principles of Communism are incompatible with the principles of the inter-American system."

This is what our beloved President John F. Kennedy meant when, less than a week before his death, he told us: "We in this hemisphere must also use every resource at our command to prevent the establishment of another Cuba in this hemisphere."

This is and this will be the common action and the common purpose of the democratic forces of the hemisphere. For the danger is also a common danger, and the principles are common principles.

So we have acted to summon the resources of this entire

hemisphere to this task. We have sent, on my instructions the night before last, special emissaries such as Ambassador [Téodoro] Moscoso of Puerto Rico, our very able Ambassador Averell Harriman, and others to Latin America to explain the situation, to tell them the truth, and to warn them that joint action is necessary. We are in contact with such distinguished Latin American statesmen as Romulo Betancourt [former President of Venezuela] and José Figueres [former President of Costa Rica]. We are seeking their wisdom and their counsel and their advice. We have also maintained communication with President Bosch, who has chosen to remain in Puerto Rico.

We have been consulting with the Organization of American States, and our distinguished ambassador—than whom there is no better—Ambassador Bunker, has been reporting to them at great length all the actions of this government, and we have been acting in conformity with their decisions.

We know that many who are now in revolt do not seek a Communist tyranny. We think it is tragic indeed that their high motives have been misused by a small band of conspirators who receive their directions from abroad.

To those who fight only for liberty and justice and progress I want to join with the Organization of American States in saying —in appealing to you tonight to lay down your arms and to assure you there is nothing to fear. The road is open for you to share in building a Dominican democracy, and we in America are ready and anxious and willing to help you. Your courage and your dedication are qualities which your country and all the hemisphere need for the future. You are needed to help shape that future. And neither we nor any other nation in this hemisphere can or should take it upon itself to ever interfere with the affairs of your country or any other country.

We believe that change comes, and we are glad it does, and it should come through peaceful process. But revolution in any country is a matter for that country to deal with. It becomes a matter calling for hemispheric action only—repeat, only— when the object is the establishment of a Communist dictatorship.

Let me also make clear tonight that we support no single man or any single group of men in the Dominican Republic. Our goal is a simple one. We are there to save the lives of our citizens and to save the lives of all people. Our goal, in keeping with the great principles of the inter-American system, is to help prevent another Communist state in this hemisphere. And we would like to do this without bloodshed or without large-scale fighting.

The form and the nature of the free Dominican government, I assure you, is solely a matter for the Dominican people, but we do know what kind of government we hope to see in the Dominican Republic. For that is carefully spelled out in the treaties and the agreements which make up the fabric of the inter-American system. It is expressed, time and time again, in the words of our statesmen and the values and hopes which bind us all together.

We hope to see a government freely chosen by the will of all the people.

We hope to see a government dedicated to social justice for every citizen.

DOMINICAN REPUBLIC:
REVOLUTION AND RESTORATION*

The following article deals with the aftermath of United States military involvement in the Dominican Republic. Lack of space makes it impossible to indulge in extensive analysis of the early path to US intervention. What follows is a brief chronology.

The assassination of the Dominican dictator, Rafael Leonidas Trujillo, on May 31, 1961, set off a complicated struggle for power. Joaquín Balaguer, Trujillo's figurehead President, was able to maneuver his position into one of real power, but was overthrown in early 1962 by a military coup d'état. This political chaos seemingly came to a close in December, 1962, with the overwhelming electoral triumph of Juan Bosch, considered by most of the American press to be part of the non-Communist democratic left. This election was widely praised, and the Dominican Republic was hailed as a showplace of democracy. Less than a year later, under the guise of crushing Castro Communism, Bosch was removed in a bloodless military coup. President Kennedy, that very day, September 25, suspended diplomatic relations and it was announced that economic aid to the Dominican Republic had been halted.

United States Dominican policy underwent a change after the assassination of President Kennedy on November 22, 1963. Five days later, the civilian junta in the Dominican Republic announced a set of future election dates. Within a month, the Johnson Administration ex-

* From *Liberation*, (September 1966), pp. 5-11. By permission.

tended diplomatic recognition to the junta. Interestingly enough, this event took place on the very same date (December 14) that Thomas C. Mann was elevated to the top Latin American post in the State Department. The appointment of Mann, known to be a "hard-liner," gave the new President his first taste of policy criticism. Since Kennedy's death it appears that the Johnson Administration may have shifted the direction of U.S. policy toward Latin America. This appearance may very well disguise a deeper continuity. It is unclear whether there was a distinct break, or a continuation under Johnson of policies that were already undergoing a hardening.

Three months later, Mann was reported to have said to a group of American ambassadors and aid officials that the United States will no longer automatically break diplomatic relations and cut off economic aid whenever a military coup takes place. Instead, as *U.S. News & World Report* put it, "To the Johnson Administration there can be good coups and bad ones" (March 30, 1964, p. 14).

No sooner said than done. On April 1, Brazil's constitutional government, headed by João Goulart, was overthrown; on April 2 the new provisional president, Raniere Mazzilli, installed by the military as their front man, received from President Johnson the following message: "Please accept my warmest good wishes on your installation as President of the United States of Brazil. The American people have watched with anxiety the political and economic difficulties through which your great nation has been passing, and have admired the resolute will of the Brazilian community to resolve these difficulties within a framework of constitutional democracy and without civil strife."

The next application of the Mann doctrine was the Dominican revolution, which began on April 24 with a military uprising by supporters of Juan Bosch (The "Constitutionalists") against the ruling junta. In reading 28, President Johnson gives his interpretation of what ensued between April 24 and May 2. An alternative view is offered by James Petras below, which carries the picture forward to include the recent election of Joaquín Balaguer. At issue is whether the United States intervened to protect American lives and prevent a popular revolution from being taken over by a small band of Communist conspirators, or whether it intervened to prevent the triumph of a popular revolution, but one contrary to what the State Department has defined as in the American interest.

James Petras has been a Research Associate at the University of California (Berkeley) Institute for International Studies. He returned in 1966 from a year in South America and now teaches political science at the Pennsylvania State University.

Santo Domingo, with its bullet-scarred buildings, its rundown commercial area, and its daylight streets full of unemployed men and broken-down wooden houses, appears like a southern Negro shantytown juxtaposed on Harlem. The difference is in the slogans on the walls: FUERA GENOCIDAS, FUERA AGRESORES YANQUIS. The houses destroyed by US mortars still lie in ruins; most restaurant windows are still boarded up. Much of the destruction was wrought by the battle of June 15-16 (1965), when US artillery and mobile units including mounted machine guns tried to carry out the US generals' boast that the revolutionaries' sector could be taken in two hours. After three nights and two days of fighting the US marines had advanced only two blocks. The ravages are still present, but many Dominican freedom fighters are not. In an interview with the author (August 25, 1966) former President Juan Bosch estimated that between three and four thousand Dominicans had been killed after the US intervention.

Today trade union leaders do not venture out of doors without carrying a pistol as protection against likely attacks while the Balaguer government is trying to pass restrictive legislation to totally disarm the populace. Today anyone who was a Constitutionalist militant is hiding the fact, for it is something worse than suspect—it can be grounds for murder. After 8 P.M. the streets are empty; the "peace and tranquility" is based on fear of the continued terror by political gangsters who now have been revived and strengthened. Before dawn hundreds of unemployed line up outside the headquarters of the *Partido Reformista* (Balaguer's organization) and around government offices, waiting for nonexistent jobs. Typical of the style of the new government is the Red Cross, which has its posters plastered on all the buildings boasting of its service to "all the community." During the Revolution when this author with a committee of doctors called the Red Cross trying to send urgently needed plasma to the Constitutionalists, they replied that they had to consult the State Department—and then refused to transmit the plasma to that side of the "community." A US businessman told me that I should come here and get rich, especially now with all the new "projects" getting under way with no taxes, cheap labor ($1 to $2 a day): "In the next five years this is the best country in Latin America to make a fortune in."

The program of the Balaguer government gives every indication of being a businessman's dream. The proposed *Ley de Austeridad* would lower salaries of public employees, freeze the wages of the working class and prohibit strikes for at least one year—while placing no limits on profits. Prices of staple foods continue to soar. According to *Listin Diario*, August 22, 1966, official prices are: regular rice 14c a pound, native beans 16c. Trade unionists and workers claimed prices were much higher—beans 24c, "poor" meat 60c, potatoes 8c a pound. The lowering of real wages and the increase in prices reverse the central planks of the Balaguer campaign: lower prices and increased salaries.

The *Ley de Tregua Política* would restrict party activities by not allowing public meetings except during the three months preceding the next election. Marches, assemblies, and public demonstrations in general would be prohibited. This would further atomize and demoralize the populace, cripple the parties of the opposition, and allow the Balaguer-controlled Congress to pass any further antipopular legislation without opposition—hence the term by which Balaguer's government is frequently referred to, the "legal dictatorship." On August 20 Balaguer signed a law that dissolves the state-owned Dominican Sugar Corporation (CAD) and makes the continuance of state ownership conditional on profitability. Under this law the enterprises could be turned over to private hands in five years. The Balaguer appointee on the new Consejo Estatal del Azúcar, Gaitán Boucher, was a top executive of the US-owned South Puerto Rico Sugar Company.

The voracious appetites unleashed by the installation of

Balaguer and the influence they can wield is seen in the following episode: In August the Appeals Court of Santo Domingo dropped charges against a son-in-law of Trujillo, Martínez Alves, who had been dispossessed of the Trujillo patrimony. This ruling would have resulted in Martínez Alves becoming the principal stockholder of the majority of enterprises that are now state-owned. But since this would have deprived Balaguer of major economic resources for governing, the Procurator General overruled the court. (*Listin Diario,* August 22-26.)

Balaguer has confirmed in their positions all the Trujillista military officers whom the US had rearmed and reorganized. The February 27 Campamento (the Constitutionalist garrison) is being totally dismantled, its officers being sent to study abroad or discharged and intimidated. Leading Constitutionalists who have been discharged from the army include Quiroz Pérez, Pericles Peralta Bueno, Lención Silverio, Polanco Alegría, Marino Almanzar, González y González, Marte Hernández, Rodríguez García and Major Calderón Cepeda. In addition, G-2 Office of the Military Intelligence Service has sent invitations to the remaining Constitutionalist officers and soldiers to visit their office, where they are subject to thinly veiled threats. (*El LJ4,* August 20, 1966, organ of the Movimiento Revolucionario 14 de Junio.) All efforts have been directed toward purging any possible dissident political force and creating a military completely loyal to the United States and to Balaguer.

In line with government policy a considerable number of militant workers have been discharged by private and state enterprises: 695 workers from Consuelo Sugar central, 2,000 workers from public works, 624 from the San Cristóbal works, 45 workers, including the trade union leadership, from the Dominican Cotton Consortium, etc.

The political arrest and selective terrorism of Constitutional leaders practiced under the provisional government of García Godoy continue unabated. A few days before my arrival in late August, Ramón Emilio Mejía Pichirilo, a Constitutionalist Comandante, and Juan Bisonó Mera, an ex-Constitutionalist official in Villa Bisonó, were assassinated. Balaguer's "investigations," like those of García Godoy, never discovered the murderers.

Other recent "unsolved" killings include a policeman of Constitutionalist sympathy, Anastasio Sosa, and Guillermo Peláez (June 14th leader) and some fourteen persons in the month of August alone. Numerous arrests of Constitutionalist leaders continued to take place in Puerto Plata, Barahona, El Leibo, and the capital. Even the middle-of-the-road weekly *Ahora* commented sarcastically on the attitude of the government toward the continuing terrorism: "nothing happens, because the authorities, including the First Executive of the nation, reduce their expressions to the traditional and inefficient 'investigations' that have always occurred." (*Ahora*, August 29, p. 66.) The reference to "always occurred" underlies the continuity of the Balaguer regime with his earlier Presidency under Trujillo.

The restoration of the old order was the primary strategy of the US invasion. The policies of Balaguer and of the military— their political gangsterism—are the fruits of the US intervention. The police state legislation, the anti-working-class measures and the totalitarian agencies and methods now in force are approved and to a large degree drawn up by US advisers who are found in the offices of every major ministry on the policy-making level, from Financial and Commercial to Military Affairs.

A discussion of politics in the Dominican Republic today must be seen in terms of three phases: 1) the revolution of April 1965; 2) the US military intervention and its aftermath; 3) the complex and continuing *process* of restoration of the old ruling classes in a permanently explosive socio-political milieu.

The physical presence of US force was the prime instrument for the resurgence of Trujillismo both militarily and politically. The elections were held in a context where 70 per cent of the population (rural) was under military occupation and only one candidate was actually permitted access to the voters. The results of the election proper were determined by the results of the first days of the revolution and of the US military occupation.

The April revolution began when a group of military officers led by Captain Manuel Pena Tavera of the February 27 Campamento revolted against the corruption of military personnel and sought popular support. The initial call of the rebel military was for a military junta which would rule for three months and then would permit free elections. The military did not "arm the people." About 100 or so civilians received arms from the military; the arming of 6,000 civilians was the result of *popular* assaults on armories, military stockades and government buildings. As in all *popular* revolutions the people armed themselves. It was this fact of armed popular power which, together with the defeat of the pro-US totalitarian military forces of Wessin y Wessin, caused Johnson to send in the marines. The revolution began as an overwhelmingly urban mass movement involving the *urban* unemployed, the industrial workers, artisans, the self-employed, the lower-level employees and the professionals. The top leadership was primarily professionals from the Partido Revolucionario Dominicano (PRD); the "comando" or command units were made up and led by Catholic trade unionists (CASC) and June 14th militants in addition to PRD militants. The US military force attacked and encircled the revolutionary forces, *confining them to the city and preventing the effective mobilization of the countryside.* The US broke an agreement that it made with the Constitutionalists, under the pretense that the US troops were establishing a zone of two blocks on either side of the US embassy to allow for the safe evacuation of US citizens. Once the US troops moved into the area they immediately extended the "passageway" into a noose around the Constitutionalist-held city. The trust placed in agreements with US political military forces indicated the predominance of the Boschists.

As a consequence, the countryside was under American political–military control from at least the middle of May, 1965, preventing the élan and solidarity of the popular forces in Santo Domingo from spreading throughout the country. The experience of a people's army defeating the tyrannical and parasitic forces of the ruling class, the program of popular reform, the arms and organization with which to confront the US marines—all these were absent from the countryside. Apart from the many areas where outright fraud was committed, Balaguer's greatest voting strength generally was found in those areas which the US marines cut off from contact with the revolutionary forces, the areas isolated and under US and Dominican military control. *Hence the urban-rural split in the vote coincided with the origins of the revolution and the geo-military positions after the US invasion.*

In reality there were two different but related "interventions" by the US: a military intervention in April, 1965; and a political one, beginning in September and reaching its peak during the presidential election campaign. The first (military) intervention continued; at the same time it established the bases for the second (political) intervention. The first phase was accomplished through the use of overwhelming power—43,000 marines, tanks, helicopters, armed mobile units, etc.—and its lightning application to rebel population centers (Northern Santo Domingo, Ciudad Nueva). Once favorable geographic positions were established, policy alternated between selected assaults and negotiations, each utilized to reinforce the other, while applying maximum pressure to force acceptance of US terms as the basis for "negotiations." The US was willing to negotiate over the formation of a provisional government, but not about the Constitution of 1963, which went by the board. The Bosch-oriented leadership (supported by the small Dominican Communist Party or PCD), fearing the continual threats of an imminent massive US attack, reluctantly agreed to negotiate for a provisional government on US terms. The June 14th Movement held out for the Constitutionalist demand. With close to 3,000 Dominicans killed and the city surrounded, the US imposed the provisional government through negotiations that were not very different from blackmail.

With the installation of the provisional government, the process of demobilizing the popular forces and reconstituting the ruling élite was begun in earnest. The army, which had gone over to the Constitutionalists en masse, defected again out of fear or opportunism when the news arrived that US troops had landed, leaving only 1,000 soldiers who actually fought with the rebels. The "meat grinder" tactics were now applied to the popular forces. During the period of the provisional government over 280 Constitutionalist leaders and activists were killed; not one of the murderers was apprehended. (These figures were given to me by Caonabo Javier, Secretary General of the Social Christian Party, and were generally supported by most Dominican political observers.)

Selective terror, the reduction of the political strength of the Constitutionalists in the armed forces, and above all the growth of an extensive network of economic-propaganda units especially in the countryside and in government offices, began to introduce the carrot along with the military stick. The more involved US political action groups mentioned to me by the education director of the Christian Democratic trade unions included CEDOECA (Dominican Center of Peasant Education), the International Development Foundation, the Community Development Organization, CARITAS, Peace Corps, Agency of International Development and Civic-Action Units (military).

Leaders of the Social Christian party, PRSC, estimated that the US–Balaguer group spent $13 million on the election. The idea of US policy makers was to establish a government subordinate to and dependent upon the United States while seeing that opposition political leadership was physically eliminated or neutralized. As "pragmatists," US policy makers took advantage of the existence of the political gangsters to further their policy goals.

In the meantime the popular forces and especially the trade union movement went through a series of militant actions, including the general strike of February (1966), attempting to stem the tide. The American military presence and its determination to stay there at all costs provided the Dominican ruling class the guarantee that the strike could not be successful: there was a force beyond the Dominican Republic which could supply the resources needed to withstand popular pressure. The overwhelming presence of the now almost universally hated US troops, and the inability of the Bosch leadership to propose any way out, began to have a reverse effect on the least political and most vulnerable sectors of the lower class: the women, the older people, the "service sector" (domestic servants, taxi drivers, etc.). Peace and price control, not Balaguer, were what most of these voters wanted; the will to resist among these strata had given way to the wish to subsist. The Balaguer "coalition" took shape amidst political assassinations and selected terror, military control and a single candidate in 70 per cent of the country; fear and confinement to the urban centers for the opposition (Bosch was so frightened of being assassinated that he "campaigned" without ever leaving his house). In the city the Balaguer vote was composed generally of exhausted lower-class women with hungry children and of older male family heads; in the countryside of intimidated peasants receiving politically controlled economic doles, and bombarded on all sides with intense anti-Communist propaganda from the radios and the pulpit. (The Catholic clergy in the countryside carried on a vociferous campaign for Balaguer.) In this context "free elections" cannot be "negotiated" with the United States. The meat grinder process predetermines the outcome, making the act of voting a means of legitimizing the superior economic and military power of the intervening US policy makers.

The meat grinder operation achieved its goal; Balaguer was "elected," authority was "restored," and the United States had created the basis for its "democracy of the gallows."

The unfolding stages—Revolution, Invasion and Restoration—had profound effects on the lower classes, many of whom had previously had little experience in political matters. *The short run results may be the restoration of US hegemony but the long run result is the creation of a great reservoir of popular anti-imperialist sentiment which is available for revolutionary movements.* The decisive age group for the revolutionary movement is between fifteen and twenty-five years old. The period from 1961 to 1965 saw the emergence of a political generation distinct in every way from its elders. This generational split reflects the tension between the "fathers" and "sons" who entered political combat at the end of the Trujillo epoch and who are indignant at their parents' subjection to the Great Benefactor. Many of the key revolutionary cadres both during and after the insurrection are drawn from the unemployed sons of the impoverished lower middle class. The four or five unemployed sons subsisting on the salary of a father who is a public employee with no employment for themselves in sight, concentrated with their peer group in *Ciudad Nueva*—this group was in the forefront of the armed struggle. Prior to "the action" it had been virtually impossible for the political parties to organize them. Rafael "Fafa" Taveras, leader of the June 14th Movement, analyzed the political role of the unemployed as follows: because of the economic insecurity and their continual "mobility" (lack of regular place of employment) they do not form the nucleus of a political organization; but they are the sector of the population most easily mobilized for *action*. It is the young unemployed (under twenty-five), politically trained during the last five or six years of struggle, who form the most explosive sector of contemporary Dominican society. With a population whose majority is under twenty-one and with official and disguised unemployment between 400,000 and 500,000 (in a population of 3½ million) this sector is of significant social weight. The socio-political force of this group has virtually no *electoral* expression; it expresses itself only through popular mobilizations.

The changes in the relationship of forces in the trade union movement both during and after the insurrection and invasion are highly revealing. The union confederation with the largest membership (roughly 40 per cent of the unionists) in 1963 was CONATRAL—formed and financed by the US embassy and the AFL-CIO. The leftist *Unión de Trabajadores Dominicanos* contained less than 5 per cent of the unionists. The Social Christian unions, the PRD unions (Boschist) and the independents controlled the rest of the organized workers. During the revolution the CASC (*Confederación Autonoma de Sindicatos Cristianos*) and the newly formed FOUPSACESI-TRADO (led by PRD supporters with Marxist nuclei) played an important role in directing the insurrectionary commandos. The CONATRAL leadership supported the US invasion and subsequently lost almost all of its union affiliates. The CASC became the leading national confederation, especially in rural organization, while FOUPSA-CESITRADO became the second major trade union force, controlling the big El Romano sugar central (13,000 workers), the transport workers, construction, cement, port, electrical and telephone workers. In total the leftist unions claim 100,000 members, more than five times their strength before the insurrection. More important, perhaps, the organization itself has changed. The PRD leadership under Miguel Soto has been replaced by younger revolutionary trade unionists led by Julio de Pena Valdez, the new secretary-general.

The trade union movement is bigger, stronger and more militant than before the Revolution. Valdez relates how prior to the US invasion only the most politicized workers were interested in the problem of imperialism; now trade unionists cannot discuss even economic matters without considering it in relation to the struggle against US domination. The mass of trade unionists have become accessible and responsive to an anti-imperialist program and leadership. In the area of the trade unions the United States has suffered a severe setback from which it will be hard to recover.

The rural populace is still divided between minifundistas,

who tend to be under the control of the Church, and the land-owners and the sugar workers, especially in the El Romano central, who have a long tradition of class struggle. While the majority of the peasantry was not actually involved in the revolution, many of the sugar workers joined the armed popular forces and two general strikes were "total." The sugar workers receive from five to six pesos a day (1 peso equals 1 dollar) but are unemployed at least six months of the year; this economic insecurity and the concentration of these rural workers facilitates political communication and produces the class solidarity and radical political culture so lacking as yet in the rest of the countryside. The first clashes between the government and the trade unions will probably occur in El Romano when their demands for wage increases at this US-owned enterprise come up against the wage-freeze law decreed by Balaguer. (El Romano is a property of the US-owned South Puerto Rico Sugar Company.) This class conscious and combative rural proletariat could become an important base linking the revolutionary urban popular classes to the exploited poor peasantry.[1]

The "middle class" is divided into various strata, each with a differing outlook: the lower white-collar workers tend to orient generally toward the PRD (Boschist), and the PRSC (Partido Revolucionario Social Cristiano), and the younger groups toward the June 14th Movement. The professionals and upper bureaucracy tend to be divided among the PRD, the PRSC and the Balaguer forces. The majority of the university students tend to be with the United Front of the Revolutionary Left (FRAGUA), which in turn is overwhelmingly June 14th. The results of the student government elections indicate the total absence of support for Balaguer and almost as little for Bosch:

University Election Results (1966)
FRAGUA	53%
BRUG (Social Christian)	41%
FURR (Boschist)	6%

The margin of victory of the FRAGUA has grown especially after the revolution, while the Bosch and Social Christian sup-

---

[1] The minifundio-latifundio pattern prevails in the Dominican Republic. 86 per cent of the landholders (392,000) own only 19 per cent of the land, while .9 per cent of the landowners (4,400) own 46 per cent of the cultivated land, 20.6 million tareas (16 tareas equal 2.4 acres).

port among the students has declined, the former precipitously. The experience of armed struggle against the US marines, in which many of the students contributed to the organization of "commandos," appears to have strengthened the revolutionary tendency among the students. The absence of any coherent ideology in the PRD, its dependence on the personal leadership of Bosch, and its perpetual indecision, make it less and less attractive to the new generation of students. The more dynamic and strongly anti-imperialist June 14th Movement appears to be the coming force among a whole generation of students. This tendency is reinforced since the post-Trujillo student body is being drawn more and more from the lowei and poorer strata of the middle class. (Students of worker and peasant origin still form less than 1 per cent of the student body.)

The ruling class in the Dominican Republic is not a "feudal" landowning oligarchy. The dominant class is primarily composed of export-importers, commercial agro-businessmen and the "pirate-capitalists" in the military caste. The overwhelming majority of this group favored the US intervention and was the social base that collaborated with the US-directed Balaguer campaign. This ruling class, dependent on the United States and fully committed to US hegemony, is linked through business contacts, privileged status and shared values with the Trujillista police and terrorist organizations, though it may disown specific actions (recent political assassinations) which compromise their US counterparts or their own political position. The US intervention saved this ruling class and hence its dependence on the United States is total. Over 60 per cent of the Dominican economy is state-owned, the former private empire of the Trujillo personalist state. The future socio-economic program of the ruling class is based on the gradual "expropriation" by private interests of these properties and of the franchises which had passed from the Trujillo family to the Dominican state.

US policy makers have been using the "grass-roots" ideology ("self-help," "community development") as a means of competing with the militant leftist and Christian trade unionists. US policy makers use "community development" as a means of consolidating the hierarchy of power and wealth by attempting to direct popular energies away from a confrontation with the

controllers of wealth and power and by obscuring the nature of
the class structure. One militant trade unionist referred to these
operations as "community corrupters" because the marginal
changes introduced attempt to weaken social solidarity that
builds organizations for struggle and structural change. The
United States has not been too effective since the leaders who
have been co-opted do not fight to better conditions; they are
not leaders selected through struggle, and they compromise
themselves by upholding "stability" against popular demands.

The four major political organizations in the Dominican
Republic are the *Partido Reformista* (PR), the US-financed and
directed organization which backed Balaguer; the *Partido Revolucionario Dominicano* (PRD), the liberal opposition directed
by Bosch; *Partido Revolucionario Social Cristiano* (PRSC),
the somewhat more reformist, Christian-democratic group; and
the radical-nationalist June 14th Movement.

The *Partido Reformista* is not so much a party as an organization mounted by US policy makers and whose leadership
personnel was largely recruited from the former Trujillo machine; Balaguer himself was the hand-picked "President" of the
Great Benefactor in his last years. The "activists" were largely
recruited from lumpen elements, the older unemployed or
semi-employed "service" sectors who saw a chance to earn
fast money and possible employment opportunities. The rural
clergy, mostly Cuban exiles and exports from Franco Spain,
and the military provided informal "electoral organizations"
along with the US-directed "Community Development" organizations. The social forces of this organization were clearly the
ruling class—US and Dominican. The party had one aim: to
legitimate their de facto return to power via US bayonets
through "free elections." The "Balaguer mass" never was nor is
today represented in a party either formally or informally. The
Partido Reformista was a one-shot deal, constructed for a single
purpose, and has never developed a structure or a program.
The only contact today between the "activists" and the *Partido
Reformista* is the line of job-hunters in front of the "party"
office. In light of this lack of firm political organization it is
understandable why the police, army, *and* restrictive legislation
are playing such a decisive role. The other side of the coin is
Balaguer's attempts to demobilize and atomize the politicalized
urban populace (ban on public meetings—*Tregua Política*)

through restrictions on the parties and a prohibition of strikes and union activity (wage-freeze law). In addition, of course, these policies directly benefit the social classes which direct Balaguer's policies, strengthening their control and increasing their economic benefits. Together with this policy Balaguer has utilized the plums of patronage to "co-opt" elements from the right wing of the PRD. Two PRD leaders have entered Balaguer's Cabinet, Minister of Finance Antonio Martínez Francisco and Minister of Industry and Commerce José Antonio Brea Pena. Both were, and some say still are, on Bosch's national committee. The combined use of repression and co-option to destroy political opposition are similar to the "salami tactics" used by Stalin in Eastern Europe during the postwar years.

Bernard Fall has analyzed an extreme application of this totalitarian strategy practiced by the United States in Vietnam. He wrote: "The new mix . . . is one of technological counter-insurgency—if you keep up the kill rate you will eventually run out of enemies. Or at least armed enemies. Of course the whole country will hate you but at least they won't resist you. What you will get is simply a cessation of resistance—an acquiescence in one's fate rather than a belief that your side and your ideas have really prevailed." ("This Isn't Munich, It's Spain," *Ramparts' Vietnam Reader*, San Francisco, 1966.) In this sense US policy had the same goal in the rural areas and among the urban women and older poor of Santo Domingo: the use of overwhelming force produced both an acquiescence as shown in their vote for Balaguer *and* an undying hatred for the United States.

The *Partido Revolucionario Dominicano* is a personalistic party, almost totally dominated by Juan Bosch and primarily geared to electoral activity. Though its leaders are mainly middle-class professionals, they are generally oriented by "modern neo-capitalist" ideas. The electoral base of the PRD is largely composed of the urban poor, the industrial workers, public employees, professional groups, shopkeepers, small (and a few larger) manufacturers. It lacks a clear ideology. It is vaguely for a welfare state, mildly anti-imperialist but with strong links with the pro-imperialist Pepe Figueres, Muñoz Marin, Leoni groups in Latin America (the self-styled "democratic left"—

neither democratic nor left). The more conservative party leadership's political position usually predominates in periods of parliamentary activity. And the result is that the class conflicts in society re-emerge in the conflicts between the militant PRD masses and the party. In 1963, after Bosch was elected, the sugar workers demanded that he live up to his election pledges and deal with their economic needs. Bosch refused to even negotiate until the workers threatened to close down sugar production. Likewise one reason why the rural peasantry did not take the risk of voting for Bosch was that he never made any gesture to relieve their rural misery as he had promised to do in 1962-63. The Bosch Congressmen are continuing this pattern. Deputy Ambriorex Díaz (PRD-Santiago) recently introduced an amendment to a proposed rural minimum wage law giving Balaguer power to lower the minimum wage below two pesos a day in areas where owners couldn't afford to pay it because of low productive land. (*Listin Diario*, August 24.) Similarly, William Nova Rosario (PRD–Indepencia) opposed overtime pay. Thus, the PRD leadership defends the profit interests of the small and medium businessmen against the hungry rural workers.

The result is that Bosch's personal prestige has declined because of his own and the PRD's debility during the coup of 1963 (he refused to prepare or lead the populace against it), the insurrection of 1965 (he asked State Department permission to lead the April revolution while US marines were landing) and the election of June 1966 (he was afraid to leave his house to campaign). As the party leadership defines itself as a bourgeois collaborationist opposition, its popular base is disoriented or tends to pass on to the other, more political forces. The non-existence of PRD student support and the sharp decline in its trade union support are indicative of the growing disillusion of the more politicalized Dominican popular forces with the PRD; these may be omens of a more general exodus.

Bosch himself in so many words admits that the PRD lacks a program under the present circumstances in the Dominican Republic. He looks for a solution not in mobilizing the laboring populace but in a future electoral victory by Robert Kennedy. While quite bitter about the Johnson interventionist policy, he tends to minimize the role of Balaguer as an instrument of US

policy, discussing Balaguer in personal rather than social terms
("Balaguer is not of the Right but his forces are of the Right")
thus perhaps justifying the collaboration in the Cabinet.

A sector of the Balaguer coalition, the Military Police Intelligence (IPM) and the air force want Balaguer to act more
forcefully against the opposition. This group has begun to intensify their plotting. Signs reading "Wessin Sí, Balaguer No"
and "Balaguer es Comunista" are generally the work of this
group. These ultras are said to have a list of five to six thousand
"Communists" that are to be eliminated. The fear which the
PRD has of this group appears to be one reason for their collaboration with Balaguer.

The *Partido Revolucionario Social Cristiano* is a party overwhelmingly made up of middle-class professionals, public employees, small businessmen and students, with little penetration
into the working class. Its program does not appear too much
different from that of other Christian-democratic parties. Because of the United States invasion, however, it has developed
an anti-imperialist consciousness that one finds all too rarely
among Christian democrats in the rest of Latin America.

Much more dynamic and with a wider influence among the
populace is the Confederación Autonoma de Sindicatos Cristianos (CASC), the Christian-democratic trade union movement. The CASC, probably the largest and most influential
confederation at the moment, has grown considerably both in
members and militancy because of its active participation in
the armed resistance against the US marines. CASC leaders like
Henry Molina and Francisco Santos played important roles in
directing the revolutionary commandos. The strength of the
CASC appears to be growing most rapidly in the countryside
where it has sixty to eighty unions organized in the FEDELAC
(Federación Dominicana de Ligas Agraria Cristiana). The Education Director of CASC pointed out that its trade union
schools have been more and more oriented toward training
rural organizers.

Though the CASC is an ideologically oriented union and is in
working alliance with the PRSC, there is a definite "syndicalist"
tendency in its orientation to the working class: in practical
terms unionism is perceived as the major vehicle for mobilizing
and defending working-class interests. CASC is both militant
and "reformist": militant in confrontations on economic strug-

gles and less clearly defined on the larger political issues—except on the question of the US presence. The revolution and the invasion had the result of causing the older conservative Catholics both in the PRSC and CASC to leave,[2] with the result that those who remained and the new members recruited during the struggle have strengthened the "militant" wing, especially in the CASC.

The combativeness of the workers who form the cadres of the CASC is tempered, however, by their strong commitment to Catholicism, and through this channel comes the major anti-Communist influence. The single most important factor preventing these workers from turning their anti-imperialism and class consciousness into a revolutionary socialist commitment is their ideological links with the Catholic hierarchy and doctrine. While liberal Catholic spokesmen encourage trade union activity and organization, the overwhelming stress is on working within Western progressive liberalism, militant anti-Communism, and avoidance of popular mobilizations for social revolution.

During the three phases of recent Dominican political history, the Papacy and the Dominican hierarchy took somewhat different approaches. The overwhelming majority of the Dominican clergy sided with Balaguer, the Dominican ruling class and the United States. The Papal Nuncio Emanuele Clarizio attempted to "mediate" between the conflicting forces and during the election the Vatican took the position that Catholics could vote for any of the candidates. Discussion with the Papal Nuncio Clarizio gives one the impression that he tends to favor a moderate Social Christian position and is less favorable to a total commitment to the Balaguer forces. Recent shifts in the hierarchy have strengthened these moderate liberal elements (the appointments of Bishop Roque Adames and Juan Antonio Flores).

The necessities of the armed struggle appear to have had the effect of overcoming some of the more conservative tendencies and influences, but they may well emerge again in the coming period.

The June 14th Movement originated as a dynamic student-based movement organized for the overthrow of Trujillo in the

---

[2] One right wing split-off group, the *Partido Demócrata Cristiano* (PDC), later supported Balaguer during the election.

late 1950s. The plan was discovered and many of the revolutionaries were tortured and executed. The June 14th Movement became a symbol of the resistance to Trujillo and grew rapidly in the period soon after Trujillo's fall. Under the influence of the Cuban Revolution, the leadership took a turn toward guerrilla warfare after Bosch was overthrown and many of the top leaders including Tavarez were killed. As the June 14th Movement defined itself as a supporter of the Cuban Revolution, sectors of the professional middle class defected; with the sudden turn away from mass struggle to guerrilla warfare the leadership lost contact with important popular sectors in or around the movement. Since 1963, however, the June 14th Movement has again been growing rapidly in numbers and cadres. Bosch estimates that the June 14th Movement had 800 followers in 1963 and 12-15,000 followers today.

The June 14th Movement is the major force in the Universities and it appears increasingly influential in the second largest trade union, FOUPSA-CESITRADO. The April Revolution and the armed resistance accelerated the influx of new members, especially from the impoverished lower middle class (self-employed, artisans, and lower-level public employees). The major social force in the June 14th Movement is this radicalized lower middle class; the dominant orientation is radical nationalism with a focus on the expulsion of all US influence and the expropriation of the foreign investors. In recent months intense discussions have been taking place in the movement on basic political and ideological questions: an analysis of the nature of Dominican society, the dynamics of revolution, and the strategy for taking power.

Rafael Taveras, a leader of the June 14th Movement, sees the petty-bourgeoisie becoming a revolutionary force—because of its growing impoverishment and the limits imposed by US imperialism. Concerning the immediate program of the movement, he says they hope to mobilize the large explosive sector of unemployed young workers and sons of the lower middle class. Taveras' orientation seems to revolve around mass mobilization politics; at the same time there appears to be a group in the June 14th Movement which is considering guerrilla warfare in the countryside. Such an orientation would probably be disastrous for the June 14th Movement, given the relatively unpolitical nature of the countryside and the existence of a revolutionary consciousness among broad layers of the urban populace. The combination of nationalism and urban mass politics would appear as the most fruitful perspective for immediate gains— barring wholesale political assassinations. The restrictions that Balaguer will impose on the functioning of the parliamentary opposition and on the reformist trade unions should confirm the revolutionary perspective of June 14th and create a wider audience for the revolutionary political viewpoint providing it can activate the mass. Taveras points to the few possibilities for democratic reforms in the Dominican Republic and hence projects the future perspective in terms of "Revolution or Dictatorship." The major weakness of the June 14th has been its internal heterogeneity, ideological indefiniteness and lack of working-class cadres. It is a youth movement which has in recent months been moving closer to class politics—especially in light of insurrectionary experience. June 14th militants view the limits of the revolution and their own shortcomings in terms of their inability to organize the major mass force in the revolution, the urban working class. According to Taveras the working class formed the backbone of the revolution but lacked the "party of the class to direct the struggle and hence the revolutionary energies were dissipated by the parties of the middle class (PRD, PRSC)." Ideological clarification and the consolidation of the organization appear however as a necessary prerequisite to the success of this organizational task. A revolutionary strategy must recognize that in the Dominican Republic the revolutionary movement of April 1965 took the form of a classic social revolution rather than rural guerrilla warfare. It was an armed uprising emanating from the union centers and based to a large degree on the trade unions, the urban employed and the university and secondary students. In Santo Domingo the high urban unemployment rate, the cleavage in the traditional basis of elite power (the army) and the availability of a highly mobilizable urban population provided the opportunity for an urban-based mass insurrection. The presence of an external occupation force exacerbates all the latent hostilities generated by externally supported national-capitalist exploitation and provides a unifying theme—anti-imperialism. In this sense the Dominican Revolution resembles the European Resistance movement during the Nazi occupation.

Of the two small Communist parties, the pro-Chinese *Mo-*

vimiento Popular Dominicano (MPD) appears the more active and has influence in the June 14th Movement. The pro-Soviet *Partido Comunista Dominicano* (PCD) is much smaller and tends to orient its activities toward supporting the "progressive" sectors of the PRD, accusing the more militant June 14th movement of being "petty-bourgeois socialists." (*El Popular,* August 8, 1966.) Neither group has much direct influence; both must rely on coalitions with the other parties, especially with the June 14th Movement. They are plagued by lack of cadres, lack of ideological sophistication of their new members, and ideological divisions. Recently the MPD split into two factions, each publishing a journal with the same name (*Libertad*) and apparently the same politics. While the MPD and PCD grew as a result of the revolution and its aftermath, the great majority of the newly radicalized populace entered into the more dynamic national-popular June 14th Movement.

With illiteracy still over 60 per cent, with at least one-third of the labor force of Santo Domingo unemployed (300,000-500,-000 out of a total population of 3.5 million), with 400,000 peasants lacking sufficient land to live on, with 200,000 school-age children out of school, and with drinkable water available for only five out of every three hundred peasants, the need for profound structural changes is obvious. The re-emergence of the old ruling class, the restoration and strengthening of the old piratical military-capitalist caste by the United States can only serve to set the stage for a new confrontation. Balaguer's restrictive legal measures are aimed at limiting and containing the challenge of the organized forces. Meanwhile, as Balaguer's promises of reform turn into political assassination and price rises, the popular unrest checked by the US onslaught is slowly beginning to express its strength. Behind the seeming acquiescence and fear there is in the popular consciousness a profound hatred of the totalitarian military and their US counterparts.[3]

[3] US white and Negro soldiers were equally brutal and equally condemned. Black Dominican workers told me that when they told North American Negroes to go back to the United States to fight for their own rights the Negroes responded, "Will you pay me $400 a month?" Conservative civil-rights spokesmen who advocate "coalition" with the Democratic Party in order to obtain promises of improvement in the immediate economic position of the North American Negro cannot and do not offer any effective political challenge or opposition to their "coalition" partners, i.e., LBJ, on crucial foreign policy matters. On the contrary, it is

There is a growing maturity in revolutionary political consciousness among the trade unions, the political militants and the young unemployed. The balance sheet of US policy in the Dominican Republic indicates that the "stability" so brutally imposed is only a transition to a new confrontation.

---

not unusual for Negro leaders to support this policy. No one put it better than Staughton Lynd when he said "coalitionism" today is "coalitionism with the marines."

IN THIS TIME OF DIRE EMERGENCY I WOULD LIKE TO MAKE THIS SOBER PLEA TO THE NATION:-

PLEASE LEAVE ME ALONE.

DISSENT HAS LONG PLAYED A RESPECTED ROLE IN OUR SOCIETY- AND I AM ALL FOR IT- BUT I CAN NOT HELP FEELING THAT MOST CURRENT CRITICISM HAS BUT **ONE** AIM:-

TO MAKE ME FEEL BAD.

NOW I DID NOT BECOME PRESI-DENT OF ALL THE PEOPLE IN ORDER TO BE MADE TO FEEL BAD.

WHY DO **I** HAVE TO HAVE A FOREIGN POLICY DEBATE WHEN **OTHER** ADMINISTRA-TIONS HAVE GOTTEN BY WITHOUT ONE FOR TWENTY YEARS?

WHY MUST PEOPLE QUESTION CHARGES OF COMMUNISM UNDER **MY** AD-MINISTRATION WHEN UNDER ALL **PREVIOUS** ADMINISTRATIONS IT WAS REASON ENOUGH TO DO **ANYTHING?**

THIS, I WARN YOU, IS A DAN-GEROUS BREAK FROM HALLOWED TRADITION!

LET ME URGE ON MY CRITICS THIS ONE REMINDER: NO MATTER **HOW** IT LOOKS- **WE** ARE THE GOOD GUYS!

LET US CON-TINUE.

VIETNAM AND THE "NERVOUS NELLIES"

(MAY 17, 1966)*

This speech was delivered at a Democratic Party fundraising dinner in Chicago against a background of disturbing developments in Vietnam. Buddhist dissatisfaction with the military dictatorship of Nguyen Cao Ky was threatening to topple the the Saigon government. And the insurgent forces battling American troops in Vietnam showed no signs of giving up their struggle. There was a danger (as Washington perceived the situation) that a new civilian government in South Vietnam might agree to a negotiated peace with the National Liberation Front and with the Hanoi government. By the spring of 1966 the Johnson Administration had developed a basic pattern of response in such situations that invariably meant further ascent on the shaky ladder of "escalation." [1]

Some Americans were aware of the inadequacies of the strategy of escalation, and President Johnson began to show noticeable hostility against his critics. But rather than grapple with their arguments, he accused these critics of speaking out from frustration or even cowardice. Meanwhile Johnson was preparing to take the dangerous

* We have used the excerpts of the President's Chicago speech as reported in the New York Times (May 18, 1966), p. 8, which differed in noticeable respects from the prepared text, released in advance by the White House, and printed in Weekly Compilation of Presidential Documents, II (May 23, 1966), pp. 657-60.

[1] See Franz Schurmann, Peter Dale Scott and Reginald Zelnik, The Politics of Escalation (Boston and New York, 1966), epilogue, and George McTurnan Kahin and John W. Lewis, The United States in Vietnam (New York, 1967), chapters VII and X.

step of bombing oil storage facilities in the near vicinity of Hanoi and Haiphong in North Vietnam. When this was done, a few weeks after the Chicago speech, the critics of his policy were dismayed and outraged. But the President was a skillful politician, and knew that at least in the short run he would gain in the context of American domestic politics. Washington newsman Tom Wicker wrote perceptively about this in the *New York Times:*

"First, [the President] . . . removed most of the uncertainty about his course and took the kind of strong action to step up the military pressure on North Vietnam that will give many Americans a sense of new decisiveness and a new vigor in the war effort.

"Second, Mr. Johnson and the majority of his party who support him probably will suffer voter defections next fall only from those who oppose the bombing and the war. Before he expanded the aerial assault to the North Vietnamese cities, the Democrats were also in danger of losing the votes of many who believed in a stronger effort to win a military victory.

"Third, since Republicans generally have urged the bombing of the Hanoi and Haiphong oil installations, an issue that appeared to be aiding their candidates has been muted and most of these candidates will have little choice but to declare their support for a President who has followed their advice.

"Finally, any dramatic turn in a foreign crisis usually causes great numbers of Americans to rally to the support of their national leader." [2]

But these short term political advantages that the President reaps by continuing to escalate in Vietnam only postpone an inevitable reckoning. One day Lyndon Johnson will be obliged to account in a more meaningful way than he has yet done to the American people for his conduct of the war in Vietnam.

◇ ◇ ◇

[2] Tom Wicker, "Bombing and Politics," *New York Times* (July 1, 1966), p. 11.

I do not genuinely believe that there's any single person any-where in the world that wants peace as much as I want it. I want the killing to stop. I want us to join hands with others to do more in the fight against hunger and disease and ignorance. But we all know from hard-won experience that the road to peace is not the road of concession and retreat.

A lot of our friends tell us how troubled they are, and how frustrated they are. And we are troubled. And we are frus-trated. And we are seeking a way out. And we are trying to find a solution.

As Commander in Chief, I am neither a Democrat nor a Re-publican. The men fighting in Vietnam are simply Americans. Our policy in Vietnam is a national policy. It sprang from every lesson that we've learned in this century.

We fought in the First World War and then we failed to build a system of collective security which could have pre-vented the Second World War.

Standing in this great city of Chicago, one of our greatest leaders ever to be produced in America, on October 5, 1937, Franklin D. Roosevelt said—and I quote him: "When an epi-demic of physical disease starts to spread the community ap-proves and joins in a quarantine of the patient in order to pro-tect the health of the community against the spread of the disease. . . . War is a contagion whether it be declared or undeclared. It can engulf states and peoples remote from the original scene of hostility." [2]

The country heard him, but did not listen.

The country failed to back him in that trying hour. And then we saw what happened when the aggressors felt confident that they could win while we sat by.

That was what President Truman remembered in 1947 in Greece and Turkey. That is what he remembered during the blockade of Berlin and when the attack came in Korea.

That is what President Eisenhower remembered in 1954

[2] This is from FDR's famous "Quarantine the Aggressors" speech, made three months after Japan attacked China. See Basil Rauch, ed., *Franklin D. Roosevelt: Selected Speeches, Messages, Press Conferences and Letters* (New York and Toronto, 1957), pp. 191-92. At that time Roosevelt was working toward a system of *collective* security against the Axis powers. Johnson here is defending a distinctly *unilateral* policy.—Eds.

when he laid before the Senate the SEATO treaty and during the crisis over Quemoy and Matsu.

That is what President John F. Kennedy remembered when in the face of Communist aggression in Laos and Vietnam he began to send American forces there as early as 1962.

Yes, we have learned over the past half-century that failure to meet aggression means war, not peace. In carrying out that policy we have taken casualties in Berlin and Korea and now in Vietnam. We have had 160,000 American casualties from World War II up until Vietnam. Now every morning I look at those casualty figures. I measure them not as statistics, but man by man. As of this morning we lost 1,705 Americans in Vietnam in the year 1966—1,705—but we lost 49,000 last year on our highways.

And I tell you that if we fail in frustrating this aggression the war that would surely come in Asia would produce casualties not in the 1700s but in the hundreds of thousands and perhaps in millions.

Your government, therefore, under your President, is determined to resist this aggression at the minimum cost to our people and to our allies and to the world.

I don't know what true men may be trying to influence and I do not seek to influence any tonight. But I do tell you here and now that we do not seek to enlarge this war, but we shall not run out on it!

America is determined to meet her commitments tonight because those commitments are right. As I said after a meeting yesterday with Ambassador Lodge just as he was returning to his post of duty, we shall continue to struggle against aggression and social misery in South Vietnam. We shall use our influence to help this young nation come together and move toward constitutional government. We shall seek an honorable peace.

Let those, though, who speak and write about Vietnam say clearly what other policy they would pursue, and let them weigh their words carefully—let them remember that tonight there are 300,000 young Americans—our own boys—out there somewhere in Southeast Asia on the land and on the sea, and in the air, they are there fighting to quarantine another aggressor, they are there fighting for the peace of the world, and let them

remember that there are men on the other side who know well
that their only hope for success in this aggression lies in a
weakening of the fiber and the determination of the people of
America.

And so long as I am President the policy of opposing aggression at minimum cost shall be continued!

I sent our ambassadors to more than forty countries. I wrote
letters to nearly 120 in the world asking for assistance, asking
for peace. My plea was well received in all the nations of the
world except the two most concerned—Red China and North
Vietnam. After thirty-seven long days, while our men in uniform waited and while our planes were grounded on my orders, while our ambassadors went from nation to nation, we
finally were forced to the conclusion that the time had not yet
arrived when the government of North Vietnam was willing or
could even be persuaded to sit down at a peace table and try to
reason these problems out.

Therefore, our arguments need to be more persuasive and
our determinations need to be more convincing and more compelling than they have been. All I can say to you tonight is that
the road ahead is going to be difficult.

There will be some Nervous Nellies and some who will become frustrated and bothered and break ranks under the strain.
And some will turn on their leaders and on their country and
on our own fighting men. There will be times of trial and tensions in the days ahead that will exact the best that is in all of
us.

But I have not the slightest doubt that the courage and the
dedication and the good sense of the wise American people will
ultimately prevail. They will stand united until every boy is
brought home safely, until the gallant people of South Vietnam
have their own choice of their own government.

More than that, not just that one little country of 14 million
people but more than a hundred other little countries stand
tonight and watch and wait. If America's commitment is dishonored in South Vietnam, it is dishonored in forty other alliances or more that we have made. So I leave you with the
assurance that we love peace and we seek it every hour of
every day.

Any person who wishes to test us can give us the time and

the date and the place and he will find us occupying our peace chair at the negotiating table with any government who genuinely and who sincerely wants to talk instead of fight.

Perhaps my sentiments and my feelings are best expressed by the words of President Roosevelt when he prepared only a day or so before he died in 1945 this speech and he never had an opportunity to deliver it. He said: "We seek peace, enduring peace. More than an end to war, we want an end to the beginnings of all wars. Yes, an end to this brutal, inhuman and thoroughly impractical method of settling the differences between governments. . . ." [3]

The men who fight for us out there tonight in Vietnam, they are trying to find a way to peace.

But they know, and I don't understand why we don't all recognize, that we can't get peace just for wishing for it. We must get on with the job, until these men can come marching home, some day when peace is secure—not only for the people of America, but peace is secure for peace-loving people everywhere in this world.

[3] FDR had prepared a radio speech for the Jefferson Day Dinner on April 13, 1945. The entire address is in Rauch's *Franklin D. Roosevelt,* pp. 388-91. Roosevelt died on April 12.—Eds.

A MIDDLE WAY
OUT OF VIETNAM[*]

While he held the post of White House Special Assistant
to President Kennedy, Arthur Schlesinger had no initial
desire to chronicle the events in which he participated,
and to which he was a witness. Yet before Kennedy was
dead the Pulitzer Prize-winning historian was already at
work on the book he was deeply grieved to call *A Thousand Days*.

In that book Schlesinger wrote of John Kennedy's early
interest in foreign affairs, and the serious view he took
of the Senate's constitutional authority in this area. As a
member of the powerful Foreign Relations Committee
Kennedy had spent many hours in study, and he had
already developed some expertise in East Asian and North
African problems.[1]

Lyndon Johnson never pretended to such attainments.
The existence of a world beyond the three-mile limit (or,
beyond the Texas tidelands) was a bit disconcerting to
Johnson. Philip L. Geyelin, in his thoughtful study of
Lyndon B. Johnson and the World (New York and Washington, 1966, p. 15), has stressed the limitations in foreign
affairs of a man who could publicly complain that the
trouble with foreigners "is that they're not like the folks

[*] From the *New York Times Magazine* (September 18, 1966). © 1966
by the New York Times Company. Reprinted by permission. The argument in the article has been developed at greater length by Mr. Schlesinger in his book *The Bitter Heritage: Vietnam and American Democracy 1941-1966* (Boston: Houghton Mifflin, 1967).
[1] *A Thousand Days: John F. Kennedy in the White House* (Boston,
1965), chap. II, especially pp. 45-57.

you were reared with." Johnson's parochialism, even before he reached the White House, revealed a malignant side. In the course of a congressional discussion of US military posture in 1948, Johnson rose to proclaim: "No matter what else we have of offensive or defensive weapons, without superior air power America is a bound and throttled giant, impotent and easy prey to any yellow dwarf with a pocket knife." (Congressional Record, 80th Congress, 2nd session [March 15, 1948], Vol. 94, Part 2, p. 2,883.) This image of giant America and the "yellow dwarfs" of Indochina remains to haunt Johnson's policy in Vietnam.

No longer in governmental service, and currently holding the post of Albert Schweitzer Professor at the City University of New York, Schlesinger finds much to criticize in this policy. Nonetheless, this criticism is from the vantage point of one in close sympathy to the overall aims of US policy. While others may use his historical analysis to conclude that American troops should be withdrawn from Vietnam at once, the tone and content of his critique suggest that he would willingly accept the call of another President Kennedy to help set right what Johnson has done in Vietnam.

◇ ◇ ◇

Why we are in Vietnam is today a question of only historical interest. We *are* there, for better or for worse, and we must deal with the situation that exists. Our national security may not have compelled us to draw a line across Southeast Asia where we did, but, having drawn it, we cannot lightly abandon it. Our stake in South Vietnam may have been self-created, but it has nonetheless become real. Our precipitate withdrawal now would have ominous reverberations throughout Asia. Our commitment of over 300,000 American troops, young men of exceptional skill and gallantry engaged in cruel and difficult warfare, measures the magnitude of our national concern.

We have achieved this entanglement, not after due and deliberate consideration, but through a series of small decisions. It is not only idle but unfair to seek out guilty men. President Eisenhower, after rejecting American military intervention in 1954, set in motion the policy of support for Saigon which resulted, two Presidents later, in American military intervention in 1965.[2] Each step in the deepening of the American commitment was reasonably regarded at the time as the last that would be necessary; yet, in retrospect, each step led only to the next, until we find ourselves entrapped today in that nightmare of American strategists, a land war in Asia—a war which no President, including President Johnson, desired or intended. The Vietnam story is a tragedy without villains. No thoughtful American can withhold sympathy as President Johnson ponders the gloomy choices which lie ahead.

Yet each President, as he makes his choices, must expect to be accountable for them. Everything in recent weeks—the actions of the Administration, the intimations of actions to come, even a certain harshness in the Presidential rhetoric—suggests that President Johnson has made his choice, and that his choice is the careful enlargement of the war. New experiments in escalation are first denied, then disowned, then discounted and finally undertaken. As past medicine fails, all we can apparently think of doing is increase the dose. In May [1966] the Secretary of the Air Force explained why we would not bomb Hanoi and Haiphong; at the end of June we began the strikes against the oil depots. The demilitarized zone between North and South Vietnam has been used by North Vietnam units for years, but suddenly we have begun to bomb it.

When such steps work no miracles—and it is safe to predict that escalation will be no more decisive in the future than it has been in the past—the demand will arise for "just one more step." Plenty of room remains for widening the war: the harbors of North Vietnam, the irrigation dikes, the steel plants, the factories, the power grid, the crops, the civilian population, the Chinese border. The fact that we excluded such steps yesterday is, alas, no guarantee that we will not pursue them tomorrow. And if bombing will not bring Ho Chi Minh to his knees or stop his support of the Vietcong in South Vietnam, there is always the last resort of invasion. General Ky has already told us that we must invade North Vietnam to win the war. In his recent press conference, the Secretary of State twice declined to rule out this possibility.

[2] "Military intervention" did *not* begin with Johnson in 1965, but with President John F. Kennedy in 1961, when Arthur Schlesinger himself was serving in the White House. See Marvin E. Gettleman, ed., *Vietnam: History, Documents and Opinions* . . . (New York, 1965), pp. 206-09.— Eds.

The theory, of course, is that widening the war will shorten it. This theory appears to be based on three convictions: first, that the war will be decided in North Vietnam; second, that the risk of Chinese or Soviet entry is negligible, and third, that military "victory" in some sense is possible. Perhaps these premises are correct, and in another year or two we may all be saluting the wisdom and statesmanship of the American government. In so inscrutable a situation, no one can be confident about his doubt and disagreement. Nonetheless, to many Americans these propositions constitute a terribly shaky basis for action which has already carried the United States into a ground war in Asia and which may well carry the world to the brink of the third world war.

The illusion that the war in South Vietnam can be decided in North Vietnam is evidently a result of listening too long to our own propaganda. Our government has insisted so often that the war in Vietnam is a clearcut case of aggression across frontiers that it has come to believe itself that the war was started in Hanoi and can be stopped there. "The war," the Secretary of State has solemnly assured, "is clearly an 'armed attack,' cynically and systematically mounted by the Hanoi regime against the people of South Vietnam."

Yet the best evidence is that the war began as an insurrection within South Vietnam which, as it has gathered momentum, has attracted increasing support and direction from the North.[3] Even today the North Vietnamese regulars in South Vietnam amount to only a fraction of the total enemy force (and to an even smaller fraction of the American army in South Vietnam). We could follow the genial prescription of General LeMay and bomb North Vietnam back to the Stone Age—and the war would still go on in South Vietnam. To reduce this war to the simplification of a wicked regime molesting its neighbors, and to suppose that it can be ended by punishing the wicked regime, is surely to misconceive not only the political but even the military character of the problem.

As for the assurances that China will not enter, these will be less than totally satisfying to those whose memory stretches back to the Korean War. General MacArthur, another one of

[3] See Philippe Devillers, "The Struggle for Unification of Vietnam," in Gettleman, ed., *Vietnam*, pp. 210-35, for the best account of the origin of the insurrection.—Eds.

those military experts on Oriental psychology, when asked by President Truman on Wake Island in October, 1950, what the chances were of Chinese intervention, replied, "Very little. . . . Now that we have bases for our Air Force in Korea, if the Chinese tried to get down to Pyongyang, there would be the greatest slaughter." Such reasoning lay behind the decision (the Assistant Secretary of State for Far Eastern Affairs at that time is Secretary of State today) to send American troops across the 38th Parallel despite warnings from Peking that this would provoke a Chinese response. In a few weeks, China was actively in the war, and, while there was the greatest slaughter, it was not notably of the Chinese.

There seems little question that the Chinese have no great passion to enter the war in Vietnam. They do not want to put their nuclear plants in hazard; and, in any case, their foreign policy has typically been a compound of polemical ferocity and practical prudence. But the leaders in Peking are no doubt just as devoted students of Munich as the American Secretary of State. They are sure that we are out to bury them; they believe that appeasement invites further aggression; and, however deep their reluctance, at some point concern for national survival will make them fight.

When will that point be reached? Probably when they are confronted by a direct threat to their frontier, either through bombing or through an American decision to cross the 17th Parallel and invade North Vietnam. If a Communist regime barely established in Peking could take a decision to intervene against the only atomic power in the world in 1950, why does anyone suppose that a much stronger regime should flinch from that decision in 1966? Indeed, given the present discord in Peking, war may seem the best way to renew revolutionary discipline, stop the brawling and unite the nation.

It is true that the Chinese entry into the Korean War had at least the passive support of the Soviet Union; but it would be risky today to rely on the Sino-Soviet split to save us from everything, including Soviet aid to China in case of war with the United States or even direct Soviet entry into the war in Vietnam. For the Soviet Union is already extensively involved in Vietnam—more so in a sense than the Chinese—and it would be foolish to suppose that, given Moscow's competition with Peking for the leadership of the Communist world, Russia could afford to stand by and allow Communist North Vietnam or Communist China to be destroyed by the American imperialists.

As for the third premise (that military "victory" is in some sense possible): the Joint Chiefs of Staff, of course, by definition argue for military solutions. They are the most fervent apostles of "one more step." That is their business, and no one should be surprised that generals behave like generals. The fault lies not with those who give this advice but those who take it. Once, early in the Kennedy Administration, the then Chairman of the Joint Chiefs outlined the processes of escalation in Southeast Asia before the National Security Council, concluding, "If we are given the right to use nuclear weapons, we can guarantee victory." President Kennedy sat glumly rubbing an upper molar. After a moment someone said, "Mr. President, perhaps you would have the general explain to us what he means by victory." Kennedy grunted and dismissed the meeting. Later he said, "Since he couldn't think of any further escalation, he would have to promise us victory."

What is the purpose of bombing the north? It is hard to find out. According to Gen. Maxwell Taylor, "The objective of our air campaign is to change the will of the enemy leadership." Secretary McNamara, on the other hand, has said, "We never believed that bombing would destroy North Vietnam's will." Whatever the theory, the results would appear to support Secretary McNamara. The northern strategy, instead of driving Hanoi to the conference table, seems to have hardened the will of the regime, convinced it that its life is at stake, brought it closer to China and solidified the people of North Vietnam in its support.

"There is no indication," General Westmoreland said the other day, "that the resolve of the leadership in Hanoi has been reduced." In other words, bombing has had precisely the effect that the analyses of the United States Strategic Bombing Survey after the Second World War would have forecast. Under Secretary of State George Ball was a director of that survey; this may well be why he has been reported so unenthusiastic about the air assault on the North.[4]

---

[4] John Kenneth Galbraith, also a director of the US Strategic Bombing Survey, suggests that the saturation bombing of Hamburg during July and August, 1943, may paradoxically have *increased* Germany's military

And, far from stopping infiltration across the 17th Parallel, bombing, if our own statistics are to be believed, has stimulated it. "It is perfectly clear," Secretary McNamara has said, "that the North Vietnamese have continued to increase their support of the Vietcong despite the increase in our effort. . . . What has happened is that the North Vietnamese have continually increased the amount of resources, men and material that they have been willing to devote to their objective."

Nor can we easily match this infiltration by enlarging our own forces—from 300,000, for example, to 500,000 or 750,000. The ratio of superiority preferred by the Pentagon in guerrilla war is 10 to 1, which means that every time we send in 100,000 more men the enemy has only to send in 10,000 or so, and we are all even again. Reinforcement has not created a margin of American superiority; all it has done is to lift the stalemate to a higher and more explosive level. Indeed, there is reason to suppose that, in its own manner, the enemy can match our every step of escalation up to the point of nuclear war.

U. S. News & World Report says in its issue of Aug. 22: "It's clear now to military men: bombing will not win in Vietnam." This is a dispiriting item. Why had our military leaders not long ago freed themselves from the illusion of the omnipotence of air power, so cherished by civilians who think wars can be won on the cheap? The Korean War, as Gen. Matthew B. Ridgway has said, "taught that it is impossible to interdict the supply route of an Asian army by airpower alone. We had complete air mastery over North Korea, and we clobbered Chinese supply columns unmercifully. . . . But we did not halt their offensive nor materially diminish its strength." If air power was not decisive in Korea, where the warfare was conventional and the terrain relatively open and compact, how could anyone suppose that it would be decisive against guerrillas threading their way through the hills and jungles of Vietnam?

The bombing illusion applies, of course, to South as well as to North Vietnam. Tactical bombing—bombing in direct support of ground operations—has its place; but the notion that strategic bombing can stop guerrillas runs contrary to experience. And we had it last winter, on the authority of the Secre-

effectiveness. See his discussion in *The Affluent Society* (Boston, 1958), pp. 161-63.—Eds.

tary of State, that despite the entry of North Vietnamese regulars the war in South Vietnam "continues to be basically a guerrilla operation."

Sir Robert Thompson, who planned the successful British effort against the Malayan guerrillas and later served as head of the British advisory mission in Saigon, has emphasized that the defending force must operate "in the same element" as their adversaries. Counterinsurgency, he writes, "is like trying to deal with a tomcat in an alley. It is no good inserting a large, fierce dog. The dog may not find the tomcat; if he does, the tomcat will escape up a tree; and the dog will then chase the female cats. The answer is to put in a fiercer tomcat."

Alas, we have no fiercer tomcat. The counterinsurgency effort in Vietnam has languished, while our bombers roam over that hapless country, dumping more tonnage of explosives each month than we were dropping per month on all Europe and Africa during the Second World War. Just the other day our bombs killed or injured more than 100 civilians in a hamlet in the Mekong Delta—all on the suspicion that two Vietcong platoons, numbering perhaps 60 men, were there. Even if the Vietcong had still been around, which they weren't, would the military gain have outweighed the human and political loss? Charles Mohr writes in the *Times:* "Almost every provincial hospital in Vietnam is crowded with civilian victims of the war. Some American doctors and other officials in the field say the majority are the victims of American air power and South Vietnamese artillery."

The trouble is that we are fighting one war, with our B-52s and our naval guns and our napalm, and the Vietcong are fighting another, with their machine guns and ambushes and forays in the dark. "If we can get the Vietcong to stand up and fight, we will blast him," General Westmoreland has plaintively said; and when they occasionally rise to the surface and try to fight our kind of war, we do blast them. But the fact that they then slide back into the shadows does not mean that we are on the verge of some final military triumph. It means simply that we are driving them underground—where they renew themselves and where our large, fierce dog cannot follow.

Saigon officials have been reporting that Vietcong morale is declining as long as I can remember; these reports need not be taken seriously now. I know of no convincing evidence that the

Vietcong lack the political and emotional commitment to keep fighting underground for another twenty years.

Our strategy in Vietnam is rather like trying to weed a garden with a bulldozer. We occasionally dig up some weeds, but we dig up most of the turf, too. The effect of our policy is to pulverize the political and institutional fabric which alone can give a South Vietnamese state that hope of independent survival which is our presumed war aim. Our method, in other words, defeats our goal. Indeed, the most likely beneficiary of the smashed social structure of South Vietnam will be Communism. "My feeling," Gen. Wallace Greene, commandant of the Marine Corps, has wisely said, "is that you could kill every Vietcong and North Vietnamese in South Vietnam and still lose the war. Unless we can make a success of the civic-action program, we are not going to obtain the objectives we have set."

Much devotion and intelligence are at present going into the programs of reconstruction, but prospects are precarious so long as the enemy can slice through so much of South Vietnam with such apparent immunity; and so long as genuine programs of social reform threaten the vested interests of the Saigon Government and of large landholders. In any case, as claimants on our resources, these programs of pacification are hopelessly outclassed by the programs of destruction. Surely, the United States, with all its ingenuity, could have figured out a better way to combat guerrilla warfare than the physical obliteration of the nation in which it is taking place. If this is our best idea of "protecting" a country against "wars of national liberation," what other country, seeing the devastation we have wrought in Vietnam, will wish American protection?

At the same time, our concentration on Vietnam is exacting a frightful cost in other areas of national concern. In domestic policy, with Vietnam gulping down a billion and a half dollars a month, everything is grinding to a stop. Lyndon Johnson was on his way to a place in history as a great President for his vision of a Great Society; but the Great Society is now, except for token gestures, dead. The fight for equal opportunity for the Negro, the war against poverty, the struggle to save the cities, the improvement of our schools—all must be starved for the sake of Vietnam. And war brings ugly side effects: inflation; frustration; angry protest; attack on dissenters on the ground that they cheer the enemy (an attack often mounted by men who led the dissent during the Korean War); premonitions of McCarthyism.

We also pay a cost abroad. Our allies naturally draw away as they see us heading down the road toward war with China. When we began to bomb the oil depots, James Reston wrote: "There is now not a single major nation in the world that supports Mr. Johnson's latest adventure in Hanoi and Haiphong." As nations seek to disengage themselves from the impending conflict, the quasi neutralism of leaders like de Gaulle gains new plausibility.

On any realistic assessment, Western Europe and Latin America are far more significant to American security than South Asia; yet the Vietnam obsession has stultified our policy and weakened our position in both these vital areas. The war has clouded the hope, once mildly promising, of progress toward a *détente* with the Soviet Union. It has helped block agreements to end underground nuclear testing and to stop the spread of nuclear weapons. It has precipitated the decision of U Thant to resign as Secretary General of the United Nations and condemns the U.N. itself to a time of declining influence.

Our rejection of the views of our friends and allies—our conviction, as Paul H. Smith has put it, "that we alone are qualified to be judge, jury and executioner"—ignores Madison's solemn warning in the 63rd Federalist: "An attention to the judgment of other nations is important to every government for two reasons: the one is that independently of the merits of any particular plan or measure, it is desirable, on various accounts, that it should appear to other nations as the offspring of a wise and honorable policy; the second is that in doubtful cases, particularly where the national councils may be warped by some strong passion or momentary interest, the presumed or known opinion of the impartial world may be the best guide that can be followed. What has not America lost by her want of character with foreign nations; and how many errors and follies would she not have avoided, if the justice and propriety of her measures had, in every instance, been previously tried by the light in which they would probably appear to the unbiased part of mankind."

The Administration has called the critics of its Vietnam policy "neo-isolationists." But surely the real neo-isolationists are those who have isolated the United States from its allies and raised the tattered standard, last flourished fifteen years ago by Douglas MacArthur, of "going it alone."

How have we managed to imprison ourselves in this series of dilemmas? One reason surely is that we have somehow lost our understanding of the uses of power. Understanding of power implies above all precision in its application. We have moved away from the subtle strategy of "flexible response" under which the level of American force was graduated to meet the level of enemy threat. The triumph of this discriminate employment of power was, of course, the Cuban missile crisis (where the Joint Chiefs, as usual, urged an air assault on the missile bases). But President Johnson, for all his formidable abilities, has shown no knack for discrimination in his use of power. His technique is to try and overwhelm his adversary— as in the Dominican Republic and Vietnam—by piling on all forms of power without regard to the nature of the threat.

Given this weakness for the indiscriminate use of power, it is easy to see why [decisions about] the application of force in Vietnam [have] been surrendered to the workings of what an acute observer of the Johnson foreign policy, Philip Geyelin, calls "the escalation machine." This machine is, in effect, the momentum in the decision-making system which keeps enlarging the war "for reasons only marginally related to military need."

The very size and weight of the American military presence generate unceasing pressures to satisfy military demands. These may be demands to try out new weapons; the London *Sunday Telegraph* recently ran an informative article comparing the Vietnam War to the Spanish Civil War as a military testing ground and laboratory. Or they may be cries for "one more step," springing in part from suppressed rage over the fact that, with military power sufficient to blow up the world, we still cannot compel guerrilla bands in black pajamas to submit to our will. Whatever the reason, Sir Robert Thompson has noted of the American theory of the war: "There was a constant tendency in Vietnam to mount large-scale operations, which had little purpose or prospect of success, merely to indicate that something aggressive was being done."

The Administration has freely admitted that such operations, like the bombing of the North, are designed in part to prop up the morale of the Saigon Government. And the impression is growing now that they are also in part undertaken in order to smother doubts about the war in the United States and to reverse anti-Administration tendencies in the polls. Americans have become curiously insensitive to the use of military operations for domestic political purposes. A quarter-century ago President Roosevelt postponed the North African invasion so that it would not take place before the midterm elections of 1942; but today observers in Washington, without evidence of shock, predict a new venture in escalation before the midterm elections of 1966.[5]

The triumph of the escalation machine has been assisted by the faultiness of the information on which our decisions are based. Nothing is phonier than the spurious exactitude of our statistics about the Vietnam War. No doubt a computerized military establishment demands numbers; but the "body count" of dead Vietcong, for example, includes heaven knows how many innocent bystanders and could hardly be more unreliable. The figures on enemy strength are totally baffling, at least to the ordinary citizen relying on the daily newspaper. The *Times* on August 10 described "the latest intelligence reports" in Saigon as saying that the number of enemy troops in South Vietnam had increased 52,000 since January 1 to a total of 282,-000. Yet, "according to official figures," the enemy had suffered 31,571 killed in action in this period, and the infiltration estimate ranged from 35,000 as "definite" to 54,000 as "possible."

The only way to reconcile these figures is to conclude that the Vietcong have picked up from 30,000 to 50,000 local re-

[5] These observers were wrong. Rightfully fearful of Congressional losses, Johnson did not escalate before the elections. Since then he has resumed ever "new ventures in escalation" by mining North Vietnamese rivers, by initiating naval shelling of its coastline, and by saturation bombing of its major steel plant near the Hanoi-Haiphong industrial complex. As of the time this book goes to press, the most significant of all possible escalations—invasion of the North—has not taken place. Yet the "logic" of the situation makes it more than probable. Johnson must either produce a quick military triumph or successfully camouflage a withdrawal by passing it off as a victory. Otherwise he faces complete repudiation at the polls. Since nothing in the Johnson temperament suggests defeat is ever acceptable, an invasion of the North seems in the cards. The decision is not Johnson's alone, however, but one which takes place within a complex institutional setting. Unfortunately, the irrationality of American foreign policy (see our introduction to this section of the book) gives little cause for optimism.—Eds.

cruits in this period. Since this seems unlikely—especially in view of our confidence in the decline of Vietcong morale—a safer guess is to question the wonderful precision of the statistics. Even the rather vital problem of how many North Vietnamese troops are in South Vietnam is swathed in mystery. The *Times* reported on August 7: "About 40,000 North Vietnamese troops are believed by allied intelligence to be in the South." According to an Associated Press dispatch from Saigon printed in the *Christian Science Monitor* of August 15: "The South Vietnamese government says 102,500 North Vietnamese combat troops and support battalions have infiltrated into South Vietnam.

"These figures are far in excess of United States intelligence estimates, which put the maximum number of North Vietnamese in the South at about 54,000."

But General Westmoreland told his Texas press conference on August 14 that the enemy force included "about 110,000 main-force North Vietnamese regular army troops." Perhaps these statements are all reconcilable, but an apparent discrepancy of this magnitude on a question of such importance raises a twinge of doubt.

Nor is our ignorance confined to battle-order statistics. We have always lacked genuine knowledge of and insight into the political and cultural problems of Vietnam, and the more we press all problems into a military framework the worse off we are. The Administration in Washington was systematically misinformed by senior American officials in Saigon in 1962-1963 regarding the progress of the war, the popularity of Diem, the effectiveness of the "strategic hamlet" program and other vital matters. It was not that these officials were deliberately deceiving their President; it was that they had deceived themselves first. Ordinary citizens restricted to reading the American press were better informed in 1963 than officials who took top-secret cables seriously.

The fact is that our government just doesn't know a lot of things it pretends to know. It is not discreditable that it should not know them, for the facts are elusive and the judgments incredibly difficult. But it is surely inexcusable that it should pretend to know things it does not—and that it should pass its own ignorance on to the American people as certitude. And it is even less excusable that it should commit the nation to a policy involving the greatest dangers on a foundation so vague and precarious.

So now we are set on the course of widening the war—even at the cost of multiplying American casualties in Vietnam and deepening American troubles at home and abroad; even at the risk of miring our nation in a hopeless and endless conflict on the mainland of Asia beyond the effective employment of our national power and beyond the range of our primary interests; even at the risk of nuclear war.

Why does the Administration feel that these costs must be paid and these risks run? Hovering behind our policy is a larger idea—the idea that the war in Vietnam is not just a local conflict between Vietnamese but a fateful test of wills between China and the United States.

Our political and rhetorical escalation of the war has been almost as perilous as our military escalation. President Kennedy's effort was to pull Laos out of the context of great-power conflict and reduce the Laotian civil war to rational proportions. As he told Khrushchev at Vienna in 1961, Laos was just not important enough to entangle two great nations. President Johnson, on the other hand, has systematically inflated the significance of the war in Vietnam. "We have tried to make it clear over and over again," as the Secretary of State has put it, "that although Hanoi is the prime actor in this situation, that it is the policy of Peking that has greatly stimulated Hanoi. . . . It is Ho Chi Minh's war. Maybe it is Mao Tse-tung's war."

"In the forties and fifties," President Johnson has said, "we took our stand in Europe to protect the freedom of those threatened by aggression. Now the center of attention has shifted to another part of the world where aggression is on the march. Our stand must be as firm as ever." Given this view, it is presumably necessary to pay the greatest costs and run the greatest risks—or else invite the greatest defeat.

Given this view, too, there is no reason not to Americanize the war. President Kennedy did not believe that the war in Vietnam could succeed as a war of white men against Asians. It could not be won, he said a few weeks before his death, "unless the people [of South Vietnam] support the effort. . . . We can help them, we can give them equipment, we can send our men out there as advisers, but they have to win it, the people of

Vietnam." We have now junked this doctrine. Instead, we have enlarged our military presence until it is the only thing that matters in South Vietnam, and we plan now to make it still larger; we have summoned the Saigon leaders, like tribal chieftains on a retainer, to a conference in an American state; we crowd the streets of Saigon with American generals (fifty-eight at last count) and visiting stateside dignitaries. In short, we have seized every opportunity to make clear to the world that this is an *American* war—and, in doing this, we have surely gone far to make the war unwinnable.

The proposition that our real enemy in Vietnam is China is basic to the policy of widening the war. It is the vital element in the Administration case. Yet the proof our leaders have adduced for this proposition has been exceedingly sketchy and almost perfunctory. It has been proof by ideology and proof by analogy. It has not been proof by reasoned argument or by concrete illustration.

The proof by ideology has relied on the syllogism that the Vietcong, North Vietnam and China are all Communist states and *therefore* must be part of the same conspiracy, and that, since the Vietcong are the weakest of the three, they must *therefore* be the spearhead of a coordinated Chinese plan of expansion. The Department of State, in spite of what has struck most people as a rather evident fragmentation of the Communist world, has hated to abandon the cozy old clichés about a centralized Communist conspiracy aimed at monolithic world revolution.

As late as May 9, 1965, after half a dozen years of public Russo-Chinese quarreling, Thomas C. Mann, then No. 3 man in the department, could talk about "instruments of Sino-Soviet power" and "orders from the Sino-Soviet military bloc." As late as January 28, 1966, the Secretary of State could still run on about "their world revolution," and again, on February 18, about "the Communists" and their "larger design." While the department may have accepted the reality of the Russo–Chinese schism by September, 1966, the predominant tone is still to regard Asian Communism as a homogeneous system of aggression. The premise of our policy has been that the Vietcong equal Hanoi and Hanoi equals Peking.

Obviously, the Vietcong, Hanoi and Peking have interests in common and strong ideological affinities. Obviously, Peking would rejoice in a Hanoi-Vietcong victory. But they also have divergent interests and purposes—and the divergencies may prove in the end to be stronger than the affinities. Recent developments in North Korea are instructive. If any country was bound to Peking by ties of gratitude, it was North Korea, which was preserved as an independent state by Chinese intervention fifteen years ago. If any country today is at the mercy of Peking, it is again North Korea. When North Korea now declares in vigorous language its independence of China, does anyone suppose that North Vietnam, imbued with the historic mistrust of China and led by that veteran Russian agent Ho Chi Minh, would have been more slavish in its attitude toward Peking?

The other part of the Administration case has been proof by analogy, especially the good old Munich analogy. "I'm not the village idiot," the Secretary of State recently confided to Stewart Alsop. "I know Hitler was an Austrian and Mao is a Chinese. . . . But what is common between the two situations is the phenomenon of aggression." The Vietnam War, President Johnson recently told the American Legion, "is meant to be the opening salvo in a series of bombardments or, as they are called in Peking, 'wars of liberation.'" If this technique works this week in Vietnam, the Administration suggests, it will be tried next week in Uganda and Peru. But, if it is defeated in Vietnam, the Chinese will know that we will not let it succeed elsewhere.

"What happens in South Vietnam," the President cried at Omaha, "will determine—yes, it will determine—whether ambitious and aggressive nations can use guerrilla warfare to conquer their weaker neighbors." The Secretary of State even described an exhortation made last year by the Chinese Defense Minister, Marshal Lin Piao, as a blueprint for world conquest comparable to Hitler's *Mein Kampf*.

One thing is sure about the Vietnam riddle: it will not be solved by bad historical analogies. It seems a trifle forced, for example, to equate a civil war in what was for hundreds of years the entity of Vietnam (Marshal Ky, after all, is a North Vietnamese himself) with Hitler's invasion of Austria and Czechoslovakia across old and well-established lines of national division; even the village idiot might grasp that difference.

When President Eisenhower invoked the Munich analogy in

1954 in an effort to involve the British in Indochina, Prime Minister Churchill, a pretty close student of Munich in his day, was unmoved. The Chinese have neither the overwhelmingly military power nor the timetable of aggression nor, apparently, the pent-up mania for instant expansion which would justify the Hitler parallel. As for the Lin Piao document, the Rand Corporation, which evidently read it with more care than the State Department bothered to do, concluded that, far from being Mao's *Mein Kampf*, it was a message to the Vietcong that they could win "only if they relied primarily on their own resources and their own revolutionary spirit" and that it revealed "the lack, rather than the extent, of Peking's past and present control over Hanoi's action." [6]

In any case, guerrilla warfare is not a tactic to be mechanically applied by central headquarters to faraway countries. More than any other form of warfare, it is dependent on conditions and opportunities within the countries themselves. Whether there are wars of national liberation in Uganda and Peru will depend, not on what happens in Vietnam, but on what happens in Uganda and Peru.

One can agree that the containment of China will be a major problem for the next generation. But this does not mean that we must re-enact in Asia in the sixties the exact drama of Europe in the forties and fifties. The record thus far suggests that the force most likely to contain Chinese expansionism in Asia (and Africa, too) will be not Western intervention but local nationalism. Sometimes local nationalism may call on Western support—but not always. Countries like Burma and Cambodia preserve their autonomy without American assistance. The Africans have dealt with the Chinese on their own. The two heaviest blows recently suffered by Peking—the destruction of the Communist party in Indonesia and the declaration of independence by North Korea—took place without benefit of American patronage or rhetoric.

In the unpredictable decades ahead, the most effective bulwark against "international" Communism in some circum-

[6] Defense Minister Lin's *Long Live the Victory of People's War!* (1965) is reprinted in Vera Reichler (ed.), *China: History and Documents* (New York, forthcoming). Cf. D. P. Mozingo and T. W. Robinson, *Lin Piao on "People's War": China Takes a Second Look at Vietnam* (Santa Monica, Cal.: Rand Corp., Memo. RM-4814-PR, November, 1965).—Eds.

stances may well be national Communism. A rational policy of containing China could have recognized that a Communist Vietnam under Ho might be a better instrument of containment than a shaky Saigon regime led by right-wing mandarins or air force generals. Had Ho taken over all Vietnam in 1954, he might today be enlisting Soviet support to strengthen his resistance to Chinese pressure—and this situation, however appalling for the people of South Vietnam, would obviously be better for the United States than the one in which we are floundering today. And now, alas, it may be almost too late: the whole thrust of United States policy since 1954, and more than ever since the bombing of the North began, has been not to pry Peking and Hanoi apart but to drive them together.

Is there no way out? Are the only alternatives widening the war or disorderly and humiliating withdrawal? Surely, our statesmanship is not yet this bankrupt. I think a middle course is still possible if there were the will to pursue it. And this course must begin with a decision to stop widening and Americanizing the war—to limit our forces, actions, goals and rhetoric. Instead of bombing more places, sending in more troops, proclaiming ever more ardently that the fate of civilization will be settled in Vietnam, let us recover our cool and try to see the situation as it is: a horrid civil war in which Communist guerrillas, enthusiastically aided and now substantially directed from Hanoi, are trying to establish a Communist despotism in South Vietnam, not for the Chinese but for themselves. Let us understand that the ultimate problem here is not military but political. Let us adapt the means we employ to the end we seek.

Obviously, military action plays an indispensable role in the search for a political solution. Hanoi and the Vietcong will not negotiate so long as they think they can win. Since stalemate is a self-evident precondition to negotiation, we must have enough American armed force in South Vietnam to leave no doubt in the minds of our adversaries that they cannot hope for victory. They must also have no illusion about the prospect of an American withdrawal. The object of the serious opposition to the Johnson policy is to bring about not an American defeat but a negotiated settlement.

Therefore, holding the line in South Vietnam is essential. Surely, we already have enough American troops, firepower and installations in South Vietnam to make it clear that we cannot be beaten unless we choose to scuttle and run, which will not happen. The opponents of this strategy talk as if a holding action would put our forces under siege and relinquish all initiative to the enemy. This need not, of course, be so. It is possible to slow down a war without standing still; and, if our present generals can't figure out how to do this, then let us get generals who can. Generals Ridgway and Gavin could doubtless suggest some names. Moreover, there is a South Vietnamese army of some 600,000 men which can take all the initiative it wants. And if we are told that the South Vietnamese are unwilling or unable to fight the Vietcong, then we must wonder all the more about the political side of the war.[7]

The object of our military policy, as observers like Henry Kissinger and James MacGregor Burns have proposed, should be the creation and stabilization of secure areas where the South Vietnamese might themselves undertake social and institutional development. Our resources should go, in the Vietnam jargon, more to clear-and-hold than to search-and-destroy (especially when search-and-destroy more often means search-and-drive-underground). We should get rid of those "one-star generals who," in the words of Sir Robert Thompson, "regard their tour in Vietnam as an opportunity to indulge in a year's big-game shooting from their helicopter howdahs at government expense."

At the same time we should induce the Saigon government to institute generous amnesty provisions of the kind which worked so well in the Philippines. And we should further increase the incentive to come over by persuading the South

[7] The editors are forced at this point to observe that not all readers will accept these conclusions (continued use of force in South Vietnam) from the evidence presented here, especially about the indigenous nature of the guerilla revolt in South Vietnam. How then is Schlesinger able to blithely affirm holding the line in South Vietnam? An explanation may be sought in the circumscribed nature of Schlesinger's dissent. Sharing the fundamental premises of American foreign policy (indeed as Special Assistant to President Kennedy he helped form them), Schlesinger hopes to persuade the policy makers that further escalation is a mistake by accepting the mildly hawkish view that a "just and honorable" solution may be facilitated by continued application of US firepower in the South. Whether this is a tactical ploy on Schlesinger's part is of little consequence. It is important, however, that a large number of critics have tempered their dissent to maintain their "respectability" and thereby are continually in the position of accommodating themselves to the next-to-last escalation. —Eds.

Vietnamese to abandon the torture of prisoners—a practice not only horrible in itself but superbly calculated to make the enemy fight to the bitter end. In the meantime we must end our own shameful collaboration with this barbarism and stop turning Vietcong prisoners over to the South Vietnamese when we know that torture is probable.

As for bombing the North, let us taper this off as prudently as we can. Bombing is not likely to deter Hanoi any more in the future than it has in the past; and, given its limited military effect, the Administration's desire to gratify the Saigon government and the American voter is surely not important enough to justify the risks of indefinite escalation. Moreover, so long as the bombing continues there is no chance of serious negotiation. Nor does the failure of the thirty-seven-day pause of last winter to produce a settlement refute this. Thirty-seven days were hardly enough to persuade our allies that we honestly wanted negotiation; so brief an interlude left no time for them to move on to the tricky job of persuading Hanoi. For Hanoi has substantial reasons for mistrusting negotiation—quite apart from Chinese pressure or its own hopes of victory. Ho has entered into negotiation with the West twice in the past—in 1946-47 and again in 1954—and each time, in his view, he lost at the conference table things he thought he had won on the battlefield.

For all our official talk about our readiness to go anywhere, talk to anyone, etc., it cannot be said that the Administration has pursued negotiation with a fraction of the zeal, imagination and perseverance with which it has pursued war. Indeed, some American scholars who have studied the matter believe that on a number of occasions when pressure for negotiation was mounting we have, for whatever reason, stepped up the war.[8]

Nor can it be said that the Administration has laid fairly before the American people the occasional signals, however faint, which have come from Hanoi—as in the early winter of 1965, when U Thant's mediation reached the point of selecting the hotel in Rangoon where talks might take place, until we killed the idea by beginning the bombing of the North. Nor, for all

[8] See Franz Schurmann, Peter Dale Scott, and Reginald Zelnick, *The Politics of Escalation in Vietnam* (New York and Boston, 1966). [Professor Schlesinger has provided a Foreword to this book.—Eds.]

our declarations about "unconditional" negotiations, have we refrained from setting conditions—such as, for example, that we won't talk to the Vietcong unless they come to the conference table disguised as North Vietnamese. Though the Vietcong constitute the great bulk of the enemy force, they have been given little reason to think we will negotiate about anything except their unconditional surrender.

It is hard to see why we should not follow the precedent of Laos, when we admitted the Pathet Lao to the peace talks, and offer the Vietcong the prospect of a say in the future political life of South Vietnam—conditioned on their laying down their arms, opening up their territories and abiding by the ground rules of free elections. Nor is there reason to see why we have been so reluctant again to follow the Laos model and declare neutralization, under international guarantee, our long-run objective for Vietnam. An imaginative diplomacy would long since have discussed the ways and means of such neutralization with Russia, France, Britain and other interested countries. Unsatisfactory as the situation in Laos may be today, it is still incomparably better than the situation in South Vietnam.

On the other hand, negotiation is not an exclusive, or even primary, American responsibility. Along with a military stalemate, the other precondition of a diplomatic settlement is surely a civilian government in Saigon. Marshal Ky is one of those Frankenstein's monsters we delight in creating in our "client" countries, very much like the egregious General Phoumi Nosavan, who singlehandedly blocked a settlement in Laos for two years. Like Phoumi, Ky evidently feels that Washington has committed itself irrevocably to him—and why should he not after the laying on of hands at Honolulu?—and that, whatever he does, we cannot afford to abandon him.

Robert Shaplen, in the August 20 issue of *The New Yorker*, reported from Saigon that the atmosphere there "is being compared to the miasma that surrounded Diem and his tyrannical brother Ngo Dinh Nhu" and that "many Vietnamese believe that the Americans, having embraced Ky so wholeheartedly and supported him so long, are just as responsible as his government for the recent repressive acts."

I am sure that President Johnson did not intend to turn over American policy and honor in Vietnam to Marshal Ky's gimcrack, bullyboy, get-rich-quick regime. The time is bound to come when Ky must learn the facts of life, as General Phoumi eventually and painfully learned them.

But why wait? In our whole time in Vietnam, there has never been a government in Saigon which had the active loyalty of the countryside. It might be an agreeable experiment to encourage one to come into existence. Instead of identifying American interests with Ky and rebuffing the broader political impulses in South Vietnam, we should long since have welcomed a movement toward a civilian regime representing the significant political forces of the country and capable both of rallying the army and carrying forward programs of social reform. We should give such a government all possible assistance in rebuilding and modernizing the political and institutional structures of South Vietnam. And if it should favor the neutralization of its country, if it should seek negotiation with the Vietcong, even if it should release us from our commitment to stay in Vietnam, we should not think that the world is coming to an end.

It is not too late to begin the de-escalation of the war; nor would the reduction of our military effort damage our international influence. "There is more respect to be won in the opinion of this world," George Kennan has written, "by a resolute and courageous liquidation of unsound positions than by the most stubborn pursuit of extravagant or unpromising objectives." France was stronger than ever after de Gaulle left Algeria, the Soviet Union suffered no lasting damage from pulling its nuclear missiles out of Cuba. And the policy of de-escalation recommended here is, of course, something a good deal less than withdrawal.

De-escalation *could* work, *if* there were the will to pursue it. . . . This is the hard question. The Administration, disposed to the indiscriminate use of power, enmeshed in the grinding cogs of the escalation machine, committed to the thesis that China is the enemy in Vietnam, obviously could not turn to de-escalation without considerable inner upheaval. The issue in the United States in the months to come will be whether President Johnson's leadership is sufficiently resilient and forbearing to permit a change in the direction of policy and arrest what is coming increasingly to seem an accelerating drift toward a great and unnecessary catastrophe.

VIETNAM IS NO MISTAKE*

Among the aspects of American society that the war in Vietnam has thrown into high relief are the shortcomings of the media of mass communications. Television has brought a vivid visual image of Vietnam, but little understanding. TV scenes of violence and brutality have, moreover, dulled the sensibilities of the American people, preparing them for yet the next stage of escalation.

Printed media have done little better. Most journalists have merely passed along official handouts as they roll off government mimeograph machines. A handful of them, however, have done honor to their profession by reporting what they saw as the truth in Vietnam—Homer Bigart, Robert Shaplen, David Halberstam, the late Bernard Fall, Harrison Salisbury, Wilfred Burchett, Neil Sheehan, Charles Mohr, and some others

The efforts of these few reporters were not enough, and by early 1965 the peace movement in the United States began to feel the need for a special news bulletin on Vietnam. *Viet-Report,* beginning monthly publication in July of 1965, attempted to fulfill this need. From the inception of the magazine, John McDermott has been Associate Editor of *Viet-Report,* and has written extensively on Vietnam in such periodicals as the *New York Review of Books.* Formerly an instructor at Long Island University, Mr. McDermott teaches at the New School for Social Research. He visited Vietnam and Cambodia early in 1967.

◊ ◊ ◊

* From *The Nation* (February 13, 1967), pp. 203-06. By permission.

Three current myths, widely held even among critics of the war in Vietnam, vitiate any effort to build popular support for new and more moderate foreign policies. The first myth holds that the continual escalation of the war by the Johnson Administration stems from the fundamental misconception that the Vietnamese crisis originated outside the South, that is, in Hanoi or, possibly, Peking. Because of this misconception, the myth concludes, events themselves will frustrate the policy, educate the policy makers and thus create, ultimately, the basis for an end to the war. Myth number two, which frequently shares billing with the first, portrays American foreign policy as containment. In this view, our policy is a minimal one, aimed merely at containing China (or Communism or whatever) until Peking gives up its expansionist propensities and learns to live in peace and harmony with the rest of the world. The third myth is the most dangerous of all. It asserts that United States foreign policy can and must be understood as an attempt to maintain a balance of power with the Communist world.

None of these is even faintly true. Contrary to myth number one, and as press reports amply demonstrate, responsible United States policy makers, far from being chagrined by the growing folly of the war, are delighted at what they consider its outstanding success to date. As for myth number two, American policy is not aimed at containing the power of China, of the Soviet Union, of the various Communist movements; it aims instead at crippling that power, at rolling it back and, where possible, destroying it. And the third myth invokes a balance of power that does not, and cannot, exist in the world today. America has no power rival in any part of the world. By contrast, the Soviet Union is at best a regional power and, in Washington's estimate, a second-line power at that.

We should not be surprised that Washington is happy with the progress of the Vietnamese War. Although its war policies have been partially rebuked by the American electorate and wholly stalemated by the Vietnamese enemy, the Administration has three very good reasons for celebration.

1. Notwithstanding the oft-voiced expectations of the critics that escalation of the war would drive China and the Soviet Union into each other's arms, the Vietnamese crisis has aggravated their differences almost to the breaking point. Since it is a major aim of Administration policy to keep its enemies divided,

the Vietnamese War has on this count been an exemplary success.

2. Moscow's inability to aid its beleaguered ally in Hanoi other than by modest shipments of arms and munitions has taught the East European states how much Soviet protection is worth. Accordingly, the escalation, again refuting the critics, has contributed to loosening still further Soviet influence in Eastern Europe.

3. By polarizing Communist and non-Communist positions in the Far East, escalation has led to a stiffening of will on the part of the non-Communists, especially in Indonesia, Singapore and Malaysia. Similarly, the escalation has helped foster internal convulsions in China, with the result that the Japanese and Korean Communist Parties have defected from the Maoist "line." US policy in Vietnam has thus contributed to the increasing isolation of China in the Far East.

The first point is true and, purely as policy, it is also unexceptionable. Any foreign office placed in the position of Mr. Rusk's State Department would try to divide the Soviet Union and China. But pressing the question further begins to reveal what is peculiar about US policy in this instance. One notes immediately that it has little to do with Vietnam itself. There is good reason to believe that policy makers in Washington, whatever their views may have been in the past, now realize that the Vietnamese War stems from long-term disputes among various Vietnamese political factions, and that the role of China, as of the international Communist movements, has been distinctly ancillary. More even than that, I am persuaded that Administration leaders know how to negotiate an end to the war on relatively favorable terms, and may even do so well prior to the 1968 elections. First, however, they want to exploit still further the differences between Moscow and Peking, and this prescribes that the war continue. We are confronted here with great-power politics of the most conventional—and ruthless— kind. The Administration is quite consciously destroying Vietnam and its people in order to gain a marginal advantage elsewhere. This is a rational choice, not a mistake or a miscalculation.

The significance of this choice should be dwelt upon. Even granting, for argument's sake, the desirability of a Soviet-Chinese split, we must ask why Administration leaders use war to accomplish it. Both the Soviets and the Chinese have made it known that they strongly desire foreign credits as well as increased trade. In addition, China must import much of its grain supply. A clever trade policy on Washington's part, forcing the Soviets and Chinese to compete with each other for substantial trade advantages, would likely exacerbate their relations quite 'as much as a war in Vietnam. Supposing this trade strategy effective, the United States would have not one enemy, China, or two, China and Russia, but none, while its major rivals would still be divided. But Washington has not chosen this course. Why?

The answer to this question is to be found in an analysis of myth number two—that is, in what poses as a policy of containment. The Administration is not trying to contain China and the Soviet Union; it is trying to reduce them further to the status of second-line powers. Holding the Soviet case in abeyance for the moment, consider China. How can one speak of the need to contain China when in fact it is not expanding? Two critical examples demonstrate the truth of this assertion.

In 1954, both North Korea and North Vietnam could reasonably be considered Chinese satellites. China had paid dearly for this influence: it fought a major conventional war in Korea, and only narrowly avoided a nuclear attack in 1953 for its efforts there; it risked a similar attack a year later as a result of its assistance to the Vietminh. The strategic location of these small nations on China's sensitive borders and their inflammable rivalries with American-supported South Korea and South Vietnam, respectively, should have guaranteed that an "expansionist" Chinese foreign office, still more its "aggressive" Communist Party, would maintain them as puppets. Nothing like that happened. Both Pyongyang and Hanoi have long since gravitated out of the Chinese orbit. Both have long pursued independent foreign policies; in both, the Communist Parties have long since been able to pick and choose among the competing views of the Communist world.

China has not been expanding—not against Japan, not against Burma and Pakistan, not even against India (and, since the late fifties, not even against Quemoy). Shrouded in truculent rhetoric, Peking's foreign policies have shown a basically moderate—even isolationist—character. But the United States has not been satisfied. Secretary Rusk and his associates want not a static Chinese international position but a declining one. They tell us this themselves when they point with satisfaction to China's growing isolation and offer it as one of the reasons to be satisfied by the course of the Vietnamese War.

A similar analysis may be made of Russia and the East European situation. Again, by their own testimony, American officials are not satisfied merely with the thaw in Eastern Europe, which was already far advanced before Soviet weaknesses were exposed in Vietnam. The war in Vietnam is a good war, in their eyes, because it exposes Soviet military weaknesses vis-à-vis the United States, and thereby encourages the East European states to make separate arrangements with Washington or its chief ally in Europe, West Germany. The Administration probably assigns no very high priority to this objective, certainly not the priority given to rolling back Chinese influence in Asia. Nonetheless, one must recognize here a milder form of the old "roll back the iron curtain" policy that John Foster Dulles tried to pursue until the development of Soviet ICBMs in 1957 forced the Eisenhower Administration to seek a *détente*.

The Johnson Administration, under its chief foreign policy theorist, Walt Whitman Rostow, has developed a new rollback policy, less crude and less bombastic than that of Secretary Dulles, but still a rollback policy and not less dangerous for being more oblique. Administration officials would deny the charge if made in these words. But, at the operating level, they accept as concrete foreign policy values, worth our bitter sacrifices in Vietnam, a systematic rollback of Soviet and, especially, Chinese influence.

That is the chief significance of the policies of counter-insurgency which grew out of the fall of Batista in Cuba in the late fifties, and which have gained such impetus from the Vietnamese War. In W.W. Rostow's still-classic presentation of the objectives of military counter-insurgency operations, given at Fort Bragg in 1961, he strongly emphasizes that a successful counter-insurgency strategy must begin long before native dissidents are ready for—or even thinking of—guerrilla warfare. Why then mount military operations against them? In Rostow's view, the answer is very simple. Native dissidents represent, at the very least, a latent Soviet or Chinese influence. Because of this, and for no other reason in Rostow's view, they must be destroyed. Counter-insurgency policy demands that America first must *expand* its influence in the underdeveloped world and, second, that it must use that influence to mount an *offensive* against Moscow's or Peking's "allies" there. From this standpoint it is not a strategy of containment (or of peaceful coexistence) since its defined objective is the diminution of Sino-Soviet influence by military means. In short, the logic of counter-insurgency has the logic of rollback built right in.

This brings up the third and critical myth, the myth that American policy is to be understood within the framework of conventional balance-of-power analysis. There is no balance of power in the world and perhaps never in modern history has the world been so distant from one. American power—military, economic, technical, political—stands at heights beyond the reach not only of its enemies separately but of the whole world together. Certainly the statement is noncontroversial if we exclude the Soviet Union. But what of the Soviets? Have they not the power to deter America in the international arena? To understand the answer to this question one must turn to one of the great disasters of our era, President Kennedy's victory in the Cuban missile crisis.

It is no quarrel with the necessity of President Kennedy's actions to call his victory a disaster. Yet it was in November, 1962, that the seeds of the rollback policy were sown. Ever since Hiroshima, Secretaries of Defense (as well as Presidents) have recited the familiar litany of America's destructive power—a power, they claimed, which dwarfed that of the Soviet Union and its allies. Until 1957, American officials really believed in the predominance of our power; accordingly, Dulles, like Acheson before him, could toy with the idea of a rollback policy. With the advent of the Soviet ICBM in 1957 the power equation seemed to change, and for several years there was serious concern in Washington, evidenced by military sniping at President Eisenhower, and culminating in the missile-gap controversy, that we had no such advantage over the Soviets. When President Kennedy won office on a pledge to restore American power in the world we should have taken that pledge seriously. JFK immediately added $6.5 billion to Eisenhower's last military budget. Later, his own first military (and space) budget exceeded Eisenhower's last by almost 50 per cent. But in spite of the impressive military build-up (unmatched by the Soviets) these fantastic expenditures represented, the Kennedy

Administration seemed at first unaware that it had broken through into a military position which promised relative freedom of action in the world.

But continued official belief in the "balance of terror" ended with the Cuban missile crisis. As Washington understood the result, the Soviets backed down. Faced with the prospect of testing the power implicit in the Kennedy rearmament program (which was not even at that time fully completed), Moscow turned away. It is not necessary to argue here whether or not this was indeed the significance of what happened. The important point is that Washington so interpreted it, and still does.

President Kennedy's victory in the Cuban missile crisis was a disaster because it persuaded high government figures that we had no serious rival, that when push came to shove, there was only one international superpower. Russian core interests did not extend to war over Cuba; the Soviet Union was only a regional power. Thus it followed that, provided Russia's regional interests were not directly threatened, the United States had a free hand elsewhere. It is now evident that elsewhere included North Vietnam. Was it an accident of timing that the Administration began bombing North Vietnam while Premier Kosygin was visiting Hanoi? Though our information on the attack is as yet incomplete, it may well have been intended as a sharp reminder to the Russians that they had neither the means nor the interest to involve themselves in a major conflict with the United States in the Far East. The Johnson Administration has learned the lesson of 1962 only too well. The bombing JFK was afraid to risk in Cuba in 1962, LBJ may risk with impunity in North Vietnam today.

To analyze our policies in Vietnam and elsewhere is also to diagnose their source and thereby to suggest, if only implicitly, the counter responses which are appropriate. Those who accept the three myths are inevitably placed in a position of arguing that in some fundamental sense only stupidity, ignorance—for some, neurosis—stand between current policy and a better, somewhat more humane and peaceful future. To accept such a conclusion is to be arrogant, abusive, unhistorical and, worse, ineffectual. The plain fact is that our current policy is led by able and determined men with coherent—if disagreeable— conceptions of the vast opportunities open to America's unchecked power, and the conscious will to use arbitrary force to achieve their ends. Accordingly, the appropriate response is not to educate them, enlighten them, psychoanalyze them, or even abuse them. Those who oppose them must begin instead to devise serious strategies for replacing them and, more important, the institutions and doctrines which have shaped them. These, the real villains of the piece, include bipartisan foreign policy, Executive supremacy in foreign affairs, congressional generosity to defense and space, the imperial mechanisms of foreign aid, the militarism of our civilian leadership, the doctrine of America's special responsibility for world leadership. It will be difficult to carry out a dramatic change in all those areas, but that program offers the only realistic alternative to the thirty-year series of "little wars" which Secretary McNamara, the Bundys and the Rostows so willfully predict.

PART **VII**

THE INNER
PHILOSOPHY OF
THE GREAT SOCITY

INTRODUCTION

The readings in this book, as we have stated earlier, have not been chosen in order to show the conflicting ideas of liberals and conservatives, or Republicans and Democrats. Instead, the Johnson Administration's image of itself has been extensively plumbed, along with a critique of that image (and the substance behind it) mainly from the left. It remains to defend this choice; and the defense first demands an analysis of American conservatism.

In the early stages of the Cold War conservatism posed a real alternative to mainstream American liberalism. The Robert Taft wing of the Republican Party disagreed fundamentally with the direction bipartisan foreign policy was taking. Senator Taft opposed American participation in NATO. He argued that rather than leading to lasting peace, ". . . it might develop aggressive features more likely to incite Russia to war than to deter it from war. . . ." [1] Taft also opposed Truman's intervention in Korea in 1950 and insisted that the United States had no vital interest there. [2] Furthermore he stated that he did not believe that

. . . we can justify war by our natural desire to bring freedom to others throughout the world. . . . There are a good many Americans who talk about an American century in which America will dominate the world. . . . If we continue our activities to the field of moral leadership we shall be successful if our philosophy is sound and appeals to the people of the world. The trouble with those who advocate this policy is that they really do not confine themselves to moral leadership. They

[1] Robert A. Taft, *A Foreign Policy for Americans* (New York, 1951), p. 91.
[2] On Taft's foreign policy, see Leonard P. Liggio, "Why the Futile Crusade," *Left and Right: A Journal of Libertarian Thought* I (Spring, 1965), pp. 23-63.

*are inspired with the same kind of New Deal planned-control
ideas abroad as recent Administrations have desired to enforce
at home. In their hearts they want to force on these foreign
peoples through the use of American money and even, perhaps,
American arms the policies which moral leadership is able
to advance only through the sound strength of its principles
and the force of its persuasion. I do not think this moral leadership ideal justifies our engaging in any preventive war, or going
to the defense of one country against another. . . . I do not
believe any policy which has behind it the threat of military
force is justified as part of the basic foreign policy of the
United States except to defend the liberty of our people.*[3]

Robert Taft died in 1953, and with him died the isolationism
that he espoused. Republicans nowadays do not attack liberal
diplomacy, except to urge that it be pursued with greater vigor.
Since the initiation of bombing raids against North Vietnam,
Barry Goldwater has found nothing fundamentally wrong with
Lyndon Johnson's foreign policy.[4] The only possible objection
to the thesis is the Republican attack on President Kennedy's
Congo policy. But even here close inspection of the actual
course of events reveals tactical rather than strategic differences.[5]

On domestic policy, the critique offered by the Republicans
as an opposition party has been complicated by the internal
divisions within the GOP. The leading Republican spokesmen
have registered carping attacks on the Great Society programs
as allegedly consisting of "novelty upon novelty, gadget upon

[3] Taft, *A Foreign Policy for Americans*, pp. 17-18.
[4] Art Buchwald's masterly satire, "If Goldwater Had Won," in *Son of
the Great Society* (New York, 1966), is highly recommended.
[5] To the accompaniment of outcries from Republicans, the Kennedy
Administration opposed the Katanga secession, led by Moise Tshombe.
This was done out of fear that another secessionist center of power might
arise in Stanleyville, led by the supporters of the murdered leftist, Patrice
Lumumba. It seemed better to forestall such a development by maintaining, against Tshombe's ambitions at that moment, a unified Congo-
lese nation. When the leftist threat was eliminated by the use of military
forces (white mercenaries, American planes flown by anti-Castro Cuban
exiles), Tshombe could take power over the entire country. American diplomacy proved to be a brilliant *tour de force*, and Republican opposition was silenced. On this, see Conor Cruise O'Brien, *To Katanga and
Back* (New York, 1966), and O'Brien, "The Congo, the United Nations
and Chatham House," *New Left Review*, May-June, 1965.

gadget, gimmick upon gimmick." [6] But these just do not amount to any principled opposition. Even the Goldwater wing would have had a difficult time in dismantling any significant part of the welfare apparatus bequeathed by previous administrations had the Arizona Senator been elected President in 1964. Liberal Republicans like George Romney of Michigan or Nelson Rockefeller of New York have been unable to carve out a political position that differs in any discernible way from the broad middle ground occupied by Lyndon Johnson.

Right-wing opinion outside the government is also beset with difficulties in trying to establish a solid ground of difference between itself and Johnson's liberalism. The attitudes expressed in the widely read *National Review* illustrate this. The principles espoused by this journal center on the concept of freedom. Freedom is defined as the absence of state interference in man's affairs, and the right to enjoy one's property. But a major concern in the columns of the *National Review*, overriding their commitment to this concept of freedom, is the fervent anti-Communism professed by the editors and contributors. Professor Murray Rothbard, himself a former contributor, has observed a progressive sacrifice of devotion to the first principle in the headlong pursuit of the second.[7] To Rothbard, the positive commitment to freedom against state control is primary;[8] an energetic foreign policy, whether directed against Communism or any other alleged evil, strengthens state power. In the essay printed below (reading 35), he lumps modern liberals with Goldwater conservatives, as servants of the Leviathan state.

Essentially, the right-winger in the age of Lyndon Johnson is in a quandary. If he hews to the original anti-statist faith, he is obliged to attack the interventionist foreign policy that the government is pursuing. But if he supports the international anti-Communist crusade (as most do, following the lead of the *National Review*), and snipes at welfare programs for the poor,

[6] Such was the conclusion of Senator Everett McKinley Dirksen, Republican minority leader, in his overall appraisal "Where Our Nation Stands at Home and Abroad," reprinted in the *New York Times* (October 23, 1966), sect. IV.

[7] Rothbard, "New Right: *National Review*'s Anniversary," *Left and Right*, II (Winter, 1966), pp. 8-13.

[8] It should be noted that Tom Hayden, speaking for the "new left" (as Rothbard does for the "old right"), is equally opposed to state manipulation of human lives. See reading 34, below.

he is in effect endorsing a net expansion of state power. From the evidence presented in this book the editors believe it is clear that the major beneficiaries of such an expansion of state power would be the giant corporations.

Thus, except for the few principled anti-statists, modern conservatism stands revealed as an ideology not far distant from that which sustains Lyndon Johnson's apparently liberal Great Society program. This judgment seriously challenges certain common views. Students in particular cherish the notion of a fundamental struggle between two opposed forces—"liberalism" and "conservatism." They see the nation's past mainly as the effort of liberals to bring about "progress," efforts usually— and often unsuccessfully—countered by conservatives.[9] Central to this commonly held view is the definition of progress as involving two coordinated principles, democracy and welfare. American liberalism is credited with having championed the two principles simultaneously, each advance in political democracy setting off a wave of humanitarian reform. In this intellectual frame of reference the Great Society program of Lyndon Johnson is merely the latest manifestation of a marvelous process at work at least since 1776. The President himself has publicly defended his policies as the extension to "the twentieth century [of] what our forefathers started in the eighteenth." [10]

Sometimes this sequence of democracy and welfare is projected into the future, and the conclusion is drawn that the gradual accumulation of welfare measure after welfare measure, reform after reform, will add up to something that can be called "socialism." Not only friends but opponents of socialism have argued that such reform programs as the New Deal, the Fair Deal, and the Great Society lead in this leftward direction. But if the problem of the interconnection between democracy and welfare is put into historical perspective, another pattern

[9] Liberal historians have generally fostered this interpretation, arguing that humanitarian efforts in the past have been coordinated with extensions of democracy. More recently a group of younger historians have suggested that these two elements—welfare and democracy—have no *necessary* connection. See David B. Davis, *Ante-Bellum Reform* (New York, 1967); Gabriel Kolko, *The Triumph of Conservatism: A Reinterpretation of American History, 1900-1916* (New York, 1963).

[10] Remarks at City Hall, Cumberland, Maryland (May 7, 1964), in *Public Papers of the Presidents, Lyndon B. Johnson, 1963-64*, I, p. 626.

altogether is revealed. Nineteenth-century Germany, and Italy in the 1920s and 1930s, show that welfare measures are compatible with a highly authoritarian political environment.[11] Italian fascism is discussed elsewhere in this volume (see p. 122); however, it is also useful to remember that the first comprehensive modern welfare state was erected in Imperial Germany in the 1880s. Chancellor Otto von Bismarck developed an elaborate program for sickness, accident, and health insurance, not from any sympathy with liberalism or socialism, but on the contrary, as part of a larger strategy of destroying the German socialist movement.[12]

Of course America under Lyndon Johnson is not Germany under Bismarck. Nevertheless historical parallels should prepare us to perceive authoritarian tendencies in such government welfare programs as those associated with the Great Society. The philosophical essay on the professionalization of reform by Daniel Patrick Moynihan (reading 33, below) is an interesting example. As an American liberal, writing for a liberal audience, his argument is free from all overt authoritarian overtones. Although no longer employed at this writing by any government agency, Moynihan expresses the Administration's view of its own benevolence. The substance of his position is that a strategy of social change initiated "from the top down" will bring about such reforms in America that a socialist program will be rendered obsolete. If this is not Bismarckian authoritarianism, it is certainly a kind of bureaucratic elitism that can be contrasted with the tradition of American pluralism and voluntarism.

Writing self-consciously in the egalitarian spirit of American democracy, Tom Hayden is led to advocate (reading 34, below) a radically different strategy of change from that offered by Moynihan. Looking beyond the benevolent sentiments expressed by designers and administrators of welfare programs, Hayden assesses the actual effects of these programs, and finds them basically authoritarian. Furthermore, adopting a perspec-

[11] Our argument here refers to the compatibility of welfare measures with political authoritarianism in a capitalist environment. We of course recognize that such compatibility might also appear under socialism, but that is irrelevant to the points we are developing here.

[12] See W. N. Medlicott, *Bismarck and Modern Germany* (London, 1965), pp. 144-46; Joseph A. Schumpeter, *Capitalism, Socialism and Democracy* (3rd ed., New York, 1950), pp. 341-43.

tive that considers foreign and domestic policy as flowing from the same source, Hayden offers a critique of the welfare rationale for anti-Communist crusades in places like Vietnam. Permeating his essay is a passionate rejection of the values of the form of modern liberalism represented by Lyndon Johnson. The liberalism of the contemporary American political establishment is committed to a domestic policy essentially designed to halt meaningful change at home, and an essentially congruent foreign policy. It poses no real alternative to something called conservatism. Hayden seeks an escape from the older, irrelevant polarities, and calls for revolutionary change to bring about the kind of society in which people participate directly and concretely in the actual decisions which determine their lives.

Thus, for Tom Hayden as well as for the editors of this volume, the old polarities are no longer valid. Traditional concepts—"liberal" and "conservative," Republican and Democrat —contribute little to an understanding of contemporary American society. Instead, it is our conviction that Lyndon Johnson's Great Society can only be understood within a framework that contrasts it with a socialist alternative.

In saying this we are sadly aware that in America socialism has become an alien idea.[13] Socialists are by no means free from blame for this. It is true however that once there was a vigorous and dynamic socialist movement in the United States.[14] But beyond that, the ideas of Karl Marx, rooted in their nineteenth century European environment, have great relevance even for our own time. Marx demonstrated that capitalism led not only to new forms of exploitation by men over other men, but also to the creation of greatly augmented productive forces.

He saw clearly that for the first time man had the ability to abolish material need, not just for a privileged few, but for everybody. He perceived also that this possibility was blocked by the possessing class's determination to resist any tampering with the basic pattern of wealth and power.

Marx freely conceded that in an earlier age the innovations

[13] See on this, Staughton Lynd, "Socialism: The Forbidden Word," *Studies on the Left*, III (Summer, 1963), pp. 14-20.

[14] See James Weinstein, *The Decline of American Socialism, 1912-1925* (New York, forthcoming).

wrought by the capitalist class constituted an immense advance over the restricted process of production under feudalism. Capitalism was a progressive force. But the system of private property erected in the capitalist era became in time a fetter on the *further* development of a free and equitable society in which goods can be distributed according to need. The notion that it was "human nature" rather than a particular institutional structure that prevented the realization of the socialist dream was rightly dismissed by Marx and Engels in *The Communist Manifesto*, where they ask rhetorically: "Does it require deep intuition to comprehend that man's ideas, views and conceptions, in one word, man's consciousness, changes with every change in the conditions of his material existence, in his social relations and in his social life?" [15] For Marx, capitalism's perpetuation was the product of the interest of a class, and this interest cannot be overcome merely by convincing argument. The agent of social change bringing about the transformation to a socialist era was the working class, which capitalism itself had created.

Socialists today are less sure that a revolutionary role will be played by the working class. Other strategies are being formulated, like that coalition of students, Negroes and alienated middle-class professionals envisaged by Tom Hayden. [16] But the conviction remains that the private ownership is outmoded and prevents a more rational organization of society. [17] It is an error, however, simply to define socialism as the nationalization of the means of production. There is no need in America today for the type of bureaucratic socialist pattern that developed in backward Russia and in other nonindustrial countries. Socialists are increasingly sympathetic to the decentralization im-

[15] Max Eastman, ed., *Capital, The Communist Manifesto and Other Writings* . . . (New York, 1932), p. 341. Even the most casual student of cultural anthropology can obtain a vivid picture of the tremendous variations in what is called "human nature" by reading such books as Ruth Benedict's *Patterns of Culture* (Boston, 1934).

[16] We do not mean to imply that Hayden considers himself a socialist. It is our view that whatever label he adopts, his analysis does lead to socialist conclusions.

[17] It should be noted that this rational organization *need not* necessarily preclude resort to the market mechanism in socialist economies. To the contrary, the recent experience of the Soviet Union and some other Eastern European countries (a phenomenon called "Libermanism," after Yevsei Liberman, a noted contemporary Soviet economist) gives every indication that the market will play a key allocative role.

plicit in the Marxist notion that under socialism the state will wither away.[18] There is a strong strain of philosophical anarchism in Marx, and this is certainly one of the most attractive elements in the socialist tradition.

Conversely, nationalization does not in and of itself mean socialism any more than does an extensive welfare program. It is easy to conceive of nationalization taking place in such a way that the economy would still be controlled by a class of state bondholders. The form of class control would be changed, but not its essential content. Nationalization in Great Britain displayed some of these characteristics.[19] A vision of a society free of exploitation is no less needed now than when Marx and Engels wrote in 1848: "In place of the old bourgeois society, with its classes and class antagonisms, we shall have an association, in which the free development of each is the condition for the free development of all." [20]

This is not the place to attempt a detailed description of what a socialist America would be like, and how that condition could be achieved. It would certainly involve the creation of a society free of authoritarianism and racism, one in which poverty could be finally eliminated along with the scourge of war. We believe it is clear from what has been presented in these pages that Lyndon Johnson's Great Society cannot evolve into the kind of humane community that we advocate. Nor can we expect such a development from the liberalism that Johnson represents. Achieving a socialist alternative is no simple task. But however difficult, it has to begin with the kind of radical critique of the present condition that we have hoped to stimulate by this book.

[18] For a recent affirmation of decentralization as a leading, humane socialist goal, see William A. Williams, *The Great Evasion: An Essay on the Contemporary Relevance of Karl Marx* . . . (Chicago, 1964). Nonsocialists too, such as Paul Goodman, have affirmed the desirability of social institutions decentralized to some "human scale." See Goodman's *People or Personnel* (New York, 1965) and *Like a Conquered Province* (New York, 1967).

[19] For example, the announcement of the terms of nationalization for the Bank of England and the British coal companies were so favorable as to have a bullish effect on their stocks. See William N. Loucks, *Comparative Economic Systems*, 7th ed. (New York, 1965), pp. 228, 297.

[20] *The Communist Manifesto* in Eastman, ed., *Capital* . . . *and Other Writings*, p. 343.

THE PROFESSIONALIZATION OF REFORM*

When President Johnson delivered his famous civil rights speech at Howard University in the summer of 1965 (see above, reading 20), Daniel P. Moynihan had helped prepare the speech, and the approach Johnson proposed closely followed Moynihan's celebrated report on the Negro family. Both the Moynihan report and Johnson's Howard University speech were special examples of a general strategy of professionalized social reform. Moynihan supplies us with a candid statement of this strategy in the essay below. In it, he gives what is intended to be a heartening report on the latest manifestation of the reform impulse in the United States.

Contemporary American social reform is the heir of a complex history. There was in the nineteenth century a sturdy tradition of individualism,—what Ralph Waldo Emerson called "an assertion of the sufficiency of the private man." [1] But alongside the spirit of manly self-reliance, there was also a repressive and aristocratic aspect to American reform. Benevolent gentlemen, convinced that they enjoyed a mandate from on high to enlighten their less deserving fellow citizens, went about their philanthropic tasks in a spirit of "Moral Stewardship." [2] In an

* From *The Public Interest*, I (Fall, 1965), pp. 6-10. © 1965 by National Affairs, Inc. Reprinted by permission.

[1] Emerson, "New England Reformers" (1844), in David B. Davis, ed., *Ante-Bellum Reform* (New York, 1967), pp. 11-18.

[2] See Clifford S. Griffin, *Their Brothers' Keepers: Moral Stewardship in the United States, 1800-1865* (New Brunswick, N. J., 1960).

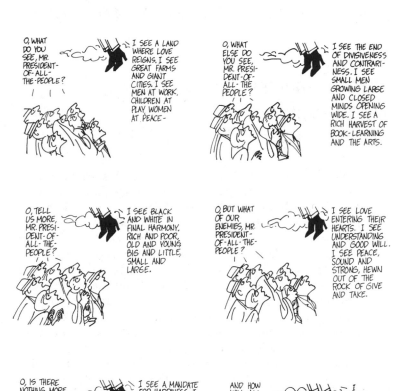

infinitely more sophisticated way, the contemporary ideology of professionalized reform shares the elitism and
tough-mindedness of nineteenth-century moral stewardship. But there is at least one important difference. In the
twentieth century, benevolent purposes are often tied to
the exercise of vast government power, whereas in the
earlier period voluntary efforts were the major expression
of reform. Harnessing state power to benevolence has
become the goal of those in modern America who call
themselves "liberal." With Moynihan, they are dedicated
to the possibilities for expert social manipulation that an
institutionalized welfare state supplies. Although he is no
longer a member of the Johnson Administration, Moynihan
provides an insiders' view of the establishment's conception of its own benevolence.

◇ ◇ ◇

I

Our best hope for the future lies in the extension to social
organization of the methods that we already employ in
our most progressive fields of effort. In science and in
industry . . . we do not wait for catastrophe to force new
ways upon us. . . . We rely, and with success, upon quantitative analysis to point the way; and we advance because
we are constantly improving and applying such analysis.

The passage above, as succinct a case for social planning as
could be made, is not a product of either the thought or the
institutions of the liberal left. It is, rather, a statement by the
late mathematical economist Wesley C. Mitchell. And it has
recently been approvingly reprinted at the beginning of a report on "The Concept of Poverty" published by—the Chamber
of Commerce of the United States.

The report itself, the work of businessmen and scholars, is
perhaps the most competent commentary on the government's
antipoverty program yet to appear. It is replete with citations
of articles in *Social Research* and *Land Economics,* and of data
from *The Statistical Abstract of the United States;* the perspective ranges from friendly references to the works of Friedrich
Engels, to more detached assessments of contemporary tracts.
("Michael Harrington, author of a widely read book on pov-

erty, *The Other America,* has written, 'Any gain for America's minorities will immediately be translated into an advance for all the unskilled workers. One cannot raise the bottom of society without benefiting everyone above.' This is almost precisely wrong.") But the report is less significant for what it says than for what it is: an example of the evolving technique and style of reform in the profoundly new society developing in the United States. Lacking a better term, it might be described as the professionalization of reform.

II

Writing for the British journal, *The New Society,* just prior to the assassination of President Kennedy, Nathan Glazer described the process:

Without benefit of anything like the Beveridge report to spark and focus public discussion and concern, the United States is passing through a stage of enormous expansion in the size and scope of what we may loosely call the social services—the public programs designed to help people adapt to an increasingly complex and unmanageable society. While Congress has been painfully and hesitantly trying to deal with two great measures—tax reform and a civil rights bill—and its deliberations on both have been closely covered by the mass media, it has also been working with much less publicity on a number of bills which will contribute at least as much to changing the shape of American society.

The vast Mental Retardation Facilities and Community Mental Health Centers Construction Act had just become law. The no less enormous vocational education bill was moving steadily through the Congress. The Kennedy Administration had earlier obtained such measures as the Area Redevelopment Act, the Manpower Development and Training Act, and the Public Welfare Amendments of 1962. "Waiting in the wings" were a domestic peace corps and an ambitious youth conservation corps, while the community action programs developed by the President's Committee on Juvenile Delinquency and Youth Crime, established in 1961, were scheduled for new and expanded funding.

It is a special mind that can as much as keep the titles of

those programs straight. But the most interesting thing about all this sudden expansion of social services was that it had behind it, as Glazer noted, "nothing like the powerful political pressure and long-sustained intellectual support that produced the great welfare measures of the New Deal—Social Security, Unemployment Insurance, Public Welfare, Public Housing." The "massive political support and intellectual leadership that produced the reforms of the thirties" simply did not exist; yet the reforms were moving forward.

Glazer accounted for this in terms of the emergence of a large body of professional persons and professional organizations that had taken on themselves the concern for the 20 to 30 per cent of the population that was outside the mainstream of American prosperity. Intellectuals knew little about the subject, and were not much interested. Organized labor, while both concerned and knowledgeable, had had but limited success in involving its membership in such efforts. As a result

the fate of the poor is in the hands of the administrators and the professional organizations of doctors, teachers, social workers, therapists, counselors and so forth. It is these who, in a situation where the legislation and programs become ever more complex, spend the time to find out—or rather have brought home to them—through their work the effects of certain kinds of measures and programs, and who propose ever more complex programs which Congress deliberates upon in the absence of any major public interest. When Congress argues these programs, the chief pressures upon it are not the people, but the organized professional interests that work with that segment of the problem, and those who will benefit from or be hurt by the legislation.

The antipoverty program that was being developed even as Glazer wrote is far the best instance of the professionalization of reform yet to appear. In its genesis, its development, and now in its operation, it is a prototype of the social technique of action that will almost certainly become more common in the future. It is a technique that will not appeal to everyone, and in which many will perceive the not altogether imaginary danger of a too-powerful government. But it is also a technique that offers a profound promise of social sanity and stability in time to come.

There are two aspects of the poverty program which distinguish it from earlier movements of its kind: The initiative came largely from within. The case for action was based on essentially esoteric information about the past and probable future course of events.

The most distinctive break with the past is with regard to initiative. War on poverty was not declared at the behest of the poor. Just the opposite. The poor were not only invisible, as Michael Harrington described them, they were also for the most part silent. John F. Kennedy ventured into Appalachia searching for Protestant votes, not for poverty. There he encountered the incredible pauperization of the mountain people, most particularly the soft coal miners, an industrial work force whose numbers had been reduced by nearly two-thirds in the course of a decade—but with hardly a sound of protest. The miners were desperately poor, shockingly unemployed, but neither radical nor in any significant way restive. It may be noted that in 1964, in the face of the historic Democratic sweep, Harlan County, Kentucky, returned a freshman Republican Congressman.

True, the civil rights movement was well established and highly effective during this period, but it was primarily concerned with just that: the demand for the recognition of the civil rights of the Negro American. While the movement would clearly in time turn to the problem of poverty and of the economic position of the Negro, it had only begun to do so, as in the March on Washington in August 1963, and its economic demands were still general and essentially traditional, as for example, an increased minimum wage.

Apart from the always faithful labor movement, the only major lobbies working for any of the programs that came together to form the War on Poverty were the conservationists supporting the youth conservation camps, and the National Committee on the Employment of Youth, an organization representing a variety of groups in the social welfare field. The essential fact is that the main pressure for a massive government assault on poverty developed within the Kennedy–Johnson Administration, among officials whose responsibilities were to think about just such matters. These men now exist, they are well paid, have competent staffs, and have access to the President. (Many of these officials, of course, were originally brought to Washington by the New Deal: they are by no means all *nuovi uomini.*) Most importantly, they have at their command an increasing fund of information about social conditions in the United States.

Almost all this information is public, but the art of interpreting it is, in a sense, private. Anyone is free to analyze income statistics, or employment data, or demographic trends to his heart's content. But very few persons in the beginning years of the present decade were able to perceive in those statistics the gradual settling of a poverty class in America. A number of officials in the Federal government (mostly academicians on leave) were. Leaving aside the question of whether or not they were right—a question which must always be open—it is clear that the judgment they reached was quite at variance, almost poles apart, from the general public understanding of the time.

Whereas the public, both high and low in the intellectual hierarchy, saw income distribution steadily compressing, saw the Negro American more and more winning his rightful place in society, saw prosperity spreading through the land, the men in the government saw something quite different: an income distribution gap that had not budged since the end of the war, and had in fact worsened sharply for Negroes, a rising measure of social disorganization among poor families and poor communities, a widening gap between the prospects of the poor and those of the middle class.

In President Johnson these officials found a chief executive who knew a good deal about poverty, and seemingly everything about politics. In a matter of weeks from the time he assumed office, the array of programs and bills Glazer had described as "waiting in the wings" were mustered into a coherent legislative program, reinforced by some entirely new ideas, and moved out under the banner of War on Poverty. It was an issue that united rather than divided, and the ranks of its supporters if anything swelled as it moved through the legislative process.

There is nothing, as such, startling about these developments. They have been foreseen, with either hope or fear, by many persons for many years. However, in recent times a number of events have occurred which very much hasten the process, and make it of greater moment. These have to do with the almost sudden emergence of the fact that the industrial nations of the world seem finally about to learn how to manage their economies, with the professionalization of the middle class, and with the exponential growth of knowledge.[3]

III

The economic revolution

Recent years, with the steady advance of technology, have given birth to a good number of neo-apocalyptic views of the future of the American economy, most of them associated with the concept of automation. No one should doubt there is something called automation going on, and that it does change things. However, there is no evidence whatever that it is in fact transforming American society, or any other society. It is simply the newest phase in a process that has been under way for at least two centuries, and will presumedly go on and on, past any immediate concern of this age or the next.

At the same time, there is a good deal of evidence, if that is the term for what are little more than everyday impressions, that in the area of economic policy there has occurred a genuine discontinuity, a true break with the past: Men are learning how to make an industrial economy work.

What is involved is something more permanent than simply a run of good luck, or specially refined intuitions on the part of persons responsible for the economic affairs of one nation, or a group of nations. Rather it is the fact that for two decades now, since the end of World War II, the industrial democracies of the world have been able to operate their economies on a high and steadily expanding level of production and employment. Nothing like it has ever happened before in history. It is perhaps the central fact of world politics today. The briefest recollection of what happened to those economies in the two decades that followed World War I will suggest why.

Moreover, it is a development that has all the markings of a scientific event, of a profound advance in knowledge, as well as of an improvement in statecraft.

In the beginning was the theory. With but little data either to support or confound them, economic theories multiplied and

3 Compare reading 18 above.—Eds.

conflicted. But gradually more and better data accumulated: progress begins on social problems when it becomes possible to measure them. As the data accumulated and technology made it possible to calculate more rapidly, the theories gradually became able to explain more, and these in turn led to the improvement in the data. John Maynard Keynes[4] at King's College, Cambridge, and Wesley C. Mitchell at the National Bureau of Economic Research in New York, are supremely good symbols of the two processes that ended up in a deeply symbiotic relationship. And then one day it all more or less hangs together and the world is different, although of course not quite aware of the change. Governments promise full employment—and then produce it. (In 1964 unemployment, adjusted to conform more or less to United States' definitions, was 2.9 per cent in Italy, 2.5 per cent in France and Britain, and 0.4 per cent in Germany. Consider the contrast with post-World War I.) Governments undertake to expand their economy at a steady rate—and do so. (In 1961 the members of the Organization for Economic Cooperation and Development, which grew out of the Marshall Plan, undertook to increase their output by 50 per cent during the decade of the 1960s. The United States at all events is right on schedule.)

The ability to predict events, as against controlling them, has developed even more impressively—the Council of Economic Advisers' forecast of GNP for 1964 was off by only $400 million in a total of $623 billion; the unemployment forecast was on the nose.

There is a temptation, of course, to go too far in presuming what can be done with the economy. The international exchange system is primitive, and at the moment menacing. The stock market can be wildly irrational. There are, as Hyman Lewis points out, competing theories of investment which could bring us to unsettling dilemmas. We in the United States have not achieved full employment. We have accepted the use of federal taxing and spending powers as a means of social adjustment, but so far only in pleasant formulations. Our willingness to raise taxes, for example, is yet to be tested. In general, the political component of political economy remains very much uncertain. Thus the British, again to cite Lewis, have the

[4] Compare the introduction to Part II, above.—Eds.

best economists, but one of the less successful economies. But the fact remains that economics is approaching the status of an applied science.

In the long run this econometric revolution, assuming it works itself out, is bound to have profound effects on the domestic politics of all the nations involved. The central political issue of most industrial nations over the past century and a half has been how to make an economy work. Almost every conceivable nostrum, from the nationalization of the means of production, distribution, and exchange, to the free coinage of silver, has been proposed, and most have been tried. Usually without success. In the United States, for one administration after another, economic failure has led to political failure. But if henceforth the business cycle has a longer sweep, and fewer abrupt downturns, the rise and fall of political fortunes may follow the same pattern. Once in power, a party may be much more likely to remain so. Or in any event, the issues that elect or defeat governments could be significantly different from those of the past.

The more immediate impact of this econometric revolution in the United States is that the federal government will be endowed, more often than not, with a substantial, and within limits predictable, rise in revenues available for social purposes. Significantly, the War on Poverty began in the same year of the great tax cut. The President was not forced to choose between the measures; he was able to proceed with both. In that sense, the War on Poverty began not because it was necessary (which it was), but because it was possible.

The singular nature of the new situation in which the federal government finds itself is that the immediate *supply* of resources available for social purposes might actually outrun the immediate *demand* of established programs. Federal expenditures under existing programs rise at a fairly predictable rate. But, under conditions of economic growth, revenues rise faster. This has given birth to the phenomenon of the "fiscal drag"— the idea that unless the federal government disposes of this annual increment, either by cutting taxes or adding programs, the money taken out of circulation by taxes will slow down economic growth, and could, of course, at a certain point stop it altogether.

Thus, assuming the continued progress of the economy in

something like the pattern of recent years, there is likely to be $4-5 billion in additional, unobligated revenue coming in each year. *But* this increment will only continue to come on condition that it is disposed of. Therefore one of the important tasks to which an Administration must address itself is that of devising new and responsible programs for expending public funds in the public interest.

This is precisely the type of decision making that is suited to the techniques of modern organizations, and which ends up in the hands of persons who make a profession of it. They are less and less political decisions, more and more administrative ones. They are decisions that can be reached by consensus rather than conflict.

The professionalization of the middle class

"Everywhere in American life," Kenneth S. Lynn reports, "the professions are triumphant." The period since the G.I. Bill has witnessed an extraordinary expansion of higher education. In the United States, a quarter of the teenage population now goes on to some kind of college, and among specific class and ethnic groups the proportion is as high as three quarters. The trend is unmistakable and probably irresistible: in the course of the coming decades some form of higher education will become near to universal. But most importantly, for more and more persons the form of education will involve professional training. This is not the same thing as traditional higher education; it does not produce the same types of persons.

The difference has been most succinctly stated by Everett C. Hughes: "Professionals *profess.* They profess to know better than others the nature of certain matters, and to know better than their clients what ails them or their affairs." And he continues:

Lawyers not only give advice to clients and plead their cases for them; they also develop a philosophy of law—of its nature and its functions, and of the proper way in which to administer justice. Physicians consider it their prerogative to define the nature of disease and of health, and to determine how medical services ought to be distributed and paid for. Social workers are not content to develop a technique of casework; they concern themselves with social legislation. Every profession considers itself the proper body to set the terms in which some aspect of society, life or nature is to be thought of, and to define the general lines, or even the details, of public policy concerning it.

As the number of professionals increase, so also do the number of professions, or neo-professions. More and more, middle-class persons are attracted by the independence of judgment, esoteric knowledge, and immunity to outside criticism that characterize professionals. As Everett Hughes puts it: "The YMCA secretary wants his occupation recognized not merely as that of offering young men from the country a pleasant road to Protestant righteousness in the city, but as a more universal one of dealing with groups of young people. All that is learned of adolescence, of behavior in small groups, of the nature and organization of community life is considered the intellectual base of his work."

There are now an extraordinary number of such persons in America. Those Americans classified as professional and technical workers have just passed the nine million mark—more than the number of "managers, officials, and proprietors," more than the craftsmen and foremen. And of this group, an enormous number is involved in various aspects of social welfare and reform. Through sheer numbers they would tend to have their way; but as professionals in a professionalizing society, they are increasingly *entitled* to have their way. That is how the system works.

One of the more powerful demonstrations of the influence of professional thinking on programs of social reform is the provision of the Economic Opportunity Act that community action programs be carried out with the "maximum feasible participation" of the poor themselves. This is one of the most important and pioneering aspects of the entire antipoverty program. But typically this measure was inserted in the legislation not because of any demand of the poor, but because the intellectual leaders of the social welfare profession had come to the conclusion that this was indispensable to effective social action. Typically also, the literature describes the process in terms of the use of the "indigenous nonprofessional"—persons identified by the fact that they are *not* professional. A somewhat ironical turn of events in this area is the role the community action programs are playing in re-creating the ethnic political-social organizations of the big city slums—the dismantling of which was for so long the object of political and social reformers in the United States! [5]

The prospect of large-scale opposition to the new professions is, for the moment at least, limited because the professionalization of the middle class has led to a no less extraordinary opening up of careers to talent. The time when any considerable number of persons of great ability and ambition have found their way out of poverty blocked by their inability to obtain an education has all but passed. (There are still many, many persons whose natural abilities are stunted by poverty, but that is another matter.) A nationwide survey of 1960 high school graduates, Project Talent, found that about 97 per cent of those in the top 1 per cent in aptitude and 93 per cent of those in the top 5 per cent, entered college within a year. Among the next 5 per cent (the 90th to 94th percentile) 86 per cent did so. As a general proposition, ability is recognized and rewarded in America today as at no time in history. (Michael Young's forecast of the revolt of the lower quartile against the ultimate injustice of a society based on merit may not be discounted, but it is not on the other hand scheduled until 2031.)

It is possible that this process, just because it is successful in drawing up talent from lower economic and social groups, will deprive those groups of much of their natural leadership, and make them all the more dependent on professionals. Kenneth Clark has noted that the degree of recruitment of civil rights leaders into "establishment" organizations verges on raiding— and has raised suspicions of hidden motives! On the other hand, there is rather a pronounced tendency for persons from such groups, when they do rise to the middle class, to settle into professions which involve work with the very groups they left behind. Thus, in a certain sense the poor are not so much losing their natural leaders as obtaining them through different routes.

[5] Compare reading 19, above.—Eds.

The exponential growth of knowledge

Among the complexities of life is the fact that the American business community, in a period when it was fiercely opposed to the idea of economic or social planning, nonetheless supported, even pressed for, the development of a national statistical system which has become the best in the world and which now makes certain types of planning and regulation—although quite different from the collective proposals of earlier eras— both feasible and in a measure inevitable. Much as mountains are climbed, so statistics are used if they are there. As an example, trade union wage settlements in recent years have been profoundly influenced by the wage-price guidelines set by the federal government.[6] This could not possibly have occurred on an essentially voluntary basis were it not that the Bureau of Labor Statistics has developed the technique of measuring productivity—and has done so accompanied, step by step, by the business and labor advisory committees that work with the bureau. A measure of the near quantum change that has only recently occurred in the information available for social planning in the United States (the development work began long ago, but the pay-off has been rather recent) may be suggested by the fact that the nation went through the great depression of the 1930s without ever really knowing what the rate of unemployment was! This was then a measurement taken but once every ten years, by the census. Today, of course, employment and unemployment data are collected monthly, and debated in terms of the decimal points. Similarly, the census has been quietly transformed from a ten-times-a-century proceeding to a system of current accounts on a vast range of social data.

Most of the information that went into the development of the antipoverty program was essentially economic, but the social data available to the President's task force was of singular importance in shaping the program, and in turn the program will greatly stimulate the collection of more such. The nation is clearly on the verge of developing a system of social statistics comparable to the now highly developed system of economic statistics.

[6] Moynihan does not discuss *how* these statistics were used, or for whose benefit. See reading 12, above.—Eds.

The use of all such statistics is developing also. A vast "industry of discovery," to use William Haber's description of events in the physical sciences, is developing in the social sciences as well. Computer technology has greatly enhanced the possible uses of such data. Just as the effort to stimulate the American economy is now well advanced, the simulation of social processes, particularly in decision making, is also begun, and may be expected to produce important, if not indeed revolutionary insights. Such prospects tend to stir some alarm in thoughtful persons, but it may be noted the public has accepted with calm, even relish, the fact that the outcome of elections is now predicted with surpassing accuracy. If that most solemn of democratic rituals may be simulated without protest, there is not likely to be much outcry against the simulation of various strategies of housing integration, or techniques of conflict resolution, or patterns of child rearing.

Expenditure for social science research was somewhere between $500 and $600 million in 1964. This was only 10 per cent of the $6 billion spent in the same year on the life and physical sciences (including psychology), and much less a proportion of the $19 billion spent on research and development altogether. Nonetheless it represents a sixfold growth in a decade. There is, moreover, some indication that social scientists are not yet thinking in the money terms that are in fact available to them. Angus Campbell suggested recently that social scientists still think in budgets of thousands of dollars when they should be thinking of millions. "The prevailing format for social research is still the exploitation of opportunities which are close at hand, easily manageable, and inexpensive." But, he adds, "there are a good many social scientists who know very well how to study social change on a broad scale and are intensely interested in going about it." The Survey Research Center at the University of Michigan, which Campbell directs, has, for example, under way a year-long panel survey of the impact of the 1964 tax cut on the nation's taxpayers, a specific example of the use of social science techniques in the development of economic policy.

All in all, the prospect is for a still wider expansion of knowledge available to governments as to how people behave. This will be accompanied by further improvement of the now well-developed techniques of determining what they think. Public opinion polls are already a daily instrument of government decision-making (a fact which has clearly affected the role of the legislature). In combination, these two systems of information make it possible for a government to respond intelligently and in time to the changing needs and desires of the electorate. The day when mile-long petitions and mass rallies were required to persuade a government that a popular demand existed that things be done differently is clearly drawing to a close. Indeed, the very existence of such petitions and rallies may in time become a sign that what is being demanded is *not yet* a popular demand.

The perils of progress

The professionalization of reform will proceed, regardless of the perils it presents. Even in the face of economic catastrophe, which is certainly conceivable if not probable, the response will be vastly more systematic and informed than any of the past.

A certain price will be paid, and a considerable risk will be incurred. The price will be a decline in the moral exhilaration of public affairs at the domestic level. It has been well said that the civil rights movement of the present time has at last provided the youth of America with a moral equivalent of war. The more general effect of the civil rights movement has been a much heightened public concern for human dignity and welfare. This kind of passion could seep out of the life of the nation, and we would be the less for it.

The risk is a combination of enlightenment, resources, and skill which in the long run, to use Harold D. Laswell's phrase, becomes a "monocracy of power."

But the potential rewards are not less great. The creation of a society that can put an end to the "animal miseries" and stupid controversies that afflict most peoples would be an extraordinary achievement of the human spirit. The argument may be made, for example, that had the processes described in this article not progressed as far as they had by 1961, the response of the federal government to the civil rights revolution would have been thoroughly inadequate: that instead of joining with and helping to direct the movement, the national government would have trailed behind with grudging, uncomprehending, and increasingly inadequate concessions that could have resulted in the problem of the Negro American becoming insoluble in terms of existing American society.

The prospect that the more primitive social issues of American politics are at last to be resolved need only mean that we may now turn to issues more demanding of human ingenuity than that of how to put an end to poverty in the richest nation in the world. Many such issues might be in the area of foreign affairs, where the enormity of difficulty and the proximity of disaster is sufficient to keep the citizens and political parties of the nation fully occupied. And there is also the problem of perfecting, to the highest degree possible, the *quality* of our lives and of our civilization. We may not be accustomed to giving political priority to such questions. But no one can say they will be boring or trivial!

WELFARE LIBERALISM
AND SOCIAL CHANGE*

Many radicals who came to maturity during the New Deal have come to accept the premise that the United States has basically solved most of its problems and that the remaining task is to perfect the existing system. A later generation, whose political consciousness was sharpened on the bitter awareness that America was offering the black man "tokenism" instead of equality, cannot so happily conclude that the system itself is beyond criticism. This new generation of radicals has produced some eloquent spokesmen. One of these is Tom Hayden.

While at the University of Michigan Hayden became one of the founding members of Students for a Democratic Society (SDS) and helped draft the famous Port Huron manifesto, stating SDS aims and goals. (See Paul Jacobs and Saul Landau, eds., *The New Radicals* [New York, 1966], pp. 149 ff.) Fully prepared to act on his radical convictions, Hayden worked with the civil rights movement in Mississippi, and then came north as organizer in the ghetto of Newark, New Jersey. He has been able in the essay that follows to distill much of the experience he has gained with the Newark Community Union Project.

But Hayden's radicalism is rooted not simply in the local agony of the ghetto environment; it extends to pro-

* Portions of this article appeared originally in *Dissent* (January–February, 1966), © 1966 by Tom Hayden. Major additions and revisions were written specifically for inclusion in this volume.

found insights into American society as a whole, and to US foreign policy as well. A vigorous opponent of American actions in Vietnam, he traveled to that ravaged land early in 1966 with Staughton Lynd and Herbert Aptheker. Hayden and Lynd have recorded their experiences and reflections of Vietnam in their recent book, *The Other Side* (New York, 1967).

◇◇◇

I

Americans find it unthinkable that their country can be corrupt at the center, guilty as a society of inhuman behavior. This is true even among American reformers, most of whom hold that discrimination, poverty, and foreign intervention are simply flaws in a generally humanitarian record. While the massacre of the Vietnamese grinds on, while Negro uprisings spread to every city, while the public looks back on August 6 as Luci's wedding and Hiroshima is forgotten, the progressive American—he may be a liberal businessman, university president, technical assistance expert, or trade unionist—is perhaps uneasy but remains basically complacent, secure in the justness of our objectives at home and abroad.

Since early in the century, the task of American leaders has been to make "peace," "self-determination" and the promise of a better life the language that explains American purposes. Probably none of them has ever willfully deprived a man of food or killed another in cold blood; they order political and economic suppression and murder—by gas, napalm, or nuclear weapons—only as a means of realizing peace and preserving democracy.

Until the day their language changes to that of naked power, it is easy to assume they are not fiends but honorable men. This is the assumption that makes reformers hope for their country. But it is sheer indulgence not to confront the consequences of our leaders' actions. We need to stop giving weight to protestations of good intentions, and to examine instead the worth of American words in the light of American deeds.

The general contradiction most worth examining is between the philosophy and the practice of the liberal–welfare state that has been constructed at home and is now being forcibly exported to other parts of the world. It is the belief in our commitment to welfare that, more than anything else, allows our honorable men to sleep at night while other men are murdered, jailed or hungry.

II

The legitimacy gained by the industrial unions, the welfare legislation passed in the thirties and forties, and now the civil rights and antipoverty reforms of the sixties—these are seen as part of a long sweep toward a society of economic and social justice. But there is, in fact, little evidence to justify the view that the social reforms of the past thirty years actually improved the quality of American life in a lasting way, and there is much evidence which suggests that many of the reforms gained were illusory or token, serving chiefly to sharpen the capacity of the system for manipulation and oppression.

Look closely at the social legislation upon which the notion of domestic improvement is based. The Wagner Act was supposed to effect unionization of workers; but today the unionized labor force is shrinking with the automation of the mass-production industries, and millions of other workers, never organized, are without protection. The Social Security laws were supposed to support people in distress, but today many are still not covered, and those who are solely dependent on Social Security payments cannot make ends meet. Unemployment compensation policies were supposed to aid men in need of jobs, but today many are still without coverage, while benefits represent a smaller and smaller share of the cost of living. The Employment Act of 1946 was supposed to guarantee federal action to provide a job for every American who needed one, but in 1966 the official (understated) unemployment rate is close to 5 per cent, and may be over 30 per cent for young men in the ghettos. The 1949 Public Housing Act, sponsored by conservative Robert Taft, was to create 800,000 low-cost units by 1953, but today less than half that number have been constructed, and many of them are beyond reach of the poor. The difficult struggle to enact even a token policy of public medical care, the hollow support for public education, the stagnation and starvation of broader programs for health, recreation and simple city services—all this suggests that the welfare state is more machinery than substance.

The trend is *toward*, not away from, increased racial segregation and division, greater unemployment for Negroes than whites, worse educational facilities in the slums, less job security for whites, fewer doctors for nearly everyone: in essence, the richest society in all history places increasing pressures on its "have nots" despite all talk of the "welfare state" and "Great Society." The real subsidies go to the housebuilders, farmers, businessmen, scholars, while comparatively, there are only scraps for the poor. The welfare recipient who cannot purchase decent furniture will not take much confort in knowing she is one of the "richest" poor people in the world. America's expanding affluence is still built on a system of deep inequalities.

The quality of the welfare state is well illustrated by the sluggish way it responds to pressure for modest civil rights reform. It required the slaughter of little girls, a bloodbath in Montgomery and Birmingham, Southern racist violence against Northern whites—students and ministers—an outbreak of Negro rebellion across the North, and the organization of an independent political party in Mississippi before the Administration and Congress began to move on the civil rights front. But even that gave little hope of real progress. The 1965 Civil Rights Bill actually shrinks the legitimate power of the federal government.[1] Under the law, the call for concrete action remains an option of the Attorney General; the burden of proof and time-consuming procedures is placed on local Negroes; no effective protection is provided civil rights workers against violence and intimidation. The rejection by Congress of the 1966 bill must be interpreted as a reflection of the national mood toward further change.

Seen in this context, the 1965 antipoverty program should evoke little optimism. The amount of money allotted is a pittance, and most of it is going to local politicians, school boards, welfare agencies, housing authorities, professional personnel and even the police; its main thrust is to shore up sagging organizational machinery, not to offer the poor a more equitable share of income and influence. Meaningful involvement of the poor is frustrated by the poverty planners' allegiance to existing local power centers. In reality, the poor only flavor the pro-

[1] This power was established long ago in such codes as Section 242, Title 18, providing for criminal prosecution of people acting under cover of law to violate the constitutional rights of others.

gram. A few are co-opted into it, but only as atomized individuals. They do not have independent organizational strength, as do the machines and social agencies.[2]

Some of the more sophisticated poverty planners believe that the involvement of the poor is essential to effective programs; thus the heavy emphasis on, and debate about, the need for "maximum feasible participation" of the poor. This policy concept rests upon the conviction that the modern poor cannot be socialized upward and into the mainstream of American life in the tradition of the earlier immigrants.

The slavery period has left the Negro poor, according to this view, without the tight-knit culture, the economic skills, and the expanding market opportunities that were so common in the life of the immigrants. The result is the breakdown of the family, at least in its function of preparing the young to take their places in the slots offered by the established industrial machine.

Though it is not officially put this way, the poverty program thus seeks to be a substitute parent more than a meal ticket, an agency of socialization more than of welfare. Not only is this the conception that underlies the Job Corps camps and the new batteries of "psychological service" counsellors; it underlies the Community Action Program as well.

Self-organization, the development of skills, helping oneself through social action, are supposedly the means by which the ghetto residents ("the target population") will be rehabilitated. The amount and kind of conscious stress on this process vary from city to city. One view is evident in testimony given to a congressional subcommittee by Denton Brooks, director of the Chicago antipoverty program. Asked whether the tactics of conflict, such as rent strikes, might be necessary for progress, his answer was negative for this reason:

Once you get the interaction of all groups, once you have a policy that something should be done for the poor, once this becomes a national policy, then you work on a problem and find a positive solution. Then the need for protest is eliminated.[3]

[2] See reading 22, above.—Eds.

[3] *Hearings before the Subcommittee on the War on Poverty Program,* Committee on Education and Labor, House of Representatives, 89th Congress, 1st session, 1965, p. 327. Emphasis added.

The practical impact of such policies was explained by Father Theodore R. Gibson, assigned as federal trouble-shooter for Newark in the summer of 1965. Gibson was

convinced that the antipoverty program was the key to racial peace in Newark this summer. . . . . "*All the things I saw that would make for trouble got their answer in the antipoverty program," asserted the Community Relations Service representative. "What saved the community more than anything else was the involvement of so many people in so many things. Even members of the most militant groups," he said, "were so busy working on antipoverty projects that they had little time to stir up dissension."* [4]

Many of the poverty planners concede that progress will involve some element of conflict and that the poor cannot be painlessly assimilated into the greater society. The feeling is that change can be accomplished through a "dialogue" between the poor and the powerful, in which the poor assert their needs as clearly as necessary. But while dialogue is promoted, final decisions remain in traditional hands. Sargent Shriver encourages "representative neighborhood advisory organizations" to give "advice on programs," which can then be "channeled" to the community action agency. This is all Shriver sees as necessary to give neighborhood people "an effective voice in the conduct and administration of neighborhood-based programs." [5]

The poverty program, in short, assumes the poor are groups of damaged individuals who need charity, relief, technical aid, or retraining. What the program cannot accept is the possibility that the poor are "natives" pitted against "colonial" structures at home that exclude and exploit them. One such "native" in Newark is Mrs. Joanne Robinson who made the following definitive comment after her first antipoverty meeting:

It seemed to me the meeting was run by politicians, whereas I thought it should be run by the poor people themselves. I

[4] *Newark News* (September 14, 1965). Emphasis added.
[5] *Hearings before the Subcommittee on the War on Poverty Program,* Committee on Education and Labor, House of Representatives, 89th Congress, 1st session, 1965, p. 78.

didn't feel free to stand up and say anything really. It was as if they wanted who they knew in, and no strangers. If you join something, you want to feel part of it, and the people at the poverty meeting just didn't give you a chance to feel part of it. It was like you're an outsider looking in.

Welfare liberalism has brought new insecurities to the American exploited. The poor are without the effective ability to control any economic resources in the welfare state. Antipoverty funds are controlled "from above" by city or federal officials. There is no unionization of tenants or welfare clients to provide financing and protection. Unable to gather independent capital from the public sector, the poor are considered unqualified for credit by banks and lending institutions. This lack of meaningful economic power divides the contemporary poor from earlier immigrant generations, who entered an expanding economy and formed unions and co-ops to advance their interests. Lacking any security or power, the "left out" whites and the poor Negroes are more likely to vote for their "masters"— those who control the public housing, welfare, and unemployment checks—or not vote at all, rather than risk an independent political initiative.

The "colonial power" maintains control of the ghetto from the outside, through the police, social agencies, and a cultivated group of colonized natives ("Uncle Toms"). The idea is conveyed, by every means, that only the governors are qualified to govern, that the only chance for self-gain, even survival, lies in trying to be like the governors, that protest is a sign of maladjustment and furthermore can never succeed. This colonialism is as real as the more traditional colonialism of Britain and France, despite our official national ideology of equality. SNCC field secretary Charlie Cobb puts it this way:

If I were trying to run things my way, I would do everything that I could to teach everybody that they were not able to run things like me. I would teach that to build something else meant that whoever wanted to do it would have to become like me. I would finally teach that I was the only person who knew enough to make other people like me. If I could manage all that, I wouldn't have to let people know they were slaves. It would be very important that the slavery I imposed be

couched in my definition of freedom, and remain unseen in
order that rebellion remained stifled, and my control intact.[6]

III

American foreign policy, in Vietnam in particular, stems
from the same framework of thought that determines domestic
welfarism. "America is building a curious empire," writes John
McDermott, "a kind which has never before been seen. It is
committed not to the exploitation of native peoples but to their
welfare." [7] The policy of the Open Door still governs. The US
denies any colonial desire, that is, direct political control of
other nations. Nor does the American government claim an interest in draining other economies for our prosperity; all that is
desired is that other nations remain "open" to American trade
and investment. Yet in Vietnam the US finances roughly 85 per
cent of the Saigon budget and is the real force holding the Ky
government in power. How can these words and deeds be consistent?

Strikingly, New Dealers were among the group that initiated
American activity in Vietnam when it became certain that the
French would withdraw. In addition to liberal reformers like
Wolf Ladejinsky, intellectuals from Michigan State University
under the auspices of the CIA were intimately involved in
building up the position of Ngo Dinh Diem. A passion for social reform evidently inspired these men; even General Lans-
dale of the Central Intelligence Agency spoke of the need for a
"revolutionary alternative" to Communism for the Vietnamese
people. For several years, the American public read about the
"miracle of social reform" in Vietnam.[8]

[6] Charlie Cobb, "Whose Society Is This?," *New Republic* (December
18, 1965), pp. 13-15.
[7] *The Nation* (July 25, 1966).
[8] This aspect of CIA activity is documented in a number of sources,
such as David Wise and Thomas B. Ross, *The Invisible Government*
(New York, 1964), and the essay by Robert Scheer in Marvin E. Gettleman (ed.), *Vietnam: History, Documents and Opinions* . . . (New
York, 1965), pp. 235-53. But the activity of the CIA is more extensive
than most Americans have suspected, including its support of the National Student Association, and a wide range of other nominally independent organizations. (See the revelations in *Ramparts*, February,
1967). The effects of this have been well analyzed by Andrew Kopkind, "CIA: The Great Corruptor," *New York Review of Books* (March

As with the New Deal, the need for a Vietnamese welfare state was defined in reaction to a threat to the social order, in this case from the Communist-led Vietminh who controlled most of Vietnam in 1954. This primary concern made two priorities precede all others: an effective police force and a stable anti-Communist government. "Sink or swim with Ngo Dinh Diem" became the watchword and (with MSU help) guns, anti-riot equipment and 10,000 American advisers were brought into Saigon. The underlying rationale was that no matter how bad Diem might be, at least improvements were possible under his government, whereas Communism would bring the end of any possibilities at all.

So the US developed a government and an army. In Saigon, a prosperous urban economy was envisioned, in which American aid would allow the Vietnamese to purchase American imports, mostly automobiles, perfumes, and other luxury items— thus creating a consumer market for American business. The strategic reason for this, as some officials observed, was to develop a new urban class in Vietnam that would identify with the government receiving the American support.

There were two problems with this economic program: (1) a new privileged class developed that was too corrupt to become a successful "nationalist" alternative to Communism; (2) the tremendous spending of American dollars has as much as doubled the Saigon cost of living in a single year.

But the real contest, most officials knew, would be in the countryside, where the bulk of the people live. The first obstacle in reaching the peasants, however, was a deep prejudice. The "prosperous" urban South Vietnamese looked with disgust upon the rural people; the French had called them *les jaunes;* and common American views were summed up as early as 1948 by Congressman Lyndon Johnson who warned that "any yellow dwarf with a pocket knife" might threaten American interests in Asia.[9]

23, 1967). President Johnson himself was forced to make some public declaration of policy on this matter, and on March 29, 1967, he ordered the CIA to halt its aid to certain private groups, except when justified on grounds of "overriding national security." Johnson did not, however, state that the CIA would refrain from promoting the overthrow by force and violence of governments it does not like.—Eds.

[9] The full quotation and the circumstances under which it was made are recited elsewhere in this volume. See p. 420.—Eds.

There is little difference today, though the United States dares not suggest racial reasons for the war. Pvt. Dennis Mora, a Puerto Rican facing three years of hard labor for refusing to fight in Vietnam, told a military court that his instructor in basic training said to "kill as many Asians as we could" and the reason for going to Vietnam was because "those small brown people were too small to carry a B.A.R. [Browning Automatic Rifle]." [10] American-trained Mobile Unit Teams take the same attitude across the border in Thailand; Alex Campbell reported that civic action has "flopped badly" there because its administrators are viewed by the peasants as tax-collectors and "have a bad habit of calling the peasants to their faces filthy, uncivilized pigs, making them squat on the ground in their presence, and making them call any policeman 'master.'" [11]

Despite this fundamental bias, some of the American planners had great dreams for the countryside. First, however, the rural areas had to be "pacified," an unusually frank term describing a plan borrowed from the unsuccessful French. The plan involved moving vast numbers of peasants from their villages into barricaded fortresses, usually despite their will and after "weeding out" subversives. But the total US plan involved more than uprooting the rural population and eliminating its traditional village government structure. Here welfarism entered to help the natives. Schools and health clinics were to be established in every hamlet, and land reform was to give the natives their own plot of land and economic security. Both the Kennedy and Johnson Administrations have had to keep coming up with new programs for the welfare of the peasants while abandoning equally hopeful older programs that had died without ever being put into effect.

The carrying out of these plans involved horrors which may never be fully recorded. Despite tuberculosis, malaria, trachoma, and more recently, bubonic plague, all spread by the war, the US has barely succeeded in bringing medical equipment to the few areas under its control. Despite mass illiteracy, despite the fact that South Vietnamese young people cannot join the civil service without a high school diploma, in US-controlled areas only a fraction of the young will finish high

[10] *New York Times* (September 8, 1966).
[11] "Thailand: Is This Something to Fall Back On?," *New Republic* (March 26, 1966).

school. The land reform program was intended to create rent control and sell plots of ground to individual peasants; but of the million acres that Ky plans to dispose of in this way, after ten years of promises, almost all of it has been parceled out already to peasants by the National Liberation Front. After an equally long period of "tax reform," the Saigon government collects less than 20 per cent of its budget from the South Vietnamese people (and even those revenues stem from American-generated income).

Ky and his government are *part of the American system,* not foreigners to it. More aid is given to Saigon than any state in the US; American businessmen, doctors and teachers are settled there; the South Vietnamese army is paid with the same funds that pay for the National Guard here; no one can deny that the whole structure of the Saigon government would collapse if American support were withdrawn; the strategic hamlets are no different from, if less stable than, the reservations where American Indians are kept.

Yet good men—liberal men—carry forward this Asian Great Society, as Hubert Humphrey calls it, year after year (or its counterpart in Latin America and Africa). Their clinching argument in support of the war in Vietnam still is that reform is underway. This is maintained despite the fact that the United States has never supported a real social revolution, but, as in Cuba, China, and recently the Dominican Republic, has been violently opposed.

What seems to happen is this: because "aid" is aimed at stopping Communism, it finds its way into the pockets of politicians whose invariable corruption matters less to American supporters than staunch anti-Communist views. As paternal as the domestic poverty program—"we are trying to create Joneses for the people to keep up with" is how the US aid officer in Laos puts it—the reforms inevitably fail to attract popular support. When insurgency, Communist-inspired or not, begins to threaten the pro-US ruling group, however decadent the rulers, the Americans call for military suppression. In the "counter-insurgency" which follows, counter-revolutionary violence takes priority—in deed, not in rhetoric—over any social construction. Americans begin to torture for freedom. What we are offering to the third world under the label of welfarism is a sophisticated barbarism. Yet Peace Corps officials can seriously

consider organizing "social revolution" in Latin America, and
Robert Kennedy can encourage a "new left." These men are
sincere. What can they mean?

IV

One way of understanding the welfare state is through its
processes of institutionalized reform. Perhaps because of its
Madisonian political traditions or its prosperity, America allows
substantial dissent, as shown, for example, in the history of the
labor or civil rights movements. Yet there are profound conti-
nuities that the tradition of dissent has not interrupted significantly: private corporation privilege, imperialist intervention
abroad, racial and class prejudice. Reform seems to follow a
typical pattern, challenging the society for a time but always
adjusting to these status quo facts.

In the postwar period, reformers have tended to be of two
types. The first are the professionals, men located in government agencies, teaching, journalism, law, social work. The second are the activists, located in reform, civil rights, and labor
politics. Their types often blend, for instance, as former civil
rights activists take desk jobs in the War on Poverty, or as professors begin to join demonstrations. Both the professional and
the activist assume that the leadership of American society can
be "enlightened" and improved through a combination of political pressure and skilled maneuver.

The term "professionalized reform" was coined by Daniel
Moynihan[12] to describe one part of this postwar pattern of
change. In his view, the poverty program was created by a
handful of concerned professionals rather than by an existing
or threatening social movement. These poverty planners typify
a "new class" precisely because they plan, they study the general needs of the system rather than defending a narrow interest. Less and less do they require "the masses" to bring issues to
their attention; research makes possible a kind of "early warning system" for the country's elite.[13]

Certainly this view reflects a real development. The poverty
legislation was conceived by a small circle of men, just as New

[12] See the previous reading, 33.—Eds.
[13] Cf. Andrew Kopkind, "The Future Planners," *New Republic* (February 25, 1967).

Deal reforms were conceived by a "brain trust." Michael Harrington's book helped to inspire it, just as earlier muckrakers focused attention on social needs. The personal compassion of JFK and LBJ made the programs possible, just as the plight of "one-third of a nation" troubled FDR. Such opportunities for "professionalized reform" are becoming more numerous than in earlier periods because of the expanding class of professional and service personnel taking part in the administration of society.

But it is not clear that these groups add more than sophistication and a white collar image to the status quo. They in fact develop their own "vested interests," as do even the social workers. Not being "of" the ghetto or the working class, they depend on information about the poor filtered through organizations of people similar to themselves. Their proposals for reform are developed not by the people who must live with the reforms (the poor themselves), but by planners with one eye on the census data and another on the political barometer. The consequence of the "new professionalism" tends to be, at best, patchwork (a young woman receives a skill through the Neighborhood Youth Corps, but her new earning power leads to a separation from her husband who is earning less) and, at worst, new public funds to shore up existing bureaucracies of the "welfare industry."

Yet these men might style themselves "participatory democrats," and so we must look at what they mean. The democracy they envision stems from modern thinking about organized society. Large-scale groups, from universities to business corporations, have been concerned increasingly with the "psychological" welfare of their employees and clients, trying to find the causes of low morale, alienation and revolt. It has become a dictum that the individual is a better citizen, worker, or student if he identifies with the large institution. In this view, grievances are primarily described as a result of misunderstanding and faulty organizational adjustment, rather than as problems of injustice. Where injustice is granted, it is seen as resulting from "backward" elements in an advanced system, such as Southern "rednecks," labor "thugs," or "savage" South Vietnamese army officers. The presupposition is that all problems can be negotiated. Society has reached the period of postrevolution. Racial violence, civil war, terror, and disruptive demonstrations are not needed if men are willing to give negotiation a try. Seen this way, violence reflects what are essentially merely personality struggles and power "grabs." Says a *New York Times* editorial, for instance:

Any leader there [in Vietnam] must always be on the defensive against his own generals and against potentially disruptive forces, such as the political leaders of the Buddhists and Catholics, the intellectuals and the outs who would like to get in and grab the power and the rewards that go with politico-military favor in South Vietnam.[14]

This is part of the reason why a liberal can sanction the use of napalm or send police with tear gas into the ghetto when the situation becomes "difficult." This is the thinking, too, that leads Sargent Shriver to celebrate the rebirth of democracy when thousands of the poor are hired as "subprofessionals," or Job Corpsmen successfully learn to be gas station attendants. Something much broader than specific property rights or a narrow organizational interest is being defended. Rather, a system of administering property and organization, a way of doing things, is projected, by men who have been trained to see the world in the same way in the universities, business firms and the Defense Department. The confidence in "managerialism" may be the closest thing to an ideology in our society.

This "professionalized reform" is a companion to the work of the activist reformers. The professionals see themselves as anticipating or translating the people's needs for the government; the activists "represent" those needs and petition the professionals and the government to do something. These activist-reformers begin with the view that the American masses are "apathetic" and can only be roused because of simple material needs or during short periods of great enthusiasm. The masses most likely to move, it is said, are those who have gained something already: the unionized workers, registered voters, property owners. Those less likely to move are the people on the absolute bottom with nothing to lose, for they are too damaged to be the real motor of change.

From this rough description of the masses, liberals go on to argue the need for certain sorts of organizations. The masses need skilled and responsible leaders, they insist. It is best if

[14] *New York Times* (March 14, 1966).

these leaders have rank-and-file experience and operate within a formally democratic system. But this grass-roots flavor must not obscure the necessity for leaders to lead, that is, to put forward a program, a set of answers that guides the movement. And because they monopolize leadership experience, it soon appears to these leaders that they alone are qualified to maintain the organization.

The perilous position of the movement, due to attacks from centralized business and political forces, adds a further incentive for a top-down system of command. The need for alliances with other groups, created in large part through the trust which sets of leaders develop for each other, also intensifies the trend toward vertical organization. Finally, the leaders see a need to screen out anyone with "Communist-oriented" views, since such individuals are presumably too skilled to be allowed to operate freely within the movement. Slowly an elite is formed, calling itself the liberal-labor community. It treats the rank-and-file as a mass to be molded; sometimes thrust forward into action, sometimes held back. A self-fulfilling pattern emerges: because the nature of the organization is elitist, many people react to it with disinterest or suspicion, giving the leadership the evidence it needs to call the masses apathetic.

The pressures which influence these leaders come, not primarily from below, but from the top, from the most powerful men in the country. Sometimes bluntly and sometimes subtly, the real elite grooms responsible trade union and civil rights leaders. The leaders' existence comes to depend upon the possibility of receiving attention from the President or some top aide, and they judge organizational issues with an eye on this possibility. There is usually no question about the leaders' primary loyalty to the "national interest" as defined by the Administration, even though they always believe their judgments are independently made. Thus most of the civil rights leadership in 1964, fearing the Goldwater movement and hoping for civil rights legislation from a victorious Johnson Administration, called for a "moratorium" on mass demonstrations. The labor leadership performed the same function for the same reasons during World War II; the irony is that their critics in that period included A. Philip Randolph and Bayard Rustin, two Negroes who pushed for the 1964 moratorium.

Some on the left tend to see each piece of social legislation as a victory which strengthens the "progressive" forces. They see a step-by-step transformation of society as the result of pushing for one "politically acceptable" reform after another. But it appears that the American elite has discovered a long-term way to stabilize or cushion the contradictions of our society. It does this through numerous forms of state intervention, the use of our abundant capacity for material gratification, and the ability to condition nearly all the information which people receive. And if this is the case, then more changes of the New Deal variety will not be "progressive" at all. Except for boosting the relative income of a few, this entire reformist trend has weakened the poor under the pretense of helping them and strengthened elite rule under the slogan of curbing private enterprise. In fostering a "responsible" Negro and labor leadership and bringing it into the pseudo pluralist system of bargaining and rewards, a way has been found to contain and paralyze the disadvantaged and voiceless people.

Defenders of the welfare state—professional or activist—say that its critics overlook (1) the political and material gains that have been made for the poor under its auspices, and (2) the relative freedom to continue organizing protest that it guarantees. The point, however, is not to deny the gains. No economic improvement or civil liberty, however small, should be underestimated. But it is something else to point to those gains in defense of an entire system. In the first place, the gains are minute in relation to what the American productive system could make available to its people. Second, the very security of those gains is not guaranteed without continuous militant pressure. Third, the struggle for those gains left most white workers with more security but at the price of remaining racist in outlook, while still working under alienating conditions. Fourth, the process of reform seemed to undermine the spirit of insurgency itself by institutionalizing and limiting it.

Consider the caseworker who tells the client she should have died in slavery, and the civic action worker who calls the peasant an uncivilized pig; the policeman beating the Negro even after he collapses unconscious; the administrator ordering shock treatment for the mental patient screaming about his rights; the executive looking for a black prostitute during lunch; the professor interviewing an Asian official while a beaten prisoner lies on the floor; the worker reading about the machine that will replace him; the judge at juvenile court deciding to put away the young delinquent until she is 21; the landlord come with the constable to evict the tenants on rent strike. These are the everyday realities of a society that preaches liberal intentions.

We see, then, that welfare liberalism is more than a system of co-optation, more than an air-conditioned nightmare. It is also a system that punishes, with whatever violence is necessary, those who balk at its embrace. In this sense its liberalism is a facade over a more coercive conservative core.

The need is not to expand the welfare state, not to incorporate the "backward" parts into it, but to replace it altogether with a political economy that serves, rather than denies, the needs of the poor and millions of other people in this country and abroad. But replacing the political economy is not a negotiable issue arrived at through institutional reform. It is a revolutionary issue, resolved by building new institutions to replace the old. What then can be done?

V

The welfare state, with all its elaborate mechanisms for containing protest, still is ridden with instabilities. Conservative forces attempt to keep social services at a minimum and their administration under archaic patronage systems. The poor, including those who are semi-employed, live in conditions that generate protest and violence. The more America becomes involved in the Vietnam-type war, the deeper these conflicts at home tend to become.

But not only the poor are affected adversely by these developments. The hypocrisy of America's role in the world is a source of discontent among intellectuals and professionals. These seeds of conflict can only become more deeply planted because of America's firm counterrevolutionary policy. There may be a short-range flexibility possible in foreign affairs, but American policy is spiraling toward a nuclear finale. In order to carry out this global policy—which requires elite control of foreign policy, massive military spending, artificial attempts at consensus, etc.—it will be necessary to repress or neglect many groups seeking change through legitimate means at home. Thus a loose opposition to "welfare imperialism" can be expected to emerge from those groups that have little to say but much to lose in an American empire. Already insurgency is a growing pattern among the poor, the students, and the new professionals.

The Negro revolt and movements of the poor

The youth of Watts and the Mississippi sharecroppers are the most visible and inspiring representatives of an awakening that is taking place among the Negro poor. Their perspective centers on Negro liberation, but they are interested as well in a movement of all the powerless and exploited.

The Southern movement stems from the conditions of the Black Belt. The people's strength comes from a stable system of family life and work, built up over generations within the framework of exploitation. Politics is new and fresh for them; they have not experienced the hollow promises of an opportunistic liberal-Negro machine. Their opposition's naked brutality keeps them constantly in a crisis framework. The broadening of their movement into Arkansas, Alabama, Louisiana, Georgia, the Carolinas, and Virginia, already underway, can be expected to challenge fundamentally the national coalition directing the Democratic Party. Already the Democrats are trying to groom moderate and liberal politicians to provide an "alternative" to the segregationists and the independent Freedom Democratic Party. Probably this effort will succeed, in the sense that political moderates will begin to compete for electoral power and leadership of the civil rights forces, mostly basing their strength in the cities, among privileged Negroes. The FDP, as a structure, may be absorbed into the national party, if only because it has no other, more effective place to go. But since the new Southern power structure will not solve the problems of poverty and race, which have plagued the North for generations, there is very little chance that this movement of poor people will be entirely co-opted or crushed.

In the black ghettos of the North, organizers face different obstacles. There work is often deadening, family life distorted: "proper" political channels are sewers; people are used to, and tired of, party organizers exploiting them. The civil rights movement does not touch these hundreds of ghettos in a deep way because of the religious and the middle-class nature of its program and leadership, though the televised Southern brutality does create much bitterness in the North. However, the Harlem rent strikes, the activities of Malcolm X and the spread of "riots" are clear evidence that there are in the ghettos people prepared to take action. Some of them are of Southern background; some are housewives with wasted talents; some are youth with no future for their energy; some are junkies and numbers men with little loyalty to their particular game. Different as the forms of their discontent may be, the discontent itself is general to the ghetto and can be the spring for action. Under present conditions, political movements among these people are likely to be based on a race consciousness that is genuine and militant—and that is based on the failure of whites to act in favor of equal rights. It will be partly violent for, as the Negro has learned too well, force is required when dialogue does not work. The ghetto consciousness, however, is intertwined with the consciousness of being both poor and powerless. Almost of necessity, the demands that the ghetto poor put forward are also potentially in the interest of the white poor, as well as of middle class professionals who depend on the expansion of the public sectors of the economy.

But will white working class and poor people take up these issues that the "Negro problem" by its nature tends to raise? SNCC sees poor whites as potentially their major ally within the United States (other revolutionary movements in the world perhaps being their main allies). The evidence for this hope is negative, but inconclusive. Poor whites, such as those in Appalachia, who are truly irrelevant to the modern economy, tend to see their plight (sometimes with accuracy) as personal rather than social: a function of sickness, bad luck, or psychological disorder. Poverty is not seen as the fate of a class, but only as the fate of individuals, each shamed into self-blame by their Protestant ideology. Working class whites, on the other hand, are more likely to be conscious of their problems as a group, but they tend to defend their scarce privileges—jobs, wages, education for their children—against what they see as the onslaught of Negro competition. While "backlash" did not split the alliance of white working people with the Democratic Party in 1964, it does serve as a barrier to an alliance with the Negro poor. But it is foolish to be rigid about these notions.

Whites *are* being organized, on a mass basis, in areas of Appalachia where there exists a common culture and an industrial union tradition, and where the blame for misery can be laid to the coal operators, the conservative United Mine Workers, and the government. They also have been organized in Cleveland and Chicago.

But these organizing efforts were led by local people or independent organizers outside the structure of the labor movement. Today there are millions of workers trapped by the organizational framework of the AFL-CIO. Their unrest at times moves the international unions slightly, but the internationals are more dependent on government and business than on their own members, and, in addition, they seem to possess effective techniques for curbing shop revolts. It is not simply the "better objective conditions" that split the white from the Negro poor, but the existence of trade unions, which actively distort the better aspirations of their members. Economic and social conditions, of course, are not improving and workers' discontent is evidenced by the recent wave of rank-and-file revolts. But whether this discontent spurs a coalition of poor whites with Negroes depends, most of all, on whether a way can be found to organize workers independent of AFL-CIO routines. Concretely, that means democratic control by the workers of their union locals, and the entry of those locals into political activities and coalitions on the community level. It also means community action and organization among the millions of low-paid workers presently outside the labor movement.

The crucial importance of community work can only be grasped if one understands the sorts of ideas the American poor have about themselves. They operate with a kind of split consciousness. On the one hand, poor people know they are victimized from every direction. The facts of life always break through to expose the distance between American ideals and personal realities. This kind of knowledge, however, is kept undeveloped and unused because of another knowledge imposed on the poor, a keen sense of dependence on the oppressor. This is the source of that universal fear that leads poor people to act and even to think subserviently. Seeing themselves to blame for their situation, they rule out the possibility that they might be qualified to govern themselves and their own organizations. Besides fear, it is their sense of inadequacy and embarrassment that destroys the possibility of revolt. At the same time, this set of contradictory feelings results in indirect forms of protest all the time: styles of dress and language, withdrawal from political life, defiance of the boss's or the welfare worker's rules and regulations.

There can be no poor people's movement in any form unless the poor can overcome their fear and embarrassment. What is required is a certain kind of organizing that tries to make people understand their own worth and dignity. This work depends on the existence of "material issues" as a fundamental organizing point—high rents, voting rights, unpaved roads, and so on—but it moves from there into the ways such issues are related to personal life. The organizer spends hours and hours in the community, listening to people, drawing out their own ideas, rejecting their tendency to depend on him for solutions. Meetings are organized at which people with no "connections" can be given a chance to talk and work out problems together —usually for the first time. All this means fostering in everyone that sense of decision-making power which American society works to destroy. Only in this way can a movement be built which the Establishment can neither buy off nor manage, a movement too vital ever to become a small clique of spokesmen.

An organizational form that suggests the style of such a movement is the "community union," involving working-class and poor people in local insurgency. Open and democratic, the community union offers a real alternative to the kind of participation permitted in civil rights groups, trade unions and Democratic party machines. It might take a variety of forms: block clubs, housing committees, youth groups, etc. The union's insistence on the relevance of "little people," as well as its position outside and against the normal channels, would create a rooted sense of independence among the members.

The chance for short-term political success for these groups is small. The people are gerrymandered, they are not stable residents of their districts, they often are afraid of or misunderstand complex election procedures, they are cynical about elections; those who do vote are usually uncritical supporters of the Democratic Party, which is carefully organized in ghetto areas.

A community union would seek positions of political power

only where really possible and where insurgency, not merely the status of an individual, might be advanced. Among the possibilities are neighborhood or municipal elections "close" to the people's experience. Where the group could not realistically seek power in that sense, it would build up at least the power of resistance at the point where colonial power is used against them, by the police, the landlords, the caseworkers who have to enter the community to do business. Besides being the only counterforce to intruding colonial authority, the community union can be a center where people can combine strength, provide services and help each other, and develop the skills of organization. By proving in practice a genuine interest in the people's welfare, by stressing the outside character of the exploiters, and by building up services and democratic activities of its own, the community union might eventually be in a position to win political power with a movement capable of using it. If not, it can be a permanent center of resistance.

A student movement

If poor people are in the movement because they have nothing to gain in the status system, students are in it because, in a sense, they have gained too much. Most of the active student radicals today come from middle to upper middle class professional homes. They were born with status and affluence as facts of life, not goals to be striven for. In their upbringing, their parents stressed the right of children to question and make judgments. And then these students so often encountered social institutions that denied them their independence and betrayed the democratic ideals they were taught. They saw that men of learning were careerists; that school administrators and ministers almost never discussed the realities the students lived with; that even their parents were not true to the ideals they taught the young.

It was against this background that young people became concerned about war, racism and inequality in the early sixties. By now, the empty nature of existing vocational alternatives has pushed several hundreds of these students into community organizing. Working in poor communities is a concrete task in which the split between job and values can be healed. It is also a position from which to expose the whole structure of pretense, status, and glitter that masks the country's real human problems. And, finally, it is a way to find people who want to change the country, and possibly can do so.

After the civil rights activities culminating in the 1964 Mississippi Summer Project and Northern summer projects, students began to find ways to create movements around other problems as well. The Berkeley Free Speech Movement and the April 1965 March on Washington to End the War in Vietnam were major departures from the inconsequential student government politics of five years before. On many campuses now students are beginning to form unions of their own, as well as independent study programs pointed in the direction of "free universities," projects located in the student community similar in direction to neighborhood organizing projects. In addition, by mobilizing antiwar activity, students are encountering their friends working among the poor. These efforts are threading the several protest movements in the country into a grass-roots coalition with students in one of the leading roles.

The fact is that student protest is becoming a normal, even legitimate, part of society. The danger involved is that the Establishment is looking for a solution that can be for students what the Wagner Act was to workers: a concession giving approval to the new student status while attempting to channel it in a "safe" direction. Private and public agencies are developing programs to "harness the energy of young people": VISTA and the Peace Corps, the Teaching Corps, "national service" ideas, etc. On the other hand, an opportunity is opened up, because the student desire for a meaningful vocation is being considered worth subsidizing. No doubt many students will boycott opportunities to be the social workers for imperialism's victims. Others will be swallowed up. Others will try these opportunities out to test their limits.

In other words, students are being treated in a way similar to previous emerging political forces. Whether the process of "institutionalized reform" can work on the affluent will be an interesting question. There is ample reason to believe that students as a rule will choose comfort over radical vocations. But on the other hand, students are rebelling against both materialism and manipulations; that is, against the root of the process by which insurgency is usually met. The society may have to choose between its counterrevolutionary policy and satisfying the desires of its younger generation.

There is a second danger facing the student movement: that of disintegration due to failure. The expanding Vietnam war may exhaust, embitter, or end in crushing the new activists. In the years 1960-1963 the student movement drew its health from the assumption that society could allow change. The war, by closing the hope for change, has exposed this assumption as naïve. If the war continues to spread, and if the majority remains comfortable, campus activism may further adopt the "opting-out" posture of the hippies. But if the expanding war causes much greater discomfort for the majority, there will be a massive right-wing demand to repress students and minorities. At any rate, even if the war is somehow ended, it has erased so much middle class innocence that a renewed student movement would perhaps be far more radical.

Middle-class insurgents

A centralized and commercial society wastes the talents and energies of millions of individuals. Some of these are women who are excluded from male-dominated vocations. Some are people with human values who cannot assert them effectively within organizations attached to the Cold War consensus. Some were politically active in the thirties, but faded away when popular movements declined. Some are part of the postwar generation which missed the experience of a radical movement altogether, and who are lodged uneasily in publishing houses, universities, and labor bureaucracies. In general, these are the professionals whose priorities are met inadequately by an inhuman society. They have a degree of conscience and shame; they want more than Moynihan's "professionalized reform."

The new movements are opening up great possibilities for these professionals to give their service directly (though some will take lucrative jobs with the Peace Corps and the poverty program). Community groups need lawyers, researchers, planners, doctors, newspapermen—in numerous ways. But these same professionals have a struggle of their own as well, against the wholesale co-option of their institutions by the national government. Professors joining students against the administration, welfare workers and teachers forming unions, muckrakers dissenting from the mass media imagery: these actions contribute to the general pressure on an Administration that talks of a Great Society while budgeting for nuclear weapons. This professional insurgency is bound to increase as the newest generation of student activists graduates and moves out of the university into careers.

VI

A summary word

It would be foolish to make of these speculations predictions-to-live-by. Revolutionaries are often among the last to know whether they are succeeding. In the 1930s radicals were surprised by the staying power of a capitalism that they had thought doomed. In the 1960s radicals may yet be surprised by the collapse of a welfare-capitalism that now seems flexible but invulnerable.

At any rate, humane opposition to the American welfare empire must be constructed not in speculative theory, but in action. Ideas, after all, are welcome commodities, easily absorbed in the new system. Only through combined action will ordinary men create the beginning of a different society. The experience and practice of solidarity is a deeper form of opposition to the welfare empire than any radical critique. Only a community contributing its own movements and institutions can fill the vacuum of local political life that the authoritarian society creates. Only men who know themselves to be capable decision-makers can consider fighting for a thoroughly democratic society. Only men able to improvise and invent vocations of their own will be prepared to demand, and live in, a decentralized, automated society of the future. Only men with experience in a universe of mixed races and cultures will be able to shed national chauvinism and ethnocentrism. Furthermore, masses of men will only be persuaded of change when some of them create a compelling, if very imperfect, example of what the future might be.

The real alternative to bureaucratic welfarism is to be found budding in the experience of men who form communities— whether a freedom school, a community union, a teach-in, or a wildcat strike—to struggle as equals for their own self-determination. Such communities come and go, existing at their best during intense periods of solidarity. But even where they fail to achieve institutional reality, these communities become a permanent part of this generation's consciousness of the possible. The new society still takes shape in the womb of the old.

THE GREAT SOCIETY:
A LIBERTARIAN CRITIQUE

One of the most hallowed dogmas entertained by those who call themselves modern liberals, is that their political position is the blessed mean between two undesirable extremes. Arthur Schlesinger, Jr., for example, has argued (in *The Vital Center: The Politics of Freedom* [Boston, 1949]) that welfare-state liberalism is the rational American alternative to a business-dominated "conservatism" on the one hand, and a Moscow-inspired radicalism on the other.

As we have stated in the Introduction to this section, it is becoming increasingly doubtful whether this "liberal" frame of reference is useful in understanding the United States of America in the age of Lyndon Johnson. Professor Rothbard, in the essay below, doubts that it can explain American politics at all since at least the Civil War. To him, true "liberalism" involves the principled commitment to individual freedom as against the power of the state. In this view the Great Society becomes only the latest in a series of reform programs that advance themselves under the banner of "liberalism," but that in reality involve the progressive limitation of freedom.

Although Rothbard's critique is based upon a belief in the kind of free-market, *laissez-faire* principles that are usually associated with the political "right," many of the points he makes could easily be assented to by the "new left"—the grim characterization of American foreign policy, the support for "black power" to be exercised by black Americans, and many other notions. So large and significant are these areas of common concern and commitment that traditional views of "left" and "right" are brought into question. An alternative to Professor Schlesinger's theory immediately suggests itself: that the great threat to America and the world emanates not from the extremes, but from the crusading reformers in Washington who want to spread a particular kind of Great Society around the world.

Dr. Rothbard, educated at Columbia University, is Associate Professor of Economics at the Polytechnic Institute of Brooklyn. He is the author of *The Panic of 1819* (New York, 1963), *America's Great Depression* (Princeton, N. J., 1963), and many other books and articles. The essay that follows was written specifically for inclusion in this volume.

◇ ◇ ◇

The Great Society is the lineal descendant and the intensification of those other pretentiously named polities of twentieth-century America: the Square Deal, the New Freedom, the New Era, the New Deal, the Fair Deal, and the New Frontier. All of these assorted Deals constituted a basic and fundamental shift in American life—a shift from a relatively *laissez-faire* economy and minimal state to a society in which the state is unquestionably king.[1] In the previous century, the government could safely have been ignored by almost everyone; now we have become a country in which the government is the great and unending source of power and privilege. Once a country in which each man could by and large make the decisions for his own life, we have become a land where the state holds and exercises life-and-death power over every person, group, and institution. The great Moloch government, once confined and cabined, has burst its feeble bonds to dominate us all.

The basic reason for this development is not difficult to fathom. It was best summed up by the great German sociolo-

[1] Recent triumphal disclosures by economic historians that pure *laissez-faire* did not exist in nineteenth century America are beside the point; no one ever claimed that it did. The point is that state power in society was minimal, relative to other times and countries, and that the general locus of decision making resided therefore in the individuals making up society rather than in the State. Cf. Robert Lively, "The American System," *Business History Review*, XXIX (1955), pp. 81-96.

gist Franz Oppenheimer; Oppenheimer wrote that there were fundamentally two, and only two, paths to the acquisition of wealth. One route is the production of a good or service and its voluntary exchange for the goods or services produced by others. This method—the method of the free market—Oppenheimer termed "the economic means" to wealth. The other path, which avoids the necessity for production and exchange, is for one or more persons to seize other people's products by the use of physical force. This method of robbing the fruits of another man's production was shrewdly named by Oppenheimer the "political means." Throughout history, men have been tempted to employ the "political means" of seizing wealth rather than expend effort in production and exchange. It should be clear that while the market process multiplies production, the political, exploitative means is parasitic and, as with all parasitic action, discourages and drains off production and output in society. To regularize and order a permanent system of predatory exploitation, men have created the state, which Oppenheimer brilliantly defined as "the organization of the political means." [2]

Every act of the state is necessarily an occasion for inflicting burdens and assigning subsidies and privileges. By seizing revenue by means of coercion and assigning rewards as it disburses the funds, the state *creates* ruling and ruled "classes" or "castes"; for one example, classes of what Calhoun discerned as net "taxpayers" and "tax-consumers," those who live off taxation.[3] And since by its nature, predation can only be supported out of the surplus of production above subsistence, the ruling class must constitute a minority of the citizenry.

Since the state, nakedly observed, is a mighty engine of or-

[2] Franz Oppenheimer, *The State* (New York, 1926), pp. 24-27. Or, as Albert Jay Nock, heavily influenced by Oppenheimer's analysis, concluded: "The state claims and exercises the monopoly of crime" in its territorial area. Albert Jay Nock, *On Doing the Right Thing, and Other Essays* (New York, 1928), p. 143.

[3] See John C. Calhoun, *Disquisition on Government* . . . (Columbia, S. C., 1850). On the distinction between this and the Marxian concept of the ruling class, see Ludwig von Mises, *Theory and History* (New Haven, Conn., 1957), pp. 112 ff. Perhaps the earliest users of this kind of class analysis were the French libertarian writers of the Restoration period of the early nineteenth century, Charles Comte and Charles Dunoyer. Cf. Elie Halévy, *The Era of Tyrannies* (Garden City, N. Y., 1965), pp. 23-34.

ganized predation, state rule, throughout its many millennia of recorded history, could be preserved only by persuading the bulk of the public that its rule has not really been exploitative: that, on the contrary, it has been necessary, beneficent, even, as in the Oriental despotisms, divine. Promoting this ideology among the masses has ever been a prime function of intellectuals, a function that has created the basis for co-opting a corps of intellectuals into a secure and permanent berth in the state apparatus. In former centuries, these intellectuals formed a priestly caste that was able to wrap a cloak of mystery and quasi divinity about the actions of the state for a credulous public; nowadays, the apologia for the state takes on more subtle and seemingly scientific forms. The process remains essentially the same.[4]

In the United States, a strong libertarian and antistatist tradition prevented the process of statization from taking hold at a very rapid pace. The major force in its propulsion has been that favorite theater of state expansionism, brilliantly identified by Randolph Bourne as "the health of the state": namely, war. For although in wartime various states find themselves in danger from one another, every state has found war a fertile field for spreading the myth among its subjects that *they* are the ones in deadly danger, from which their state is protecting them. In this way states have been able to dragoon their subjects into fighting and dying to save them under the pretext that the *subjects* were being saved from the dread Foreign Enemy. In the United States, the process of statization began in earnest under cover of the Civil War (conscription, military rule, income tax, excise taxes, high tariffs, national banking and credit expansion for favored businesses, paper money, land grants to railroads), and reached full flower as a result of World Wars I and II, to finally culminate in the Great Society.

The recently emerging group of "libertarian conservatives" in the United States have grasped a part of the recent picture of

[4] On various aspects of the alliance between intellectuals and the State, see George B. de Huszar, ed., *The Intellectuals* (Glencoe, Ill., 1960); Joseph A. Schumpeter, *Capitalism, Socialism, and Democracy* (New York, 1942), pp. 143-55; Karl A. Wittfogel, *Oriental Despotism* (New Haven, Conn., 1957); Howard K. Beale, "The Professional Historian: His Theory and Practice," *The Pacific Historical Review* (August, 1953), pp. 227-55; Martin Nicolaus, "The Professor, The Policeman and the Peasant," *Viet–Report* (June–July, 1966), pp. 15-19.

accelerated statism, but their analysis suffers from several fatal blind spots. One is their complete failure to realize that war, culminating in the present garrison state and military–industrial economy, has been the royal road to aggravated statism in America. On the contrary, the surge of reverent patriotism that war always brings to conservative hearts, coupled with their eagerness to don buckler and armor against the "international Communist conspiracy," has made the conservatives the most eager and enthusiastic partisans of the Cold War. Hence their inability to see the enormous distortions and interventions imposed upon the economy by the enormous system of war contracts.[5]

Another conservative blind spot is their failure to identify *which groups* have been responsible for the burgeoning of statism in the United States. In the conservative demonology, the responsibility belongs only to liberal intellectuals, aided and abetted by trade unions and farmers. Big businessmen, on the other hand, are curiously exempt from blame (farmers are small enough businessmen, apparently, to be fair game for censure.) How, then, do conservatives deal with the glaringly evident onrush of big businessmen to embrace Lyndon Johnson and the Great Society? [6] Either by mass stupidity (failure to read the works of free-market economists), subversion by liberal intellectuals (e.g., the education of the Rockefeller brothers at Lincoln School), or craven cowardice (the failure to stand foursquare for free-market principles in the face of governmental power.) Almost never is *interest* pinpointed as an overriding reason for statism among businessmen. This failure is all the more curious in the light of the fact that the *laissez-faire* liberals of the eighteenth and nineteenth centuries (e.g., the Philosophical Radicals in England, the Jacksonians in the United States) were never bashful about identifying and attacking the web of special privileges granted to businessmen in the mercantilism of their day.

In fact, one of the main driving forces of the statist dynamic of twentieth century America has been big businessmen, and this long before the Great Society. Gabriel Kolko, in his path-

[5] Thus, cf. H. L. Nieburg, *In the Name of Science* (Chicago, 1966); Seymour Melman, *Our Depleted Society* (New York, 1965); C. Wright Mills, *The Power Elite* (New York, 1956).

[6] See reading 11.—Eds.

breaking *Triumph of Conservatism*,[7] has shown that the shift toward statism in the Progressive period was impelled by the very big business groups who were supposed, in the liberal mythology, to be defeated and regulated by the Progressive and New Freedom measures. Rather than a "people's movement" to check big business, the drive for regulatory measures, Kolko shows, stemmed from big businessmen whose attempts at monopoly had been defeated by the competitive market, and who then turned to the federal government as a device for compulsory cartellization. This drive for cartellization through government accelerated during the New Era of the 1920s and reached its apex in Franklin Roosevelt's NRA. Significantly, this exercise in cartellizing collectivism was put over by organized big business; after Herbert Hoover, who had done much to organize and cartellize the economy, had balked at an NRA as going too far toward an outright fascist economy, the US Chamber of Commerce won a promise from FDR that he would adopt such a system. The original inspiration was the corporate state of Mussolini's Italy.[8]

The formal corporatism of the NRA is long gone, but the Great Society retains much of its essence. The locus of social power has been emphatically assumed by the state apparatus. Furthermore, that apparatus is permanently governed by a coalition of big business and big labor groupings, groups that use the state to operate and manage the national economy. The usual tripartite *rapprochement* of big business, big unions, and big government symbolizes the organization of society by blocs, syndics, and corporations, regulated and privileged by the federal, state, and local governments. What this all amounts to in essence is the "corporate state," which during the 1920s served as a beacon light for big businessmen, big unions,

[7] New York, 1963. Also see Kolko's *Railroads and Regulation* (Princeton, N. J., 1965). The laudatory reviews of the latter book by George W. Hilton (*American Economic Review*) and George W. Wilson (*Journal of Political Economy*) symbolize a potential alliance between "new left" and free-market historiography.

[8] The National Recovery Administration, one of the most important creations of the early New Deal, was established by the National Industrial Recovery Act of June, 1933. It prescribed and imposed codes of "fair competition" upon industry. It was declared unconstitutional by the Supreme Court in 1935. For an analysis of the inception of the NRA, see my *America's Great Depression* (Princeton, N. J., 1963).

and many liberal intellectuals as the economic system proper to a twentieth century industrial society.[9]

The indispensable intellectual role of engineering popular consent for state rule is played, for the Great Society, by the liberal intelligentsia, who provide the rationale of "general welfare," "humanity," and the "common good" (just as the conservative intellectuals work the other side of the Great Society street by offering the rationale of "national security" and "national interest"). The liberals, in short, push the "welfare" part of our omnipresent welfare–warfare state, while the conservatives stress the warfare side of the pie. This analysis of the role of the liberal intellectuals puts into more sophisticated perspective the seeming "sellout" of these intellectuals as compared to their role during the 1930s. Thus, among numerous other examples, there is the seeming anomaly of A. A. Berle and David Lilienthal, cheered and damned as flaming progressives in the thirties, now writing tomes hailing the new reign of big business. Actually, their basic views have not changed in the least. In the thirties, these theoreticians of the New Deal were concerned with condemning as "reactionaries" those big businessmen who clung to older individualist ideals and failed to understand or adhere to the new monopoly system of the corporate state. But now, in the 1950s and 1960s, this battle has been won, big businessmen are all eager to be privileged monopolists in the new dispensation, and hence they can now be welcomed by such theorists as Berle and Lilienthal as "responsible" and "enlightened," their "selfish" individualism a relic of the past.

The cruellest myth fostered by the liberals is that the Great Society functions as a great boon and benefit to the poor; in reality, when we cut through the frothy appearances to the cold reality underneath, the poor are the major victims of the welfare state. The poor are the ones to be conscripted to fight and die at literally slave wages in the Great Society's imperial wars. The poor are the ones to lose their homes to the bulldozer of urban renewal, that bulldozer that operates for the benefit of real estate and construction interests to pulverize available low-

---

[9] Part of this story has been told in John P. Diggins, "Flirtation with Fascism: American Pragmatic Liberals and Mussolini's Italy," *American Historical Review*, LXXI (January, 1966), pp. 487-506.

cost housing.[10] All this, of course, in the name of "clearing the slums" and helping the aesthetics of housing. The poor are the welfare clientele whose homes are unconstitutionally but regularly invaded by government agents to ferret out sin in the middle of the night. The poor (e.g., Negroes in the South) are the ones disemployed by rising minimum wage floors, put in for the benefit of employers and unions in higher-wage areas (e.g., the North) to prevent industry from moving to the low-wage areas. The poor are cruelly victimized by an income tax that left and right alike misconstrue as an egalitarian program to soak the rich; actually, various tricks and exemptions insure that it is the poor and the middle classes who are hit the hardest.[11] The poor are victimized too by a welfare state of which the cardinal macro-economic tenet is perpetual if controlled inflation. The inflation and the heavy government spending favor the businesses of the military–industrial complex, while the poor and the retired, those on fixed pensions or Social Security, are hit the hardest. (Liberals have often scoffed at the anti-inflationists' stress on the "widows and orphans" as major victims of inflation, but these remain major victims nevertheless.) And the burgeoning of compulsory mass public education forces millions of unwilling youth off the labor market for many years, and into schools that serve more as houses of detention than as genuine centers of education.[12] Farm programs that supposedly aid poor farmers actually serve the large wealthy farmers at the expense of sharecropper and consumer alike; and commissions that regulate industry serve to cartellize it. The mass of workers is forced by governmental measures into trade unions that tame and integrate the labor force into the toils of the accelerating corporate state, there to be subjected to arbitrary wage "guidelines" and ultimate compulsory arbitration.

The role of the liberal intellectual and of liberal rhetoric is even more stark in foreign economic policy. Ostensibly designed to "help the underdeveloped countries," foreign aid has served as a gigantic subsidy by the American taxpayer of Amer-

[10] See Martin Anderson, *The Federal Bulldozer* (Cambridge, Mass., 1964).

[11] Thus, see Gabriel Kolko, *Wealth and Power in America* (New York, 1962).

[12] Thus, see Paul Goodman, *Compulsory Mis-Education* and *The Community of Scholars* (New York, Vintage paperback edition, 1966).

ican export firms, a similar subsidy to American foreign investment through guarantees and subsidized government loans, an
engine of inflation for the recipient country, and a form of massive subsidy to the friends and clients of US imperialism in the
recipient country.

The symbiosis between liberal intellectuals and despotic statism at home and abroad is, furthermore, no accident; for at the
heart of the welfarist mentality is an enormous desire to "do
good to" the mass of other people, and since people don't usually wish to be done good to, since they have their own ideas of
what they wish to do, the liberal welfarist inevitably ends by
reaching for the big stick with which to push the ungrateful
masses around. Hence, the liberal ethos itself provides a powerful stimulant for the intellectuals to seek state power and ally
themselves with the other rulers of the corporate state. The liberals thus become what Harry Elmer Barnes has aptly termed
"totalitarian liberals." Or, as Isabel Paterson put it a generation
ago:

*The humanitarian wishes to be a prime mover in the lives of
others. He cannot admit either the divine or the natural order,
by which men have the power to help themselves. The humanitarian puts himself in the place of God.*

*But he is confronted by two awkward facts; first, that the
competent do not need his assistance; and second, that the
majority of people . . . positively do not want to be 'done
good' by the humanitarian. . . . Of course, what the humanitarian actually proposes is that he shall do what he thinks is
good for everybody. It is at this point that the humanitarian
sets up the guillotine.*[13]

The rhetorical role of welfarism in pushing people around
may be seen clearly in the Vietnam War, where American liberal planning for alleged Vietnamese welfare has been particularly prominent, e.g., in the plans and actions of Wolf Ladejinsky, Joseph Buttinger, and the Michigan State group. And the
result has been very much of an American-operated "guillotine"
for the Vietnamese people, North and South.[14] And even *Fortune* magazine invokes the spirit of humanitarian "idealism" as

[13] Isabel Paterson, *The God of the Machine* (New York, 1943), p. 241.
[14] See John McDermott, "Welfare Imperialism in Vietnam," *The Nation* (July 25, 1966), pp. 76-88. Cf. readings 32 and 34.

the justification for the United States' falling "heir to the onerous task of policing these shattered colonies" of Western Europe, and exerting its might all over the world. The will to make this exertion to the uttermost, especially in Vietnam and perhaps China, constitutes for *Fortune*, "the unending test of American idealism." [15] This liberal–welfarist syndrome may also be seen in the very different area of civil rights, in the terribly pained indignation of white liberals at the recent determination of Negroes to take the lead in helping themselves, rather than to keep deferring to the Lords and Ladies Bountiful of white liberalism.

In sum, the most important fact about the Great Society under which we live is the enormous disparity between rhetoric and content. In rhetoric, America is the land of the free and the generous, enjoying the fused blessings of a free market tempered by and joined to accelerating social welfare, bountifully distributing its unstinting largesse to the less fortunate in the world. In actual practice, the free economy is virtually gone, replaced by an imperial corporate state Leviathan that organizes, commands, exploits the rest of society and, indeed, the rest of the world, for its own power and pelf. We have experienced, as Garet Garrett keenly pointed out over a decade ago, a "revolution within the form." [16] The old limited republic has been replaced by Empire, within and without our borders.

[15] *Fortune* (August, 1965). As the right wing of the Great Society Establishment, *Fortune* presumably passes the Berle–Lilienthal test as spokesman for "enlightened" as opposed to narrowly "selfish" capitalism.

[16] Garet Garrett, *The People's Pottage* (Caldwell, Idaho, 1953).

THE POVERTY OF
THE GREAT SOCIETY*

Poet, novelist, architectural theorist, psychologist, professor, Paul Goodman likes to think of himself as an old-fashioned man of letters. In his mid-fifties now, he is one of the few adults whose ideas seem relevant to young radicals. He has written *Growing Up Absurd* (New York, 1959); *Communitas: Means of Livelihood and Ways of Life*, with his brother, Percival Goodman (2nd ed., New York, 1960); *Utopian Essays and Practical Proposals* (New York, 1962); and many other books and articles. His latest book of social criticism is *Like a Conquered Province* (New York, 1967). An excellent biographical study of Goodman by Richard Kostelanetz appeared in the *New York Times Magazine* (April 3, 1965).

◇ ◇ ◇

I

A reasonable function of government is to see to it that the conditions of life are tolerable. In modern societies this might involve considerable government intervention, to prevent or remedy social and physical evils, like urban poverty, exploitation of labor, traffic congestion, air pollution. But such a safeguarding function is entirely different from government's trying to make life excellent, to make society moral, civilized, or magnificent. Intellectual or moral excellence is not a likely province for rulers of any breed, and certainly not for Ameri-

* From the *New York Review of Books* (October 14, 1965). © 1965 by Paul Goodman. Reprinted by permission.

can politicians who have risen to power by speaking banalities, making deals, and pandering, and who stay in power by avoiding the risks of sharp definition, imagination, scrupulous integrity, or even too much wit. Political arts have their use, but they are not the way to spiritual excellence.

Yet the last three Administrations have kept dabbling in this direction. President Eisenhower, who was hardly literate, ordered a commission to map our National Goals, and under him government agencies began to improve the school curricula and speed up intervention in scientific research. John Kennedy, who was stylish and had academic connections, called us to service and he wanted us to be respected for our civilization as well as our military and economic power. He was a champion of art centers, neo-classic architecture, and concerts at the White House; above all, he speeded up the harnessing of academic social sciences to government policy. And now Lyndon Johnson, who is culturally noted for monograms and driving fast, is going to inaugurate for us the Great Society.

I do not think this was only a campaign slogan. Even if it were, we must note the change in slogans. "Fair Deal" and "New Deal" used to refer to political economy and were a legitimate bid for votes; "New Frontier" and "Great Society" are more spiritual. (Barry Goldwater, correspondingly, threatened to restore us to Moral Order.) In any case, the President has carried his slogan over into 1965, and when his oblique eyes become dreamy and his voice avuncular on the theme of our future greatness, I am insulted by his pretension.

Do not misunderstand me. When the President speaks of trying to dissolve hard core poverty, assuring equal rights, opening to every child the opportunity for an education, or coping with the blight of cities, I assent. (It is said that this populist strain in LBJ is authentic,[1] and I hope so.) But that is not the program of a great society but of any decent society. It should be urged modestly and executed resolutely. There is no cause for fanfare in doing justice where we have been unjust, conserving where we have been vandals, and spending for neglected public goods what a small country like Denmark or Holland provides as a matter of course.

But the fact is that every element of the Great Society, including its war on poverty and its conservation, is contami-

[1] See the discussion of Johnson and "populism" above, p. 4.—Eds.

nated by, compromised by, and finally determined by power lust, greed, and fear of change. No good thing is done for its own sake. Let me give half a dozen examples—I could give a hundred. The drive to schooling, even in its propaganda, is not to liberate the children and to insure that we will have independent and intelligent citizens (this was the educational aim of Jefferson); it is apprentice-training of the middle class for the corporations and military, and a desperate attempt to make slum children employable and ruly. Beautification and area development are treated as adjuncts of the automobile business. We will curb the billboards but multiply and landscape the highways that destroy country and city both. Eighty per cent of the billion for Appalachia is going for highways. Yet almost acute emergencies, like air and water pollution and the insecticides, are bogged in "research" because of hostile lobbies and because there is no money to be made of them. The cities are overcrowded, yet farm policy persistently favors food chains and big plantations and drives small farmers out, so beautiful, vast areas are depopulating and returning to swamp. In the cities, housing, renewal, and community development are tied to real-estate bonanzas, the alliance of national and municipal political machines, and even the aggrandizement of the welfare bureaucracy. In the crucial test case of Mobilization for Youth in New York, the move toward grass-roots democracy was swiftly crushed and brought under professional control, staffed by City Hall, Washington consenting. (As Edgar and Jean Cahn have pointed out, in the War on Poverty, as in all wars, the invading army ensures its own welfare before that of the occupied population.)[2] In communications, there has ceased to be any attempt to decentralize television and get some variety, if not foliage, into the wasteland. Indeed, by temperament President Johnson hankers for consensus and managed news; he says he welcomes responsible criticism, but it's an angry welcome; and the projection of his personality and icons is beginning to resemble the style of Russia or Cuba. In forwarding the fine arts, the government neglects the traditional, useful, and safe method of underwriting standard repertory and editions of the American classics, but it toys with the obnoxious official art of Arts Councils, glamorous culture centers, and

[2] Edgar and Jean Cahn, "The War on Poverty: A Civilian Perspective," *The Harvard Review*, II (Fall, 1964), pp. 34-54.—Eds.

suppers for the famous. Meantime, free lances are bulldozed from their lofts and it is harder for creative people to be decently poor in their own way. The Department of Justice keeps whittling away at civil liberties, and the emasculation of Congress proceeds. The arms budget continues to increase. Now a spaceship will explicitly become a new grotesque weapon, and we explicitly use the adventure of exploration for propaganda. And it is hard to believe the President's moral commitment to civil rights at home when he dispatches marines and bombers to subjugate foreign peoples whose civil rights threaten what he sometimes calls the Free World and sometimes our National Interests.

Perhaps most alarming is the bland affirmation of clashing contradictories, as if people were already imbeciles. When we bomb hospitals and burn villages, the President is bound to make an unusually tender announcement about cerebral palsy (and the marines give out candy). When we allot 1.7 billions for a new space weapon, our astronauts are at once sent on a world tour for peace.

The theory of the Great Society is obvious enough. Lyndon Johnson came in during an unparalleled prosperity, with a consensus of businessmen and liberals and, seemingly, money for everything, including tax cuts to encourage investment. He made a fairly graceful capitulation for the Negro protest. Thus, the Great Society could re-invest unprecedented profits in new fields, including the public sector; could provide unskilled and semi-skilled jobs; and could consolidate the votes of the urban poor. But if we examine this happy formula, we find that money, power, and fear of change are the determinants. We do not find the magnanimity, disinterestedness, and imagination of a great society. Worse, it is less and less an American society. Instead of tackling the political puzzle of how to maintain democracy in a complex technology and among urban masses, it multiplies professional–client and patron–client relationships. Worst of all, if we watch, during ten minutes of television, the horrors of the world, the piggish commercials, and the nightly performance of the President, we do not see even a decent society. As the Connecticut Circuit Court recently put it succinctly, in clearing some tabloids of charges of obscenity: "Coarse and puerile these tabloids are, but so is much of our civilization. We doubt that they will pollute the social atmosphere."

II

Nevertheless, the concept of a national mission cooked up by the past three Administrations is not merely a fraud. It is an ideology made necessary by contemporary history. In the first place, there has developed a dangerous vacuum of political–moral values, dangerous especially for the young. To give an important example: there must be *some* human use of our galloping high technology better than the infinite expansion of a hardware Gross National Product; affluence is no longer enough. One purpose of the big slogans has been to meet this moral demand and yet contain it, as we have seen, in the control of the same leaders and corporations. So far, the official moralists have not hit on anything believable, but that may come.

Secondly, however—and this, I think, is the essence—there must be some general ideology, whatever it is, to give a warrant to an amazing new grouping that has emerged in our society, the American Establishment. For this purpose, the Great Society might prove good enough, and it is virulent.

An Establishment is the clubbing together of the secular and moral leaders of society—in industry, the military, labor unions, the cities, sciences and arts, the universities, the church, and state—to determine not only the economy and policy but the standards and ideals of the nation. The role of an Establishment is to tell what is right, accredited, professional, British (German, Russian, etc.), and to rule out what is not (not *Kultur*, not Leninist, etc.). An important part of an Establishment is a large stable of mandarins to raise the tone, use correct scientific method, and invent rationalizations. Also, the literate mandarins write the speeches.

There is no doubt that such an interlocking accrediting club has attained enormous power in the United States. Its genius is to go round and round and be self-enclosed. The job in the want ads says "M.S. required," for industry respects the university; but meantime the university is getting contracted research from industry and the government. Cities or settlement houses will get funds from Washington if they employ accredited staff. (I am laying stress on school credentials because education is probably the biggest business in the country; there has been no

such class of monks since Henry the Eighth.) Retired generals
become vice-presidents in charge of contracting; they know
whom to talk to and how. A broadcaster seeks his license from
the FCC, but the Administration has a healthy respect for the
power of the broadcaster—hardly one license has been rescinded. Meantime, by FCC mandate, a commercial sponsor
cannot censor the program he sponsors, but he does have the
right to expect that it will not tarnish or jar the image of his
firm. Tax-exempt foundations support what *is* art or research,
as recommended by those who are accredited, and they will
underwrite a pilot project if it is carried out by a proper institution. But woe to a project that has nothing to recommend it but
that it is a good idea, and whose inventor carries his office
under his hat. In principle such a project cannot exist, and soon
it does not exist.

Now our country has had neither a traditional aristocracy
nor a totalitarian dogma, so it is not easy for the American
Establishment to find moral justification for so much omni-
science and exclusive power. It has really thrived on quiet expansion and being taken for granted, like creeping socialism. It
is not surprising that its ideology should be mere campaign slogans, future and hortatory, half public relations and half corny
dreams.

But however hazy its justification, the personnel of the Establishment has specific properties: it must be rooted in the
baronial institutions and it must be conspicuously idealistic. It
was with uncanny precision—in fact, the candidates are pre-
selected for him from 25,000 *vitae* by computer—that Johnson
chose John Gardner as Secretary of Health, Education, and
Welfare. Gardner was the head of the Carnegie Corporation,
and he is the author of a book called *Excellence.*

Thus, the process of spelling out and implementing the
vague national mission is as follows: From the Establishment,
the President chooses task forces. The task forces think up programs and these are given for execution to those accredited by
the Establishment. It is not astonishing, then, if a major function, if not purpose, of the Great Society is to aggrandize the
Establishment, the education barons, the broadcasting barons,
the automobile barons, the shopping center barons. In a youth
employment project, more than three-quarters of the appropriation will go for (accredited) staff salaries and research; not

much is left for wages for the kids. Of course, sometimes there is an hilarious exception, as when some SNCC youngsters I know got $90 a day as consultants at a conference on poverty in Washington.

So a practical definition of the Great Society is: to provide professional employment and other business for card-carrying members of the Establishment. *This* is not a fraud.

Of course, the Great Society is strictly for domestic consumption. Abroad, our friends are drifting away because we have lost our reputation; persuasion gives way to brute force. Thus, by a grim devolution, the Great Society turns out to be a liberal version of the old isolationism of Fortress America.

III

In conclusion, let me return to a thought mentioned above, the need to fill the moral vacuum. The technical, urban, and international premises of modern life have changed so rapidly and markedly that the old elites, who cling to their power, inevitably seem morally bankrupt, especially to the young. I have no doubt that this is the case everywhere—it has been persistently reported from the Soviet Union during the last ten years —but since ours is the most advanced country, we reveal the moral bankruptcy worst.

By the middle of the Administration of Eisenhower, it was impossible for a public spokesman to say "the American Way of Life" with a straight face. And there occurred the flood of social criticism, often devastating, which left us morally dank indeed. It was in this context that the President's Commission on National Goals made its report. But it was a feeble effort that influenced nobody, certainly not the young. The beat generation withdrew. And there began the spiritual defection of college youth from the corporations that has increased steadily. (In 1956, according to a survey by David Riesman, the great majority of collegians wanted to work for a big organization. Just now, at Harvard, more students want to go into the tiny Peace Corps than into business!)

John Kennedy hit on the Posture of Sacrifice, which was what young people wanted to hear, something to give meaning to the affluent society. But apart from the token of the Peace Corps—filled largely, as it turned out, by youth of the upper middle class—he could not produce anything to sacrifice *for*, not with so many credit cards around. Indeed, when they asked what they could do for their country, many of the best youth found that they wanted to serve precisely against the government, sometimes illegally, in the Negro movement and protesting against fall-out. And the majority of the returning Peace Corps itself have proved to be critical of the society they have come back to.

The Great Society, as we have seen, started with more moral ammunition: an electoral campaign against Black Reaction, a bill for Civil Rights, a war against poverty. Yet once again many of the best youth have remained unconverted. During the nominating convention, the militants of the Freedom Democratic Party rejected the Humphrey compromise.[3] Shortly after the electoral triumph of the Great Society, the students at Berkeley raged in their thousands. This year, there have been student troubles on a hundred campuses, East, Middle West, and even South. The Students for a Democratic Society have thrown themselves into undermining precisely the War on Poverty, which they consider undemocratic and insincere.[4] And both many students and many teachers seem to want to undermine even the war for the Free World in Vietnam. Some writers refused to go to the President's party.

In brief, as a moral incentive for youth, the Great Society, like its predecessors, is unpersuasive. It does not square with the obvious facts; it is too corrupt. Fatally, it avoids the deep problems that demand real changes. The political–moral problems that deeply interest youth are of the following kind: How to use high technology for human advantage? How to regain substantive democracy in modern cities and with mass-communications? How to get rid of the Bomb and the whole atmosphere of the Cold War? How to be educated without being processed? How to work at something worthwhile outside the rat race of an infinitely expanding GNP? How to avoid 1984?

The Establishment in America and its President do not cope with these questions because they *are* morally bankrupt.

[3] See on this, reading 22.—Eds.
[4] See an expression of such a view in Tom Hayden's piece, reading 34. —Eds.

A DANGEROUS
CONCENTRATION OF POWER*

In the spring of 1966, when this essay appeared, there was little visible opposition to Johnson's policies at home or abroad. Since then, in response to such criticisms of the President as those of Hans Morgenthau, a highly visible opposition has developed. Some in the President's own party are openly talking of "dumping Johnson" in 1968. But whatever the fate of the man who became President in November of 1963, the problem of the exercise of vast executive power will continue to plague the American polity.

Hans Morgenthau, who graphically outlines this problem in the essay below, has served as adviser to the US Department of State. Currently he holds the position of Albert A. Michelson Distinguished Service Professor of Political Science and Modern History at the University of Chicago. Long an advocate of policies based upon realistic considerations of national interest rather than sentiment or ideology, Morgenthau is the author of such books as *The Purpose of American Politics* (New York, 1960), *Politics Among Nations* (3rd ed., New York, 1961). Recently he has been a vigorous critic of US policy in Vietnam. *Vietnam and the United States* (Washington, D.C., 1965) is a collection of Morgenthau's essays.

◇ ◇ ◇

*Slightly abridged from the *New York Review of Books*, VI (March 31, 1966), pp. 11-14. Copyright © 1966, The New York Review. By permission of Hans J. Morgenthau and the *New York Review of Books*.

"Someone has said," wrote Lord Bryce in *The American Commonwealth*, "that the American government and Constitution are based on the theology of Calvin and the philosophy of Hobbes. This at least is true, that there is a hearty Puritanism in the view of human nature which pervades the instrument of 1787. It is the work of men who believed in original sin, and were resolved to leave open for transgressors no door which they could possibly shut. Compare this spirit with the enthusiastic optimism of the Frenchmen of 1789." And compare it with the spirit and the political practices of the Americans of 1966!

The American system of government reposes upon two premises, which are in strict logic mutually exclusive: first, that the government must be strong enough to govern, and second, that it must not be so strong as to be able to abuse its power. Thus on the one hand, the Constitution, supported by the dynamics of American politics, confers upon the President powers which, as the Founding Fathers recognized with awe, are the equal of those of any king; on the other hand, it confines those powers within a strait jacket of checks and balances, which interposes seemingly insuperable obstacles to their effective exercise. The dynamic interplay between these two contradictory principles has called forth a dialectic in which the Supreme Court and Congress have tried to shackle the President's powers while the President has tried to free himself of these shackles.

In the short run, Congress and, more sporadically, the Supreme Court have been able to hamstring a succession of Presidents, to delay, water down, and divert their policies. When Woodrow Wilson published his *Congressional Government* in 1885, he saw Congress as the center of governmental power and the President as a mere appendix to it. "The President," he wrote, "is no greater than his prerogative to veto makes him; he is, in other words, powerful rather as a branch of the legislature than as the titular head of the executive." This was written, of course, under the impact of the experience of a succession of weak Presidents. Yet in the twentieth century a succession of strong presidents—Wilson himself, the two Roosevelts, Truman, and Kennedy—could have recognized more than a grain of truth in Wilson's analysis. And where the President and Congress were able to cooperate, as in the early New Deal legislation, the Supreme Court struck their legislation down as unconstitutional.

In the long run, however, strong Presidents have known how to mobilize their constituency, that is, the nation as a whole, in support of their policies, and Congress and the Supreme Court have not been able to resist that combined pressure of President and people for long. After three decades, the radical innovations of the New Deal have become the orthodoxies of the American consensus. Yet after each new departure, Congress and the Supreme Court have known how to reassert their limiting functions, calling forth a new presidential initiative.

Thus the American political system seems to have fulfilled the intentions of its founders: it continuously oscillates between the ascendancy of the President and that of Congress and the judiciary. It is indeed a system of checks and balances. In consequence whenever the presidential scales are heavy, one must wish for an increase in the weight of the congressional and judicial ones, and vice versa. Thus I could write in 1962:

It is for the President to reassert his historic role as both the initiator of policy and the awakener of public opinion. It is true that only a strong, wise and shrewd President can marshal to the support of wise policies the strength and wisdom latent in that slumbering giant—American public opinion. Yet while it is true that great men have rarely been elected President of the United States, it is upon that greatness, which is the greatness of its people personified, that the United States, from Washington to Franklin D. Roosevelt, has had to rely in the conduct of its foreign affairs. It is upon that greatness that Western civilization must rely for its survival.

These words I addressed in 1949 to Mr. Truman and in 1956 to Mr. Eisenhower. It is the measure of the chronic weakness of presidential leadership that the same words must be addressed to Mr. Kennedy in 1962, at the beginning of his second year in office.

Obviously I would not write these words today. For today the President's power sweeps all before it. The Supreme Court has become his ally, and Congress stirs but halfheartedly and ineffectually in its bondage. Mass communications, with very few and again halfhearted exceptions, are at his service. The individual citizen, opposing the President's powers and policies, may fulfill the mission of keeping the voice of conscience alive, but as for his political effectiveness, he might as well talk to himself. When Theodore Roosevelt said that he had only one wish, to be for twenty-four hours President, Congress, and the Supreme Court at the same time, he was daydreaming. Lyndon B. Johnson has achieved what Theodore Roosevelt was dreaming about, and for more than twenty-four hours.

What is so ominous in our present situation is not that the President has reasserted his powers, but that in the process he has reduced all countervailing powers, political and social, to virtual and seemingly permanent impotence. What the Founding Fathers feared has indeed come to pass: the President of the United States has become an uncrowned king. Lyndon B. Johnson has become the Julius Caesar of the American Republic.

> *Why, man, he doth bestride the narrow world*
> *Like a Colossus, and we petty men*
> *Walk under his huge legs, and peep about*
> *To find ourselves dishonorable graves.*
> *Men at some time are masters of their fates:*
> *The fault, dear Brutus, is not in our stars,*
> *But in ourselves, that we are underlings.*

What makes opposition to such a concentration of power particularly burdensome is its exercise on behalf of aspirations commonly possessed by the great majority of the American people. Quantitatively, Lyndon Johnson's Great Society signifies the consummation of the great social reforms which the New Deal initiated for the first time on a broad scale. Qualitatively, the Great Society seeks the restoration of man's dignity in an environment worthy of him. These aspirations are not selfish even in the sense that they are limited to a particular nation; in truth, they embrace mankind, and for the time being at least individual doubts and parochial dissatisfactions cannot prevail against the attractiveness of these great designs, so much in tune with the humanitarian aspirations of America. If Lyndon Johnson were a selfish tyrant, protecting, say, "the interests" against the popular aspirations, the people, Congress, and the Court would cut down his powers, for they would find distasteful the ends on behalf of which those powers are being used. If a contemporary Mark Antony were to tell us what Caesar has done and will do for the people and for mankind, who cares that Caesar is "ambitious"; that is, that he has, and seeks, too much power?

Lyndon Johnson's power is benevolent at least with respect to the President's intentions. Who could quarrel with him if his policies designed to bring peace, security, justice, and nationhood to South Vietnam had a chance of succeeding? But this is not the issue here. Even if the President's great designs could be realized, they would require a concentration of presidential powers that would stagger the imagination. Thus the benevolence of inordinate power must not blind us to the dangers inherent in such power, regardless of the intentions and purposes of its holder. For no man, however good and wise, is good enough and wise enough to be trusted with unlimited power. This is the perennial truth which the Founding Fathers wrote into the structure of American government. "Th'abuse of greatness is, when it disjoins remorse from power." This is what Brutus feared in Caesar; that is what we must fear in Lyndon Johnson.

This astounding imbalance in the distribution of governmental powers has become obvious in Lyndon Johnson's administration, but it has not been created by it. Comparing the powers of Napoleon III and the President of the United States, the London *Economist* remarked on January 27th, 1866:

The keynote of the American Constitution is the existence of an executive which during its term of office is responsible to the people, which acts by its own volition, which can pursue if necessary a policy diametrically opposed to the wishes of those who elected it. That also is the keynote of the system established by the Second Empire. The President does as he pleases in all matters within his province just as the Emperor does, and like him is irresponsible to the Legislature—need not, indeed, explain to the representatives of the people his own official acts.

Almost a decade ago, a French writer, Amaury de Riencourt, referred to the President's "powers of truly Caesarian magnitude."

The objective conditions for the ascendancy of presidential powers have been long in the making; they only awaited a

President willing and able to make full use of them. First of all, the President has a natural advantage over the other branches of the government because he can take the initiative, he can act, while the others can only prevent and delay. This natural advantage of the executive has since the beginning of the republic been particularly marked in the conduct of foreign policy.

Secondly, and most importantly, our age has witnessed a drastic shift in power from the people at large to the government, within the government from the legislative to the executive branch, and within the executive branch from the democratically responsible officials to certain technological elites. These shifts of power are the result of the revolutions in the technologies of transportation, communication, and warfare. These revolutions have transformed the business of government into an esoteric undertaking, unintelligible to the uninitiated and far removed from the experience of the man in the street. The issues of whether or not to build an anti-missile system or fallout shelters are different in quality from, say, the issue of the prohibition of child labor of more than half a century ago. In contrast to the former, the latter was intelligible to the man in the street, and he was capable of passing moral judgment on it and translating the judgment into political action. In consequence, political participation has given way to apathy, and "consensus" has taken the place of political controversy.

Thus the stage was set for a new Caesar to bestride it. Only Caesar was missing. Presidents Truman and Kennedy could not fill the role because they were unable to manipulate Congress, and President Eisenhower, even though he created the administrative machinery of the contemporary presidency, was not interested in using it for the actual enlargement of the President's powers. It is the signal contribution Lyndon Johnson has made to American political life that he has taken advantage of the objective conditions of American politics with extraordinary skill and with an extraordinary taste for power. He has well-nigh exhausted the possibilities of power of the modern presidency, dwarfing the other branches of the government and reducing the people at large to helplessly approving bystanders. . . .

An impotent opposition is a mere function of an all-powerful presidency. To affirm the latter and to call for a strong opposition to check it is a contradiction in terms.[1] It is the very existence of an all-powerful President that reduces the opposition to impotence. The opposition can criticize the President's conduct of the Vietnam War. But it can do nothing but talk, and it is the President who acts. By virtue both of the constitutional arrangements and the dynamics of American politics, the congressional opposition cannot prevail against the President as a parliamentary opposition can. The remedies are both broader and narrower than that.

On the one hand, the congressional opposition can mobilize the people at large who will render their verdict in the next congressional and presidential elections. On the other hand, Congress can refuse to grant the President the financial means with which to implement his policies. Both the general remedy of bringing about a change in policies by changing the policy makers and the specific one of forcing the President to give up certain policies by withholding financial support from them must be nurtured by a spirit of political realism and of democratic independence, which recognizes both the need for presidential powers and the necessity to restrain them. At this point we return to the wisdom and dilemma of the Founders: a system of checks and balances which will promote the effective use, and prevent the abuse, of presidential power.

[1] Morgenthau here is criticizing some of the formulations in James M. Burns, *Presidential Government: The Crucible of Leadership* (Boston, 1966).—Eds.

GALLOPING CONSENSUSOCRACY*

Lyndon Johnson has been widely hailed as an exponent of the politics of consensus—the process of absorbing all viewpoints into his own. A foreign observer writes that Johnson "is, by trade, a conciliator. Everyone in Washington was bored long ago by the word consensus, but it does indicate what the President is after." [1]

Consensus is not only a tool of presidential strategy, but part of a powerful ideological tendency in the United States. Historians of this persuasion view the nation's past as the pleasing record of general harmony, and the sociologists of consensus are happy to find that present-day America has solved all its basic problems.[2] It should be clear that, whether used by an energetic president or by contented academics, "consensus" is basically a conservative notion.

◇◇◇

Contrary to the predictions so freely made in the months immediately after the last election, the Republican Party has not died.

Visitors to Washington may see it by calling any weekday between 9 and 5 at the Bureau of the Consensus, where President Johnson keeps it in warm storage, along with two dozen newspaper columnists, a large nest of hawks, the leaders of organized labor, a pride of Southern Democrats and such miscel-

* From the *New York Times* (May 6, 1965), © 1966 by the New York Times Company. Reprinted by permission.

[1] Michael Davie, *LBJ: A Foreign Observer's Viewpoint* (New York, 1966), p. 75.

[2] See John Higham, "The Cult of the 'American Consensus,'" *Commentary*, XXVII (February, 1959), pp. 93-100.

laneous phenomena as Everett McKinley Dirksen, the television networks and Prime Minister Harold Wilson.

"It's odd, when you think about it, that none of our earlier Presidents ever thought of government by consensus," one of the bureau's deputy directors explained the other day during a guided tour. "The old two-party system had been creaking badly for years, and since the differences between the two parties had become negligible anyhow, it was much more practical to merge all the major factions into one lovely jelly of agreement."

How does the Consensus Bureau do it? "Quite simply," said the deputy. "Observe the Republican party, for example." He indicated several rooms overflowing with Republicans awaiting the summons to a Consensus shape-up on the latest armed hostilities.

"Vietnam!" he shouted, and the Republicans immediately began delivering speeches praising the President's policy in Southeast Asia. "You see," the deputy explained, "they plunge readily into the consensus because the President is carrying out what they believe to be the Vietnam policy urged by Senator Goldwater last fall. Now, listen."

And he cried, "Dominican Republic!" Instantly, the Republicans broke off their commendations for the President in Vietnam and most fell to praising his intervention in Santo Domingo.

A few, however, remained silent. "Communists in the Caribbean!" the deputy shouted at them. "Castro!" At these cries, the sluggish Republicans began applauding for Lyndon Johnson.

"There you see the basic elements that brought the Republicans into the Consensus," the deputy explained. "A dash of Barry Goldwater, a smidgen of Theodore Roosevelt and just a pinch of Joe McCarthy."

The politically unsophisticated may ask how the Republicans were able to enter the Consensus for Armed Hostilities so readily when for years they had denounced the Democrats as "The War Party." The explanation is that the more fighting they can cheer the President on to, the easier it will be for them to call the Democrats "The War Party" when the next elections occur.

"We don't insist that they consense in everything," the deputy explained. "We let them out regularly to go to the Capitol and vote against the Great Society. There aren't enough of them to make much difference, and it keeps them from feeling regimented."

How are the Democrats brought into the Consensus? "We let them spend a great deal of money," the deputy explained. "Oh, it's all spent in good causes, of course. There's nothing that keeps a Democrat quite as happy as spending a great deal of money, particularly if it's in a good cause."

The deputy paused at an oak-paneled clubroom. "We're very proud of this," he said. Inside, industrialists and financiers were clipping coupons and boasting how they had tricked de Gaulle by reducing the dollar flow to Europe.

"Two years ago nine out of every ten men in that clubroom were firmly committed to the Eastern internationalist wing of the Republican Party," the deputy said. "Now they consense happily with Democrats, Goldwaterites and Texans."

What made these tycoons see the light? "The President's decision to turn off light bulbs in the White House," the deputy said. "He cut the electric bill by $12.73 and brought $40 billion worth of businessmen into the Consensus."

The consensus, clearly, is the most astounding political creation since Charles de Gaulle, and the man who built it is just as clearly a genius. Is it possible to see this man? "Almost any hour of the night or day," said the director, turning on all three television networks.

There he was, explaining the latest troop movements, invoking the Pedernales, firing the blood with passionate defense of human rights, introducing the Cabinet, sorrowing for the poor, demonstrating how to sign a check and mow the lawn.

The effect was magnetic, overwhelming. It was impossible not to murmur, "A great President, a great Democrat."

"No," the deputy whispered. "A great Consensusocrat."

SELECTED BIBLIOGRAPHY

BEN H. BAGDIKIAN. "The 'Inner Circle' Around Johnson." *New York Times Magazine*, February 28, 1965. [A study of Johnson's varied demands on friends and acquaintances.]

LEONARD BAKER. *The Johnson Eclipse: A President's Vice Presidency*. New York: Macmillan, 1966. [A vivid evocation of the frustrations Johnson labored under as Vice President.]

PAUL A. BARAN. *The Political Economy of Growth*. New York: Monthly Review Press, 1957. [A penetrating Marxist analysis of economic development in advanced capitalist countries as well as in the third world, and of the retarding influence of imperialism.]

PAUL A. BARAN and PAUL M. SWEEZY. *Monopoly Capital: An Essay on the American Economic and Social Order*. New York: Monthly Review Press, 1966. [A stimulating critique of American society from a Marxist standpoint.]

ROBERT L. BRANYAN and R. ALTON LEE. "Lyndon B. Johnson and the Art of the Possible." *Southwestern Social Science Quarterly*, XLV, December, 1964, pp. 213-25. [Abject homage is paid to the way Johnson made the legislative machinery "work" during his Senate years, "whether or not one agreed with his ends. . . ." The "ends" are not discussed by these authors.]

Roger H. Davidson. " 'Creative Federalism' and the War on Poverty." September, 1966. [A study, presented to the annual meeting of the American Political Science Association, of political tensions.]

Michael Davie. *LBJ: A Foreign Observer's Viewpoint.* New York: Duell, Sloan and Pearce, 1966. [This London correspondent's viewpoint has brought little in the way of deepened understanding of Johnson.]

Ronnie Dugger. "The Johnson Record: A Summing Up." *Texas Observer,* June 3, 10, and 24, 1960. [Careful investigations of Johnson's legislative career.]

Economic Report of the President. Washington, D.C.: US Government Printing Office, annual each January. [An indispensable source, despite its aim of providing a rationale for the President's economic policies. Contains both a popular exposition "by" the President, and more technical analyses by his Council of Economic Advisers.]

Rowland Evans and Robert Novak. *Lyndon B. Johnson: The Exercise of Power.* New York: New American Library, 1966. [Although thin on the early years, this biography is rich with revealing data on LBJ and the Washington scene. The most serious limitation is the inability of the authors, who deal brilliantly with *how* power is exercised, to discuss *in whose interest* it is exercised.]

Henry Fairlie. "A Cheer for American Imperialism." *New York Times Magazine,* July 11, 1965. [A frank acceptance of the reality of American imperialism, along with praise for it.]

Henry Fairlie. "Johnson and the Intellectuals." *Commentary,* XL, October, 1965, pp. 49-55. [A view by a British journalist, hostile to American intellectuals, who argues that attacks on Johnson are unwarranted and gratuitous.]

D. F. Fleming. *The Cold War and Its Origins, 1917-1960.* Two vols., Garden City, New York: Doubleday, 1961. [A courageous and comprehensive history, rich in its sense of the missed diplomatic opportunities and the openness of the political process.]

Marvin E. Gettleman. "The Johnson System." *The Nation,* CCIV January 30, 1967, pp. 150-52. [A review of three recent LBJ books, focusing on their implicit assumptions.]

Marvin E. Gettleman, ed. *Vietnam: History, Documents and Opinions on a Major World Crisis.* New York: Fawcett, 1965; 2nd ed., Harmondsworth, England: Penguin Books, 1966. [A comprehensive collection concentrating on the post-World War II period, and American policy.]

Philip L. Geyelin. *Lyndon B. Johnson and the World.* New York and Washington, D.C.: Frederick A. Praeger, 1966. [An important book, by the diplomatic correspondent of the *Wall*

Street Journal, rich with insights into Johnson's foreign policy, but within a range bounded by the assumptions of official Cold War policy.]

CHARLES H. GRAY. "A Scale Analysis of the Voting Records of Senators Kennedy, Johnson and Goldwater, 1957-1960." *The American Political Science Review*, LIX, September, 1965, pp. 615-21. [Handy compilation of interesting comparative data.]

MEG GREENFIELD. "LBJ and the Democrats." *The Reporter*, XXXIV, June 2, 1966, pp. 8-13. [A rather colorless study of political tactics.]

J. EVETTS HALEY. *A Texan Looks at Lyndon: A Study in Illegitimate Power*. Canyon, Texas: Palo Duro Press, 1964. [An anti-Johnson campaign document, dripping with invective, and based essentially on the proposition that LBJ, alas, is not Thomas Jefferson.]

MICHAEL HARRINGTON. *The Other America: Poverty in the United States*. New York: Macmillan, 1962. [President Kennedy was said to have been moved by Harrington's poignant descriptions of those stricken by poverty.]

MICHAEL HARRINGTON. "Taking the Great Society Seriously." *Harper's Magazine*, CCXXX, December, 1966, pp. 43-49. [Although a self-proclaimed socialist, Harrington succumbs to the comfortable notion that a radically transformed America is further to the left along the same continuum that includes Lyndon Johnson's Great Society.]

SEYMOUR E. HARRIS. *The Economics of the Political Parties: With Special Attention to Presidents Eisenhower and Kennedy*. New York: Macmillan, 1962. Also *Economics of the Kennedy Years*. New York/Evanston/London: Harper & Row, 1964. [Standard liberal Keynesian apologetics for the Democratic Party establishment.]

WALTER W. HELLER. *New Dimensions of Political Economy*. Cambridge, Mass.: Harvard University Press, 1966. [The former chairman of the Kennedy and Johnson Council of Economic Advisers gives an insider's account of the economic policies of the New Frontier and the Great Society.]

H. STUART HUGHES. "The Messianic Pose: Post Cold-War Delusions." *The Nation*, January 3, 1966. [A sharp critique of US policies abroad.]

LYNDON B. JOHNSON. *Public Papers of the Presidents, Lyndon B. Johnson, Containing the Public Messages, Speeches, and Statements of the President, 1963-64*. Two vols., Washington, D.C.: US Government Printing Office, 1965. *1965*. Two vols., Washington, D.C., 1966. [Splendidly edited reference works.]

LYNDON B. JOHNSON. *A Time For Action*. Intro. by Adlai E. Stevenson. New York: Atheneum, 1964. [A collection of a decade of public speeches, including only four made as President. Published also in a Pocket Cardinal edition (New York: Pocket Books, 1964) "in association with the Democratic National Committee."]

LYNDON B. JOHNSON. *My Hope For America.* New York: Random House, 1964. [A selection of passages from LBJ's presidential speeches, brought together, without indication of when the utterances were first made, for the electoral campaign of 1964.]

ROBERT LEKACHMAN. *The Age of Keynes.* New York: Random House, 1966. [The last chapter of this important and well-written biography of John Maynard Keynes and the impact of his economic theories on the postwar era, includes a critique of the Great Society programs.]

ROBERT LEKACHMAN, "Death of a Slogan—The Great Society, 1967," *Commentary,* XLIII, January, 1967, pp. 56-62. [An economist's lament for the passing of humanitarian reform.]

WILLIAM E. LEUCHTENBERG, "The Genesis of The Great Society," *The Reporter,* XXXIV, April 21, 1966, pp. 36-39. [Survey of how, in advancing his Great Society program, LBJ also created a distinct political identity.]

WILLIAM C. LEWIS, JR. [pseudonym]. "Anatomy of Decision—a Fictionalized Study of the Executive Decision Process in an International Security Crisis." Congressional Record, CIX:6 (88th Cong., 1st Sess.), May 1, 1963, pp. 7, 525-37. [An amazing revelation into the decision-making process, with interesting observations on Lyndon Johnson's behavior during the Cuban missile crisis. Read into the Record by Senator Margaret Chase Smith (Republican of Maine).]

NORTON E. LONG. "Local and Private Initiative in the Great Society." December 7, 1965. [In this paper, prepared for the Arthur F. Bentley Seminar on the Great Society of the Maxwell Graduate School of Citizenship and Public Affairs of Syracuse University, the validity of Great Society goals is assumed, and an elaborate structure of speculation is erected. Arthur Bentley's realistic approach, unfortunately, is not followed.]

HERBERT MARCUSE. "The Individual and the Great Society." *Alternatives: The New Magazine of Politics and Society.* (University of California, San Diego, 92038) Issues #1 and 2, 1966. [A searching critique by the distinguished author of *Eros and Civilization: A Philosophical Inquiry Into Freud* (1955, reprinted, New York, 1962) and *One Dimensional Man* (Boston, 1965).]

KENNETH MCNAUGHT. "American Progressives and The Great Society." *Journal of American History,* LIII, December, 1966, pp. 504-20. [An historical perspective of the way in which radicals contributed to the defeat of American radicalism.]

LOUIS MENASHE and RONALD RADOSH, *Teach-ins U.S.A.: Reports, Opinions, Documents.* New York/Washington/London: Frederick A. Praeger, 1967. [A well-edited collection, revealing the extent of academic disenchantment with LBJ.]

DAVID MERMELSTEIN. "The Economic Policy of the Liberal Democrats." *Science & Society,* XXVII, Fall, 1963, pp. 457-64. [A critique of standard liberal Keynesianism.]

WILLIAM C. POOL, EMMIE CRADDOCK and DAVID E. CONRAD. *Lyndon Baines Johnson: The Formative Years.* San Marcos, Texas: Southwest Texas State College Press, 1965. [With many of the parochial limitations of local history, this volume is nevertheless essential. It is based upon original archival research and extensive interviewing.]

CHARLES ROBERTS. *L.B.J.'s Inner Circle.* New York: Delacorte, 1965. [Pro Johnson, and revealing much of the inside gossip that is considered favorable to him, such as his decision to escalate the war in Vietnam *before* the 1964 elections.]

ALVIN ROSEMAN. "Foreign Aid under Lyndon Johnson." *Current History,* June, 1966, pp. 335-41, 364-65. [A study of the wide gap between presidential statements and performance.]

STEPHEN W. ROUSSEAS. "The Great Society: An Old New Deal." *The Nation,* May 10, 1965. [Viewing the Johnson program as a belated version of an already obsolete vision.]

HOBART ROWEN. *The Free Enterprisers: Kennedy, Johnson, and the Business Establishment.* New York: G. P. Putnam's Sons, 1964. [A careful, informative study by a *Newsweek* correspondent of the pressures put on Kennedy and Johnson by the Business Establishment.]

FRANZ SCHURMANN, PETER DALE SCOTT and REGINALD ZELNIK. *The Politics of Escalation in Vietnam.* Boston: Beacon Press, 1966; New York: Fawcett, 1966. [Nine of the ten chapters of this book, dealing with the domestic US political pressures on Vietnam policy, discuss the Johnson Administration. Highly recommended.]

BEN B. SELIGMAN, ed. *Poverty as a Public Issue.* New York: The Free Press, 1965. [An outstanding collection of articles on poverty, one of which—that by Elinor Graham—we have included in this volume.]

PATRICIA CAYO SEXTON. *Education and Income: Inequalities in our Public Schools.* New York: Viking/Compass Books, 1964. [Brilliant examination of class bias in American education.]

ROBERT SHERRILL. *The Accidental President.* New York: Grossman, 1967. [An acid portrait of LBJ by *The Nation's* Washington correspondent.]

LAWRENCE STERN. "L.B.J. and the F.C.C. . . ." *The Progressive,* XXVIII, June, 1964, pp. 21-24. [Excellent survey of the Bobby

Baker scandal in the context of Johnson's own TV station investments in Texas.]

I. F. STONE. "The Making of a President." *New York Review of Books,* June 30, 1964. [Insightful biographical essay.]

WILLIAM S. WHITE. *The Professional: Lyndon B. Johnson.* Boston: Houghton Mifflin, 1964; New York: Fawcett, 1964. [A pseudo biography, creating a stylized hero-Johnson. One of a large number of such books.]

INDEX

ABOUT THE EDITORS

MARVIN E. GETTLEMAN was educated at the City College of New York and Johns Hopkins University. He is currently Assistant Professor of History at the Polytechnic Institute of Brooklyn. Professor Gettleman is a former consultant to the Association of the Bar of the City of New York. He is the editor of the book *Vietnam: History, Documents and Opinions* (1965). His articles and reviews have appeared in *The Nation, The American Journal of Economics and Sociology, Social Research,* and *Science and Society.*

DAVID MERMELSTEIN was educated at Amherst College and received his Ph.D from Columbia University. He is Assistant Professor of Economics at the Polytechnic Institute of Brooklyn. Formerly, Professor Mermelstein was a Lecturer in economics at Hunter College, Columbia University, and Fairleigh Dickinson University. He is the author of articles on economic policy and contemporary Cold War propaganda.

Professors Gettleman and Mermelstein have served as organizers and officers of the Socialist Scholars Conference, an independent association of scholars and students dedicated to the promotion of original research, analysis and theory within socialist perspectives.